Arnold Toynbee
on Judaism and Zionism

Arnold Toynbee
on Judaism and Zionism

A critique

Oskar K. Rabinowicz

W. H. ALLEN
London
A division of Howard & Wyndham Ltd
1974

The family of Oskar Rabinowicz wishes herewith to express its deep gratitude to John Shaftesley, an old friend of the author, whose efforts were indispensable in the preparation of the manuscript for publication. Drawing on his considerable editorial experience, and giving generously of his time, he guided the book from original typescript to final publication. He concerned himself both with details and with general matters of style, and he made a notable contribution to the book as it now appears. In Dr Rabinowicz's name as well as its own, the family wishes to record its profound appreciation of Mr Shaftesley's valuable assistance.

PRINTED AND BOUND IN GREAT BRITAIN BY
W & J MACKAY LIMITED, CHATHAM FOR THE PUBLISHERS
W. H. ALLEN & CO, LTD, 44 HILL STREET, LONDON W1X 8LB
ISBN 0 491 01550 X

Contents

It is difficult for anyone brought up in the Christian tradition to shake himself free from the official Christian ideology. He may have discarded Christian doctrine consciously on every point; yet on this particular point he may find that he is still influenced, subconsciously, by the traditional Christian view in his outlook on Jewish history . . . I am conscious that my own outlook has been affected in this way.

—TOYNBEE, *Reconsiderations*, p. 478

This contrast between the historical facts and the conventional Christian and ex-Christian view of the history of the Jews and Judaism shows how difficult it is for anyone brought up with a Christian background to look at Jewish history objectively.

—*Ibid.*, p. 482

We may say with our lips that, when we are making an historical study of our fellow human being, we suspend our moral judgments and suppress our feelings; but, if we fancy that we can do that, we are deceiving ourselves.

—*Ibid.*, p. 54

However able, open-minded, and humble-hearted an inquirer may be in analysing himself, many of his fundamental prejudices—and these are the most warping prejudices of all—are likely to escape detection, just because they are buried at as deep a level of the subconscious abyss of the psyche.

—*Ibid.*, pp. 60-61

Philip Toynbee: Now it has been said that you have a particular prejudice against Judaism. We'll get on to the question of Israel and so on later. It's said that in your treatment of religions you always have a slight 'down' on this particular one. If this is true, is it because you feel that religious intolerance springs from Judaism?

Arnold Toynbee: I do think it springs from Judaism, and in that sense I suppose I do have a 'down' on Judaism—I have a 'down' on the Jewish streak—it's more than a streak, it's more like the metal rods in reinforced concrete—in Christianity and in Islam.

—A. AND PH. TOYNBEE, *Comparing Notes*, p. 22

Author's Note

In the second volume of his *Study of History*,[1] published in 1934, Toynbee summarised his view on Zionism in the following passages:

> The ultimate aim of the Zionists is to liberate the Jewish people from the peculiar psychological complex induced by the penalisation to which they have been subject for centuries in the Gentile world. In this ultimate aim, the Zionists are at one with the Assimilationist School among the 'emancipated' Jews in the enlightened countries of the West. They agree with the Assimilationists in wishing to cure the Jews of being 'a peculiar people'. They part company with them, however, in their estimate of the Assimilationist prescription, which the Zionists reject as inadequate for coping with the malady.
>
> The ideal of the Assimilationists is that the Jew in Holland, France, England or America should become a Dutchman, French-man, Englishman or American, as the case may be, 'of Jewish religion'. They argue that there is no reason why a Jewish citizen of any of these enlightened countries should fail to be a completely satisfied and satisfactory member of Society just because he happens to go to synagogue on Saturday instead of going to church on Sunday. To this argument the Zionists have two replies. In the first place, they point out that, even if the Assimilationist prescription were capable of producing the result which its advocates claim for it, it is only applicable in the enlightened

countries in which the Jews have been granted 'emancipation'. It offers no solution for the Jewish problem in Eastern Europe, where the regime of the ghetto still virtually prevails where bona-fide 'emancipation' is not in prospect.[2]

In the second place—and this is the more trenchant of the two Zionist attacks upon the Assimilationist position—the Zionists contend that, even in the most enlightened Gentile community in the world, the Jewish problem cannot be solved by a Gentile-Jewish 'social contract' under which the Gentile 'emancipates' the Jew and the Jew 'assimilates' himself to the Gentile. This attempt at a contractual solution is vitiated, in the Zionists' view, by the false premise which vitiates the classical 'social contract' theory of Rousseau. It presupposes that human beings are social atoms and that a human society is an aggregate of these atoms which is held together by a legal nexus between the individuals as, in the physical universe, an aggregation of physical atoms is held together by the laws of Physics according to the 'classical' physical science of the nineteenth century. The Zionist, arguing *ad hominem*, insists that the Jew, at any rate, is not in fact an autonomous individual who can make and unmake his social relations as he pleases. To be a Jew is to be a human being whose social environment is Jewry. It is an essential part of the Jew's individuality that he is a member of the living Jewish community and an heir to the ancient Jewish tradition. He cannot cut off his Jewishness and cast it from him without self-mutilation; and thus, for the Jew, an emancipation-assimilation contract with a Gentile nation has the same kind of consequence as the legal instrument which turns a free man into a slave. It 'deprives him of his manhood'.[3] A Jew who, by process of emancipation and assimilation, attempts, in a social contract with his Gentile neighbours, to turn himself into a Dutchman or a Frenchman or an Englishman or an American 'of Jewish religion', is simply mutilating his Jewish personality without having any prospect at all of acquiring the full personality of a Dutchman or whatever the Gentile nationality of his choice may be.

Thus, in the Zionist view, the emancipation and assimilation of the Jew as an individual is a wrong method of pursuing a right aim. Genuine assimilation is indeed the true solution for the Jewish

problem and ought therefore to be the ultimate goal of Jewish
endeavours; but the Jews can never escape from being 'a peculiar
people' by masquerading as Englishmen or Frenchmen. If they are
to succeed in becoming 'like all the nations',[4] they must seek
instead assimilation on a national basis and not on an individual
basis. Instead of trying to assimilate individual Jews to individual
Englishmen or Frenchmen, they must try to assimilate Jewry itself
to England and France. Jewry must become a nation in effective
possession of a national home, and this on the ground from which
the historic roots of Judaism have sprung. When a new generation
of Jews has grown up in Palestine in a Jewish national environment,
then, and not till then, the Jewish problem will be solved by the
reappearance in the world of a type of Jew which has been almost
non-existent for the past two thousand years: a Jew who has
genuinely ceased to be 'not as other men are'.[5]

Though the Zionist Movement as a practical undertaking is
only half a century old, its social philosophy has already been
justified by results. In the Jewish agricultural settlements that have
been founded in Palestine within the last fifty years, the children
of the ghetto have been transformed out of all recognition into a
pioneering peasantry which displays many of the characteristics of
the Gentile European colonial type in the New World. The
Zionists have made no miscalculation in their forecast of the effect
which the establishment of a Jewish national home in Palestine
would have upon Jewry itself. The tragic misfortune into which
they have fallen, in company with the Mandatory Power, is their
inability to arrive at any understanding with the existing population of the country: prior claimants and possessors who have been
roused to resistance by the very spirit of Western Nationalism
which has been the inspiration of Zionism itself.

This was the primary intensive description of Zionism in Toynbee's
Study of History. When he touched on the Zionist issue in the subsequent
ten volumes of his *magnum opus,* he referred to it as his basic evaluation.[6]
Twenty-seven years later he maintained that he had not diverted from
it. 'On reconsideration,' he wrote, 'I do not find that I have changed
my view of Zionism.'[7]

In the light of these remarks, it seems appropriate to investigate Toynbee's evaluation of Zionism and to test both the accuracy of the assessment and the later claim to consistency.

There are accurate and fair assessments of assimilationist and Zionist views to be found in the quotation above, and in the course of this analysis reference will be made to them. On the other hand, some parts of the evaluation are vague or ambiguous and are therefore open to various interpretations. They subsequently served Toynbee as a basis for a gradually developing anti-Zionism which broke into the open in the eighth volume of his *Study* and in later writing. On the 'road of his conversion to anti-Zionism' the correct assessments in the quotation above somehow got lost, so that his assertion of an unchanged view of Zionism does not stand up to scrutiny. The evidence which I intend to submit in the following pages will show this clearly.

Part I

Theoretical Foundations

Goethe is my Shakespeare, I don't
know why. I read him at school and
he got an everlasting hold on me
. . . I have carried Faust with me
ever since.

Toynbee in A. and Ph. Toynbee, *Comparing Notes*, p. 86.

Die Hexe:	*The witch:*
Du musst verstehn!	This understand!
Aus eins mach' zehn,	From one make ten,
Und zwei lass gehn,	And drop two then;
Und drei mach' gleich,	The same with three,
So bist du reich.	And rich you'll be.
Verlier die Vier!	Omit the four!
Aus fuenf mach sechs,	From five make six,
So sagt die Hex',	So said the witch,
Mach' sieben und acht,	Make seven and eight,
So ist's vollbracht:	Which clears the slate:
Und neun ist eins,	And nine is one,
Und zehn ist keins.	And ten is none.
Das ist das Hexen-Einmaleins.	This is the witches' 'one-times-one'.

Mephistopheles:
Ich kenn' es wohl, so klingt das ganze Buch
Ich habe manche Zeit damit verloren.
Denn ein vollkommener Widerspruch
Bleibt gleich geheimnisvoll fuer Kluge wie fuer Toren.
Mein Freund, die Kunst ist alt und neu.
Es war die Art zu allen Zeiten,
Durch drei und eins und eins und drei
Irrtum statt Wahrheit zu verbreiten.

Mephisto:
I know it sounds like that for many pages.
I lost much time on this accursed affliction,
Because a perfect contradiction

Intrigues not only fools but also sages.
This art is old and new, forsooth:
It was the custom in all ages
To spread illusion and not truth
With Three in One and One in Three.

Johann Wolfgang von Goethe, *Faust*, Erster Teil, 'Hexenkueche' ('Witch's Kitchen'), lines 2540–2553 and 2555–2562. (The translation of the witch's words is by my son [Professor Theodore Rabb]. Mephistopheles' are taken from Walter Kaufmann's translation of *Faust*, New York [Doubleday], 1961, pp. 252–253.)

1

A Superficial Approach

Let us now analyse the summary of Zionism quoted above. Even a perfunctory glance reveals that Toynbee has omitted to consider the deeper philosophical, religious, and national aspects of the problem. In fact, as these five paragraphs reveal, he has not submitted a serious analysis of the Zionist ideology at all, but has made a purely superficial assessment. This superficiality is evident in the very first sentence of the quotation, in which he defines the 'ultimate aim' of the Zionists. It appears from this that he attributes to Zionism no affirmative purpose whatever. He defines it as a purely negative concept, as a reaction to 'penalisations', as a banding together of Jews desirous of liberating the Jewish people from a 'peculiar psychological complex'. The definition is not only superficial but it also provides one of the many examples of a peculiar method which we shall frequently encounter in this study: Toynbee makes an unwarranted and uncorroborated statement and regards it as proved because he has made it. He then bases subsequent conclusions on his statement. In this case his uncorroborated assumption that Zionism is a negative concept serves him as such a basis. And as assimilationism in its very essence is obviously a negative term, he simply joins together what he now feels justified in accepting as negative concepts: Zionism and assimilationism. Having thus arrived at a common denominator for both these 'schools', Toynbee then switches the order of priority and reaches the conclusion that Zionism is fundamentally assimilationism because Zionists regarded 'genuine assimilation . . . as the true solution of the Jewish problem [which] ought therefore to be the ultimate goal of Jewish endeavours'. This whole thesis is incorrect in its assumption and wrong in its conclusion, as will be shown.

There is, of course, no doubt that Jews have been affected by the sufferings inflicted on them by non-Jews. Yet they have also been affected by the good treatment they have received, and by many other influences from their surroundings.[8] It is inherent in the nature of man to react to everything that happens to him and around him. In order to react, however, an organism must be alive. And no valid conclusion can be drawn about the reaction of this organism unless there is an understanding of what it is or what it stands for. Only then can one determine how it absorbs external influences and to what extent it is affected.

On this Toynbee has kept silent. One can, of course, understand why. For if he had regarded the Jews as a living organism, he would have had to reverse the theory that Jews constitute a 'fossil of the Syriac civilisation', a description which at the time of writing the passage above he still advanced in its accepted meaning of a 'dead relic'.[9] He therefore sought the easy way out and did not concern himself with the question of the organism's essence, notwithstanding the fact that his contention that Zionists and assimilationists react to 'penalisations' by aiming to liberate the Jewish people from a psychological malady presupposes the existence of such a living organism.

He was no less superficial in the terms he used in the quotation to describe other characteristics. When he spoke of a Jewish 'malady', for instance, with which Zionism aims to cope, he omitted to tell us what kind of malady it was or how it expressed itself.

He also omitted to define the 'peculiar psychological complex' of the Jews of which, he said, both Zionists and assimilationists wished to rid themselves and the rest of Jewry. As we have seen, he attributed this 'complex' to the effect which those 'penalisations', inflicted on them by the Gentiles during the Diaspora, had had on the Jews. This, however, does not help to clarify the 'complex'. To do so, he would first have had to specify the 'penalisations' which were said to have caused the 'complex', and then, on this basis, describe the nature of that 'complex', how it had influenced or become part of the Jew, and finally how it had

caused what he termed the 'malady'. Thus he would have had to begin
with an exhaustive analysis of 'penalisations' in Jewish history and their
effects on Jews. But he did nothing of the kind, although 'penalisations' in general received a prominent place in his work. He formulated a special theory[10] around them with the help of which he
endeavoured to trace the influence of 'penalisations' on individuals and
on groups, and thus implicitly on the Jew in the Diaspora as well.
But not even in this special section did he clarify the origin and essence
of the 'penalisations' as far as the Jews were concerned; he treated them
only as 'punishments' already sustained.

2

The 'Penalisation' Theory

According to his theory, variations in the severity of 'penalisation' have resulted in variations in the intensity of the Jewish ethos. Mild 'penalisations' have led to a weakening of Jewish life; severe ones, on the other hand, have strongly contributed to the survival of Jewry. He concluded from this that 'penalisations' served as a Stimulus to survival. To accentuate this, Toynbee headed this chapter of his work with the significant title 'stimulus of Penalisations'.[11] He presented the essence of that theory in the following simile:[12]

> We may remind ourselves, once again, of our simile of 'the pillared willow'. The more ruthless the execution that is done by the pruner among the shoots that he finds sprouting in spring-time out of the willow's head, the more abundant will be the vitality that the tree will concentrate into the shoots which are spared, and the more vigorous, therefore, will be the growth of these surrounding shoots in the course of the season.

The application of this simile to Jewry is obvious: the 'ruthless execution' in the Diaspora of the Jews throughout the ages by 'the pruning' Gentile world is the secret of Jewish vitality and survival. In fact, the Jewish Diaspora served Toynbee as the paramount evidence of this theory:[13]

> In Jewry, we find a graded sequence of types . . . in which the ethos varies in intensity through all the degrees from maximum to vanishing point; and we observe that these variations in the intensity of the Jewish ethos

correspond to variations in the severity of the penalisations to which Jewry has been subjected by the Gentiles.

From these general statements, we may describe his conclusion as follows: Jews survived in the Diaspora as the result of the 'penalisations' which they had sustained. This secret of their survival has stimulated them to suffer more, and thus they continue to survive to this day. This is the underlying idea of his statement that[14]

> on the economic as well as on the spiritual plane, penalisation has proved to be an unusually powerful stimulus [in the Jewish Diaspora].

It may as well be made clear at this point that, as will be shown,[15] the first part of Toynbee's 'penalisation' theory coincides with Zionism's concept of Jewish misery—namely, that external forces (antisemitism) do constitute an important contribution to the awakening and/or maintaining of Jewish consciousness. But the extraordinary conclusion which Toynbee derives therefrom, Jewish acceptance of continuous sufferings as a stimulus to survival, is foreign to Judaism and thus *eo ipso* to Zionism. It is a Christian concept.

With the help of his 'penalisation' and 'stimulus' theories, Toynbee has tried in his *Study* from Vol. VIII onwards, and is still trying, in his articles and lectures, to persuade the Jews to reject the alternative for survival represented by Zionism, and to accept the fate of the Diaspora. He bases his advice on the following consideration:[16]

> The vitality of the Jewish diaspora, and its significance for mankind as a whole, as being the probable 'wave of the future', is brought out by the contrast between the steady success of the diaspora in surviving—in spite of penalisations, persecutions, and massacres—and the unsatisfactoriness of all attempts up to date, since the Babylonian Captivity, to re-establish a Jewish state on Palestinian soil.

It is an interesting sidelight that the contrast of which Toynbee speaks in this quotation was emphasised forty years earlier by one of the leading 'Nazis' of pre-Hitlerite Germany, Theodor Fritsch, when he argued[17] that the Jews

> virtually at no time, and when they did, only in a limited form, possessed the ability to organise themselves into a State or live in their own State. As

long as history has spoken of the Jews, their great mass has always lived in the Diaspora . . . dispersed all over the world, yet has been able to manage to survive . . . This is one of the most admirable acts of human tenacity, and, if I am permitted to say so, in this sense one of the greatest human virtues of Jewry.

These two elements as characteristic of two thousand years of Jewish history—denial of the ability to establish a State and praise for the Diaspora—dominate Toynbee's and Fritsch's statements. They subsequently became tenets of Nazism[18] in a most sinister context; as the Jews, according to this theory, are fated to remain in the Diaspora, *i.e.* among other peoples, they must be annihilated as 'parasites on the body of pure races'. Toynbee, as we shall show, does not even think in such brutal and inhuman terms; he expects the disappearance of Jewry by peaceful means rather, by a process of 'suicide from within' through de-Judaisation and intermarriage with others.

Any attempt at proving the ability of Jews to establish a State of their own, or its actual establishment in 1948, therefore stands in direct contradiction to Toynbee's Diaspora theory. Therein we find one of the major causes of his anti-Zionism.

This becomes still more obvious if it is recalled that, as already quoted, Toynbee had identified Zionism with an endeavour to *liberate* the Jewish people from the 'complex' which was caused by Gentile 'penalisations'.

Of course, he also considered assimilationism as a similar attempt at liberation. However, since the beliefs of the 'non-consequential' assimilationists (*i.e.* those who, in contrast to 'genuine' assimilationists, did not wish to disappear entirely as Jews) were based on a self-contained and self-supporting Diaspora without the necessity of a territorial centre for the Jewish people, they did not pose any difficulties for his Diaspora 'penalisation' theory. On the other hand, a territorial centre was indispensable to the Zionists, even if a substantial Diaspora remained in existence. This requirement destroyed Toynbee's 'penalisation' theory, because it provided an alternative for all Jews in the hour of need: once 'penalisations, persecutions, and massacres' are feared or actually begin, they do not have to be sustained; the national centre provides every Jew with the opportunity to choose whether or not to remain in the Diaspora. Because of Zionism, 'penalisations' cease to be a stimulus for survival in the Diaspora, and the principal basis of Toynbee's theory is thereby destroyed.

It is therefore not surprising that with his Diaspora 'penalisation' concept he appeals to anti-Zionist Jews and to those who cannot discern the pitfalls of this vague and nebulous theory. Toynbee understands how to appeal to the sentiments of both these types of Jew, and he promises them that the Jewish Diaspora, if it accepts his ideas of the 'stimulus of penalisation', will serve as an example which will be emulated by the rest of the world for the sake of mankind's survival. The Jews in the Diaspora are to serve as the beginning of what in the quotation above is described as the 'wave of the future'. In this he visualises the 'Pioneer Destiny of Judaism'.[19] Jews will not only be rewarded for serving as examples, but, out of gratitude for this sacrifice, he promises his Jewish readers, Jews will one day be recognised by mankind as the pioneers, builders, and leaders of the 'new age in the human history' which, he maintains,[20] is at hand and which he had already christened the 'age of world-wide Diasporas'.[21]

Toynbee is not the first Gentile in history (nor will he be the last) to try to lull Jews into enduring 'penalisations' in lieu of a better future that never comes. Symbolic of all such attempts is Archbishop Ruthard's invitation in 1096 to all the Jews in Mainz, Germany, to take refuge in his palace area in order to save their lives and possessions from the Crusaders marching towards them.[22] When, however, the Crusaders arrived, the palace gates were opened to them and all the Jews, men, women, and children, were massacred. They had been lured to the palace by the Church dignitary in order to be handed over to the murderers' arms. The Jews of Mainz believed the Archbishop when he promised them a safe future for enduring some 'inconvenience' in the present. In similar fashion, Toynbee's conception of the 'age of Diasporas' promises the Jews a bright future, and gratitude for being the 'pioneers' who have maintained the Diaspora, even though it means enduring the 'inconvenience' of 'penalisations'. But he is obviously interested only in keeping the Jews trusting and believing promises, for, as we show further, he actually rejects the Jewish Diaspora both in the present and in the future. Let us not concern ourselves at this moment with whether a single Jew, even the most ardent anti-Zionist, could be found who would accept this recipe, or who would not perceive the humorous clumsiness of such an attempt at missionary persuasion. It is referred to here in order to indicate how Toynbee deals with Jews and Judaism. At this point it is worth stressing that Toynbee conceived the idea and developed it into a full theory during a time (1934-1961) when he was observing and evaluating the most modern results of 'penalisations, persecutions, and massacres' which, as he has said,[23] the term 'Diaspora' entails in Jewish history: the loss of one-third of Jewry at the hands of the Nazis during the short period of one decade. Contrast the answer given in 1942 by Toynbee's contemporary, the Archbishop of Nitra (Slovakia), Mgr Karol Kmetko, to the local Chief Rabbi, Shemuel David Unger. The latter, accompanied by two leaders of the Jewish community, called on the eighty-two-year-old Church dignitary to implore his intervention with his former secretary, Mgr Jozef Tiso, then Prime Minister of Slovakia, to prevent the banishment of Slovakian Jewry to 'labour' camps in Poland. The Archbishop replied:[24]

> This is not only a banishment—there you will not die of hunger and epidemics—there they will slaughter you in one day, all of you, the old ones and the young, men, women and children—and this is the penalisation due to you for the killing of our Saviour.

From the point of view of Jewry's 'destruction' and as a concept it surely makes no difference whether it is achieved through the enforced torture methods of a Ruthard, Hitler, or Kmetko, or through a voluntary endurance of that torture by the Jews as proposed by Toynbee.

Toynbee's thesis is, in fact, a variant of the archaic Christian concept which the Slovak Archbishop so brutally presented in the quotation above. According to this, Jews have sustained 'penalisations' ever since Jesus's curse against Cartafilus, and since his death on the cross, and as they rejected Jesus they are rejected by God. The Jews, therefore, will continue so to suffer until they accept Christ's messianism. Accepting this messianism in essence has no other meaning than that Jewry's separate existence would become superfluous. It remains, of course, a question whether, if 'penalisations' (persecutions and massacres) were to continue, any Jews would be left to 'accept' Christ's messianism. From Toynbee's writings one rather gains the impression that he combines both the orthodox Christian view and his own 'Diaspora' theory. He thus seems to visualise Jewry as a collective community of Jesus Christs or 'Suffering Servants',[25] the latter, as distorted by Christian theologians,[26] ready to sacrifice their lives for the Toynbee 'wave of the future'.[27] Israel Zangwill once illustrated this old prescription now emulated by Toynbee by ridiculing the idea of 'the People of Christ becoming the Christ of the People'.[28] But the basis of his concept remains the archaic, orthodox Christian, as Toynbee himself confesses:[29]

> It is difficult for anyone brought up in the Christian tradition to shake himself from the official Christian ideology. He may have discarded Christian doctrine consciously on every point; yet on this particular point he may find that he is still being influenced, subconsciously, by the traditional Christian view in his outlook on Jewish history . . . I am conscious that my own outlook has been affected in this way.

Toynbee's description of this traditional Christian (and Moslem) view is as follows:[30]

> Upon the advent of Christianity or, alternatively, of Islam, the 'mandate' of Judaism and the Jews 'was exhausted' (to use an apt Chinese formula). Now, in God's own good time, the true 'Chosen people' had arrived on the scene, and the Jews' duty was clear. They ought to have accepted Jesus or, alternatively, Muhammad at the valuation placed on him in the official doctrine of the Judaic religion of which he was the founder. In declining to accept him on these terms, the Jews were failing to respond to the supreme challenge in their history, and were thereby putting themselves permanently in the wrong and on the shelf. Jewish history and its Israelitish antecedents down to the beginning of Jesus's or, alternatively Muhammad's ministry still has validity and value as a prelude, arranged by God, to the Christian or, alternatively, to the Muslim, dispensation. Jewish history since one or other of those climactic dates is without significance except as a classic example of perversity on the part of the people that, of all people, ought to have known better.

This is the archaic 'rejection' theory clearly formulated. It goes far beyond the most ultra-conservative Christian concept because it doubles the 'rejection' by not confining itself to Jesus but also adding Mohammed. The 'rejection' theory is the most pernicious reason for antisemitism in its brutal forms because, as Toynbee's description suggests, Jews, having been rejected by God, have since been superseded by a new elect of God and therefore put 'themselves permanently in the wrong', and accordingly there is no reason for their further existence. Even the fundamentalist Catholic Church felt the necessity to prohibit the 'rejection of the Jews' as deriving from the Gospels.

'Penalisations' in Jewish Tradition

The phenomena mentioned by Toynbee, such as persecutions, diaspora, survival, and so on, are age-old and well known. Jewish thinkers, too, have studied and interpreted the meaning and the impact of, for instance, recurring persecutions on individual Jews and on the Jewish community in the process of their survival in the Diaspora. A well-known *Midrash*[31] summarised it symbolically with a comment on the words 'Thy Name is as oil poured forth' (Song of Songs i, 3), which compares Israel with oil:

> Just as oil is improved only by pounding, so Israel is brought to repentance by chastisements; just as oil will not mix with other liquids, so Israel will not mix with other nations of the world.

Jews, as they understood their history, regarded this as the motif that guided them through the Diaspora persecutions. In their religious creed, all their misfortunes resulted from their own sins and apostasy, which they were still perpetrating, and not from one supposedly 'great sin' which their ancestors are said to have committed hundreds of years ago and for which they were to have been cursed. They were and are punished for the purely internal reason of not obeying the God of Israel, and not for any external factors like curses. The 'chastisements' were the sole 'penalisations' of the Jews for deserting the God of Israel. 'There is no affliction without preceding transgression against God,' said the Talmud.[32]

Throughout their history, Jews have heeded the words of God spoken through Moses:[33]

> I call heaven and earth to witness against you this day: I have put before you life and death, the blessing and the curse. And you should choose life that you and your descendants should live.

Jews feel it their duty not to die but to live for a better future for their own people and for mankind, as their tenacious vitality proves in history. Theirs is a conception of *Kiddush ha-Hayyim*, the sanctification of life, and not of *Kiddush ha-Shem*, the holiness of martyrdom, that had been their response when it was forced upon them from outside.[34] For centuries they studied, absorbed, and believed in what was foretold them in *Leviticus* and *Deuteronomy* and subsequently repeated in prophetic variations: the fate that awaited them if they deserted God. In minute detail, all the bestialities of persecution and suffering in the Diaspora were enumerated in these twenty-six verses of the twenty-sixth chapter of *Leviticus* and in the last fifty-four verses of the twenty-eighth chapter of *Deuteronomy*, centuries before they occurred. They still read as realistically as though they were written today in the light of past experience. But Jews also believed that, although individual members of their people would die in the course of the 'chastisement',[35] the people itself would never disappear because[36]

> for all that, when they be in the land of their enemies, I will not cast them away, neither will I loathe them, to consume them, and to make void My covenant with them; for I am the Eternal their God. But I will for their sakes remember the covenant of their ancestors, whom I brought forth out of the land of Egypt in the eyes of the nations, that I might be their God: I am the Eternal.

In the light of this traditional Jewish belief, 'penalisation' does not indicate a means of survival in the Diaspora nor a 'stimulus' for continuous existence in and the perpetuating of the Diaspora. It is a reminder that at any moment God's promise can be fulfilled and both 'penalisations' and the wandering ended. With the return to God through repentance, the Jews would be redeemed and brought back to their land, and would re-establish Jerusalem and Eretz Israel. Only this development would bring the Messianic era and thus the end of 'penalisations'. Nowhere in the holy literature, Biblical or post-Biblical, do we find any indication of the end of 'penalisation' otherwise than by the re-establishment of Jewish nationhood through the people's return to Palestine. Therefore the situation that is variously referred to by the Greek term 'Diaspora' or the Hebrew 'Gola' or 'Galuth' and their anglicised Latin equivalent 'Exile' has the precise meaning that these terms stand for: the temporary character of its existence. Jewish history is replete with Diasporas which existed, contemporaneously or consecutively, in all parts of the earth; they rose and disappeared. None persisted. Sometimes they lasted for short periods, sometimes for centuries, as in Babylon, Egypt, Spain, Yemen, or Germany. But without exception and however much they had differed from other contemporary ones and from previous ones, they all ended in oblivion. Thus Jewish history testifies to the fact that 'exceptions' or 'differences' do not affect the essence of Diaspora; a fact which is rooted in Jewish existence and inherent in the tenets of Jewish religion, Jewish nationalism, and Jewish tradition. And the essence of Diaspora is that, in addition to its above-mentioned temporary character, it means dispersion, atomisation, minority existence,[37] in contrast to the greatest force in Jewish continuous existence: the hope for concentration and unification in Eretz Israel.[38] It is irrelevant whether some badly informed or malevolent Gentiles or a few or many Jews for reasons of their own deny or reject this historical truth. Denial or rejection does not make it non-existent. It is this truth in which Jews believed, as every page of their experience and their literature testifies. Toynbee himself is aware of this traditional Jewish article of faith, for he wrote:[39]

> In the past the theory of the Diaspora has, in truth, been that it is essentially a transitory regime. Its reason for keeping itself in existence has been, in theory, not to exist permanently, as a Diaspora, but to hold itself in readiness to return to Eretz Israel as soon as God wills that it should.

This statement is erroneous in its larger part; it is not only 'in the past' that Jews believed the Diaspora to be a 'transitory regime'—great masses still believe so today; the reason for Jewry keeping itself in existence in the Diaspora was not and is not 'in theory' but in conviction and hope; and the 'readiness to return' was not to be passive, because repentance which abolishes this Diaspora situation in Jewish law demands 'practice' and 'deeds'.[40] But despite the statement's erroneousness, it testifies to Toynbee's awareness of the transitory character of the Diaspora in Judaism.

The Inadequacy of 'Penalisation'

Being aware of this 'transitory regime' does not in Toynbee's work mean that he would draw definite conclusions from it. On the contrary, he retains his basic principle of the 'continuous survival' of the

Jewish Diaspora through 'penalisation' even if this leads him into an unavoidable contradiction. One cannot free oneself from the thought that Toynbee enjoys contradictions between his own ideas or between reality and his hypotheses, for we encounter them in the most unexpected places. Thus, at this point not only does the 'transitory regime' clash with the 'continuous survival' but it also clashes with another thought which is based on his theory of the 'stimulus of penalisations' as the strong force keeping the Diaspora going. He maintains, as we know, that the Jews are not the only 'fossils' nor is the Jewish the only Diaspora. What is it, however, that keeps these other Diasporas going? We shall see that the propelling force is almost anything but 'penalisation', which leads to the conclusion, which he neither draws nor rejects, that the 'stimulus of penalisations' is, after all, not that great force which should induce Jews to suffer in order to maintain their Diaspora.

However, whatever the merit of comparisons between the various 'fossils' and the various 'diasporas', there is no doubt that none but the Jewish Diaspora fits into his concept of the survival 'through penalisations', as described above. How does he overcome this obvious difficulty? In his comparative study of the various 'fossils', Toynbee simply omits his 'penalisation' theory altogether, as it is obviously impossible to show that all diasporas are victims of 'penalisations' and have survived thanks to them. But as he classifies them as 'fossils' and these 'fossils' have survived, he has been forced to devise some different reason or reasons for their survival. This has necessitated the 'concealment' of the 'survival-through-penalisation' theory with regard to Jews, whom he otherwise could not keep in the same category as every other 'fossil'. Thus he writes:[41]

> In these similar crises in their history the Jews and the Parsees had preserved their identity by the same creative feat of improvising new institutions and specialising in new activities. They had found in the elaboration of their heritage of religious law a new social cement to replace a political bond that had perished with their state, and they survived the disastrous economic consequences of being uprooted from the land of their fathers by developing, in the land of their exile, a special skill in commerce and other urban business in lieu of a husbandry which these landless refugees were no longer able to pursue.

Elsewhere and in a wider context, Toynbee writes:[42]

After the temple-state at Jerusalem, in its turn, had gone the way of the original Kingdom of Judah, Jewry still contrived to preserve its communal identity in diaspora thanks to a corporate religious life that survived the loss of its historical ecclesiastical citadel . . . If we now call to mind other examples of the general phenomenon that is exemplified in a post-Exilic Jewry, we shall observe that a majority of our 'fossils' had been preserved in an ecclesiastical sheath. [He then enumerates a number of such 'fossils' and concludes:] The Monophysite, Nestorian, and Zoroastrian fossils of an extinct Syriac Civilisation managed, like Jewry, to retain their identity in diaspora by maintaining corporate religious organisation.

On that basis it was not 'penalisations' but the specific positive method of organising their own life that made them all, including the Jews, survive. Toynbee cannot but bow to this result from this comparative 'fossil' study:[43]

The historic Jewry was the Diaspora and the distinctively Jewish ghettos and institutions . . . A meticulous devotion to the Mosaic Law and a consummate virtuosity in commerce and finance were those which the Diaspora in the course of ages had wrought into social talismans endowing this geographically scattered community with a magic capacity of survival.

From this description we conclude that the theories which Toynbee has developed as regards Jewish survival in the Diaspora differ considerably from each other. They were formulated so as to fit into those aspects of general history which Toynbee happened to be dealing with at a particular time: if necessary, 'penalisations' are a welcome stimulus; if required, the entire Diaspora history is one comprehensive field of pogroms and persecutions; if called for, commerce, the ghetto, or religion have preserved the Jews. We do not intend to analyse these theories, for they are not relevant to our present investigation, apart from the fact that we do not know which of these can be accepted as *the* one. As in many of his contentions, there are some ingredients of truth in every one of these theories. This only aggravates the situation of the student of Toynbee's works.

What Kind of Diaspora?

In this connection we must also ask ourselves another question. Throughout the labyrinth of the various Toynbee theories and descriptions of the 'diaspora', the Jewish reader is induced to believe that it is not only chosen as a subject for theoretical discussion, but also that it is the Jewish diaspora which is the one to be finally emulated by mankind. Nothing, however, is further from the truth than this assumption.

If one reads his works, Toynbee's contempt for the 'Jewish Diaspora' cannot fail to command one's attention. See, for instance, the following passages:[44]

> . . . The Jews of the 'Diaspora' have successfully responded to the human challenge of religious penalisation and have been compensated for their Babylonian captivity among the Gentiles by the presence of those fleshpots to which their ancestors used to look back with such regret after Moses had led them forth into the wilderness out of the land of Egypt. The exercise of holding their own in a hostile environment has not only stimulated the Jews of the Diaspora to activity; it has also enabled them, in diverse Gentile societies, in successive ages, to keep their footing in the market-place and their seat in the counting-house, and to take their tribute from the golden stream of commerce and finance, instead of having to put up with the poverty-stricken life of the wilderness that has been led by their Abyssinian and Caucasian co-religionists.
>
> . . . like the Jewish 'Diaspora' again, they are being compensated for their endurance of this human ordeal by 'reaping where' they have 'not sown', inasmuch as they are participating in the material prosperity which has been built up by the work of other men's hands in a country which is not the immigrants' home.

We shall deal with the antisemitic aspect of this evaluation, as it is echoed in the Nazi literature, elsewhere. At this point it interests us only in connection with Toynbee's theory of the 'Stimulus of Penalisation' and the 'age of the world-wide Diasporas'. Judging from the tone and phraseology of these quotatations it is inconceivable that it can really be the 'Jewish' Diaspora that Toynbee wishes to see emulated by the Gentiles, even if, as we have seen, he repeatedly finds words of praise for Jewish survival in the Diaspora. That it is inconceivable also emerges from a further study of those parts of his writings in which he touches on the question of Jewry's future. We find there, as will be shown, that Toynbee despises the Jewish Diaspora not only from the standpoint of their 'moneylending' pursuits, as implied in the quotation above, but he also wishes it to disappear from purely religious motives. Only that Diaspora is acceptable to him as an 'example for mankind' that has surrendered everything Jewish except the last 26 chapters of Isaiah, and only then if these are blended with the teachings of Jesus and Paul. He was, therefore, quite frank in his statement when, after reconsidering his writings, he retrospectively wrote that[45]

> The treasure that the Jews have to give is not the Talmud or the written Torah or the Jewish diaspora or a Jewish national state in Palestine. It is the Prophet's vision of God's character.

Presenting his concept of the 'Age of the Diasporas' with all the phrases of a glorious future in a Jewish periodical to Jewish readers, Toynbee counts heavily on the fact that people do not study his *Study*. Dangling these sweet hopes and future honours before Jewish eyes—there are many more instances of such efforts—he expects Jews to be lulled into taking seriously promises of this sort which appear as innocent in their external expression as they are destructive in their essence. In fact, if proof were still required of the temporary character of the Jewish Diaspora and the undesirability of its permanency, Toynbee has, in the quotation above, provided it with the strongest possible arguments.

3
The Complex

In the light of this excursion into Toynbee's 'penalisation' theory, we now return to the question of the essence of the 'complex' from which Zionists and assimilationists, according to him, wish to liberate the Jewish people. He cannot see how the premise of 'religious penalisation', dealt with in the preceding section, and upon which Toynbee founded his theory, could cause a 'psychological complex' in the Jews. This premise may have some influence on the psychology of the Christians or on Toynbee's own psychology,[46] because those like him not only believe in these 'penalisations' and 'sufferings', but are also participants in, or responsible for, inflicting such 'penalisations' on the Jews through acts, words, or silence. They have therefore, out of necessity, developed a 'complex' influencing their feelings and acts in a kind of *mental vertigo* as defined by Renouvier.[47] But as a Christian concept, based on the Ahasver curse or on the 'penalisation' invention of Christian theologians, it has in that meaning no bearing at all on the Jewish psychology, for the Jews do not know of any such curse, and, if told about it, do not believe in it. As Nahum Goldmann once put it:[48]

> The Jew reacted to persecution, attacks and humiliation as to the barking of a dog; one protects oneself against a mad dog or runs away, but one does not feel humiliated because one is threatened by a dog—

apart from the fact that Jews are quite familiar, from their history, with the knowledge that persecutions against Jews, whether called 'penalisations', 'massacres', or 'pogroms', had taken place long before Jesus was born and before Christianity was organised. Toynbee himself knows this full well.[49] The 'complex' of which the Zionists would wish to free the Jewish people, if indeed they would desire to do so, as Toynbee suggested, would thus have to result from different causes.

There is no doubt that the suffering for the sake of the redemption of the Jewish people (the only meaning for those who endured it and no other, 'to hold itself in readiness to return to Eretz Israel', as Toynbee wrote) had a psychological effect on its victims. But the effects of 'penalisations' comprehended in this way and willingly accepted differ considerably from what might be expected if Toynbee's Christian or any other meaning of the term 'penalisations' is accepted. For, as we have seen, the Jews believe that their survival is secured through faith in God and the hope of redemption, and not through curses or external influences such as meaningless 'penalisations'. Conscious of these Jewish teachings of repentance, the Jews are dominated by feelings of faith and hope; and any 'complex' arising therefrom would differ from one created in people who undergo persecutions for reasons unknown to them. The one is positive, ending in liberation; the other is negative, causing despair. Above all, it is questionable whether people possessed by such a 'complex' of faith and hope would wish to 'liberate' themselves from it at all.

Toynbee should have been well acquainted with the fundamental difference between these two types of complex, because he has admitted to an admiration for Carl G. Jung, who was a pioneer in the elaboration of the distinction of the two.[50] But he completely disregarded the distinction and kept the entire issue vague. Nor did he trouble to describe the essential nature of the 'complex' of the Jews or make it clear how it expressed itself. He did not even attempt to prove that a 'complex' actually existed. Above all, while he wrote that both Zionism and assimilationism aimed at liberating the Jewish people from a 'psychological complex', it is not clear from his description whether the cause of the 'complex' or the 'complex' itself was the same when modern assimilationism was born, one hundred and fifty years ago, or when the Zionist movement was created some eighty years later; or whether the 'complex' is or is not the same today (Toynbee wrote in the paragraph quoted above:[51] 'The ultimate aim . . . is', i.e.

in the present). It is preposterous for Toynbee to take it for granted that Jews, Zionists, or assimilationists all wish to rid themselves of a 'complex' which he did not even define. There is no reason and no ground on which to accept this as a given fact. For the Jewish character has been moulded in the course of Diaspora history by a host of external and internal influences and developments that finally produced the Jew of today. Some produced bad characteristics; others good ones. This is only natural. But the conscientious Jew feels that the former are primarily the result of the abnormal conditions under which Jews had to live in the Diaspora; they did not constitute a 'complex' but were a corollary of Israel's 'sin against God' and therefore removable through repentance accompanied by a normalisation of the Jewish people's existence. And he feels and is proudly aware of the predominating characteristics of the Jew: his sense of family life, his unswerving optimism, the sincerity of his friendship, his love for knowledge, his concern with education, his adaptability, charity, sense of brotherhood with fellow-Jews, and so on. Which Zionist or, indeed, which Jew would really wish to 'liberate' himself or his people from these phenomena? Are they the symptoms of the 'psychological complex' of which Toynbee wrote? Or is this innocent-sounding term chosen as an oblique description of the 'Jewish ethos' which Toynbee has presented elsewhere in his work? Although he made a general study of the ethos of human nature,[52] he did not bother to apply serious research when this Jewish ethos was to be dealt with. Instead he wrote:[53]

> At the present time, the Jews who display most conspicuously the well-known ethos which is commonly called 'Jewish' and which in Gentile minds is popularly assumed to be the hall-mark of Judaism . . .

These lines indicate that it is the author rather than the Jews who is possessed of a 'complex'. This, to no small degree, is further confirmed by what Toynbee's son Philip has described as the tendency of those people[54] who 'would never describe themselves thus [antisemites] but who vaguely feel and say that there must be much to be said against the Jews'. This tendency is undoubtedly revealed in a passage in which Toynbee states:[55]

> In the unhappy relations between Jews and Gentiles, which is the classic case, the Gentile who is disgusted and ashamed at the behaviour of his

anti-Semitic fellow Goyyim is also embarrassed at finding himself constrained to admit that there is some element of truth in the caricature which the Jew-baiter draws as a justification for his own bestiality.

If, in addition, we recall what Toynbee has said about his own prejudices, as quoted in one of his maxims introducing this study,[73] we can see that, when speaking about the 'complex' of the Jews, Toynbee does nothing other than emulate the customary phrase 'Judaic complex' of which psychoanalysts talk, and which certain intellectual Jews themselves mention as an 'inferiority complex'. Jean-Paul Sartre, dealing with this 'complex', had the following to say about those who had coined the term and those Jewish intellectuals who accepted it uncritically:[56]

Inauthentic Jews . . . are those whom other men regard as Jews and who have chosen to flee from this unbearable situation. As a result, they follow various modes of conduct, which are not all manifested at the same time in the same person, but each of which may be characterised as a *way of escape*. The antisemite has collected and bracketed together all these distinct, and sometimes incompatible, ways of escape, and through them has sketched a monstrous portrait, which he claims to be that of the Jew in general . . .

We are prepared to recognise that the choice to take flight entails among certain Jews, for the most part intellectuals, an attitude as often as not due to a conditioned reflex. For this conditioned reflex is not inherited: it is a way of escape; and it is we who force the Jew to flee.

[Wilhelm] Stekel, in company with several other psychoanalysts, talks, in this connection, of a 'Judaic complex'. I see no harm in employing this expression as long as it be understood that the complex is not received from outside[57] and that the Jew *places himself in a state of complex* when he chooses to live his situation in an inauthentic manner. He has then, in short, allowed himself to be persuaded by the antisemites, and is the first victim of their propaganda. With them he admits that, *if there is a Jew*, he must have those characteristics which popular ill-will ascribed to him,[58] and he attempts to set himself up as a martyr, in the proper meaning of the word, or, in other words, to prove through *his own person* that there is no such thing as a Jew. The anguish he feels often manifests itself in a special form—as the fear of acting or of feeling as a Jew . . . Certain Jews . . . have let themselves be poisoned by a particular representation others have made of them, and they live in fear that their actions will conform to it.[59]

Is this then the meaning of the word 'complex' which Toynbee has employed in connection with the Jews? And is this the reaction that he expected in Jewish circles? But with the exception of a few intellectuals, who are anyhow on their 'way of escape' out of Jewry, no Jews who adhere to their Jewishness accept the existence of this popular 'Judaic complex'. Therefore they would not wish to liberate themselves and the Jewish people from something that, in their minds, does not exist.

After having been analysed himself,[60] and in the process been 're-leased . . . from a sense of guilt', Toynbee became 'enormously interested in it [psychology] intellectually' and agreed

> that psychology is probably the most important science which has been developed in our lifetimes.
>
> . . . psychology is like a new dimension, a fourth dimension. It gives sense to everything that one knows about human nature. It's a new instrument for looking at human nature and, when one applies it, everything takes on a new light.

While thus recognising the great importance of psychology in our time, he laid particular stress on its value for modern historiography. For its practical application, he compared the historian to the analyst who, in order to get[61]

> rid of one's psychic disorders . . . must know as much about the psyche's inner universe as possible.

To attain this position, Toynbee insisted that

> the maximum, not the minimum, amount of knowledge is what he needs in pursuit of his . . . objective; and the duty of acquiring as much knowledge of his subject as he can is enjoined upon him.

Yet, while fully understanding the importance of such a treatment of human psychology in history in general, Toynbee has not applied this same sensible approach to Jewish affairs. He has submitted no evidence in his work that he has endeavoured to gather even a minimum amount of knowledge of the Jews for an assessment of their 'psychology', their 'complex', etc. This he would have had to gather from the literature, history, philosophy, economy, and every other activity of those past periods with which he intended to concern himself. On his own confession, he has not done so.[62] If, on the other hand, he had intended to 'analyse' contemporary Jewry, he would have had to study, in addition to the historical sources just mentioned, contemporary Jewish works and activities in every sphere. Further, he would have had to acquire a personal comprehensive knowledge of the Jews and Jewry by living among them, talking with them, observing them, studying their reactions, and so on: in short, by gathering what he has termed 'the maximum . . . amount of knowledge' as the necessary instrument for psychological assessment. Toynbee has done nothing of the kind. He has used the phrase 'psychological complex' about the Jews in the same way as it had become fashionable to do so in recent years at cocktail parties, when terms like 'conscious' and 'subconscious', 'introversion' and 'extroversion', 'archetype' and 'complex', were bandied about, obviously without corroborative justification. His whole treatment of the Jewish 'psychological complex' is therefore, apart from the anti-semitic spirit it shows, nothing else than another example of what has been characterised above as the superficiality with which Toynbee, in his *Study of History*, has approached Jewish affairs.

4

Assimilationism and Nationalism

There is no evidence, and Toynbee has not presented any, that Zionism and assimilationism were born out of a reaction to 'penalisations', as he maintains. Let us look at the assimilationists.

Emancipated Jews became assimilationists not because they reacted to 'penalisations', but because they reacted in their own way to the friendly attitude of enlightened Governments which, in the last century, legally recognised the rights of Jews to live as they wished as free men. There were no pogroms in the 'emancipated' areas of the West, and there had been no persecutions there for some time when the Jews were officially given these rights.[63] Many among them were gasping for freedom. They believed that legalised emancipation also meant equality in real life, and that their integration among the nations of the world was expected and would be welcomed by their neighbours. In the early period of this 'romance', many of them parted with everything that externally or formally 'made' them Jews, including their religion. They were genuine assimilationists. They became Christian Frenchmen, Germans, or Englishmen. Their personal problem was solved. They voluntarily ceased to be Jews. Many others went only half-way; they decided to part with everything but their religion. But, for all of them, it was not 'penalisations' but friendliness on the part of the Gentiles, or the prospect of the equality they had hoped for, which was the underlying motive in their decision. By the time antisemitism was revived, some fifty years later, 'emancipated' Jews felt no 'peculiarity' or 'separateness'. They did not understand why they were to suffer as Jews in France of the Dreyfus period or in Germany under Hitler, having long since regarded themselves as Frenchmen or Germans. Even before they were fully assimilated, they did not regard themselves as members of a 'peculiar people'; they did not believe, as today's assimilationists also do not, that they were members of a Jewish people or that Jewry constituted a people. But in every period, assimilationists have been Jews who have made an individual decision with regard to their own present and future. They never intended, as Toynbee suggests,[64] to 'cure the Jews of being a peculiar people'. Assimilationists were not concerned with the Jews as a 'people'. In their vast literature they developed an 'ideology' based on and aiming at the problem of individual Jews in the majority society; but they never devised a philosophy or programme appertaining to all Jews. They had no desire to 'cure' anyone else, but were concerned only with themselves. For the conception of assimilationism is primarily based on individualism, not on group-consciousnessness—on spreading out individually in wide areas because concentration would block its success.[65] Toynbee was fully aware of this when, in the principal quotation given above,[66] he contrasted Zionism, a national movement, with assimilationism, an individual concept. Yet, despite this contrast, he intermingled in his text both the collective and individual aspects when he spoke of the desire of both the Zionists and the assimilationists 'to cure the Jews of being "a peculiar people".'[67]

Not even organised assimilationism as it emerged in the post-emancipation period could be regarded as desiring to solve any other problem than that of its individual members. There were, of course, attempts by assimilationists during the emancipation century to band together for the purpose of achieving assimilation with the people around them—to become, in Toynbee's words,[68] 'Dutchmen, Frenchmen, Englishmen or Americans, as the case may be, "of Jewish religion",' and it is useful to understand their way of thinking and its practical application.

Before doing so, it seems opportune to remind ourselves about the distinction between 'nationality' and 'nation' which we draw in this study. The former is ethnic in its nature, the latter is identical with statehood or citizenship. Assimilationists have never needed, and do not need today, to assimilate with the nations—*i.e.* with the countries in which they live. They belong to the country; still truer: the country belongs to them. They are fully fledged citizens of the country, as are all other citizens, including also those Jews who do not aim at ethnic assimilation. The intention to assimilate, therefore, cannot mean the pursuit of something which is already possessed—*i.e.* nationhood or citizenship. It is obviously the pursuit of something hitherto unattained (let us omit in this connection the adoption of another religion, which, in the final analysis, is not assimilationism): membership of a specific ethnic nationality which either dominates a nation (country) absolutely —a rare specimen—or is part of a multinational State, and this applies to most countries. According to this theory, an assimilator would thus not strive to band together with other Jews to become a Swiss, Belgian, or British national (citizen), because he is already one by birth or naturalisation; but he would strive to become a member of the German, French, or Italian nationality in Switzerland; or of the Fleming or Walloon nationality in Belgium; or of the English, Welsh, Irish, or Scottish nationality in Britain. These nationalities, including those Jews who regard themselves as members of the Jewish nationality, jointly constitute the respective nations (States), and jointly contribute their best to the civilisation that is Swiss, Belgian, British, and so on. All of them together, and thanks only to their common effort, are the architects and builders of these nations.

Assimilationism in a Changed World

This was the general aspect of assimilationism when Toynbee wrote volumes I-V of his *Study*. In the subsequent volumes he did not take cognisance of the changes that have taken place. For him it remained more or less a European problem in the strict division of ethnic nationality and political nationhood. But the situation has undergone fundamental changes thanks to the developments in the last fifty years, the emergence of a new society in the United States, and the internal change in Jewry's structure (the destruction of Continental Jewry, the emergence of the State of Israel, and the rise of American Jewry to its dominant position). These events, which, as mentioned, did not secure serious consideration in the Jewish sections of Toynbee's work, should have caused fundamental changes in the thinking and working of Jewish assimilationists. One cannot, for instance, pursue the old theory and speak of an assimilationist in the United States as a Jew who retains his religion and desires to assimilate to another ethnic nationality such as Polish, Dutch, Russian, Italian, Irish, Spanish, and so forth, who to this day reside in large areas of the States where they maintain the concentrated cultural activities of their respective peoples. Reality teaches us that the old theory applies nowhere. A Jewish assimilationism directed towards merging with one of the existing ethnic nationalities is therefore non-existent in the United States (and in some other countries also, for that matter), not only because Jews do not desire to merge ethnically into these nationality groups, but also because of the particular trend in the United States. Many barriers against merging have in fact fallen; there are now more openings for entry. Yet Jews still remain Jews. What direction this trend in United States society will take, what indeed it is or will be, and when it will reach a clear form, cannot be foretold. Fifty years ago it was believed that the 'melting pot'[69] conception would take effect and thus bring to an end the separate existence of the various nationality groups. This concept has now been generally recognised as a fallacy, having failed to materialise, and been given up. Whether it is at all realisable is a matter of pure speculation. As it has recently been put:[70]

> . . . the sense of ethnicity has proved to be hardy. As though with a wily cunning of its own, as though there were some essential element in man's nature that demanded it—something that compelled him to merge his lonely individual identity in some ancestral group of fellows smaller by far than the whole human race, smaller often than the nation—the sense of ethnic belonging has survived. It has survived in various forms and with various names, but it has not perished, and twentieth-century urban man is closer to his stone-age ancestors than he knows.

Factually we are today *Beyond the Melting Pot*.[71] At present the United States is predicated as a 'cultural pluralism', as advanced by Randolph Bourne and Horace Kallen,

> in which the ethnic groups cherish their own traditions while refusing to isolate themselves from the larger culture.[72]

This obviously confirms the failure of a full merger and corroborates the Zionist conception of a separate Jewish nationality and its acceptance of 'assimilationism in the dative'—*i.e.* absorbing external cultural influences while preserving one's folk personality, as elaborated elsewhere in this study. It is not without significance that this view has been confirmed in the American scene. For the assimilationist Jew in the United States it causes immense difficulties, because, for a start, it is extremely uncertain whether this latest trend will be the final stage of development, particularly as the cultural elements in the 'pluralism' are simultaneously also predominantly ethnic. These latter considerations have remained in existence and have even been fortified by the influx of Spanish-speaking Puerto Ricans and by a growth in the national consciousness of the Negroes accompanying their 'revolt' for total equality.[73] Finally, there is the question: what is the United States *per se*? Today it is still a political entity with a very heterogeneous population. It is quite possible that it will develop into a special entity according to the assumption that:[74]

> the United States is rapidly assuming that character of relative homogeneity which marks a fully matured nationality. Whether that American nationality which is being born before our eyes will englobe all sections of the population, or whether some or all of the marginal groups mentioned above will be kept at arm's length, sharing citizenship status but not becoming part and parcel of the new ethnic entity, is a problem apart, and certainly a very weighty one. But it does not affect the central fact. After having decried nationalities and nationalism as a European anachronism, America herself is becoming 'nationalised'. Nor is the nascent American nationality free from that heightened self-awareness, from that emphatic and emotion-laden concentration on its typical values (usually referred to as 'the American way of life'), from that insistence that the interests of the national community be made the major yard-stick of policy, which is certain to comprise the overwhelming majority of the population, the United States is about to become a nation-State such as we find in Britain, France, Spain, Italy and the Germanys and several smaller European countries. It is easily understood, therefore, that the conceptual distinction between the nation in the ethnic sense and the 'nation' in the sense of the sum total of the States' citizenry, just as in the case of these European States, continues to be blurred in the mind of the average American; the more so since the United States has never gone through the phase of fighting the cause of the nation against a hetero-ethnic State. None the less,

glimpses of a more exclusivist nationalism, with all its inherent excesses, have been appearing in the United States ever since the 'Know Nothing' movement and are certainly noticeable today, a nationalism in which the alleged values and interests of the dominant ethnic group were knowingly distinguished from those of the country as such. The more the marginal groups will be kept out of bounds of the nascent nationality, the more American nationalism will lift itself out of a more generalised, State-and-geography-oriented patriotism, and will come increasingly to resemble the nationalisms of the dominant nationalities of Eastern and Central Europe. The more the marginal groups will be permitted to integrate, the more nationalism and patriotism will tend to merge after the fashion of most of Western Europe. At present we encounter a self-styled American nationalism used ambiguously in both meanings, with the adjective 'national' applied more frequently to the politically circumscribed group of the inhabitants of the whole country (as distinct from the population of a single 'State' or region), and 'nationalist' to an ethnically determined group with exclusivist proclivities.

In such uncertainties with regard to the United States and thus *eo ipso* to the present and future, the Jew in the United States will, because of them, become a candidate for a sort of 'assimilationism' which he will find most difficult to define even if he tries. But does he try? I cannot think of a single Jewish community in history whose members had the wish or urge to assimilate with other majority groups which did not know how to define this wish or urge. The emancipation and post-emancipation assimilationists in Europe developed a definite 'ideology' of their own which was based on their consciously being Jews and consciously desiring to assimilate, knowing precisely with whom and to what end to assimilate. They took their decisions seriously. They created a literature of lasting value from both the point of view of scholarly approach to Judaistic studies ('Wissenschaft des Judentums'), the philosophical, sociological, cultural, religious, and national investigation of Judaism, and that of the position of the Jew in a non-Jewish world. They knew Jewry and Judaism thoroughly, even if some of their prominent leaders came to the conclusion that Jewry would not survive in the 'new era'.[75] For the first time in history it now happens that the Jewish assimilationist knows nothing or almost nothing of Judaism, of his religion, history, culture, language, etc., nor can he define the direction of his life as a Jew in the non-Jewish surroundings.

His is a faceless, empty, drifting existence which cannot even be termed assimilationist, because he has neither the will to be a Jew nor the will to cease to be one. At best he remains a negative Jew, who, without being able to say positively what he wants to be, defies other Jews if he feels that they endanger his position of 'nothingness' in which he pretends or somehow even believes to feel well. The Orthodox is too religious for him, the Zionist too nationalistic, and the rest of the Jews too Jewish. This is not the place to investigate the causes of this development and to suggest a solution. We are dealing with Toynbee's view of assimilationism and his obvious inclination to suggest it as the solution of the Jewish problem. It certainly *is* a solution if it is carried out honestly and consequentially; it leads to the disappearance of the Jew as Jew. For this reason the lesson of assimilationism, learned in Europe, which is the core of Toynbee's approach, has its important meaning for our days also. The phenomenon is the very same. Only it must be adapted to the present. It may even one day, if the above-quoted prognosis of an ethnic American nationality comes to be realised, be of practical help to *a future* generation of today's largest Jewish community on earth.

A new approach in the light of the old may help many a 'drifting Jew' to find himself. And from this point of view, not everything is bleak. In addition to a strong conscious Jewish feeling among large masses particularly of American Jewry, a kind of American version of 'Juedische Wissenschaft' is in the making, primarily characterised by a positive approach to Judaism and Jewry with regard to both the past and the future. There is no doubt that these factors will, in the end, force the 'drifting Jews' to seek and find an 'ideology', as their predecessors in Europe were forced to do, for the justification of their existence. The situation today is in more than one respect reminiscent of that of European, particularly Central European, Jewry on the eve of the emergence of Zionism. Even the method followed by Jewish assimilationists in the 1960s, negatively defying other Jews while hiding (probably not even knowing) their position behind generalities, is almost identical with that of the 1890s, in the second—or third, if we accept Dubnow's divisions[76], phase of post-emancipation assimilationism. They were then forced into daylight by the progressive deepening of Jewish consciousness and by the emergent conditions in the non-Jewish society around them. If one observes intently and with a discerning eye the trend in American Jewry and in some other lands, one can see the similar contours of the new investigation in the same directions. In the search for positive values in Judaism by all sectors of conscious Jewry and in the investigation of the Jews' relationship to a pluralistic world, the 'drifting Jew', too, will be forced to investigate what he really is and where he actually wants to go. For there is no other way to that knowledge than the study of one's own people's history and literature, the old well-trodden method which, experience tells us, is the only way to know oneself.[77] Experience of the past may thus to a large extent help to clarify the situation of today and to-morrow. It is therefore not least for this reason that this excursion into assimilationism can serve its purpose even if it is restricted to Toynbee's limited scope.

What Is An Assimilationist?

We can now return to the description of assimilationism which we interrupted.[78] We pointed out there that assimilationists are individuals or 'groups' of individuals who want to submerge in one of the ethnic nationalities of their country. We had in mind, of course, the assimilationists who consciously desired to assimilate. This now leads us to a further question. Through the very fact that assimilationists are striving for assimilation, they reveal that they are not yet assimilated. What are they meanwhile? Toynbee has not hesitated to describe them as members of 'Jewish national or . . . ethnic solidarity'. He wrote:[79]

> A sense of national—or, as some Jewish scholars call this in its Jewish context, ethnic—solidarity still continues to be one of the elements in the Jewish communal consciousness, and this among Western Jews as well as others, though among Jews in Western countries the ethnic, as compared with the religious, aspect of their Jewish consciousness has perhaps become less prominent than it still is among most Jews elsewhere.

That this is so is strongly confirmed by the efforts of those who band together for the purpose of assimilating. Experience reveals that such efforts have not brought those Jews nearer to their aim, but have kept them away from it. For they were forming groups of Jews, organisations of Jews, movements of Jews, thus strengthening Jewish consciousness and reinforcing segregation by their togetherness confined to themselves. They retained a form of 'community'—*i.e.* group-distinctiveness from the non-Jews, which they admittedly did not want, but is separation nevertheless.[80]

In addition, their banding together was to be of a temporary nature only, a step towards one day fully assimilating with the surrounding people. If they took their own aims seriously, they could not remain assimilationists for ever—*i.e.* Jews striving to assimilate. After all, a moment must arrive when they achieve their dream and become assimilated—*i.e.* absorbed as individual members of a new nationality without a 'hyphen'—not even a religious one. As Prof. Bruno Bettelheim confessed:[81] 'If one prefers to remain an American citizen, as I do, one has to face the fact that one's Jewishness may become less and less important as the generations pass'. For not only is the religion which dominates the lives of Gentile nationalities non-Jewish, but the Jewish religion itself is essential to the distinctiveness of its adherents. However, once their conscious absorption has been achieved, they cannot claim to be full-fledged members of a new nationality and still retain a distinct separateness (in particular, a Jewish religious separateness) within it. Genuine assimilation can have this meaning only, and many sincere people have drawn the conclusion from their belief in honest assimilationism: they disappeared as Jews.

Whether, therefore, it is possible to be a genuine assimilationist and still retain one's 'community distinctiveness' is purely speculative. History and experience have shown the impossibility of such a union. Toynbee thought that it was possible, without the Jews disappearing as Jews; although when he attempted to devise a practical way, he ran into an unavoidable contradiction. He recently emphasised that the Jews[82] in

> the Diaspora still have a future in Western countries, and this still as a distinct community. It has a magnificent future on a religious basis if it bases itself on religion alone ... So far from being threatened with extinction, the Diaspora today has before it the prospect of retaining its identity in the role of a religious community open to all men and winning converts all over the globe.

Even a superficial glance at these few lines in comparison with the first quotation at the beginning of this chapter[83] shows the basic contradiction. For, in Toynbee's new garment, the assimilating Jew would not aim at 'curing' Jewry of being a 'peculiar people', but would remain a member of a 'distinct community' through his religion. In this connection it is conveniently overlooked that, in the concept of assimilationism which rejects Jewish nationalism, both the essence of the 'peculiar people' and of the 'distinct community' derive from the very same source: Jewish religion. Toynbee, too, made this quite clear himself when he wrote that[84]

> their present distinctiveness can be seen to have originated in particular social and religious innovations . . .

How an assimilating Jew, who anyhow believes that Jewry constitutes a 'religion' only, can remain within a 'distinct community' yet cure himself of belonging to a 'distinct community', is one of those questions which remain unsolved and buried in the graveyard of the *Study*.

The problem, basically, hinges on what is understood by Jewish religion and by a distinct community. In the light of our experience, it is not surprising to find that these terms, too, have escaped a clear definition by Toynbee.

A. The Religious Aspect

Toynbee surely cannot claim innocence with regard to Jewish religion. He is fully aware of the various religious conceptions within Jewry.[85] For a clear analysis of religion in Jewish life would have unavoidably led to the conclusion that his edifice of an 'integrated' yet 'distinct Jewish community based on religion' would have collapsed. Apart from the widely different Jewish religious denominations, there is a great mass of Jews who are not affiliated with any of these Jewish religious groups, many are altogether atheistic, and yet all these regard themselves and are regarded by others as Jews.[86]

But even if, as a pure supposition, one of the various religious denominations in Jewry were to declare itself the basis of the 'distinct Jewish community', that would be tantamount to accepting the exclusion of the other denominational groups from that 'community', and this would of itself lead these other denominations to create communities of their own. Accordingly, Jewry throughout the world and in each country would be split into a host of 'distinct communities based on religion' as understood and practised by each of them. Assuming that the miracle were possible of one existing religious group being accepted as representing religiously the 'Jewish community', it would not have any impact whatever on the distinction between Jews and Gentiles as it exists today, because historically, conscientiously, and factually, Jews, through religion more than through any of the other attributes that make them Jews—ethnic, racial, social, cultural, psychological, historical, etc.—have remained a 'distinct community'. And each of the various religious shades within Jewry has contributed through its very existence to this 'distinctiveness' of which they form an integral part. For, by its nature, religion is not something formal or mechanical, adhered to occasionally at special times, let us say on a Saturday or Sunday between ten o'clock and twelve o'clock, chosen by its adherents. If it is intended in its true meaning as the relationship between man and God, it must, in the same spirit, also shape man's relation to man. For religion, professed sincerely and practised genuinely, profoundly influences its adherent in everything he does and thinks. One cannot be religious for an hour or two in the mosque, church, or synagogue, and disregard religious tenets outside. And in view of the fact that Jewish religious principles differ fundamentally from those of the Christian, Moslem, or other religious majorities because they are the result of their different experience and understanding of the meeting and subsequent relationship between God and man, the Jew, any Jew, to whichever of the Jewish religious denominations he may adhere, is 'distinct' from his neighbours. This is not only accidentally, as Toynbee mentioned,[87] 'because he happens to go to synagogue on Saturday instead of going to church on Sunday', but unavoidably and all the time. Naturally, this influences his position vis-à-vis his non-Jewish friends and neighbours, as well as in society at large and in the State. Based on the regulative principle of holiness ('Ye shall be holy'—*Leviticus*, xix, 2), the Jew's thoughts and feelings are permeated by an unqualified monotheism, by a sense of absolute justice, by a standard of conduct, by ethics, morals, by a balance between individual and society, and other standards derived from and based on that principle. But these are not the monotheism, justice, standard of conduct, ethics, morals, balance between individual and society, that are derived from Christian, Moslem, or other teachings, however similar some or many of them may seem to be on the surface. The differences condition and justify the separate existence of these religions. As Judah L. Magnes once put it:[88]

> To a Jew, the interesting part of Christianity is the part that he rejects. The morals are the morals of Judaism . . . But the other part—the Hellenistic and pagan and sacramental—that is new and interesting and strange . . . and for the life of us, literally, we and our fathers have not been able to believe it, and we reject it with both hands.

In accordance with their respective teachings, and based on them, religions devise codes of right and wrong and guiding principles to be followed by their adherents. We therefore speak of a specific 'way of life' rooted in religion. This applies to Judaism more strongly than to any other religion, because Judaism insists on the duty of all adherents to a fulfilment; it is a commitment not only to believe but to practise and thus to accept a self-imposed discipline. 'Ye shall therefore keep My statutes, and My judgments which man shall carry out and live by them' (Leviticus, xviii, 5). Accordingly, Jewish religion, which, in fact, is the Jewish way to religion, dominates the daily activities of the Jew.

In this connection it must be emphasised that we are refraining from considering those Jews for whom a declaration that 'We are Jews by religion' is only an excuse or apology for being different from the Gentiles yet are unable to conceal their Jewishness or seriously explain their identity. We are concerned solely with persons who genuinely regard themselves as Jews by religion and take their religion seriously, in spirit and in practice.

It is natural that all those who adhere to a religion or to a specific interpretation of it should join together for its observance. They form organisations and establish institutions for specific synagogal, cultural, philanthropic, social, financial, medical, and other pursuits that may be required to fulfil the objectives arising out of their common ideal and approach to the various aspects of life. They also endeavour to bring up their families in the spirit of the religion's teachings and according to its code of standards. This entails, in addition to the institutions mentioned, the establishment of schools,[89] of houses, of learning, of youth centres, headed by rabbis, teachers, youth leaders, trained in special academies which the groups build,[90] and taught from a literature in Hebrew[91] and in the vernacular, specially created by competent writers in the respective religious denominations. In these schools and institutions the child and the student are taught the basic tenets of Judaism, often not only from the Jewish Bible, with its prophecies of a great Jewish future in Eretz Israel, but also Talmud and other relevant literature. They will thus absorb that which constitutes Jewish religion. And while they live in non-Jewish surrounding the basic difference between their religion and that adhered to by the surrounding majority will glaringly come to notice. Apart from this spiritual aspect, special formal practices are introduced and traditional customs and ceremonies adhered to (in some cases less rigid; in others faithfully; but none[92] without) with regard to such *Mitzvoth* (Commandments) as Sabbath, Festivals, circumcision, *Bar Mitzvah*, marriage, *kashruth*, burial, sanitary and sex regulations, and so on. The practice in synagogue and schools and family observances and celebrations at home are no less an indispensable part of adherence to religion, because family life is the central characteristic of Jewish religion. It is therefore particularly in the home, where people spend the greater part of their lives, greater by any measure than in synagogue, that the endeavours to live a religious life would be made and become obvious. For this is the basis of the unified Jewish family system, which has become exemplary in every direction. And for this purpose domestic rituals of singular beauty and inspiring practise have been and are being introduced. On such occasions 'homes turn into synagogues'. He who has not witnessed a Sabbath or Festival ceremony in a Jewish home, with mother lighting the candles and father reciting the age-old songs; or a family *Seder* on *Pessach*; or the joy on *Chanukkah* accompanying the lighting of the *Menorah*; or any of the other domestic celebrations, cannot evaluate the great importance of religion in the daily life of the Jews. And one of the strongest elements in the inner feeling of Jewish unity is the awareness of Jewish families that when they practise this or that ceremony or *Mitzvah*, in thousands of other Jewish homes it is performed at the same time.

Through the teaching of Judaism in the above-mentioned institutions, from childhood on, and through all the other practises deriving from Jewish religion, the distinctiveness from the non-Jews grows with the Jewish child and becomes implanted in the Jew's being. This distinctiveness also makes itself felt in the non-Jewish surroundings of the Jew. It becomes, in mixed settlements, as it was once defined,[93] a kind of 'five o'clock iron curtain' which 'separates Roman Catholics, Jews and Protestants after they have been working together all day' in areas of general, local or business affairs or at school. And this arouses questions and curiosity, which already begin with the children talking about it or when challenged to 'explain' the difference to their non-Jewish friends, who are usually mystified by Jews not living 'like ourselves'. Adults are not less involved through their separate activities and way of life arising out of their 'belonging' to a different religious group and through the influence that religion has on the character and the mentality of its adherents. As Charles Singer once put it:[94]

> All religions produce certain special patterns of character in those they affect. The peculiar history of the Jewish people and the peculiar teachings of the Jewish religion have combined to produce a pattern of distinctive type.
>
>   The special pattern of character created by a religious tradition can perhaps be traced in its simplest outline and therefore be seen most clearly in the conduct of men who, though born within that tradition, are little moved by its actual expression and little interested even in its products. This is quite as true of Judaism as of Christianity . . . The Jewish pattern of life, like the Christian pattern of life, can often be seen even in those who have formally separated themselves from the religion.

Therefore the distinction based on and arising out of religion does not remain a strictly Jewish affair. It will apply equally in the Gentile sector which takes its religion seriously and will, for the same reasons mentioned with regard to the Jewish religion, also deepen the Gentiles' own creed and strengthen their own communal conscious distinctiveness. We can observe this trend, for instance, in the U.S.A., where the Christian churches are not only places of worship, visited on Sundays for religious services, but are also clubs, centres for various functions of a public, social character, which gives them the clear stamp of a distinct entity. Apart from the activities arising out of their 'belonging' to their churches, Christians will, like Jews, adhere to their basic teachings and practise them faithfully. Many of them will no doubt in all honesty accept or retain the basic Christian attitude towards Judaism which is inherent from the first in Christianity, destined to supersede

Judaism as the true religion, to eliminate it through missionary effort, and finally, to take possession of its heritage.[95] This purely religious aspect will, of course, deepen, not ease, the distinction between them and the Jews.

In short, it can be accepted as an axiom that religions by their very nature separate the adherents of the various denominations. As Israel Zangwill once put it:[96]

> Whoever heard of a religious sect that did not yearn to live as compactly as possible, whether for communion or self-defence? Why, in my *Times* Atlas, there is a map of Europe coloured according to religions, and the division is almost as clear as that of countries.

There is nothing wrong or bad in that 'difference', provided that it is not concealed or denied for opportunistic reasons. The honest adherence of people to their religions, however far apart these may be and however deep the spiritual and social gulf between them, leads to mutual understanding and respect, and probably to many a healthy compromise in social interchanges if it is openly and frankly stated and honestly faced.

This also applies in no less a degree to the areas of possible friction. Such friction does not necessarily arise. But to exclude the possibility may be a wishful escape from reality. As experience shows, occasional frictions, not always significant or of the same importance, have resulted in the past from the normal religious practice of individuals or of small groups—an experience many religious Jews have encountered in one way or another wherever they have lived.[97] On the other hand, there also arose more general controversies which reached beyond individuals and small groups and embraced the entire Jewish community in a given place or land. Experience in this respect shows that it has happened not seldom that the free, undisturbed practice of religion has led to bitter controversies, to court proceedings between Jews and Gentiles, and has even turned into local or statewide political issues.[98] Moreover, areas of distinctiveness, as mentioned above, cannot be confined to religious practices (worship) in a synagogue, a church, or the home, because religion is *prima facie* a strong spiritual force with a great lesson for its adherents, who, as believers, would wish others to share it as well. Thus, as good citizens, adherents of a particular religion would endeavour to get their country to accept their thoughts (derived from their religious concept) on such vital matters as family life, birth control, education, capital punishment, Church-State relations, civil liberties and rights, ethical and moral conduct,[99] and so on, as guiding ideals for the various legislation appertaining to the welfare of all its citizens. This is not only the self-evident desire of a religion's adherents but also their duty as citizens. These are to no less a degree political issues, involving Jews as Jews, Christians as Christians,[100] or Moslems as Moslems, each with their distinctive approach to these questions, than the organisation of, let us say, Jewish defence against antisemitism, with which Jews in every country are confronted whether they regard themselves as Jews by religion, by nationality, or by any other mark; or the organised protests of, let us say, Jews in the U.S.A. or in France or in other free countries against antisemitism in Soviet Russia (although the Jews there are recognised not as a religious community but as an ethnic nationality),[101] in the course of which Jewish leaders invoke the intervention of their respective Governments, the press, public opinion, and so on, in support of their protests.

In a recent study Professor Fuchs, investigating the political aspect of American Jewry, came to the conclusion that because of the difference between the Jewish religion and the Christian concept, their respective political behaviour differs fundamentally.[102] He believes that the three basic roads leading a Jew to be a Jew arose out of the Jewish religious tradition of learning (*Torah*), charity (*Zedakah*), and the positive attitude to life. He wrote:[103]

> In probably no other American subculture is so high a value placed upon learning and intellectuality, or upon the helping of the poor by the rich and the weak by the strong, or upon living a good life upon earth in full use of one's body. These three values, taken together or regarded separately, have helped to guide Jewish political behaviour in recent decades along what in the discourse of our times would be called 'liberal lines'.
>
> Considered separately, it is possible to see how each dominant value has had influence in shaping the Jewish position on issues and candidates in recent decades.[104]
>
> Taken together with the other Jewish values of learning and *Zedakah* the non-asceticism of the Jews has, along with their insecurity, helped to pro-

duce a distinctive Jewish political style which has characterised a liberal position in our time.[105]

We therefore see from all that has been said hitherto that from whatever angle one approaches Jewish religious communal activity it ends in 'politics'. The Jew who regards himself as a Jew by religion only and derives honest and sincere conclusions from his adherence to it is deeply involved. Thus the very future that Toynbee foresaw for the Jews once they confined themselves to a purely religious community, namely, that[106]

> in a western country, the basis of the local 'Jewish' community is bound to be wholly unpolitical,

cannot happen and does not happen. *Nolens volens* they enter the political field. After all, the very principle of religious freedom is a political struggle; it can only be achieved by political means. Moreover, to pretend the absence of political ways and means in religious communities in Western countries, as Toynbee does in the quotation above, amounts to concealing the fact of what Western countries really are like. Unless, of course, it is to be assumed that in Toynbee's structure only the 'Jewish community based on religion' is to be wholly unpolitical while all other religious communities are to remain political. But a Jew who is told by Toynbee that by confining himself to his religious community he becomes a full-fledged equal member of a given society would not understand why this equality in political activities should not extend also to his 'religious community', if it applies to all other 'religious communities' in that society. But Jew and non-Jew alike is aware of the fact that politics is very much a factor in every human being's life: so also in the Western world of which Toynbee speaks. Some concrete examples of this effect have been referred to before; not can it be denied that the conjunction of religion and politics in, for instance, a Western country like England is a proven fact,[107] and so is the strong combination of religion and politics in American life.[108] It is natural that a religious community by virtue of its existence must maintain a certain relationship with the other communities next to whom it lives, particularly if it pursues activities which could be advanced or prevented from realisation by all or some of these other communities. A great many of such activities, as has been shown, become party matters of political interest, apart from the fact that if a religious community wishes or is forced to deal with local or State government authorities, it will do its utmost to win government sympathy for its practices and demands, and for this purpose will wish to disseminate information leading to a deeper understanding of its beliefs, ideas, and programme—all this is a matter of uninterrupted political contacts.

If therefore a religious community wishes to exist and practise its religion, strong political activity is, in many respects, the basis of its success. The question is, therefore, not whether political work is necessary but only what kind of politics should be pursued. And the form and method will vary according to the urgency of the issue and to the opposition against it. As the few examples which we have selected above (at random, from a host of many more possible) show, Jews have fought and are fighting for their religious rights by political means: they organise political campaigns, the lobby is alerted, the vote of Jews in municipal and statewide elections plays a role. Often Jewish communities in other countries endeavour to assist their coreligionists through diplomatic interventions,[109] and so on. In Toynbee's writings it appears[110] that such political activities take place primarily in America, by Zionists on Jewish national grounds only, and in connection with Israel. But, as shown in the examples above, and as reality teaches us, the very same political activities and methods, in no way connected with any Jewish national, racial, ethnic, or similar issues and especially not with the affairs of the State of Israel, are employed on purely religious grounds.[111] The strictly religious issues turn into political problems, with Jews and non-Jews mostly on different sides of the fence. The Jew, basing his Jewishness on religion only, would thus, contrary to Toynbee's premise, not tear down the barrier that separates him from the others. The barrier of difference will remain. For it exists and will exist as long as Jewish religion exists, a religion which in so many respects differs from other religious concepts. There is, therefore, no substance to Toynbee's assertion[112] that if the Jews were to confine themselves to being only a religious community

> the age-old friction between Jews and non-Jews would then surely disappear.

For at the outset Jews are very well aware of the fact that this friction was very noticeable during the centuries when nationalism in its modern connotation was still unborn, and the issue was thus a purely religious one (whether or not the Jews were willing to accept Christianity). But the examples quoted in the preceding pages also show the impact that adherence to religion did and can have on the Jews in their relationship to their surroundings. In some respects this led to serious implications, as other examples show, in which opponents of Jewish religious demands went beyond legal or political argument and indulged in open threats against the Jewish community as such.[113] In this connection it cannot be sufficiently emphasised that all this appertains to Jews as a purely religious community.

Neither the trivial nor the significant examples enumerated above will necessarily be repeated in the future or superseded by others. But no one can state today with certainty that frictions will not arise any more. Both Jews and non-Jews strive, of course, towards reducing the areas of possible clashes and much has already been achieved in this respect.[114] And it is hoped among all religious denominations that as time goes on and understanding of and respect for each other's differences grows, many more areas of co-operation will be opened, accompanied by a simultaneous reduction of actual frictions. In one specific field particularly, the attack in contemporary society against all religions, it is equally important to Christians, Moslems, Jews, and every other religion to seek cooperation. One example is in the establishment of an Inter-Religious Committee Against Poverty by Roman Catholic and Jewish religious leaders in the U.S.A.[115] But in all this, in the dreams of a future world and in the realities of today, the situation remains clear even if the emphasis in contemporary society in general has been shifted from religion to nationalism: the fundamental and, therefore, permanent religious differences are sufficiently strong to make the distinction emphatic. And as long as this prevails, and religions are adhered to by their members, the Jew by religion remains separated from the Gentile. This is especially so, as it is beyond dispute that adherents of the Jewish religion are only Jews and not members of any other nationality or people. But the Jewish position in this historical division remains undisturbed ever since the Prophet Micah defined it as follows:[116]

Let all the people walk each one in the name of his God, and we will walk in the name of Adoni, our God, for ever and ever.

It was Toynbee who asserted that the friction resulting from religious distinction can only be abolished if toleration dominates motivations in human society.[117] Otherwise

there is no guarantee that intolerance will not raise its head again. If it does not re-appear in Religion itself, it may take its appearance in some psychological substitute for Religion in the shape of a secular 'ideology' such as Nationalism, Fascism, or Communism.

On these grounds alone, the suggestion that Jewry confine itself to a religious community only, and wait for toleration, loses all its meaning. Because, if the age of toleration keeps us waiting as it does, then the abandonment in the meantime of everything outside religion (even if it were possible) would not bring tranquillity and make the 'age-old friction . . . disappear'. On the other hand, once toleration dominates human society, it should make no difference what anybody—Jew or non-Jew—believes and practises. For what other meaning can toleration have than that a person can choose to remain distinct from the others?[118] It is for this toleration that civilised man strives. But it cannot be attained through the insistence that, long before its attainment, Jews should surrender one or more of those elements which they know or believe to constitute the essence of their existence. Jews who all along have stood in the forefront of the struggle for toleration could accept such advice only at the price of self-dissolution.

Many a Jewish generation has fallen victim to tempting propositions, similar to Toynbee's, promising tranquillity, the end of friction with Gentiles, the age of toleration. We have already referred to some such suggestions by him. There is nothing new in these propositions; even the method of 'temptation' is the same. Jews in their hope and trust have sacrificed many of the best of their youth and some of their outstanding talents to every one of the great 'world-saving' ideas: liberalism, communism, universalism, and many others. They all promised the abolition of what Toynbee has called 'the age-old friction between Jews and non-Jews',[119] but with respect to Jewry they all failed tragically because they had to be accompanied or preceded by the supreme sacrifice: the surrender of the Jewishness of the Jew, or his outright disappearance as a Jew. But these and other high ideals can only be attained if they are not conditioned on the sacrifice of those principles for which, in fact, these very same high ideals stand. Then only can they and, we hope, will they, be pursued in honesty and sincerity and thus finally prevail. This at least is the conception of traditional Judaism, which maintains[120] that 'a Godly command attained through sin is not regarded as fulfilled'. But to revert to the present: toleration, although it constitutes only a first step towards universal peace, is, in the world of today, notwithstanding many advances, not much nearer to, and in some areas even further from, realisation than a century ago. Toynbee's admired Carl Jung[121] even maintained that 'it may reasonably be doubted whether man has made any marked or perceptible progress during the known five thousand years of human civilisation'. It is, however, a blatant contradiction of the facts if in this connection Toynbee maintains[122] that as regards Jews the fault lies 'on both sides'. It does not. It lies squarely on Gentile shoulders. Jews have honestly tried to accept the promises or what they believed to be the promises accompanying all the lofty ideals, and to live up to them, ready to make and actually making great sacrifices. The last one hundred and fifty years testify to this beyond any doubt. Toynbee himself feels obliged to confirm that[123]

> In a bourgeois and secular modern Western Society in which the now all-important field of business activity had been reopened to the Jews on equal terms with the Gentiles, while Religion had sunk into being a matter of secondary importance or no importance at all, why should not the individual Jew become socially uniform with the individual Gentile by evolving into a Western bourgeois of the Jewish religious denomination, or of no religious belief or allegiance of any kind? In the Western World in the course of the nineteenth century of the Christian Era the process of assimilation on this basis did in fact go very far, and it was conceivable that it might have ended in a complete obliteration of the historic communal distinction between Jews and Western Christians if the process had not been cut short through the sudden and unexpected seizure of the Western World by a fresh paroxysm of trouble as severe as the previous bout from which it had emerged towards the close of the seventeenth century. Nineteenth-century Western hopes of solving the Jewish problem, like nineteenth-century Western hopes of abolishing the institution of War, proved in retrospect to have been a delusion.

The reason for this great failure simply is that toleration is not a legal but a moral question, and laws, however well-meaning and however imbued with lofty ideals, cannot enforce moral conduct, mutual respect, and understanding. To have that force, legislation would have had to be promulgated only *after* the lawgivers had recognised and confessed that a great injustice had been perpetrated on the Jews, and only after they had accordingly prepared and educated their citizens to understand the issue and accept the solution. But in reality legislation has not had that force because it has preceded the confession of guilt and the education of the people. As a matter of fact, this confession and education have not even followed it. It was thus only an imposition from above. It was never demanded by the mass of the people. Many of the Western countries put the 'emancipation' of the Jews on their statute-books, as Max Nordau once emphasised,[124]

not out of an inner desire but as an imitation of a fashion of the time.

But whatever the reasons, or whatever historical circumstances or other determining factors may have moved these governments, laws were passed by all of them. 'Emancipation' is a legal fact, but the people's feelings towards the Jews have remained basically what they were before, even if many important improvements have been made in practice. Anti-Judaism has been condoned or practised in their minds. After all, even in the quotations above, written in 1954, Toynbee himself expected that the freedom granted to the Jews would result in their disappearance ('It might have ended in the complete obliteration of the historic communal distinction between Jews and Western Christians'), which only proves that the guilt lies not 'on both sides', as he stated, but that 'emancipation' is understood by him, in contrast to the very meaning of 'emancipation',[125] as absorbing the Jews into the majority population so that they finally disappear as Jews. And this confirms our contention that Jewish history shows that if complete liberty, equality, and so on, are to be attained by way of promises and suggestions by Gentiles and based on any conception other than Judaism the surrender of the Jewishness of the Jew is the expected 'sacrifice', if not always by the non-Jewish initiators of these ideals, then definitely in the subsequent period of practical application. It also confirms our conclusion that in truth Toynbee cannot really wish for the existence of 'a distinct Jewish community . . . based on religion', as he professes, if through 'emancipation' he expects Jewry's disappearance.

All these contradictions in Toynbee's thoughts about assimilationism, religious community, and the Diaspora are, of course, closely connected with his own ultimate motives. We can catch a further glimpse of these if we consider carefully the following statements made by him, between 1934 and 1962, on the question of the success or failure of 'emancipation' and its impact on the Jewish Diaspora:

He wrote in 1934:[126]	He wrote in 1954:[127]
. . . when we consider how short a time has passed since the legal emancipation of the Jews took place, and how far from being complete their moral emancipation still is, even in the enlightened countries of the West . . .	By A.D. 1914 the official emancipation of the Jews on all planes of human activities was a long since accomplished fact in all provinces of the Modern Western World . . .

Such contradictions were not just accidental matters of style, as another two statements also made within these twenty years show:

He wrote in 1934:[128]	He wrote in 1962:[129]
This appalling recrudescence of militant anti-Semitism in one of the leading countries of the Western World still further strengthens the already strong Zionist case. For the German outbreak of 1933 can only be compared—in its brutality, its hysteria, and its thoroughness—with the Castilian outbreak of A.D. 1391. If this could happen in the present age in a country in which the Jews had long since been emancipated, then where in the World can the Jewish Diaspora feel itself secure?	Is it true that emancipation has proved a failure? This assumption is surely refuted by the facts.

Thus we see that Toynbee kept for himself the best of both worlds; Jews were and were not 'emancipated', and therefore have and have not a future in the Diaspora. How he could draw 'definite' conclusions under these circumstances is beyond comprehension. For the contradictions here are not matters of interpretation but of fact. Either the Jews were completely 'emancipated' before 1914 or they were not. There is no room for 'explaining' why it subsequently failed. For it could have failed if it were in a state of experimentation, but it could not have failed once it was an 'accomplished fact', as he had stressed.

The only way to understand these contradictions is, I believe, to see them in the light of Toynbee's method of applying 'facts' to his momentary requirements. Thus in 1934, as we have seen in the quotation at the beginning of this book,[130] and in the second of the quotations above of that year, he believed in the correctness of the Zionist assessment of the Jewish position, and accepted its success unequivocally. ('The Zionist Movement['s] . . . social philosophy has already been justified by results.' And '. . . still further strengthens the already strong Zionist case'.) If, therefore, the Zionist conception was right and 'emancipation' and 'assimilation', to repeat a phrase from Toynbee's 1934 statement,[131] were 'wrong method[s]', there was no future for them, and therefore no future for the Diaspora.

By 1954 and 1962 Toynbee had changed his stand and unequivocally emphasised his 'hostility towards Zionism'.[132] Consequently 'emancipation' was now declared to have been an accomplished fact forty years previously (before 1914), and was promoted from a position of doubt and doom in 1934 to a challenging alternative in 1960: the bearer of 'The Pioneer Destiny of Judaism',[133] bound to become a rallying cry for Jewish survival through a new Diaspora.

We can look in vain, of course, for Toynbee's own explanation of these contradictory statements. For it appears that while, on the one hand, making such definite statements in 1954 and 1962, on the other, also in 1962, he made statements which softened up the 'definite' ones, in this way only deepening the confusion over where he actually stands. Thus, in a speech in Philadelphia, he said:[134]

> Unfortunately, emancipation has not been a one-hundred per cent success during the century and a half that has passed since emancipation was inaugurated . . .

Why was he so indefinite on this occasion? The explanation is simple.

This last statement was made before a Jewish audience in Philadelphia, which, though strongly anti-Zionist, nevertheless could not be presented with a picture of Jewish 'emancipation' as an 'accomplished fact in all provinces of the Modern World' when, to the personal knowledge and experience of his Jewish audience, this was not so.

But the matter does not rest there. Toynbee seems to have counted heavily on his readers' poor memory. The few examples quoted above from widely separated volumes of his *Study of History* would probably not have been detected by general readers of his work, nor would they have detected the one which lay hidden in a footnote in which Toynbee, taking Professor Geyl to task in connection with the question of whether the Nazis were 'Westerners' or not, wrote:[135]

> If German Western Christians or ex-Christians could do, and did do, what the Nazis did, no other Western Christians or ex-Christians can now be sure that, in similar circumstances, they might not find themselves doing the same.

If this is applied to the Jewish case, it means that there is no hope for the future of Jews in the Diaspora, because a holocaust can happen again at any time and at any place, and this confirms what we tried to make clear when we dealt with the temporary character of Diasporas, and doubted whether any Jew anywhere could say today, 'it cannot happen here'. This is identical with the statement which Toynbee made in 1934, when he announced the doom of the Diaspora and the victory of Zionism.

And thus we are back where we started.

But Toynbee *ad hominem* also teaches us another lesson. A man of his calibre who ranges over the earth with the vision of a world of toleration, equality of men, and universal peace, has revealed his own feelings in the matter when speaking about his preconceived Christian view of Judaism and when openly confessing in 1960 and 1961 his prejudice against Jews and Judaism, as the quotations show from his writings which we have selected as maxims for this section of our analysis.

What, in such circumstances, can one expect of people brought up under less fortunate conditions, far less conducive to independence of thought, than Toynbee—people nurtured in prejudices from the cradle? After such an admission, we can realise why, even though numerous laws in numerous countries have been promulgated granting equality and other rights, prejudice still prevents Jews and other minorities in so many places from sharing in genuine equal rights and equal opportunities.

A host of other religious, ethnic, and racial minorities all over the globe have also been denied even the most primitive human rights although they too were to benefit from the great liberation of mankind as foreseen by the prophets of these 'new ages'.

It should not be forgotten that it is upon the Jewish prophets' vision of a universal peace that all these conceptions are based, including Toynbee's, as he himself has confirmed.[136] And if mankind thus accepts these Jewish prophets' visions, even if only as a dream and a hope for the future, it cannot but accept also the fundamental precondition appertaining to the Jewish people. This vision is not based on the disappearance of those who received these prophecies in the first place and for whom they foretold a continuing existence; it is not based on the disappearance of its primary and representative force, Jewry, but, on the contrary, on the re-establishment in freedom of the Jewish people in Palestine, as a first step towards toleration, peace, and a God universally accepted. Indeed, no other prophecies awaited fulfilment but the return of Israel to Eretz Israel. This high ideal for Jewry and the world has not before been tried and found wanting. It has merely been untried until our day.

Toynbee is, of course, aware of the clash between his aim of dissolving Jewry and the prophets' vision which he accepted, and he therefore attempts to give a complete Toynbeean meaning to this vision:[137]

> If He is the creator and lord of the Universe, all His creatures must be His concern. If He is good as well as almighty, He cannot have limited His loving care to a tiny minority of his human creatures and have turned His back on the rest. If the whole world is His and is embraced in His plans, the supreme objective of these plans cannot be the re-establishment of a Jewish state on Palestinian soil.

What shortsightedness! Having repeatedly emphasised his admiration for and acceptance of Amos's teachings, Toynbee has obviously forgotten what this great prophet of the Jewish people told his brethren:[138]

> Are ye not as the children of the Ethiopians unto Me, O children of Israel? saith the Lord. Have not I brought up Israel out of the land of Egypt, and the Philistines from Caphtor, and Aram from Kit?

And it is surely not without deep significance that these words are always read by Jews in their synagogues on the same Sabbath on which they read of God's bestowal of holiness upon them as a people.[139]

Jews throughout the ages have understood that through such prophecies as these they have been made to see clearly that it is not only Jews who were to be led from Egypt to Palestine, from slavery to freedom, but other nations as well, because all nations, all races, are dear to Him, are 'His children', and in the migrations of all of them to their respective liberties, and not only in that from Egypt, is God's guidance discernible.

From a complete misunderstanding of this fundamental Jewish conception Toynbee's misrepresentation of the concept of chosenness also emanates.

The Chosen People

We know from his writings[140] that time and again he emphasises his strong rejection of the uniqueness of any people.

> I reject the pretension to be a 'Chosen People' in whatever people's name it is made,

he claims.[141] But in his enumeration of peoples who make a claim to be a 'chosen People', his deepest resentment is reserved for the Jews in this connection. He cannot conceal his bitterness when he states[142]

> I reject with particular vehemence the claims to uniqueness that are made by the Judaic religion . . . For a Westerner brought up in the Christian tradition, the Jews' claim to be 'the Chosen People' is the classical case of pretension to uniqueness of the objectionable kind.

He resolved therefore to fight against the 'pretension' to chosenness wherever he found it:[143]

> I acknowledge, without misgiving or apology, that I tilt against pretensions to uniqueness wherever I encounter them.

In this connection it would again appear to be in vain to argue on a scholarly basis with Toynbee about the meaning of the term 'Chosen People' in Judaism, because it would become a one-sided controversy between knowledge and the lack of it; and this we want to avoid. Let it be pointed out, however, that, while 'chosenness' can and does have a variety of meanings, we are concerned here with the Jewish aspect only, and Judaism rejects racial discrimination, exclusivism, personal superiority claims, or earthly uniqueness. Nor does it lead to power and physical domination. Even the extreme orthodox Jew believes that God did not intend all non-Jews to become Jews today or at the end of days. Any sincere believer in any religion has his own road to salvation. And in the 'messianic' era the acceptance by all of one religion— Judaism—is neither expected nor desired; at that time it will be only one God who rules the world. Judaism believes that the selection of the Jewish people by God was not due to favouritism or to physical or intellectual superiority, but was the result of their acceptance of the Torah offered by God and their readiness to remain faithful to the covenant made at Sinai. Jewry believes therefore that it was chosen to be loyal to the Torah. After all, which Jew could believe in physical or racial superiority through 'chosenness' while for centuries undergoing physical sufferings and pogroms? What 'superiority'! The Jewish concept of the 'Chosen People' means chosenness for responsibility, not for privilege; it means holiness through service to God—and nothing else. No outsider, particularly one who, like Toynbee, has confessed to ignorance and prejudice, has the right to tell the Jews what they should or should not, what they do or do not, believe in. They have at least the same right as Toynbee claimed for himself in a debate on the London B.B.C.,[144] as we have repeatedly mentioned:

I suppose I must be the last judge on what my own beliefs are.

Yet, when all this has been said and written, we find that Toynbee himself has become the foremost repudiator of his own theory, at least as far as Jewry is concerned. While denying Jewry's 'Chosenness', he repeatedly elevates the Jewish people (if we are to take his words seriously) to a special place in his work and in the history of mankind. There is rarely a chapter in his thousands of pages, dealing after all with millennia of history of the entire human race, without reference to

Jews, Jewry, Judaism. In fact, he himself has made the Jews 'unique', has chosen them to be the 'Chosen People', to whom God has 'vouchsafed' His light,[145] to serve as examples to others ('A Jewish Alternative Model for Civilisations'),[146] as bearers of a 'Pioneer Destiny'[147] for the future of humanity, as the 'oldest example . . . of the new type of community that is surely destined to supersede the earth-bound local tribe in the age of annihilation of distance and of the conquest of outer space',[148] and as a religious concept the attainment of which, 'becoming a world-wide religion', he regarded as the 'manifest destiny' of Judaism.[149]

I cannot see that it is my task to explain psychologically or otherwise the reason for Toynbee's denial of 'Chosenness' in theory while employing it in practice. The Duke of Gloucester was probably struggling with this very same problem when he whispered:[150]

> I moralise two meanings in one word.

From the quotations above of Toynbee's universal concept of God it becomes clear not only that he completely misrepresents the Judaic teaching but that the form of his combination of this universalism with the creation of a Jewish State in Palestine reveals the same absence of understanding of the issue. There is more, in Jewish religion, in the re-establishment of Jewry in the Holy Land than the occupation of a geographical area.[151] It seems that Toynbee has never seriously asked himself the question, which lies at the core of the problem, of why Jewry has been preserved throughout the ages and through all its vicissitudes. Was it really for no other purpose, as Toynbee now projects, than not to return to Palestine but rather to become Frenchmen, Englishmen, Germans, and so on? Was Isaiah's prophecy of the 'return to the Land' really given to any other people than the Jews? In any other language than Hebrew? Did he prophesy about the future of Israel, asking future Jewish generations to return to God and to the Land of Israel, knowing all along that this people to whom he spoke would disappear or be superseded by Christians or Mohammedans, as Toynbee maintains?[152] And above all, are the Jews now to be the only ones who will not return and see their glorious future as Isaiah, Amos, Micah, and the other Jewish prophets foretold? And if Jews do not 'return', who will? Who else is referred to in these eternal words?

Apart from all this, however, Toynbee is obviously blind in the face of the great ideal which reveals that neither 'loving care to the tiny minority', as he puts it, nor the 're-establishment of a Jewish state' are ends in themselves in the prophetic vision. Both 'the tiny minority' and the Land were preserved in history for a reunification which is not without a deeper meaning for Jews and for 'all His creatures'. And the meaning is that mankind cannot be free if even a 'tiny minority' is not free. Jewry, which in the fifteenth chapter of Exodus sang the first Song of Freedom in the history of man, symbolises all 'tiny minorities' on earth, all small peoples oppressed or deprived of their freedom. 'The Eternal did not delight in you, nor choose you, because you were more numerous than any other people; for ye were the fewest of all the peoples'.[153] Progress towards toleration, and finally towards universal peace, can therefore be most appropriately measured by the degree of freedom enjoyed by that 'tiny minority'. Indeed, it is a measuring-rod of mankind's progress towards a better world, as the great philosopher-statesman Thomas Garrigue Masaryk once emphasised:[154]

A nation's attitude towards the Jews is the measure of its cultural maturity.

This is, in fact, a paraphrase of Lord Acton's ('one of the great minds among Western historians')[155] statement that[156]

The most certain test by which we judge whether a country is really free is the amount of security enjoyed by minorities.

And when Acton attempts to prove this contention by an example, he finds it 'in the history of the Chosen people'—*i.e.* the Jews.[157]

Therein lies the deeper significance for mankind of Zionism and of the re-establishment of the Jewish State in Palestine, which Toynbee fails or refuses to see. In the cause of this 'blindness', he even disregards his own theory in which he maintains that it is not the totality of mankind, not 'all His creatures', but only the 'creative minority' which is capable of finding[158]

opportunities for expressing itself in effective action for the benefit of all participants in the society.

Without the deeper significance of Zionism and Jewish nationhood in Palestine, as mentioned above, the re-establishment of a Jewish State would, in the prophetic vision, have no other meaning than the disregard of the rest of mankind in favour of the Jews that Toynbee indicated. But because it is foreseen that the Jewish State in Eretz Israel would be only a beginning, a first step towards the great future, Toynbee's rationalisation of this great vision, and his reducing it to a geographical term, becomes so meaningless. To help him in 'tearing heaven down to earth', he even dejudaises the great Jewish prophet Isaiah and selects him, of all the great visionaries, as the symbol of a non-national, anti-Zionist conception:[159]

> They [the Jews] will have to give up the national form of the Jewish com- munity's distinctive identity in order to become, without reservation, the missionaries of a universal church that will be opened on an equal footing, to anyone, Jew or Gentile, who gives his allegiance to Deutero-Isaiah's God and seeks to do His will. In our time the Zionist movement has been travelling just the opposite direction to this. It has not only clung to, and accentuated, the national form of Jewish communal life. It also has put it back on the territorial basis.

For Toynbee, as we see, Deutero-Isaiah is what he wants him to be, and not as he appears in the only source available about him, in Hebrew and spoken to his own people—his great prophecies in chapters xl–lxvi.[160] Not one of those chapters fails to promise or to imply the redemption of the Jewish people combined with its return to Eretz Israel, to re-establish its nation, as the precondition of the universal belief in God that will emanate from there once this is accomplished. A number of verses, selected at random from Deutero-Isaiah, will serve as examples:

> I will bring thy seed from the east and gather thee from the west; I will say to the north, Give up; and to the south, Keep not back; bring my sons from afar, and my daughters from the end of the earth (*Isaiah*, xliii, 5, 6).

> And they shall bring all your brethren out of all the nations for an offering unto the Lord, upon horses, and in chariots, and in litters, and upon mules, and upon swift beasts, to My holy mountain Jerusalem, saith the Lord, as the children of Israel bring their offering in a clean vessel into the house of the Lord (*Isaiah*, lxvi, 20).

> And the ransomed of the Lord shall return, and come with singing into Zion, and everlasting joy shall be upon their heads; they shall obtain glad- ness and joy, and sorrow and sighing shall flee away (*Isaiah*, li, 11).

They shall build houses, and inhabit them; and they shall plant vineyards, and eat the fruit of them (*Isaiah*, lxv, 21).

I will give salvation in Zion, and my glory unto Israel (*Isaiah*, xlvi, 13).

For as the new heavens and the new earth, which I will make, shall remain before Me, saith the Lord, so shall your seed and your name remain (*Isaiah*, lxvi, 22).

And it shall come to pass that from one new moon to another, and from one Sabbath to another, shall all flesh come to worship before Me, saith the Lord (*Isaiah*, lxvi, 23).

Let all the nations be gathered together, and let the peoples be assembled: who among them can declare this, and show us former things? Let them bring their witnesses, that they may be justified: or let them hear, and say: It is truth. Ye are My witnesses, saith the Lord, and My servant whom I have chosen (*Isaiah*, xliii, 9, 10).

And I will set a sign among them, and I will send those that escape of them unto the nations . . . that have not heard My fame, neither have seen My glory: and they shall declare the glory among the Gentiles (*Isaiah*, lxvi, 19).

This is the only true meaning of the great prophet's vision: the universal worship of One God, with Jerusalem, restored by the returning Jews, as the devotional capital of mankind. As it is said in the great work of Kabbalah.[161] Through the blessings which come over Jerusalem, the whole world will also be blessed.

That future in Jewish tradition is expected to arrive after the unification of Israel and Eretz Israel. And it can arise only then and there. For Palestine is the Jewish people's birthplace, and it gave birth to no other people. Nor did the Christian or Mohammedan religion arise in Europe or in the West; they came from Palestine. And Palestine owes its place in history only to the Jews and to no other people. The combination of Jewish spiritual creativity and the soil of Palestine have in the past brought to life the great religions of Judaism, Christianity, and Mohammedanism. The re-establishment of the same combination of the Jewish people and the Jewish Land—if the Jewish prophets' vision is to be fulfilled—is bound to bring about some new forces, whose first effects can already be felt, despite most difficult conditions, only these few years after the establishment of the State of Israel. They are at work in the moulding of a new society out of the most diverse cultural and social elements settling there: where the old and the new cross each other, as do the different streams within Judaism, and the old traditions meet new times; a human and sociological experiment that in years to come will be emulated by other countries in similar circumstances, or by those who one day may realise the age-old dream of 'one world', notwithstanding the heterogeneous character of its constituents. And they are at work in the enormous progress which the young State has made, for instance, in the field of utilising atomic energy for peaceful purposes, such as the transformation of a wasteland into a region of prosperity and the desalting of ocean water. But the new forces are not only at work in the newly created State. It is in the shape of educational, medical, sanitary, technical, and social ideas for instance that the State of Israel is already exercising an influence on millions and millions of Africans and Asians, who, neglected and oppressed for centuries by Western Gentiles, look up to Zion for guidance.[162] As the late President Kennedy stressed in a message he wrote shortly before his assassination:[163]

> The energies and skills, the minds and hearts of the Jewish people that went into the building of a new society based on timeless principles of freedom and justice . . .
> We are united by the common bonds of freedom and we give of our abundance to rescue the hopes of others. In the same spirit Israel has brought the skills and resources of its working men and women to the service of emerging nations around the globe.

And it was President Johnson who called Israel[164]

> an example in the ways and means of the free society to the emerging nations of the world.

True, all this is not yet the great spiritual revival that Jewish tradition expects to emanate from Jewry's restored national independence in Eretz Israel; this is not yet the 'Torah that comes forth from Zion, and God's word from Jerusalem';[165] but there is no doubt in the belief and hope of conscientious and faithful Jews that one day this State and this Land is going to be 'the house built by the Lord',[166] where His people will again 'declare Thy greatness' and 'sing of His righteousness'.[167]

This to no small degree is one more reason for Toynbee's struggle against Zionism and its spiritual impact. For it creates new ideas in that wide geographical area from which Toynbee has foreseen the emergence of quite a different conception:[168] a mixture of a Toynbeean-Christian-Muslim-Buddhist-Hindu religion as the saviour of mankind. It is for this that he strives and not, as would appear from his various statements quoted above, for the acceptance by mankind of the Jewish religion, which, he says, would become a 'community open to all men and winning converts all over the globe'—a view that he presents to Jewish audiences and writes in Jewish magazines. This advice should be read in the light of the following passage:[169]

> It is difficult and painful to renounce aims and practices to which one has remained faithful, at the cost of penalisation and persecution, for hundreds of years. But the Jews have at their command a spiritual instrument that, in the past, has enabled them to perform feats as difficult as this. The unwritten Torah was dormant for 1,400 years, from the date of the closing of the Babylonian Talmud till the 'emancipation' of the Jews in the West in the Napoleonic age. Yet, considering that it proved possible to bring the unwritten Torah to life in Ezra's time, and again in the Age of the Pharisees, it is not surprising that it should also be proving possible to revive it today; and it is an instrument that is equal to the task that has been confronting Jewry by now for 2,500 years. The treasures that the Jews have to give is not the Talmud or the written Torah or the Jewish Diaspora or a Jewish national state in Palestine. It is the Prophet's vision of God's character; the relation of human souls to God as the Prophets have seen Him; and the ideals of human conduct that follow from this.
>
> In equipping itself for its universal mission, Judaism might have something to learn from two great Jews whom it has disowned hitherto. It might recall that, at the zenith of the Pharisaic Age, one Pharisee, Paul, was singular in already anticipating the change of outlook that is perceptible among Jews today on a broader front. Paul perceived that the Torah, which had once been a spiritual panoply for the preservation of Judaism, had lately become a spiritual impediment to the propagation of the Jewish faith, and that therefore the time had come for the Torah to be reinterpreted again. Present-day Jews should recognise in Paul a forerunner of theirs in this field, without having also to accept Paul's belief that Jesus

was a divine being. The Jews might also at last lay claim to Jesus, whom they have allowed the Christians to appropriate without any Jewish protest. Jesus was not a Christian; he was a Jew in belief and practice, though, being a Galilean, he may have been a gentile by descent.

Now at least we can see a little clearer, and understand what Toynbee means when he pleads with Jews to renounce most of the elements that constitute, in Jewish belief, tradition, and reality, an integral part of the essence of their existence, and to confine themselves to a 'distinct community based on religion' only. He does not mean the Jewish religion at all as the Jews know it. This emerges clearly not only from the statement above but also from other sources, where, for instance, he characterises the Jews' observance of religious laws as 'a pathologically meticulous observance',[170] or where he suggests the elimination from the 'Old Testament' of the books of Joshua,[171] Ezra,[172] Judges,[173] Samuel, and Kings,[174] and pleads for a 'reinterpretation of the Torah',[175] whereby[176]

> the god of Abraham, Isaac and Jacob has become transfigured in Deutero-Isaiah's vision into the god of Ikhnaton, Jesus and Mohammed.

Once this 'reinterpretation' on the part of the Jews were to be completed, one could dispense also with the rest of the 'Old Testament', for[177]

> a Christian Church's reconservation of the Jewish Scriptures as the Old Testament of a Christian Faith was the weak spot in Christianity's armour through which the shaft of Jewish criticism went home to Christianity's heart.

This is precisely the position taken by the Nazi ideologist Rosenberg, who, interpreting the Nazi conception of 'positive Christianity', wrote:[178]

> Therefore once and for all the so-called Old Testament must be abolished as a religious book . . . [It is part of] the unsuccessful attempt of the last one and a half millennia to make us spiritually Jews, an attempt which, among other things, is also responsible for our terrible materialistic domination by Jews.

It is in keeping with the regret expressed over the 'Jewish influence' (a role ascribed to the 'Old Testament' by both Toynbee and modern antisemites, as shown in both quotations above) on Christianity that Toynbee agreed that his prejudice against Judaism was to no small degree influenced by the belief that 'Old-Testament Judaism' was ethically far lower than latter-day Judaism.[179]

Toynbee pleads with the Jews, in the long quotation above, to be guided in their approach to the Torah today by the experience of Paul, and suggests that the only difference between Paul and the Jewish concept is that of the recognition of 'Jesus as a divine being'. This is a contradictory and misleading statement: (1) if Toynbee regards it as the tragedy of Judaism that at that time it declined[180] to recognise its expected Messiah in Jesus, and therefore 'renounced its birthright' as representative of monotheism, would Judaism regain its 'birthright' as representing monotheism if it accepted Jesus as a human and not 'as a divine being'? How is this possible if they have forfeited this 'birthright' because they have always regarded him from the beginning as only a mortal human being?; (2) presented in this way, the plea is apt to conceal the primary aspect of Paul's teaching, which for Judaism is more significant than his attitude towards Jesus, an aspect which Toynbee himself has emphasised elsewhere in his work,[181] stating that Paul

made himself notorious by repudiating and denouncing the Mosaic Law.

And this repudiation of the Torah, the Jewish Law, is, of course, un-equivocally emphasised in Paul's *Epistle to the Romans;*[182] an effort which, as we have seen, fully accords with Toynbee's own aims.

Thus again we find confirmation of what has repeatedly been stated in the preceding pages, that it is not the Jewish religion which Toynbee has in mind when he speaks of a 'Jewish community based on religion' only, but a religion without the Torah, without the Jewish Law.

He makes it clear that mankind has really nothing more to expect from Judaism, and Judaism has nothing more to give mankind. These are his words,[183] which he has not retracted to this day:

At the present day the Parsees, like the Jews, survive as a mere 'Diaspora'; and the petrified religion which still so potently holds the scattered members of either community together has lost its message to Mankind . . .

Not only has he not retracted the words, but in his *Reconsiderations,* where he has undertaken his own analysis of what he presented as his theories in the preceding volumes of his *Study of History*, he confirmed them unequivocally. The first proof of this is in his statement already quoted, in which he stressed that, because they had rejected Jesus, Judaism and the Jews

> were thereby putting themselves permanently [*sic*] in the wrong and on the shelf.

He further stressed the unimportance of Judaism and the Jewish Diaspora for mankind in terms no less strong when he pointed out:[184]

> In this historical perspective the peculiarity of the Post-Exilic Jewish dias-pora, like the distinctiveness of Post-Exilic Judaism, looks as if it were no more than a passing phase. Distinctiveness was not an original characteristic of either the people or its religion; for their present distinctiveness can be seen to have originated in particular social and religious innovations that are of relatively recent date; and it is not a permanently acquired charac-teristic; for the monotheism that is the essence of Judaism has already become the religion of half the World in its Christian and Islamic versions, while the social structure that is characteristic of the Jewish diaspora seems to be now on the way to becoming the standard pattern of all mankind.

Thus it is clear that Jewry, as a 'passing phase', is not worthy, either as a religion or as a Diaspora, of further existence. It would be better if it disappeared, which in fact is the same conclusion that necessarily emerges from his statement about the essence of the Diaspora which we analysed in a previous section.

Those Jews who have thought or are thinking of playing along with Toynbee's conception because they believe that on this one point— Jews by religion only—his idea meets their own (for whatever reason they may proclaim religion as their mark as Jews) should know what the religion of Toynbee's 'distinct Jewish community based on religion' is expected to be. It cannot be denied that some Jews and Jewish writers may to a certain extent have even encouraged Toynbee in the belief that a chance existed of putting his idea over. There is, to begin with, the heritage of Claude Montefiore, whom Toynbee so frequently consults in his assessment of Jewish affairs and with whom he found an identity of thought. However, while Montefiore's 'Liberal Move-ment' has moved far from its original tenets in the sixty years of its existence, Toynbee may have found consolation in another more recently formed group of individuals, organised in the 'American Council of Judaism', who regard themselves as Jews by religion only and were primarily drawn to him because of his anti-Zionism, which they shared.

Apart from this group and a number of so-called 'intellectuals', I cannot think of any Jew who, having a positive attitude towards his Jewishness and wishing to continue to be a Jew, would or could become a victim of this clumsy missionary method. Nor does Toynbee strengthen his case when he writes:[185]

> The Ugaritic Baal and the Byblian Adonis, not the Israelite Yahweh, were the historic models for the Galilean Jesus Christ.

This theory has long been discredited by scholarship,[186] but has been a favoured theme for antisemites.[187]

Intermarriage with a Promise

Toynbee has also endorsed another traditional means of sapping Judaism, intermarriage, for he has suggested:[188]

> A Jewish community that had abandoned the ethnic basis of its distinctive identity would still retain the religious basis of it. It would simply be completing the long-drawn-out process of its transformation from a local community, based on 'blood and soil', into a world-wide community based in a distinctive common religion . . . If Judaism did become a world-wide religion, whose membership was based, no longer on physical descent, but on individual conviction of choice, and if intermarriage between Jews and non-Jews, in the previous racial meaning of the terms, became frequent, I can foresee two great spiritual gains for us all . . . the age-old friction between Jews and non-Jews would then surely disappear and . . . the great spiritual treasures of Judaism, in their original form, would at last become one of the common spiritual possessions of the whole human race.

This statement clashes right away with the one which we quoted earlier,[189] and according to which Judaism was said to have already 'become the religion of half the world'. This great acceptance obviously happened without the necessity of Jews giving up their existence as a people and without intermarriage between Jews and non-Jews. Why then should this process not continue in the same way that, in Toynbee's opinion, had already led to these world-wide successes? Of particular interest is a comparison of the figures:[190] today there are some 12,867,000 Jews all over the world, while the religions representing the Toynbeean 'true Judaism',[191] amount to 916,370,000 Christians (of all denominations) and 437,278,000 Mohammedans. Even if it were possible of realisation for all Jews—men, women, and children—to intermarry with non-Jews tomorrow, they would still become, if we include their spouses, only 25,734,000 individuals in contrast to the 1,353,648,000 members of what Toynbee calls the 'true "Chosen People!"';[192] and in contrast to 2,307,481,000 members of all major religions put together. This would amount to no more than a little over one per cent. What a prospect this makes for a 'world-wide religion' to be represented by a little over one per cent of mankind!

We have already mentioned that with Toynbee's suggestion of intermarriage combined with the promise of a glorious Jewish future, he has simply emulated past missionary attempts. It is surprising that he has not been able to think of a different, more modern form for his suggestion, but has simply pulled this one out of the old collection of junk where it has lain for centuries. It may, however, be worthwhile comparing Toynbee's suggestion of intermarriage, not with these old proposals, but with the one made by another important countryman of his who—like Toynbee—had a classical education,[193] who—like Toynbee—had a critical approach to Christianity,[194] and who—like Toynbee—had a deep admiration for Isaiah and Paul:[195] James Arthur Balfour. Over half a century ago the latter said in the British Parliament:[196]

> The right hon. Baronet Sir Charles Dilke had condemned an anti-Semitic spirit which disgraced a great deal of modern politics in other countries of Europe, and declared that the Jews of this country were a valuable element in the community. He was not prepared to deny either of these positions. But he undoubtedly thought that a state of things could easily be imagined in which it would not be to the advantage of the civilisation of the country that there should be an immense body of persons who, however patriotic, able and industrious, however much they threw themselves into the national life, still, by their own action, remained a people apart, and not merely held a religion differing from the vast majority of their fellow-countrymen, but only inter-married among themselves.

At that time, in 1905, no Jewish State was in existence, most British Jews regarded themselves as 'Englishmen of the Jewish persuasion', and a Jewish ethnic nationality was not even mentioned in the speech or the debate. It was solely the religion of the Jews that made them a people apart, and their refusal to intermarry with Gentiles that elicited Balfour's remarks. But his greatness consisted in his willingness to learn. In 1905 he did not know the Jews, their philosophy, their way of life. Twelve years later, in 1917, he had filled that gap, and was great enough to draw an honest conclusion: he became the 'godfather' of the 'Balfour Declaration', which not only welcomed Jews as members of a 'distinct people', but also established the Jewish community, in international law, as a 'distant people' ('the establishment in Palestine of a national home for the Jewish people'[197]).

Toynbee went in the other direction. We know that many of his critics believe that in his spiritual make-up he has not moved from the nineteenth century.[198] However, with regard to the above aspect of Jewish life, he first joined the twentieth century but then returned to the previous one after a serious encounter with reality. Thus he began as a pro-Zionist in Balfour's 'progressive' 1917, but by 1961 had regressed to Balfour's 'outdated' 1905 view. Like Balfour, he was never even interested, on his own confession,[199] in becoming acquainted with Jewry in literature or in life. As the poet wrote:[200] 'Like—but oh how different!'

In one respect, however, Toynbee differs from both the missionaries and Balfour. These thought of intermarriage between Jew and Gentile in the sense of the physical disappearance of the Jew through the merger, and possibly the acceptance of the majority religion, and were frank about it in their statements. It was and is in this sense that Jewry, too, understands every claim made by outsiders for intermarriage. After all, this is a problem that has interested Jewry ever since Abraham, Isaac and Jacob sent their representatives to find brides for their sons from within the fold. Experience over the millennia has taught them to see in intermarriage one of the principal external threats to Jewish survival as a people, and it is for this reason that so much concern about intermarriage is discernible in Jewish families and communities to this day. From this viewpoint, the endeavours of Jewish communities must be evaluated to stem the tide of intermarriage, which has in recent times assumed proportions beyond the 'safety coefficient' of Jewry's survival.[201] Anyhow, it is a generally accepted axiom among Jews today (without reference to statistical correctness) that intermarriage leads away from the Jewish fold, if not always directly through the marriage act, then certainly in the following generation.[202]

Aware of this attitude, deep-rooted in Jewry, Toynbee has devised a diversionary method by which he hopes to achieve the same results. He suggests—what on the surface seems 'tempting'—a combination of intermarriage with efforts at proselytisation, at making converts to Judaism, and promises as a result an increase in the number of Jews, and thus a strengthening of Judaism. He wrote:[203]

> If the door to conversion to Judaism were thrown open, multitudes would, I believe, come to drink at the fountain-head. So the numerical balance-sheet of conversions would be likely to work out in Judaism's favour. Again, if the abandonment of ethnic reservations were complete and genuine on both sides, the traditional caste-barrier between Jews and non-Jews would be likely to be broken down by more frequent intermarriage.

Before analysing these statements it seems opportune to note that they constitute another example of what has repeatedly been described in these pages as Toynbee's combination of a desire for Jewry's dissolution with superlative praise of Jewry's importance. It is worth noting in the above quotation he asserts that the Jews are permanently right because they are the only monotheists, that their 'mandate' is still valid because Christianity and Muhammadanism represents only derivative forms of Judaism, and that accordingly Judaism would also win numerically. How it could do that in view of the comparison already referred to between 12,867,000 Jews and 1,353,648,000 Christians and Moslems is one of those puzzles which Toynbee has failed to solve.

The only real result that would come from efforts directed, as Toynbee suggests, towards winning converts to Judaism all over the world, would be a 'war of conversions', because no religion can stay inactive when attacked by attempts to deprive it of its membership.[204] The enormous danger in such a 'war' that would confront Jewry, which everywhere outside Israel is in a minority, cannot even be imagined. The State of Israel itself may serve as an example of resentment against conversion attempts by Christians, a minority, among the Jewish majority of the country.[205] It is inconceivable that, as Toynbee wishes us to believe, non-Jews who believe in their religion as ardently as Jews in theirs could be persuaded to waive their objections to their own conversion if Jewish men married the Gentile daughters or Jewish women married the Gentile sons. But even if such an unlikely attitude on the part of the Gentiles were to be forthcoming, there is not the slightest chance of Jews accepting this amazing proposition. For it is particularly religious Jewry that resents intermarriage.

In fact, the information shows clearly that intermarriage between Jews and Gentiles takes place in an overwhelming number of cases among Jews who are not religious or do not practise religion. The conclusion is also drawn from this information that Jews who do not regard their Jewishness in religious terms but in national or non-denominational terms take more easily to intermarriage than individuals who regard themselves as Jews by religion. As Joseph Maier put it:[206]

> Ethnicity is closely allied with religion, perhaps especially so in the case of the Jews. While the coincidence of religion and ethnicity tends to reduce out marriages, it must be agreed that marriages across ethnic lines are more frequent today.

And he quoted Marcson's remark[207]

> that intermarriage patterns tend to be endogamous in religion and class, but exogamous ethnically.

On such a basis Toynbee, in his advancement of intermarriage, should have supported the strengthening of the ethnicity of Jewry and not demanded its abandonment and the confinement of Jews to a purely religious community. But, of course, it is hard to expect logic in all the confuting theories which we have uncovered in this study. One is reminded of Kipling's description:[208]

> Very rarely will he sparsely push the logic of a fact
> To its ultimate conclusion in unmitigated act.

We have just mentioned that we could not conceive of any Christian group accepting Judaism through the intermarriage of its children with Jews. Toynbee shows as great a disrespect towards Jewry if he believes that Jews (however few) could be tempted to intermarry in the hope, as he promises, that in this way they would acquire peace on earth for themselves and worldwide conquest. It must be pointed out at once that Jews have a good memory and know from experience that this way of attaining the end 'of the friction' is a false one. An example in our own day shows this clearly: Sweden is a country with very few Jews (13,000 out of a population of seven million), with the highest percentage (40 per cent) of intermarriage in any country in the world. Sweden's Jews are free and play their modest role in the country's life as law-abiding, respected citizens. Yet Sweden has become one of the main centres for the publication and dissemination of antisemitic literature, financed mainly from within.[209] There intermarriage does not lead to peace between two coexisting religions or groups; nor do any other 'surrenders' on the part of the Jews. For antisemitism, or what Toynbee calls the 'friction', has nothing whatever to do with Jewish efforts to abolish it. It is a sickness of non-Jews. Furthermore, Toynbee's assumption that the Jews could be tempted to intermarry so as to obtain for the sake of buying the abolition of the 'friction between Jews and non-Jews'[210] reveals how completely he has mis-understood the essence of Jewish survival. For had the Jews wanted to barter belief for peace, they could have done so centuries ago through simple desertion. Had they, however, done so and accepted what Toyn-bee suggests they accept, who would have remained as living witnesses to what Toynbee himself has proclaimed before Jewish audiences as his vision of the 'glorious role' that Judaism has still to play in the world of the atomic age?[211]

Intermarriage, like marriage itself, is not something that one can organise in the fashion of an electoral campaign. Nor can it be arranged for the purpose of spreading a religious philosophy, because people are 'people' and not philosophers or angels. They marry for other reasons than to spread religion.

Judaism, however, while not encouraging proselytisation, does not prohibit it. After all, it is natural that Jews who believe in their religion's greatness should not remain indifferent to whether or not their religious ideas make progress, particularly if in the ultimate they wish to serve mankind. But this wish was never, in Jewish history, combined with the aim of turning other nations into Jews, especially since the occasion when John Hyrcanus I, after conquering Idumaea in 129 B.C.E., forced all its inhabitants to be converted to Judaism.[212] The consequences, as Jewish tradition recounts, were tragic. Herod, although as second-generation Judaean,[213] nevertheless was regarded as a 'foreigner' and 'half-Judaean'[214] because he was descended from those Idumaeans who, as a people, were converted to Judaism *en masse*, without, therefore, the necessary preceding conviction. Jewish tradition attributes to this mass conversion the lack in acquiring a true knowledge of Judaism and the subsequent cruelties, murder, and tortures of the Herod regime in Judaea—so very much against the principles of Judaism.

Jews themselves testify to the unfeasibility of mass conversion, as Toynbee has noted with amazement in a note regarding the forced mass baptism of Jewry on the Iberian Peninsula:[215]

> The survival of crypto-Jewish communities in the Iberian Peninsula over a span of more than four centuries is amazing; and our amazement will be increased when we consider that, throughout the sixteenth and seventeenth centuries of the Christian Era, this subterranean Jewish community was being weakened all the time by a steady drain of its more active and enterprising members, who lost no opportunity of emigrating in order to return publicly to their ancestral religion in a Dutch or Tuscan or Otto- man asylum.

Forced mass conversions, which lacked the required preceding conviction, were thus of no avail. Even after centuries, the converted returned to the fold, and, as Sephardim, contributed considerably to the enhancement of Jewry and Judaism. Names such as those of Spinoza, Disraeli, de Medina, Nieto, and many others come to mind in this connection.[216] And Herzl family tradition also maintained that Theodor Herzl, the founder of the Zionist Organisation, was a descendant of Spanish Marranos.[217]

As stated, Jewish proselytisation does not concern itself with the conversion of peoples or large masses in order to ensure that 'the numerical balance-sheet of conversions would be likely to work out in Judaism's favour', as Toynbee suggested.[218] Jewry believes that the ideas of Judaism in their purest form can be represented only through the Jewish people, and that it is its duty to uphold these ideas, centred on strict monotheism, until mankind, in the course of its progressive spiritual development, adopts them, once Jewry is physically re-established as a nation in Palestine. As Deutero-Isaiah, whom Toynbee regards as the repository of the Judaic religion, foretold:[219]

> The Lord God who gathereth the outcasts of Israel saith Yet will I gather others to him beside those that are gathered unto him.

There have been many Rabbis and scholars who, because of prophecies of this sort—in which the Prophetic books abound—rejected active proselytisation in the conviction that monotheism as taught by Judaism will be accepted anyhow if only Judaism maintains uncompromisingly its physical existence, and stands uncompromisingly by its God, until it is redeemed in Eretz Israel. The more resolutely Jews maintain their Judaism in all its aspects, the more certainly will the Gentiles become aware of the fact that their ethical, moral, and other elements derive from Jewish sources, and they will draw the proper conclusions.

But proselytisation is not prohibited in Judaism, as has already been pointed out. It concentrates rather on individuals than on peoples. Proselytisation is not just the superficial capture of a non-Jew to join a kind of 'Foreign Legion' in lieu of a consideration, be it money, position, or marriage. Becoming a Jew must be an act of voluntary desire and must be based on a full knowledge and awareness of what it is that the 'neophyte', as the proselyte is called, is taking upon himself. If this sincere and honest conversion takes place, the proselyte becomes a *Gertzedek*, a righteous or pious proselyte, for whose well-being Jews pray in their synagogues three times a day,[220] in a prayer equally devoted 'to the righteous and pious, to the elders of thy people the house of Israel, to the remnant of their scribes . . . and to us also'. For this kind of proselyte the house of Israel always stood open.

Conversion to Judaism must be purely out of conviction, without even a thought of a consideration. Accordingly, marriage is nowhere foreseen as a condition of a consequence of proselytisation. If it arises after the sincere and honest acceptance of Judaism by the convert, it ceases to be 'intermarriage', for then it is a marriage between Jew and Jew. In this respect Judaism and Jews are very particular, because they never lose sight of the basic tenet: that marriage and family life are their keystones.

After all, Toynbee himself may serve as an example, if we accept his laudatory statements about Judaism at their face value. Without 'inter-marriage', he came to describe Judaism as 'a great spiritual treasure'[221] which 'is meant for all mankind',[222] and to proclaim 'its manifest destiny to become a worldwide religion'.[223] He did not even hesitate to state that his own religious beliefs are 'nearer to Judaism than they are to orthodox Christianity'[224] and if it were only possible to change one's 'lineage' he might be willing to change it; 'I might find myself tempted to barter my Anglo-Danish birthright for a Jewish'[225] and other examples. But of course, when challenged[226] to live up to what he preached, he quickly withdrew behind the 'natural' impossibility of giving up one's 'lineage' (which immediately put a different complexion on his suggestion that Jews give up their 'lineage' and confine themselves to religion only).

The strong stand and belief in themselves of the Jews has caused and still causes many Gentiles to take cognisance of this fact and to ask themselves what power it is that creates the inexhaustible capacity of the Jew to survive and wherein lies the source of this unique manifestation. People in their thousands, without active proselytisation, have come not only to admire and respect Judaism, but, contrary to Toynbee, also to draw practical conclusions and implement convictions—without 'marriage licences'.

Summarising Toynbee's diverse statements as regards proselytisation and intermarriage, we are confronted (how typical of him!) with both exceeding praise for and strong objections against them. This is, of course, the result of the usual vagueness of his suggestions. Therefore one cannot state whether Toynbee expects a proselytisation based on Jewish Judaism or on a combination of Deutero-Isaiah and Jesus; whether he expected Jews to be united with the Gentiles through inter-marriage and in this way increase their own ranks, or to be united with them in order to disappear in the great mass of humanity.

B. The Jewish Community

Having so far dealt with the meaning of the term 'religion' in Toynbee's phrase, 'distinct community based on religion', and with the consequences which his suggestion entails, we shall find strong confirmation of our conclusions if we now turn to an investigation of the term 'community' in that phrase. What is its meaning? Does it describe a religious group? And how does it apply to Jewry and Judaism?

The first conspicuous confusion comes to mind if one compares Toynbee's description of other religions with that of Judaism. For instance, he refers to a Christian Civilisation,[227] to a Protestant Church,[228] or to a Catholic Church,[229] but not to a Christian, Catholic, or Protestant community embracing all their respective members. When searching for a name to describe these religions, he chooses, as he pointed out,[230] 'to label it "a church" ', although some of his critics contested the correctness of this description, and he himself agrees with this criticism.[231]

He applies similar descriptions to Mohammedanism. He speaks of the Islamic State,[232] of the Islamic Empire,[233] of the Islamic Civilisation,[234] but not of the Islamic community, embracing all its adherents all over the world.

This in itself shows that Judaism does not fit into the pattern of a Church or a Synagogue or an ecclesiastical organisation, but has to be treated by him, like no other religion, as a 'distinct community based on religion'.

But even with regard to the use of the term 'community' Toynbee is not consistent. Thus he uses it to describe various ethnic groups living in one country;[235] one such ethnic group living in a part of a country;[236] the inhabitants of a certain locality;[237] or as a description of the Zionist ethnico-national concept whereby a 'Jew . . . is a member of the living Jewish community'.[238]

When, as a result of criticisms, he wrote *Reconsiderations*, he was also obliged to explain the meaning of his use of the term 'community', and he devoted a section of a chapter to it.[239] But even the 'clarification' does not clarify the issue. Thus we read that

> participants in a community may have a distinctive religion, language, state, or other institution that is not shared with them by other participants in the same society. For example, the English people are a community within the Western Society; but other Westerners are not natives of the Kingdom of England, do not have the English Episcopalian Church as the established church in their respective states, and do not speak the cis-Tweed cis-marine dialects of English.

That means, in other words, that the term 'community' covers everything, and not only religious adherence. And here follows the classical way in which Toynbee tries to extricate himself from this confusion:

> Some word is needed to denote what I mean by 'communities'. But I confess that my definition of both 'communities' and 'societies' is arbitrary. Every definition of them is and must be. The popular usage of both words is vague, yet at the same time it is almost impossible to avoid conscripting and regimenting both words for use as more precise instruments if one is trying to make a systematic study of human affairs.

Here Toynbee is obviously reserving to himself the right to retain the term without explaining its meaning, and leaving it open to any 'arbitrary' interpretation. And because of this he finds it most suitable, with regard to the Jewish question, to use it to mean 'nationality', 'state', or 'religion', and probably a number of other things. The conclusion that one can draw from this is that Toynbee himself is confused both as to the meaning of 'community' and as to the nature and essence of Jewry and Judaism. Hiding behind this vague term, he has obviously sought refuge for his ignorance. A glance at the formulation of his principal thesis confirms this. He wrote:[240]

> The Diaspora does still have a future in Western countries, and this still as a distinct community. It has a magnificent future on a religious basis if it bases itself on religion alone. So long as its basis was only semi-religious and was still semi-political, the Diaspora was a closed community—in practice, though already no longer in principle.

The first conclusion that one must draw from this statement is that in Toynbee's opinion today Jewry constitutes a distinct community which is based on a number of characteristics, including religion. It will change its present status only when it gives up everything else and 'bases itself on religion alone'. But today it is still precisely what those maintain who regard Jewry as a 'distinct nationality' or 'people' embracing every characteristic. This conclusion may be derived not only from this last quotation but also from a number of statements in Toynbee's works, a few of which should be mentioned:

> Yet, without the political framework of a state or the territorial basis of a home, the Jews have managed to preserve their separate identity as people

from 586 B.C.—the year that saw the obliteration of the Kingdom of Judah—*down to the present day.*[241]

Even since the fearful national disaster the paramount aim of Judahites deported to Babylon and their Jewish descendants has been to preserve, unbroken, their distinctive national identity. In this they have been brilliantly successful. The Jewish people has managed to survive, as a people, a long series of successive ordeals . . . This record is recognised, by friendly and hostile observers alike, as being an extraordinary monument of steadfastness and obstinacy—whichever of the two words the observer may feel inclined to use. *The achievement has been possible only because the Jews have always consistently given priority over other aims of theirs to this aim of preserving their distinctive national identity.*[242]

The survival and vitality of the diaspora has been a *tour de force* but, just on this account, the diaspora has been, *and still is,* the supreme and characteristic instrument and monument of the Jewish people's persistent will to maintain its distinctive communal identity.[243]

A sense of national—or, as some Jewish scholars call this in its Jewish context, ethnical—solidarity *still continues* to be one of the elements in the Jewish communal consciousness, and this among Western Jews as well as others . . .[244]

Jewry today is a combination of ethnic and religious elements.[245]

From these statements it is clear beyond doubt that Toynbee's term 'distinct community' has today one meaning, and one meaning alone: the distinct Jewish nationality, the distinct Jewish people. And it is also clear beyond doubt that it has not the meaning of a unification of individuals through religion alone. It is, as already pointed out, Toynbee's suggestion that Jews now give up all other elements that constitute what he has termed in the quotations above 'the Jewish people', and retain in the future only the religious ingredient. If this were possible, however, a 'distinct community' could not continue to exist in the Diaspora, because the 'distinct community' is his definition of Jewry today—which includes all other ingredients also. Toynbee soon recognised that by using this phrase—and by speaking in 1960 to a Jewish audience of a 'distinct community based on religion only'—he laid himself open to an absurd contradiction in terms, and therefore, two years later, when addressing the same Jewish audience, Toynbee shifted the emphasis. He stated:[246]

A Jewish community that had abandoned the ethnic basis of its distinctive identity would still retain the religious basis of it. It would simply be completing the long-drawn-out progress of its transformation from a local community, based on 'blood and soil', into a world-wide community based on a distinctive common religion.

He confirmed this ultimate development that he expected, when he wrote in another connection:[247]

There is only one solution for the antinomy between the nationalism which is the Jews' will and the universalism which is an involuntary but inevitable corollary of their nationalism. The Jews must constitute themselves the One True God's missionaries to the rest of mankind, and must make it their paramount aim to convert the World to the vision that has been vouchsafed to the Jews themselves. But the pursuit of this aim by the Jews would require them to unite with their gentile converts in a world-wide religious community of followers of the pure religion of Deutero-Isaiah, and this transformation of a closed national community into an open religious community would run counter to the Jews' hitherto para-mount aim of preserving their community's distinctive identity in the form of a nation.

This 'open religious community' is a far cry from the 'distinct Jewish community based on religion' which, according to Toynbee, was to secure the Jewish Diaspora's 'future in Western countries'. And it is quite obvious from these quotations that Toynbee does not even expect the continuation of any Jewish Diaspora at all, once its members merge or, as he puts it, 'unite with their gentile converts in a world-wide religious community', for in this way they would disappear as Jews, even religiously.

In this negative aspect—the disappearance of Jewry—Toynbee pursues the consequences, as he pursues the consequences in his positive suggestions noted earlier: their adopting a new religion. The ways leading to this suggested final result differ in form and in their diversified routes, but if one reads his writings and does not forget related passages among the thousands of pages, one unavoidably obtains the picture which is presented here.

It is interesting in this connection that in all his suggestions for changing their present status—nationally or religiously—Toynbee does not once consider the possibility of external forces to induce Jews to take the road to disintegration. In every case he expects these paths to be accepted and trodden by Jews themselves; they should surrender their national characteristics, they should give up the *Torah*, the *Talmud*, most parts of their Bible, with the exception of Deutero-Isaiah, they should intermarry, they should unite with Gentile converts in a new religion, and they should merge into a world-wide community. All this must come from within Jewry, because it is his conviction that no people, no culture, no civilisation, no religion, can be destroyed without being destroyed from within. These are his words:[248]

> I find myself unable to cite a single case of the breakdown and the disintegration of a civilisation in which I think it is certain that this was the work of some external agency. In all cases in which our knowledge of the course of events is sufficient to enable us to diagnose the causes of breakdown and disintegration with any assurance, I believe now, as before, that the verdict suggested by the evidence is one of suicide, not one of murder.

Jews who want to live as Jews will, of course, not heed these suggestions in any of their proposed forms. Some may innocently fall victim when reading Toynbee's praise of Jews, Judaism, and the Diaspora, remaining ignorant of the condemnation of these same values in other parts of his works. There is, however, a third category of Jews mentioned before, whose way leads anyhow in the direction of cessation. From sources such as these, Toynbee may derive encouragement for his conclusions. He may also not be unaware of the attempts made within Jewry at these same effects in Europe during the period of 'emancipation'. Religion as the sole earmark of Judaism was a conception born in Germany and was brought over from the last century. It is a little over a hundred years since the death of Samuel Holdheim,[249] who in his works sought to remove from Judaism all its ethnic or national elements and to confine Jewry to a 'religious community only'. To this purpose he practised a simple method: he marked out as national all those elements which, not being universally acceptable, were found burdensome and disagreeable. He finally became the prototype of the Toynbeean self-destroyer ('suicide from within'), whom a great Jewish historian characterised as follows:[250]

> He contemplated turning upside down the whole of Jewry in its threefold formation, with its Biblical, Talmudic, and Rabbinic sections, to confuse its ideas, to stupefy its conscience. Jewry had not had since Paul of Tarsus

such an internal enemy, who was thinking of undermining its entire structure from its base.

Holdheim simply suggested the abolition of everything with the exception of some sort of universal religio-moral-ethical ideals, open to all, which he did not define either. Toynbee may not have learned this theory from a study of the relevant literature or of Jewish history, for he did not study them, on his own confession.[251] But he has without doubt taken over its basic principle from the writings of Claude G. Montefiore, whom he has frequently referred to in his work.

Jews, accordingly, have experienced the impact and the results of such 'progressive' ideas as a sole concentration on a vague universal religious ideal. The adherents of Holdheim in Germany and Europe left no trace of their Judaism in subsequent generations, and those who remained alive became the victims of the destruction of European Jewry whether they were Jews by nationality, by religion, or by any other distinguishing mark. And the collapse of the conception advanced in England by Holdheim's epigone, C. G. Montefiore, is dealt with in a separate section because of its significance in Toynbee's attempts at emulating it without regard to its fate.

There is, however, one fundamental aspect of the issue which neither Holdheim nor Montefiore had assumed in their theories: they accepted nationalism *per se*, but they approved only of a German or English nationalism respectively. Toynbee, on the other hand, has a strong element in his favour, based on what appears in his writings as a vehement opposition to nationalism *per se*, when, for instance, he writes:[252]

> But, in an age when political nationalism has come to be a threat to the human race's survival, our paramount loyalty must be transferred from our local nation to mankind as a whole.

And although he emphatically stated that[253]

> I myself hold, and have always held, that the future course of human affairs is unpredictable,

nevertheless with regard to the national problem he assumed the role of 'a prophet unto the nations'[254] and started to predict that future course:[255]

Perhaps we can already begin to make out what the world of the future may be going to be like. It seems likely to be 'one world' because mankind, in the Atomic Age, will have, as we know, to choose between 'one world or none' and we are hardly likely, when it comes to the point, to choose race-suicide. In this probable future 'one world', people's paramount political allegiance will be their loyalty to the world-community. Mankind's danger of extinction by its own hands will focus patriotic feelings upon the human race as a whole and will drain these feelings away from the race's factious national fragments. . . .

Those once romantic goddesses, the local states—Britain, Nicaragua, the United States, Israel, and the other ten dozen of them—will still be on the map, because they will still have local jobs of work to do, such as minding and mending the drains and administering other local public utilities. But the romance will have gone out of them.

In another section of his work, it is true, he visualised for the 'local states' more important activities than looking after 'public utilities':[256]

In the world-wide society into which we are now moving, national units will have the same part to play that the states have in a federation, and the countries or departments in a unitary national state. National loyalties in such fields as literature, art, and sport can continue to enrich our common human life without being the menace to the human race's existence that national loyalties are today when we are still indulging in them in the fields of politics and war.

The first thing that catches the eye in this 'vision' in Toynbee's prophecy' of the future is the emergence of a 'world-community' consisting of all hitherto sovereign nations or states. It is hard to imagine how a 'distinct Jewish community in the Diaspora' which would constitute neither a State nor a nation would fit into this new world structure and remain as the sole exception among the thousands of millions of people, and 'distinct' through something other than Statehood.

But there is another aspect also to be considered which is no less characteristic. On his prophetic way to the 'one world', Toynbee failed to give his denationalisation advice to the Gentiles. When condemning nationalism in general, as we have seen, he does so only with regard to its political aspect, thus identifying nationalism with Statehood ('Britain, Nicaragua, the United States, Israel, and the other ten dozen of them'), whose sovereignty he would like to see subordinated to a higher authority.[257] But in his work one cannot find a single piece of advice offered to the non-Jews to surrender the ethnic basis of their existence and cease to be Frenchman, Englishmen, Poles, and every other nationality, and become members of a 'world-community'. It is only the Jews he advises to abandon the ethnicity of Judaism right away, while he keeps silent on the question of whether all the others should retain their ethnic basis now, before the emergence of the 'one world', and also after it, had been achieved. Once again, Jews alone among the nations are chosen to make the necessary sacrifice today for the sake of a 'glorious future for mankind'. If it were not so obvious that this frequent choosing of the Jews for the various experiments for the alleged benefit of humanity is closely connected with Jewry's 'suicide', one might wonder whether Toynbee in reality does not believe in the Jews as a 'chosen people', which he otherwise emphatically denies in his writings.

There is, moreover, a further contradiction underlying his condemnation of nationalism when it comes to the issue of Jews and non-Jews. We have mentioned that in his principal theory of nationalism *per se* he wishes to see it abolished. In contrast to this, however, he has repeatedly maintained that Jews who confined their Judaism to religion alone would become fully-fledged 'Dutchmen, Frenchmen, Englishmen, and so on'. Jews are therefore advised by him to give up their ethnic identity and become (not citizens of Holland, England, or France, which they are already), but members of a new ethnic identity 'whatever that newly chosen nationality may be'.[258] Thus in the case only of Jews, it is not ethnic nationalism *per se* that is bad, but Jewish ethnic nationalism, which should be given up and exchanged for another one.

Let us suppose for argument's sake that the Jews would agree to such adoption of a new nationality and would declare today: we surrender the ethnic basis of our existence. Is it really certain that this new nationality would be willing to accept them as they are, particularly if they came in groups and in the mass, as Jews, with their specific character, way of thinking, and distinct religion? Jewish history, which in its long endurance has encountered every kind of 'solution' for every occasion, also provides us with answers to this question. A hundred and forty years ago Jews were praised as members of a different ethnic nationality and condemned solely for their different religion. The Archbishop of Canterbury then welcomed their attaining equality with all other Britons on a Jewish ethnic national basis, but strongly opposed their political equality because of their adherence to their religion. He said in the House of Lords:[259]

> Even if they turn their eyes ever so earnestly towards that quarter ['the return to the promised land'], who is there that will not think more highly of them on that account? Who will not approve of their conduct in not forgetting the promises originally made to their race, and in still entertaining hopes of recovering those advantages of which they have so long been deprived? For my own part, my Lords, I do not think that, if this be so, it at all follows that the Jews should be less attached to the country in which they at present reside—that they should be less loyal, as subjects to the State which protects them—or less capable than others of fulfilling all the relations of society. . . . though, in point of doctrine and morale, the Jewish religion is superior beyond all comparison, yet, considered in its relation to Christianity, it is not mere unbelief, but a direct contradiction of the truth. Its profession involves the assertion that the Saviour, adored by Christians as the Most High God, was a wicked imposter, who justly suffered death. Christianity in the eyes of the Jews, is the offspring of a falsehood, which has brought disgrace to his name, and ruin and exile on his nation. That the professors of a religion which must cease to exist when these anti-Christian positions are abandoned, should be empowered to legislate for a Christian people, much more for a Christian Church, is surely, my Lord, an absurdity!

Gradually, with progressive 'enlightenment', religion receded as the dominating spiritual and cultural force in the Western world, and was superseded by a nationalism which led from religious universalism to the national State. This became the political frame of what is known as the 'ethnic nationality'. Not having found full equality, because of their religion, Jews now felt there was an opportunity of joining the new ethnic nationalities among whom they lived, which had de-emphasised religious affiliations. Again, the distinction made in this study between 'nation' as a country or State and 'nationality' as an ethnic entity should be recalled. Jews in 1833 and later were citizens of the various 'nations' (States). There was, therefore, no necessity to obtain permission to settle there or to join these 'nations'. But Jews, citizens of all these countries, joined the German, Dutch, French, and other nationalities, simultaneously declaring their own Jewish ethnic nationality void. We know today that they did not succeed anywhere, for Germans, Frenchmen, Englishmen, and all the others had for generations developed what finally emerged as their nationality. They grew with it and in it; it bore their specific stamp, culturally, spiritually, in character, in common experience, sufferings, and joys, in war and peace, in proverb and folk-song. And suddenly the Jews came, strangers up till now, and expected to be equal with the members of these nationalities through a declaration: 'We give up our national basis and join you'. They did not wait for an invitation, they did not receive official acceptance. They simply declared their joining, disregarding the fact that one does not join a nationality; it belongs to one, it is one's own creation, it is one's life. Therefore, however much and however loudly they proclaimed their belonging to the new nationality, they remained apart and different, and were, and are to this day, instinctively recognised by what Toynbee has called 'the ethos of the Jews'.[260] They were not accepted as equals, not only because they were 'different' but also because those who surrender such vital essentials of their own existence are usually suspected of ulterior motives rather than respected by those for whom similar essentials in their own existence play so important a role and which they would never surrender so light-heartedly. Characteristic of this trend is a controversy that took place eighty years after the debate referred to above in the House of Lords. A Jewish writer, Moritz Goldstein, complained in the Berlin *Kunstwart*,[261] in an article dealing with Jews in German art, literature, and culture, that

> we Jews are guardians of the spiritual treasures of a people which denies our right and ability to be so.

In the discussion following this article, the magazine's editor, Ferdinand Avenarius, summarised the non-Jewish German's position as follows:

> If the Jews think that we Germans have no reason to be dissatisfied with their guardianship of culture, we must contradict them. In trade and industry . . . and in many other fields of practical life we can daily live next

to each other and also together in peace; and help each other to our joint advantage. But the areas where the imponderabilia come together of the imagination and the emotions, in accordance with the national character ('Volksart'), which are not only differently coloured but also differently shaped, are greatly underestimated by those who deny the fundamental difference between both peoples. . . . Can we, the others, really be blamed if we fear that through the 'guardianship' of our 'spiritual treasure' by the Jewish spirit a foreign and, to our cultural anxiety, spurious feeling might penetrate?

Despite the passage of time, which might seem to outdate them, these examples are important documents of trends which time and again repeat themselves in one form or another, based on this or that 'objection'. They are therefore as valid today as they were in 1833 and in 1912. This is because the essence of the Jew has not changed. It has developed, it has been broadened and deepened in many respects, and, thanks to Zionism and to the creation of the State of Israel, has become considerably strengthened. But it has been there all the time, definitely and visibly, for otherwise Toynbee would not lay so much stress on the necessity today of denouncing and demanding the surrender of the ethnic-national basis of Judaism. But it is also valid because fundamentally, in their essential values, the non-Jews have not changed either. They too have developed, deepened, broadened their horizons, and strengthened their positions in our day, but essentially they have remained Frenchmen, Englishmen, or German, as they were before.

We wonder what the reaction would be if they were to receive similar proposals to surrender their ethnic-national bases. After all, Dutchmen, Englishmen, Frenchmen, and members of the other nationalities have their own feelings of history, their common past, a sense of common fate, a common language, their own State, and so on; it might be interesting to follow the reactions to advice by Toynbee to these nationalities to abandon their ethnic basis, join another nationality, then begin waiting for the denationalised 'one world' of the future and, after its attainment, again give up the newly acquired nationality in favour of a nebulous 'world-community'. These are the people with whom he might begin, to whom he might preach, whom he might attempt to persuade to accept his idea. For Toynbee, the Westerner, is culturally and spiritually closer to them than to the Jews.[262] Why come along unwanted and undesired, to bother Jews and Jewish audiences? Let, for once, a single Gentile nationality begin to prepare the Toynbeean 'glorious future' as Jews used to do in the past whenever someone invented 'world-saving' ideas; they were usually the first to believe in them and to set out to implement them, with disastrous results.

One instance may enlighten us about the probable reaction of Western Gentiles to Toynbee's denationalisation suggestions. It is given by Toynbee himself in a conversation with his son Philip,[263] in which the father had to accept the complete failure of any such possibility:

> The English in Italy didn't want to live in England, they wanted to live in Italy. Yet they didn't want to become Italians, and this seems to be a hateful way of living.

These are harsh words against his fellow-countrymen, and not justified at all if one considers that Toynbee himself has confessed[264] that if it were possible to give up one's 'lineage' he might give up his Anglo-Danish birthright and adopt another. The main aspect of this confession is that he regarded its implementation as impossible and—remained an Englishman. As he exclaimed:[265]

> As I myself have been born and brought up an Englishman . . . myself am an Englishman, after all.

And he so regards it notwithstanding all the unkind words which he employs against his country and people; and notwithstanding his own 'prophecy' of the denationalised 'one world' of the future, which anyway should have begun with the 'prophet' himself.

In the light of this, Jews are forced to doubt the genuineness of his suggestion and to emphasise his lack of understanding of human nature if he pretends to expect anyone else, or even a whole people which has a little more love and respect for its 'lineage', to agree to the surrender which he proposes.

But to return from the 'vision of the future' to reality, we see that Toynbee's 'one world', which he can 'already make out', and which is to be based on nations that surrender their sovereignty, is far from appearing in our day. The West and particularly the nations of Europe remain persistently divided, unable to unite ever since Charlemagne, notwithstanding the milder nationalism which emerged after World

War II, and notwithstanding the fact that 'tribal' nationalism, as Toynbee calls it, is out of fashion and has become obsolete, as he maintains. On the other hand, since he expounded his 'vision'[266] in 1952, some sixty nationalities and nations have emerged, have attained sovereignty, and have entered the United Nations as distinct national States.[267] 'We live today in this nuclear world—in this world of a hundred new nations', as President Johnson recently emphasised.[268] And Toynbee himself had to confess:[269]

> Asians and Africans are now rushing to take the Kingdom of Western materialism by storm; and they are regarding their success or failure in reaching this exotic objective as being the measure of their success or failure in life.

All these are, however, external matters. The primary question remains: Are the Jews a community? If so, what kind of community? And can they give up one or more of the ingredients that make them a community? We can best illustrate Toynbee's answers to these questions if we refer to two examples which serve Toynbee as confirmation of his theory of a denationalised Jewish community based on religion only.

C. Two Examples

Toynbee selected two movements in Jewry for this purpose; and they are completely opposed to each other in religious beliefs and practices: Agudath Israel and Liberal Judaism. He admires the strictly Orthodox Agudath Israel and admires no less its antithesis. And he presented these examples as parts of an historical development within Jewry, on the one hand, and as a confirmation of his theory of 'challenge and response' on the other. He therefore went back over eighteen hundred years to find an analogy between the reactions of these two modern movements to the pressures and influences of the modern world, and those of the Zealots and Herodians in ancient Palestine towards similar external forces inherent in Hellenism. He asserts that[270]

> These two Jewish antithetical reactions to a pressure exercised by Hellenism were so sharply pronounced that they can be used as indicators for detecting and sorting out other instances of the same psychological

phenomena in other passages of the histories of encounters between contemporaries.

He then compares Agudath Israel with Zealotism of old because of its 'meticulous observance of the Mosaic Law', and Liberalism with Herodianism because of the 'whole-heartedness and . . . virtuosity with which . . . it participated in the secular activities'.[271]

> At the time of writing on the morrow of the Second World War, both the Herodian 'non-Aryan' and the Zealot Ritualist survivors of the Jewish diaspora in the Western World had lost the lead in a Western Jewry to a Zionist movement that differed from both these other diasporan reactions alike in displaying an ambivalent affinity with both of them simultaneously.
>
> It will be seen that Zionism betrayed its ambivalence by laying itself open to simultaneous charges of Herodianism and Zealotism which, unfortunately for the Zionists, did not cancel one another out.

Toynbee follows this up with an elaboration of the fundamental differences between the orthodox Zealots and the liberal Herodians on the one hand, and the Zionists on the other. Faithful to his usual method, he showers praise, of course, on both the Agudath Israel and Liberal Judaisms in order to make the distinction from Zionism more conspicuous. However, not only does Toynbee base his theory on incorrect facts, but his contention that both movements have lost their lead in Western Jewry since World War II because Zionism has 'displayed an ambivalent affinity with both of them' is a product of his fantasy and has no foundation in fact. This is simply because both Agudath Israel and the particular branch of Liberal Judaism Toynbee has in mind were created after the foundation of the Zionist Organisation, and never, in fact, either before or after World War II, attained any leadership in Western Jewry or in any other geographical area. Indeed, notwithstanding their opposition to Zionism, both have in the course of time come to accept the Zionist conception of the re-establishment of the Jewish nation in Palestine, and thus implicitly to accept its dominance in Jewry. Both these movements laid the strongest emphasis on their respective brands of Jewish religion; but Agudath Israel never denied ethnic Jewish nationalism, and from its inception recognised the importance of the national territorial aspect in Jewish reality; while Liberal Judaism, in response to the denial of legal 'emancipation' to ethnic Jewish nationalism, gradually, with the growth and success of Zionism, progressed from bitter opposition to neutrality, the first stepping-stone, and thence to clear support of this politico-national movement.

(a) Agudath Israel

In a description of the aims and objects of Agudath Israel, Toynbee has this to say:[272]

> The *Agudath Israel* are a strictly orthodox sect who believe implicitly that an ultimate restoration is God's will, and that He is certain to accomplish this purpose of His in His own time.
>
> The . . . principle of abstaining from all attempts to promote the fulfilment of God's will in This World by the work of human hands has become so fast ingrained in the Jewish tradition that the strictly orthodox *Agudath Israel* at this day look askance at the Zionist movement and are holding rightly aloof from any participation in the work of building up a material Jewish 'national home' under a British mandate in Palestine.

Toynbee repeated this fundamental description in one way or another in a number of his references.[273] It is, however, false, with no foundation in fact. It is worthy of note that this same incorrectness and absence of familiarity with the facts appear in a description of the aims of Agudath Israel written nine years previously (1930) by the Nazi theoretician, Alfred Rosenberg, in terms almost identical to those of Toynbee.

Let us now look more closely at Toynbee's description quoted above. To begin with, Agudath Israel was not and is not a religious 'sect'. It is a political world organisation formed in May 1912 in Kattowitz (Poland).[274] In the same year (July 1912) it established its first branch in Palestine,[275] and went ahead with general activities. In its structure (Congress ['Kenessio Gedaulo'], executive board, financial instruments ['Keren Hatorah'], territorial groups, and so on) it became an imitation of the Zionist Organisation, which by then had been in existence for fifteen years. Agudath Israel is opposed to Zionism not because this movement was national and began to build a Jewish national home in Palestine, but because the Zionist Organisation had not accepted the Torah and Jewish religious principles as the dominating factor in its programme nor as the determining factor in its activities. Agudath Israel, therefore, rejected, and still rejects, collaboration with the Zionist Organisation, but has not rejected working for and in Palestine, or now Israel.

Agudath Israel did not expect a restoration in 'His own time' without Jews doing anything towards it, nor did it refuse to work in Palestine under a British mandate for the building of a Jewish National Home there. In 1936, three years before Toynbee published the description above, Agudath Israel submitted to the Royal Commission[276] a memorandum in which it said, among other things: Agudath Israel recognises the Mandate in its totality, as approved by the League of Nations, as in accord with the old historical rights which no authority on earth can alter or doubt. At the same time Poale Agudath Israel, the Labour Organisation of the movement, also submitted a memorandum to the Royal Commission on Palestine[277] in which it stated, *inter alia:*[278]

> The Balfour Declaration is to it [Poale Agudath Israel] a miraculous deed by God, who has begun to fulfil His promises and has honoured the British Empire by causing it to take upon itself the world historical task of standing in the service of that promise. The Mandate is in full accord with this service.

And in his introductory remarks to these memoranda, Chief Rabbi Joseph Dushinsky, representing the World Agudath Israel, told the Royal Commission[279] of the

> wording and spirit of the Mandate, which in so wonderful a way confirms the prophecies of the prophets.

These quotations alone reduce Toynbee's contentions to an absurdity. Nor is it insignificant that the *Survey of International Affairs for 1936*, of which Toynbee was the editor (assisted by V. M. Boulter), dealt comprehensively with the conclusions of the Royal Commissions, with quotations and references from the *Report* and the *Evidence*. It is inconceivable that a responsible editor should have failed to study so far-reaching a *Report* as that of the Royal Commission before permitting its analysis to be issued in important publications. It is impossible to miss the statements made by the Agudath Israel and their Labour

Organisation when perusing these documents. And the Report of the
Royal Commission stated unequivocally:[280]

> In giving evidence before us, the representatives of *Agudath Israel* supported
> on all major points the case presented by the Jewish Agency. Zionism, in
> fact, is Jewish nationalism, and like nationalism elsewhere—in post-war
> Turkey, for example—its driving force is political rather than religious.

Should, however, this unlikely omission have taken place and the responsible editor of the *Survey* not have seen all this, there is no escape
from the fact that Toynbee's *Survey for 1925* had this to say about the
Agudath Israel:[281]

> The situation [in Palestine] was complicated by the fact that there was a
> certain number of Jews who did not recognise the authority of the Jewish
> National Council.[282] These Jews belonged almost entirely to the pre-war
> population of Jerusalem. They were distinguished by their rigid adherence
> to the Pentateuchal Law, and they saw in Zionism, as a national movement
> inspired by modern ideas, a challenge to the theocratic concept of Jewish
> life which was, in their view, of the essence of orthodox Judaism. They
> were separately organised under the name of the Ashkenazi Jewish Com-
> munity of Jerusalem, which claimed to speak for 1,000 heads of families.[283]
> They had behind them an international organisation known as the *Agudath
> Israel*, which had a considerable membership in Poland, as well as in
> Frankfurt, Vienna, and certain other centres of conservative Jewish
> thought.[284] These two bodies made parallel representations both to the
> mandatory Power and to the Permanent Mandates Commission.[285] Their
> main contention was that the adherent of the *Agudath* should not only be
> free to remain outside the jurisdiction of the Jewish National Council,
> but should also have official recognition as a separate and independent
> community.

Thus he has been fully aware, ever since 1925, that Agudath Israel was
a practical political organisation which not only was not waiting
passively for the Almighty to re-establish the Jewish people in Palestine,
but was seeking recognition as an independent section of Palestine
Jewry and as a negotiating political factor on an international basis in
the League of Nations. Accordingly, if Toynbee stated in 1939 (Vol. V)
and in 1954 (Vol. VIII) that Agudath Israel was 'abstaining from all
attempts to promote the fulfilment of God's will in This World by the

work of human hands in Palestine', he was obviously making a statement which is not borne out by documents cited in a volume produced by colleagues of his under his direction.

In the light of Toynbee's misconception of the aims and objects of Agudath Israel, it is not surprising to find that the conclusions which he draws therefrom cannot but also be completely without foundation. Thus he wants us to believe that[286]

> it will be seen that *Agudath Israel's* religious scruples and the Palestinian Arabs' political anxieties alike could have been reconciled with a latter-day Jewish nationalism *alla Franca* if the Zionists had decided to seek a site for the Jewish national state of their dreams, not in Palestine, but in some no-man's-land.

For the surrender of Palestine, not only the Aguda but Zionism also could have received the blessings of the Palestinian Arabs, and of Toynbee, for that matter, just as they would have received his blessings for many other 'surrenders' which he has proposed and which we have been able to demonstrate. However, Agudath Israel and Zionism were ideologically if not religiously or organisationally 'reconciled' on a national basis: the establishment and final emergence of the State of Israel. This was not an imitation of *Franca* but was based on adherence to Jewish historical nationalism, described further below, and in no other country but Palestine, which both movements were in no circumstances prepared to give up.

Members of Agudath Israel have sat in Israel's Parliament since the first day of independence, were represented in Israel's Government from the outset, and are today represented in it through Poale Agudath Israel. They participate, in their specific way, in every stratum of national and religious activity, and are deeply convinced that this is the will of God.

(b) Liberal Judaism

Liberal Judaism serves as the second example of a group of Jews whom Toynbee came to regard as allies in his efforts against Zionism.

There is, of course, a fundamental difference between the two examples and the purpose which they serve in his edifice. Toynbee, when emphasising (incorrectly, as we have seen) the refusal of Agudath

Israel to participate in the building up of a Jewish National Home in Palestine because of its belief that God would do so in His Own Time, pursues, as we have said, no other purpose than to place religious tradition in antithesis to Zionism. Toynbee could not deny, nor did he, that Agudath Israel and Orthodox Jewry *per se* accept the fact that they belong to a separate people, that the Land of Israel is the historic home of the Jewish people, and will be so once again (however long that may take). Even if we had not been able to prove that Agudath Israel declined to wait passively for the future, its philosophy of the re-established Jewish nation in Palestine is that of historical national Zionism.

Nor could Toynbee utilise Agudath Israel's opposition to Zionism for his theory of individual or national assimilationism; the distinct religion and peoplehood espoused by Agudath Israel, 'Gottesnation' (God's nation), as it was termed in their literature, defies any thought of assimilationism as interpreted by Toynbee.

The difference between the two examples, Aguda and Liberalism, is further inherent in the strict adherence of the former to religious orthodoxy. Thus it could not serve Toynbee in his attempts at revising Jewish religion so as to make it indistinguishable from the religion which he wishes Jews to adopt: a combination of Deutero-Isaiah, Jesus, and Paul.

In contrast to Agudath Israel, in Liberal Judaism Toynbee appears to have found all those ingredients he required for his designs against Zionism and against the survival of Jewry, including antagonism to the existing Jewish religion and to Zionism, and approval for assimilationism.

Before elaborating the theme it must be pointed out that what in Britain is called 'Liberal Judaism' is known in America as 'Reform Judaism'. But it would be erroneous to assume that all Liberal and/or Reform sectors have identical conceptions with regard to Jewish religion, nationalism, Zionism, and assimilationism. There are wide and deep differences! It is therefore important to stress that it is only from the brand of Liberal Judaism represented within Liberal Judaism by Claude Goldsmid Montefiore in England that his fellow-countryman Toynbee has no doubt derived information, inspiration, and encouragement. As if he sensed the difference between these conceptions, Toynbee himself has drawn a distinguishing line by proclaiming Liberal and Reform Judaism as two different conceptions.[287] The term 'Liberal Judaism' is retained here for the purpose of this analysis, it being clearly understood that it constitutes only the Montefiorean sector within Liberalism and Reform.

We have already indicated some aspects of the identity of outlook between Liberal Judaism and Toynbeeism in matters of Jewish religion and Jewish nationalism, and have also pointed to the many references to Montefiore's ideas in Toynbee's writings. No doubt, an acquaintance with Montefiore's ideas encouraged Toynbee to believe that he may have found, and may still find within Jewry, people willing to accept the Judaeo-Christian religion which he propounded, a religion based on the preceding surrender of Jewry's ethnicity and leading to a purely religious community. It is pretty obvious that in such theories as those espoused by Montefiore, Toynbee found his 'Jewish source' behind which to hide in his propagandist pursuit of an assimilationism which would make the Jew indistinguishable in almost every way from the surrounding majority population and from the majority religion, an assimilationism which would inevitably lead to the disappearance of Jewry.

The parallelisms in ideas and phraseology between Montefiore and Toynbee in their writings are striking and frequent. In order to justify the advancement of the idea that Judaism move in the direction of adopting Jesus and the Gospels, Montefiore and, following him, Toynbee had first to attack the fundamentals of Judaism, the historicity and validity of the Bible, so as to remove the stumbling-block on the road to fulfilment of their desire. It is of no relevance to our investigation that the negative criticism of the Bible did not originate with Montefiore. As mentioned before, he based his ideas on those expressed by the leaders of the extreme Jewish Reform Movement in Germany, which, in turn, leaned on the concepts developed by the 'School of Higher Criticism' which flourished in Germany in the nineteenth century.[288]

It was this group of German Protestant professors who, through indiscriminate dissecting of the Bible, caused the denigration of Holy Writ and thus laid the foundations and opened the way for the latter-day 'scientific' antisemitism in Germany, which drew heavily on the

method and results of these 'scholars' in its endeavours to denigrate the
faithful adherents of the Bible—the Jews. As Schechter once put it:[289]
'Higher criticism, higher antisemitism'. Toynbee in this respect follows
the 'line' almost literally when he says[290] that Hitler's

> main idea—the fanatical worship of a jealous tribal god, at the bidding of
> a prophetic leader—is the original (though not ultimate) *Leitmotiv* of the
> Old Testament.

Whatever the reason, therefore, the 'Old Testament' is the source
of all evil. And this conclusion has obvious implications for Jewish
survival:[291]

> To accept Judaism without accepting the Mosaic Law is not a 'contra-
> diction in terms', if by the 'Mosaic Law' one means the Torah as reinter-
> preted by the Pharisees' method.[292] A new Jewish interpretation of the
> Torah—this time as being a symbolic expression of the religious ideals of
> Judaism—is a necessary condition for Judaism's achievement of its destiny.
> Judaism's destiny is too accessible to, and accepted by, the gentiles. It may
> be true that, without the carapace of the Torah and the Talmud, it is im-
> possible for the Jews to maintain their distinctive communal identity in its
> national form; but there are two ways in which a community's distinctive
> national identity may disappear: the Israelite way and the Roman.

Toynbee thus recognises the Bible and Talmud as sources of Jewish
physical existence and openly stresses that a reinterpretation of these
works such as he suggests would lead to the disappearance of Jewry.
The way to this end thus lies in the invalidation of the Bible. At this
point Montefiore, with his own negative critiques, renders Toynbee a
most valuable service. Able to quote him extensively, Toynbee sees in
Montefiore his 'Jewish witness' for his anti-Jewish crusade, and therefore attributes to him greater importance than his works justify. Indeed, Toynbee in his works elevates him to a rare honour for a Jew by
declaring him[293] to be one of the 'notable exceptions' among Jews
and Gentiles who had risen above the prejudice of their ancestral
tradition.

One or two comparative statements out of many that could be
quoted show something of the identity of thought between Montefiore
and Toynbee:

MONTEFIORE	TOYNBEE
It is true that the religion of Israel is professedly an historical religion, and possesses documents which claim to give an historical account of its origin and fortunes. But the earliest portions of these documents, like the sacred traditions of other races, embody not history but legend, the unhistoric character of which, in the light of comparative religions, is pretty easily determined.[294]	Moses may be a historical character; but if he is not legendary, his alleged literary work is. A critical analysis of the Pentateuch shows that it is a composite work; that each of these books in which it is now arranged has been spliced together out of pieces of older written documents, and that these sources are not older than the ninth century B.C., or the tenth century at the earliest.[295]
These books contain isolated documents . . . their earlier portions may belong to the ninth, a very small element to the tenth century. They are derived from many sources, and these sources had themselves a history, during which they did not retain their original shape, but, in the process by which they were fused together to form each of these so-called books, underwent revisions, and that they incorporate increments from different centuries.[296]	The Torah as we have it today has been edited and re-edited to make it conform with successive phases through which religion passed in Judah and in the subsequent Jewish diaspora in and after the eighth century.[297]

Having thus disposed of the historicity of the Torah and the Bible, and relegated it to a world of legend, the authors' next step is clearly indicated: a work that has been compiled over centuries by various authors, that has been subject to change and consists of a diversity of fragments, has no eternal or permanent validity. It can therefore undergo further changes to comply with the requirements of what Toynbee termed the 'successive phases'. Our days are such a new 'phase' and therefore in the minds of these two authors, further new editing is called for.

Montefiore, of course, drew practical conclusions from his critical, vastly negative approach to the Torah and Bible, and particularly from the contention that it should be adapted to contemporary requirements. Symbolically he called one of his works *The Old Testament and After*.[298] Through a new revision the Bible could eventually become the foundation of a 'Judaism of the future', which, according to him, would be derived from a radical elimination of all 'superfluous' parts and from a selected compilation of the remainder, mostly a collection of ethical and moral precepts as laid down in the Books of the Prophets. Such a revision of the Bible would then be synchronised with a similar revision of the New Testament, the result of which would be a compilation of virtuous principles based on Hebrew prophets, the Gospel, Jesus, and Paul. Thus, so Montefiore believed, would emerge a universal religion. This is, of course, a faithful copy by Montefiore of the 'religious universalisms' preached by his German Jewish Reform predecessors. It goes without saying that it was particularly in this area that Toynbee recognised the spiritual bond of a common approach.

The universal Judaeo-Christian religion based on vague ethical principles which emerges from the parallelism of Montefiore's and Toynbee's writings is so far from the Judaism of yesterday and today, and so near to Protestant Christianity, that there is only one last link needed to obliterate the distinction: the Jewish bearers of the new religion would also have to disappear physically as a people and give up the ethnic basis of their existence, to become, as Montefiore visualised it,[299] 'the herald-soldiers of a world-wide Theism which . . . will proclaim the truth of man's kinship and communion with the Father of all', or, as Toynbee visualised it,[300] 'to become the pioneer and pilot community of the new kind'. But the preceding denationalisation of the Jew—his dissociation from Palestine—is for both the *conditio sine qua non* of this happy future. As in his other ideas, Montefiore in this respect too emulated his German Jewish Reform predecessors and Toynbee simply followed him.

The best way to achieve this denationalised Jewish community is not simply to issue a statement to that effect, important as this form of abandonment it appears in the writings of both men. It requires practical steps to become effective and final. The safest way to this end is through the erasure of any possible remaining national element in the Jew— *i.e.,* through intermarriage. In this respect Montefiore and Toynbee do not agree fully, although it would be difficult if not impossible to describe the points of disagreement. They are so close to each other in their reasoning and suggestions that the spiritual dependence on Montefiore's vagueness of Toynbee's consequential stand in the matter is clearly discernible.

The conclusion which both Montefiore and, following him, Toynbee derive from their religio-theologico-philosophico-ethnological parallelism is that Jews who regard themselves as Jews by religion only, after abandoning the ethnic basis, in the words of Montefiore,[301]

hold themselves to be Englishmen or Frenchmen of the Jewish faith;

or, as Toynbee put it,[302]

The new obligation is that he shall now abandon all Jewish ethnic reservations and shall become an American or a Dutchman one hundred percent.

It goes without saying that this concept leads them both straight to their bitter anti-Zionism. Even in this respect Toynbee follows the lead of Montefiore—whose fight against Zionism dates back to the days of Herzl[303] and attained full strength and vigour at the time immediately preceding the Balfour Declaration in 1917.[304] It is, however, to be noted not without irony that at the time when Montefiore headed this fight against Zionism during World War I, Toynbee strongly supported the Zionist case. There cannot be any doubt that in those days he was fully aware of Montefiore's anti-Zionist ideas, because, as an employee of the British Government, Toynbee was concerned with Near Eastern affairs, primarily Turkey, to which Palestine then belonged, and with the anti-Zionist activities of Montefiore, who then occupied an important position in the Anglo-Jewish community and caused no little upheaval in official circles, in the general press, and in Jewish quarters.[305] Toynbee, espousing then the official pro-Zionist line as well as expressing his own personal attitude[306] towards the Palestine issue, supported Zionism and for that reason rejected the opposition against it. And then, twenty years later, he rediscovered the old Montefiorean brand of anti-Zionism. Without any consideration about whether he himself had already reduced it to an absurdity when espousing the Zionist cause, and without any regard for whether these ideas of World War I were valid or outdated, Toynbee used them to serve as the 'Jewish testimony' in his later anti-Zionist crusade. After all, as we have shown, for the holy war against Zionism Toynbee did not hesitate to make Agudath Israel and Liberal Judaism bed-fellows.

Jewry, Zionism, and Liberal Judaism went ahead quickly into the new era, leaving behind the old dead ballast which Toynbee has now tried to revive. Had he tried to study these developments, he would immediately have found, among other valid replies, the brilliant analysis and complete demolition of Montefiore's religious and anti-national structure by Ahad Ha'am, whose essay culminated in the demand:[307]

> Let them who still have this feeling [i.e. the spirit of the Jewish people] remain within the fold; let them who have lost it go elsewhere. There is no room here for compromise.

Not only did opponents of Liberal Judaism such as Ahad Ha'am, who was not an Orthodox Jew, reject its religious and national conception; even the foremost Reform spiritual leader of his time, the author of the 'Pittsburgh Program' which became the ideological basis of American Jewish Reform, Professor Kaufmann Kohler,[308] rejected it outright:

> [In Montefiore's work] concessions are made to a creed which totally differs from our monotheistic faith, and which for more than eighteen hundred years stood out as a hostile force to Jew and Judaism, sowing hatred instead of fostering the spirit of justice, of love and humanity in the name of God, the Father of mankind.

All this, and much more, would have emerged, had Toynbee the historian wished to write history and not indulge in developing his theory—without regard to what had happened to ideas pronounced earlier by individuals. For he would have found a complete rejection of the Montefiorean concept by every Jewish denomination as well as by the laity, and not only in its literature but also in a fundamental break with that concept in the very movement founded by Montefiore himself. For Liberal Judaism has come a long way back to Judaism and Jewry since Montefiore's time. Its spiritual leader, Rabbi Isidore Mattuck, whom Montefiore brought over from America to serve as the first minister of the Liberal Synagogue in England,[309] took cognisance of these fundamental changes when he pointed out in his book[310] that

> All Jews have a common possession in the history of the Jewish people [sic] and in the Jewish tradition [sic!], and all Jews are united by their faith in God, their attention to His Law [sic] and their belief that the Jews have a religious contribution to make to the life of humanity.

And further on he added:[311]

> The individual Jew can come to God through his attachment to the Jewish people. . . . The Jew is brought nearer to God by belonging to the Jewish people. His relation to the Jewish people is established by his adherence to the Jewish religion. Judaism is a personal religion, and also the religion of a people. When an individual possesses it personally, it binds him to the Jewish people; and when he feels his membership in the Jewish people it strengthens his personal hold on the religion. To be a Jew, therefore, means adherence to the Jewish religion with an effective sense of relation to all Jews in the universal community of Israel.

This may have been a new and late development of Liberal Judaism, but vast sectors of Reform Judaism had taken the turn towards Jewish tradition and Jewish nationalism much sooner. For them, ceremonials, originally completely rejected, assume meaning; non-religious and purely national festivals such as Purim, celebrating the victory over the antisemitic Haman's bands, all of whom were executed in Shushan;[312] or Pessach (Passover), recalling the exodus from Egypt, the destruction of Pharaoh's army, and the re-establishment of Jewry as a free people;[313] or Shavuoth, the Festival of Torah and Land, of the giving of the Torah, and of the first fruits (not in France or England or America but in Palestine); or Hanukkah, rejoicing in the victory of the Maccabees over the Assyrian armies, the victory of Jewish nationalism over assimilationism, the regaining of national independence, and the victory of monotheism over paganism[314]—all these are celebrated today by both young and old of those Liberal and Reform movements which originally had rejected them. Liberal Judaism in England, however, went even a step further. They have not yet given Zionism important leaders, as the other Reform movements have done, but they have finally adopted the basic tenets of Zionism, and thus broken completely with their Montefiorean past. At their conference in Brighton in April, 1963,[315] they adopted a platform in which the centrality of the State of Israel in Jewish life was recognised in the provisions that Liberal religious schools should have 'a special Israel content, so that children should be taught a love for Zion'; that their student ministers 'should spend some time in Israel'; that the ministers should be given their Sabbatical leave to enable them to 'refresh themselves in Israel'; that schemes should be worked out for congregants 'to go see the Land and the people that dwell therein'; that Liberal Judaism 'devise some new form of religious observance to commemorate the independence of Israel'; that scholarships, named after the late Leo Baeck, be established at every Liberal Synagogue 'for immigrant children in Israel not able to get into secondary schools there'; that the Liberal Movement should have 'its own forest in Israel and plant trees there, in addition to the aid given to various organisations in the State by the Union' [of Liberal and Progressive Synagogues].

The conference went even further. Conscientious Jewish education, based on the new conception, and Hebrew as a living language and not that of occasional usage in religious services were also adopted.[316]

From all this it follows that however far Jews wander from their Jewishness, and however much they try to become indiscernible from the 'others', as long as they regard themselves as Jews, by whatever definition, they are not lost. The logic of life and history prescribes their way of return to the fold sooner or later. Herzl prophetically foretold this development in his controversy with Montefiore over seventy years ago:[317]

> It is regrettable that Mr Montefiore influences through his example a number of narrow-minded intellectuals or drags behind him those weak-minded people who love to be in such good company. So robust a national movement as ours can put up with such losses. All these lost ones will join us when we have been proved right, and we shall then welcome them with a smile.

What prophetic vision! Sixty years later, Zionism welcomed back those who had gone astray.

In sum, Toynbee has utterly failed as an historian and, above all, in the evidence required for his theory and expectations, with regard to both Jewish religion and Jewish nationalism. He chose two examples,

Agudath Israel and Liberal Judaism, as countering Zionism; and, as we have proved, these two examples show beyond any doubt the strength, depth, and Jewishness of the Idea of Zionism which prevails, and by necessity must prevail, wherever Jewry's existence and the Jewish future are at stake.

D. The Wrong Method and the Wrong Aim

We have quoted statements from Toynbee's writings in which he has pointed out that the Jews today constitute a community not based exclusively on religion. Moreover, he has also conceded Jewry's enduring ethnic basis. He has strengthened this opinion, finally, by his suggestion, in which otherwise there would be no sense, that Jews give up the ethnic basis. Surely they could not be asked to give up something that they do not possess. Not only does he confirm all this but he is also fully aware of the nature of this community's strength when emphasising:[318]

> A sense of national—or, as some Jewish scholars call this in its Jewish context, ethnic—solidarity still continues to be one of the elements of the Jewish communal consciousness.

It is for the preservation of this national or ethnic solidarity that the Jews have been and are striving; as he correctly perceived:[319]

> Throughout, the Jews have concentrated on their paramount aim of preserving their distinct national identity. This focusing of Jewish efforts has been rewarded by success for more than two thousand five hundred years up to date.

In the light of the quotations above it seems strange to find Toynbee characterising Jewish nationalism as a copy of 'Gentile nationalism' and, above all, as having emerged only about seventy years ago with the birth of political Zionism. If Jewish nationalism was born seventy years ago, how could Jewish 'distinct *national* identity' have been preserved for twenty-five centuries, as he wrote in the quotation above? To befog this obvious contradiction, Toynbee falls back on a device and its argument runs as follows:[320]

> In the Zionist view the emancipation and assimilation of the Jew as an individual is a wrong method of pursuing the right aim. Genuine assimila-

tion is indeed the true solution for the Jewish problem and ought therefore to be the ultimate goal of Jewish endeavours. . . . Instead of trying to assimilate individual Jews to individual Englishmen or Frenchmen, they must try to assimilate Jewry itself to England and France. Jewry must become a nation in effective possession of a national home . . .

Before analysing these contentions, it must be emphasised that in this text we again find an imaginary premise on which Toynbee bases his argument, when he begins his description with the words 'In the Zionist view'. I am not aware of a single instance in the entire Zionist literature which could be regarded as corroborating Toynbee's description of the desired 'national assimilation' in the 'Zionist view'. Zionism is the very antithesis of a belief in the future of Jewry through assimilation, whether individually or *en masse*. It is not a case, therefore, in the Zionist view, of the 'wrong method pursuing the right aim', as Toynbee puts it, but the wrong method and the wrong aim.

Zionism does not deny that 'genuine assimilation' of individuals is possible, but assumes that under 'genuine assimilation' is meant the progression already described according to which a Jew, by his own decision, merges fully with the Gentiles around him, nationally, ethnically, and religiously—and thus disappears as a Jew. This can be attained on an individual basis. But, contrary to Toynbee's view, Zionism, faithful to the Jewish heritage, does not believe in the possibility or desirability of a 'genuine assimilation' of the Jewish people as a people; nor does it regard it as a means of solving the Jewish problem. The father of Zionism wrote:

> The folk personality of the Jewish people cannot, must not, and does not want to go under. It cannot because external enmity keeps it together. It does not want to—this it has demonstrated in two thousand years of frightful suffering. It must not: that is what I attempt to establish with this book, following in the footsteps of many Jews who have not given up hope. Whole branches of the Jewish people can perish: the tree lives.

Toynbee could not but be aware of this, because in the same paragraph in which he spoke of Zionism's supposed aim at 'genuine assimilation' he pointed out that Zionists believe that Jews 'can never escape from being "a peculiar people" by masquerading as Frenchmen or Englishmen'. Thus within ten lines on one page, Toynbee stated that Zionists regarded 'the people's' assimilation as their ultimate aim, and at the same time stated that they regarded their 'people's' assimilation as unrealisable. All that Toynbee does therefore is to confuse the issue. He uses the term 'assimilationism' to describe the desire of individual Jews to become members of the peoples among whom they live—and so ultimately disappear; and uses the same term to describe the preservation of Jewish national consciousness and separateness through striving at becoming a nation like other nations. There is no other explanation of these contradictions than that he has created a terminological confusion through the application of different meanings for one term (a method in which he obviously indulges): he has used the generally accepted meaning of 'Assimilation' for both 'becoming absorbed' and 'to imitate', as well as for the process of continuing a self-centred, unaltered existence which has neither of these meanings.

However, instead of making the difference clear and investigating whether any of them are applicable at all, Toynbee has done nothing but simply retain the term which, as we have argued, implies the disappearance of Jewry.

The same superficiality betrays his insertion of Rousseau's 'social contract' theory into the discussion.[321] He maintains that the Zionists reject 'an emancipation-assimilation contract with a Gentile nation'. Toynbee thus presupposes that such a 'contract' actually exists, or has in the past been the basis of a *quid pro quo*—i.e. in return for the granting of emancipation, the Jews would assimilate and merge with the people who grant it. This is an imaginary supposition, which, like many other ideas on Judaism, he took over from Claude G. Montefiore. There has never been a 'contract', either written or unwritten, connected with emancipation proclamations. Accordingly, there has never been any reason for Zionism to approve of or to oppose a non-existent 'contract'.

At that time there was in any case no Jewish 'address' anywhere in the world which could have acted as a contracting party; nor has any local Jewish 'address' with central pretensions existed in any of the countries which granted emancipation. Further, Jews were emancipated because these enlightened countries proclaimed equality for all people and in the end it was impossible to exclude any portion of the existing population. As Adrien Du Port expressed it when on September 27, 1791, he moved the resolution which became France's second and final declaration of Jewish emancipation:[322]

> You have laid down, gentlemen, what are the qualities necessary for all citizens of France. But there is one resolution which seems to contradict the general laws thus laid down. I refer to the laws affecting the Jews. I demand the repeal of that decree,[323] and I wish the House to declare that the Jews, like all other persons, can become citizens by fulfilling the conditions laid down by the Constitution.

'Emancipation' was thus a one-sided proclamation by Gentile nations. It was neither 'bargained about' beforehand with the Jewish population of a given land, even if often and loudly demanded by individual Jewish leaders, nor was its approval by Jews or their consent expected. Assimilation, accordingly, was not a 'payment' requested as part of a contract or bargain. Assimilation was a purely voluntary act on the part of the Jews, who believed that legal equality meant social and moral equality as well, and felt the urge to become 'like other nationals'.

Toynbee is also blatantly wrong and, of course, unable to submit evidence in asserting that Zionism rejects emancipation. Zionism does not reject the concept of emancipation if it is meant sincerely and carried out honestly: each person to enjoy equality and personal freedom and to remain what he is. A struggle for such ideals is one of the tenets of Zionism. But Zionism is aware of the fact that 'emancipation', and not only with regard to Diaspora Jewry, has so far failed for reasons which are dealt with elsewhere in this study.[324] The historic 'emancipation' of one hundred and fifty years ago[325] proclaimed the emancipation of the Jew as he then was; it never pretended to be nor was it an instrument for the transformation of the Jew into something else. For, if he was not worthy of emancipation, why give it him? I have read the decisions appertaining to 'emancipation' in France, Germany, and England. I have nowhere found it laid down as a condition that the Jew must change from his then existing national, religious, cultural, moral, or social essence *qua Jew* in return for personal freedom or for full rights as a citizen of his country. And how did the non-Jewish legislator, deciding on 'emancipation', view the Jews whom he emancipated? As we see from the debate quoted in the British House of Commons,[326] and as is also clearly discernible from the contemporary literature in these respective countries, the 'emancipation' legislator was fully cognisant of the religious thoughts and practices of the Jews as well as of their existence as a separate community. The reference to Jews praying and hoping for a restoration of Jewish statehood in Palestine can be found in almost all the relevant literature and Sir Robert Grant has clearly emphasised this.[327] Thus Jewish nationalism was then an element of Judaism and recognised as such. Accordingly, it is beyond doubt that the legislator 'sanctioned nationalism and conceded civic equality to Jews in the full knowledge that Jewish nationalism was part of the Jewish religion, and in the conviction that Jewish nationalism was quite consistent with loyalty and patriotism as a citizen of the country where the Jews lived'.[328] It was assimilationist Jews who failed to understand this meaning of 'emancipation': that they could remain full Jews and be free. Nor is there any evidence that these Gentile peoples ever wanted or invited them to become part of their ethnic nationality or of their religion.

This is the meaning of Herzl's statement at the Second Zionist Congress:[329]

> The laws were kindlier than the usages. And we witnessed the reaction, this tremendous growth of regret on the part of those nations which only recently received us so graciously. But from emancipation, which cannot be rescinded, and from antisemitism, the existence of which cannot be denied, there arose for us a new, great conclusion. It could not have been the historic signification of emancipation that we cease to be Jews, for we were repulsed whenever we wanted to intermix with the others. The historic signification of emancipation was rather that we provide a home for our liberated nationality. This we could not have done before; we can do it now if we so will it with full vigour.

The conclusion from all this is self-evident: Zionism rejects assimilationism not only for the reason that it is beyond the dignity of man to infiltrate into another nationality while neither invited nor welcomed nor appreciated there—apart from the basic question of whether this is biologically and spiritually possible at all—but because assimilationism became a vehicle for the loss of Jewish cultural creativity as individuals and as a people; a vehicle for the loss of true identity, and thus a means of the obliteration of Jewry. In contrast, Zionism's basic concept is the continuous existence of the Jewish people and its creativity in every field of human endeavour.

On the other hand, there is no doubt that Zionism accepts 'assimilationism' in a reverse direction. As it was once put: 'A Zionist assimilates *sibi*, not *se*'. It is 'assimilation' in the *dative*, not in the accusative. It absorbs, as human beings in general do, ideas, thoughts, practices from its surroundings. It recognises the great values which individuals, peoples, and nations the world over create in the fields of literature, art, and social progress, and in every other stratum of human endeavour; and is aware of the fact that these external influences exercise a great impact on the Jews. But everything depends on the way these influences are absorbed—whether the absorption is accompanied by a surrender of one's own values or personality; or whether it is used to strengthen and invigorate one's being. After all, the whole of Jewish history in the Diaspora constitutes a continuous process of encounters with the peoples and cultures among whom Jews dwelt—in the Hellenistic period, in Babylon, in Arabic Spain, in Christian Europe, and so on—accepting many of their values without surrendering its specific, distinct Jewish individuality. Zionism thus recognises reality, and this shows that no people in the world lives in isolation but takes from and gives to the progress of mankind. As Martin Buber put it:[330]

> It would be senseless to wish to free oneself from the surrounding culture, which is permeated by the innermost forces of our blood and is part of us. We want and are permitted to be conscious of the fact that we, more than any other people, are a cultural mixture. But we do not want to be slaves, we want to be masters of this mixture.

The Oldest Nationalism

Therefore it is erroneous to say, as Toynbee does, that Jewish nationalism is an imitation of modern nationalism and Zionists 'alien converts to this Modern Western Nationalism'.[331] With phrases of this sort he simply emulates a thought of the Nazi theoretician, Alfred Rosenberg, who described Jewish nationalism as propounded by Zionism as 'an alien infection [by the Zionists] of the national feeling and conception of State of European nations'.[332] But both are wrong. For Jewish nationalism, the basis of Zionism, was in existence long before modern nationalism arose and long before any of the modern nations were born. The idea of nationalism was the contemporary concept with which Moses set out to create and unify the Jewish people as a nation, in its own State, in its own territory. He was 'the first Zionist', as an official British publication once emphasised.[333] He was the leader and teacher of the Jews when they were moulded into a nationality and nation, and he laid down, formally and philosophically, the foundations in which nationalism, Jewish and non-Jewish alike, in whatever form it appeared in the subsequent millennia, was rooted and shaped. The Jewish Bible contained all the basic elements inherent in the terms 'people', 'nation', 'nationality', to which modern usage applies, whatever interpretations are put on them, be they in the sense of descent, race, religion, culture, language, or country. In the same way, it contains the detail of all the basic functions of 'nations' in their widest interpretation, appertaining to family life, moral code, social problems, minorities, taxation, diplomacy, patriotism, State administration, trade, war, security, treason, army, peace, and much more. All this, of course, in addition to being the source for answers to man's spiritual needs as well as the fountain of the great prophetic messages for mankind of toleration, universal peace, and the world-rule of monotheism. As Franz Rosenzweig once expressed it in a nutshell:[334]

> The Bible is a parable of man's advance to the family, to the tribe, to a nation with a national ideal, to a nation with a universal ideal (prophets).

The Jewish Bible is thus a blueprint of nationalism in its all-embracing meaning and has played a significant role in keeping the national concept of Jewry alive. This is probably a further reason why Toynbee desires the abolition, abandonment, and revision of the various Biblical books, as we have mentioned before. Only a lack of knowledge and understanding of Jews and Judaism, and of the role of the Bible in this connection, could permit the putting of such unreal thoughts on paper. For the Bible to the Jew is not just a book that one borrows from a library and then returns and forgets its contents. It is the Book with which Jewry became interwoven through that special and unique relationship which the *Zohar* summarised in the words:[335]

> 'God, the Torah, and Jewry form one unity'.

The Jew and the Bible stayed together throughout the ages; they went to every place on earth together; it thus became the Jews' guidebook to everyday life and thought. It was, therefore, not something of the remote past to the Jew, but of the constant present. The patriarchs and the prophets, the thinkers and lawgivers, the fighters and organisers, all the men of the Bible without exception, great or small, important or insignificant, were for the Jews not mythical figures but living humans, 'contemporaries'; the precepts in the Bible were not ancient outdated rules but as if given 'today'; and Palestine was always 'the Land of Israel', the Jews' land, where they once lived and would do so again. The whole life of the Jew was patterned on the Bible and on the subsequent literature which is based solely on it: the Talmud, the philosophical, ethical, legal, and other writings. The Bible *per se* and through its commentaries and interpretations thus became an integral part of the Jew. Accordingly its national concept is the Jews' life. This has never been lost or given up, either in Rome, or in Babylon, or in Nazi Germany, or in Siberia. This Jewish nationalism was implanted in the Jews' soul throughout the ages, from their childhood, and it developed in them and with them. Thus the idea of nationalism remained an ever-present part of Jewish feeling and thought, as Toynbee aptly stressed in saying that it 'has been rewarded by success for more than two thousand five hundred years up to date'; and as Jewish literature and Jewish existence, in Ahad Ha'am's correct assessment,[336] prove convincingly enough. Though the conception of 'nationalism' in its current sense is modern, the national sentiment itself has existed in our people all the time. And its existence and value have been realised in our literature in every period, from the Bible and the Talmud to the literature of the Hassidim.[337]

When in the world at large the modern State emerged, and nationalism ripened and was finally recognised and accepted as a way of life by Gentile peoples, at the time of the French and American Revolutions, this was not a sudden new invention. Almost four hundred years earlier, John Wycliff understood that[338]

> The Bible is for the government of the people, by the people, and for the people.

The idea of modern nationalism grew out of the past in combination with the social, economic, and political conditions of the time. And that past was considerably influenced, as far as the spiritual life of these peoples was concerned, by the Jewish Bible and by the New Testament, by their religious content and message, and therefore could not but also deeply and decisively influence the emergence of the new national idea. Thus the Puritan revolution in seventeenth-century England is, in Hans Kohn's words,[339] 'the first full manifestation of modern nationalism'; it was 'the influence of the Old Testament [that] gave form to this new nationalism', and it was, as he said elsewhere,[340]

> the Covenant . . . between God and the whole [Jewish] people, every member in complete equality . . . a symbolic act of the highest pregnancy, revived three thousand years later as the root of modern nationalism.

Also Thomas Masaryk, in an analysis of the development of modern nationalism, emphasised[341] that 'we all live spiritually from this Jewish heritage', meaning the Jewish Bible and its conception of nationalism closely knitted with religion. As he put it, with regard to his own people, in one of his major studies:[342]

> Only in the Reformation period does the whole nation appear for the first time as a nation on the scene of modern history. Nationality,[343] the idea of nationality, is closely connected with the Reformation, it emanates from it. It is self-evident that nationality cannot be comprehended biologically only; nationality is an idea, a state of mind.[344] Nationality is a moral idea. The idea of nationality is in the end love, mutual relationship based on language and descent, a moral idea, and this idea has been strengthened and consecrated through the Reformation and, in particular, through Hus,[345] through the very fact that the Bible was translated, which to the nations is the book of books, and that the national language became the language of religion.

Lord Acton goes even further. Not the Bible alone but also the history of the Jewish people constitutes a continuous lesson in practical nationalism. He said:[346]

> The example of the Hebrew nation laid down the parallel lines on which all freedom has been won—the doctrine of national tradition and the doctrine of the higher law; the principle that a constitution grows from a root, by process of development, and not of essential change; and the principle that all political authorities must be tested and reformed accord-

ing to a code which was not made by man. The operation of these principles, in unison, or in antagonism, occupies the whole of the space we are going over together.

Taking a panoramic view (which is his preferred method) of Toynbee's prejudice against Jewry and Judaism, one wonders whether his present-day contempt for nationalism in general is not to a large degree influenced by the facts to which reference has been made in the preceding quotations on the roots of modern nationalism and democracy in the Jewish Bible and in Judaism. In this case, however, he would have to reverse the challenge and accuse Western nationalism of imitating historical Jewish nationalism, and this in itself would reduce to nonsense his theory of a 'Zionist assimilationism'. But logic is not a strong point in Toynbee's work.

Misused Nationalism

If nationalism, as it has progressively developed, has become a tool in our day in the hands of sinister forces and is being misused to the detriment of humanity, the fault lies not with nationalism *per se*, just as it does not lie with religion *per se* if it is being similarly misused. Neither religion nor nationalism nor any other high ideal is 'bad', 'destructive', or to be 'disdained'; their leaders, or some of their adherents, are or may be so. In dealing with the essence of any of these ideals, the emphasis, however, must be put on the ideal, not on its blasphemous abusers. It is therefore no solution to demand loudly the abolition of nationalism or religion (even if that were possible), just as it would be no solution to demand the abolition of love because lechery exists or the disappearance of mankind because individual human beings sin. There is room for an honest and true appreciation and realisation of these ideals in life. So progress is secured not by surrender out of despair or disappointment but by continuous effort to realise it. For there cannot be anything fundamentally wrong, bad, or sinful in the fact, which constitutes the basic motive of nationalism, that people long for freedom and desire their own territory to foster and develop their own culture and lives in accordance with their own ideals and hopes. Nationalism constitutes the free development of a people's creative forces in pursuance of its own continued existence and in the final analysis in pursuance of the benefit of mankind. Sentiments and feelings of this sort are not the results of artificial external influences but are born in the hearts of the people, grow in them and with them, and undergo changes progressively with the inevitably increasing complexities of political, social and economic development. Seen from this vantage point, Jewish nationalism, rooted in the Jewish Bible and growing and developing progressively as Jewry's existence grew and developed over the centuries, remains the classic model for Jew and non-Jew alike. Zionism appeared in modern times at the end of an epoch, or probably when a new one was emerging, as the culmination of this growth and development. Its national ideal, like that of Jewish nationalism since the beginning of the Diaspora, differed from all others known under that name because, apart from what has already been mentioned, it did not develop within the limits of a territory where its members lived. Therefore, in contrast to every other, it was nationalism at its purest, because it constituted the strongest protest against the oppression of peoples and thus emerged as the absolute in freedom for enslaved man. In this lies the importance for mankind of the 'tiny minority' striving for freedom which Toynbee, as we have shown, did not understand. That is because a nationalism of this sort became a symbol of national freedom and social justice. One should not overlook the fact that when World War I came to an end it was the conception of Zionist nationalism of the 'tiny minority', then only about twenty years old, that was applied by the League of Nations as the ideal solution for establishing the freedom of all small nationalities and nations, on the principle of 'national minorities' and 'national self-determination'. Toynbee himself at that time became an ardent supporter and propagator of these ideas.[347] It was thus something that the Western peoples have learned from Zionism, an aspect which Toynbee now conveniently overlooks when talking about a Zionism emulating others. Nothing that Hitler and the other sinister forces of our age have done can stain the purity of these ideas. Jewish nationalism 'is one of those eternal truths which came out of Zion to show mankind a way'.[348] And Zionism, rooted in the Jewish Bible, leads directly to these eternal truths. It may make mistakes, it may err in this or that assessment or practical step, and, indeed, it has made many mistakes and has badly sinned against its principles and ideals. But sinning is human and man-made; it in no way reflects on the greatness and soundness of the idea.

In view of what has been said, it is a fundamental misjudgment of the historical development of the national idea for Toynbee to maintain that Jewish nationalism espoused by Zionism was or is 'national assimilation'. Max Beloff emphasised this when stating[349] that 'the early exponents of Zionism were on the whole more impressed by the uniqueness of what they were doing than by the parallels that could be drawn between what Jews were demanding in the secular sphere and what other submerged nationalities—Czechs, Poles, Ukrainians— were claiming.' And indeed, Zionism 'is the oldest nationalist move- ment in history', as the British *Handbook* quoted before aptly formulates it;[350] and this is, as we have shown in the short survey above, a correct evaluation. Jewish nationalism constitutes a continuation of and identi- fication with what had existed in Jewry uninterruptedly before, during, and after the development of modern nationalism which came to life in the eighteenth century. Today's Jewish nationalism is therefore not new but historic, as a scholarly study on the subject pointed out:[351]

> The modern Jewish national movement is the heir both of the Exodus from Egypt and of the Return from Persia. It owes a great deal of its impetus to the desire of masses of Jews, particularly in Europe, to escape from intolerable conditions; but it springs also out of a need to 'build the house of the Lord'—or, in modern terms—to restore to the Jewish people the unhampered power of self-expression, the possibility of shaping a life of its own in accordance with its own ideals and beliefs. If the material need is the more urgent and apparent at the present time, it is none the less true that the spiritual need has largely determined the character of the national movement, and in particular its direction towards Palestine.

Zionism, as an organised force, arose at a moment when, thanks to the general atmosphere surrounding 'emancipation', Jews were able to proclaim and demand aloud formally what for centuries they had been prevented by the Gentile world from demanding and pronouncing. Theodor Herzl, the founder of political Zionism, made use of the opportunity and of the methods which the world around him offered. 'This we could not have done before', he wrote, 'we can do it now.' Modern techniques, the slogan of freedom of speech, of liberty and democracy, enabled the Jews for the first time in their history to utilise these elements for the presentation of their problems in the language of this new age, with the arguments familiar to the non-Jewish world, and comprehensible in the new terminology. 'Electric light was not invented merely that a few snobs might illuminate their salons with it', wrote Herzl,[352] 'but rather that the problems of mankind might be illumined and solved thereby.' But what he and his followers presented as Zionism's national concept has always been there; it was not artificially created for momentary requirements as a copy of other nationalisms. It based itself solely on the continuous existence of the Jewish people. Thanks to the spiritual and psychological change in the minds of Western peoples at the time, Zionism was not only able to lay before them openly, in their language, the long-existing Jewish question but also to elevate it into a world problem concerning all of them.

Surrender—Impossible

In the light of this, it is therefore absurd to suggest, as Toynbee does, that Jews give up the nationalism which has been part and parcel of their essence for 'over two thousand five hundred years', in his own words. This national or ethnic element in Judaism is, as has been stated, not something that has been artificially acquired and could therefore be given up at will. Present-day Jews are the result of an uninterrupted development—they descend from Jews, are linked with Judaism by countless generations of common history, and are linked with other Jews by kinship and age-long experience as well as by faith. This historical parallelism of attributes that make up the Jew is unique, as we have shown in our comments on religion, where it was stressed that Jews not only have a peculiar religion, but are also a peculiar people because this religion, in all its denominational interpretations, is confined to this people only, and this people has none other but this religion. Members of many races and nationalities are Catholics or Protestants; Judaism is the sole religion of the Jewish nationality. The teachings and practices of these other religions are of a metaphysical nature or are interwoven with various sets of ethical principles. The highest and deepest teachings of Judaism, its religious daily customs and ceremonies, are, from time immemorial, closely connected and interwoven with Jewish nationalism, and aim at preserving Jewry as a separate people. Even if there are Jews who do not practise religion, do not belong to any of the religious denominations, regard themselves as atheists, or proclaim themselves Jews by nationality only, they think and practise and live in almost every aspect of their activities on the basis and in the spirit of what Jewish religion throughout the ages has contributed to and shaped in Jewish nationalism. Therefore the physical Jew and the Jewish religion remain interwoven because the Jew alone created it. He did not join it. It grew together with him, developed with him, and regulated his existence as he regulated its perpetuation. No division is thus possible between the Jew in his physical aspect and Jewish religion, nor is it possible to make a division within any or all of the other attributes that constitute the essence of Jewry, because no borders exist between these ingredients; each is an integral, yet completely absorbed, part of the whole. It is for this reason that Zionism envelops the whole of Jewish life, and not only one aspect such as, for instance, the territorial or linguistic, however important each may be. In these circumstances, if any such division as Toynbee suggests were to be achieved within the Jewish people, it would lead inevitably to the obliteration of Jewry; and this in itself would lead to the disappearance of the Jewish religion—whatever Toynbee may promise to a 'community based on religion only'. For Jewish religion without the physical Jew is a contradiction in terms and of life. The term 'nationality' or 'people' employed for Jewry, therefore, embraces every element that makes them a people, religion predominantly included. Toynbee was indeed right when, as we quoted before, he said[353] that

> throughout the Jews have concentrated on their paramount aim of preserving their distinctive national identity.

Zionism, A Progressive Movement

If this is correct—and it is—then the uninterrupted concentration by Jews on their national preservation cannot be classified as an imitation of a Western nationalism which was born fifteen hundred years after such 'concentration' on that aim had begun. Nor can Zionism be classified as a 'regressive movement'[354] or 'archaic' when it regards as its aim the furtherance of this continuous preservation of the Jewish national identity. Yet once again Toynbee does not hesitate to disregard history and logic and chooses rather to contradict himself when he says in respect of Zionism:[355]

> Archaism . . . is always a perilous pursuit, but it is most perilous of all when it is taken up by members of a community that is a fossil of a dead civilisation, since the Past to which the archaists have it in their power to cast back in such case may be more sharply at variance with present realities than even the remotest past state of a society belonging to the living generation of the species. A Western-inspired archaism carried the twentieth-century Zionist faction of a Jewish diaspora back to the aims and ethos of the generation of Joshua . . .

If Zionism is thus a movement casting back to Jewry's beginnings, or to the time of Joshua, thousands of years ago, how could it be a movement of 'alien converts'[356] to nineteenth-century Western nationalism? Of course, we seek in vain for an answer. In fact, we do not expect one. The question is raised here so as to add one more item to the collection of Toynbeean superficiality which characterises also the rest of the quotation above. For there is no reason to accept Toynbee's opinion, without evidence, that archaism is perilous, or that it is more perilous in the fossil of a dead civilisation than in a living civilisation, or that the past must of necessity be at variance with present realities. All that is apart from the undiscriminating use by Toynbee of the term 'fossil', which to this day he himself confesses not to know how to apply.[357] Nor, of course, is it acceptable at all that what Toynbee contemptuously calls the 'ethos' of the generation of Joshua is necessarily bad as is obviously implied in his quotation, especially if we remember how undiscriminatingly he has used the term 'ethos'. After all, the paramount aim of the Book of Joshua is summarised in the verses (i, 7–8):

> only be thou strong and very courageous, that thou mayest observe to do according to the law, which Moses my servant commanded thee: turn not from it to the right hand or to the left, that thou mayest prosper whithersoever thou goest. This book [Torah] of the law shall not depart out of thy mouth; but thou shalt meditate therein day and night that thou may observe to do according to all that is written therein . . .

In the end, however, Toynbee's whole quoted passage collapses on the statement that Zionism supposedly 'carried [its ideology] back to the aims and ethos of the generation of Joshua'. This is because, as we have shown above,[358] there is neither possibility nor desire nor necessity for Jews or Zionists to hark back to anything specific in the past, as—and for this Jews have not needed 'a Western-inspired' impulse—no generation in any period of Jewish history has ever ceased to live within Jewry. It is precisely what Toynbee himself, when not yet haunted by a desire to reformulate every concept in order to attack Zionism, once described as follows:[359]

> We shall admit, then, without hesitation, that in the life of a nation, just as in that of an individual, past experience conditions to an overwhelming degree each present moment, as it comes and goes, and that the absence of tradition and, still more, a positive break with the past, are always symptoms of weakness and defect in the ideals of the contemporary generation.

The usual contradiction between two Toynbee statements once again becomes obvious ('The past . . . at variance with present realities' and 'past experience conditions . . . each present moment'), and thus makes his whole theory of 'archaism' appear ridiculous.

'So quick bright things come to confusion'![360]

The last-mentioned Toynbee quotation serves him as the basis of his own formula for describing the essence of 'nationality' and 'nation', without attempting to define them precisely. As we shall see, the past emerges here not as an 'archaism' but as the strongest force of life. This formulation might be usefully applied to an understanding of what Zionism, rooted in the millennia of Jewish national development, has attempted to explain in modern terminology. Toynbee wrote:

> . . . what is a nationality? Like all great forces in human life, it is nothing material or mechanical, but a subjective psychological feeling in living people. This feeling can be kindled by the presence of one or several of a series of factors; a common country, especially if it is a well-defined physical region, like an island, a river basin, or a mountain mass; a common language, especially if it has given birth to a literature; a common religion; and that much more impalpable force, a common tradition or sense of memories shared from the past.[361]
> Nationality is a 'will to co-operate', and a nation is a group of men bound together by the immanence of this impulse in each individual.[362]

This is the will bequeathed by the past that gives its incalculable momentum to the will of the present.[363]

And indeed, the underlying impulse to Jewry's self-preservation is will to live and to continue to live. That means, not to create something new *ex nihilo* but to perpetuate existence. This will was present in the people when the Jews had their State in Palestine. It continued also to direct Jewry after the loss of political independence, because it was based on and accompanied by faith in the future. The attraction and daily recall of past national independence was sufficiently strong to enable the Jew to stick stubbornly to continued existence because that memory became part of his contemporary thinking and feeling, of his uncompromising belief in the future of his people. His nationalism therefore had only a practical meaning, because it did not suddenly arise out of what Toynbee calls 'archaism' and did not confine itself to memories of a glorious past but at every second of its existence, without interruption, it looked consciously and with unbroken faith towards the future. This is the deeper meaning of the 'Messiah to come'. Thus Israel became a people of hope, as has been shown elsewhere in this study,[364] for it was always a living community and had the will to perpetuate its life. Throughout Jewish history this basic motif repeated itself in various forms.

A Natural Corollary

The will to renewal as a living community is closely interlinked with the memory of the territorial, national, and political life in Palestine and the hope for its revival. Like nationalism, this concept of the national territory has been present also at all times in the Jews' hearts. Spiritually the Jew has never left Palestine. The Holy Land, the Land of Israel, is close and real to him in his daily life, like the great figures of the Bible, as has already been shown.[365] The return to Palestine was, as Toynbee correctly stated,[366]

a natural corollary of the Jews' paramount aim of preserving their distinctive national identity.

It is, therefore, mere paralogism to say, as Toynbee does in the quotations above,[367] that, even in aiming at creating a 'national home' in

Palestine for the Jewish people, Zionists pursue 'assimilationism on a national basis', thus imitating other peoples who have the desire to possess their own country. Palestine, as we have said, has always been regarded by the Jews as 'belonging' to Jewry; they did not have to learn from others their longing for the Land and for their re-establishment there. Jews have lived with the belief that the Land was given them by God, by Covenant with their ancestor Abraham 'Unto thy seed will I give this land' (*Genesis*, xii, 7), 'to thee will I give it, and to thy seed for ever' (*ibid.*, xiii, 15) 'to inherit it' (*ibid.*, xv, 7). And they knew that this ownership was subsequently confirmed through Moses ('I have given you the land to possess it'—*Numbers*, xxxiii, 53), and that this possession was to be perpetuated for all time by what Isaiah prophesied on the future unity of the people of Israel and of the Land of Israel:[368] 'You people shall all be righteous, they shall inherit the Land for ever'. This was pronounced some two and a half thousand years before the emergence of the modern territorial state nationalism. One wonders: who assimilated whom?

This feeling of the unity of the Jewish people with the Land of Israel, and the belief that the division between them is only of a temporary nature, is so strong that, while dispersed all over the world (and in large masses to this day) Jews have always said all their prayers with their faces turned towards Jerusalem; they continue to pray for rain and dew —in Palestine; they continue to celebrate the first fruits and the harvest —in Palestine; they continue to pray three times a day for the return—to Palestine; when painting his dwelling the Jew still leaves an unpainted patch, and when his son gets married, ashes are still placed on his head—both in memory of the destruction of Jerusalem. And throughout his life the Jew continues to preserve in his home a little bag of Palestine soil to be put into his grave on his burial if interred outside the Holy Land. There are dozens more similar national customs which have become religious tradition, and religious observances that have become national practices, stressing the interrelationship of religion and nationalism and the close connection of Israel and Eretz Israel. Never for one moment has the thought of the Land been absent from the mind of the Jews. 'Next year Free Men' has always in Jewish homes on Passover night followed the annual call, 'Next year in Jerusalem', the sum-total of all the love and hope for a re-established

Palestine. And this hope has to an extraordinary degree kept the Jewish people alive.

There is also another aspect of the 'return of the people to its Land' which shows the absurdity of degrading it, as Toynbee does, to an assimilationism by trying to distinguish on this ground between Jewish nationalism and Jewish religion. For it is not the physical Jew only who aims at returning to his national centre; Jewish religion, too, if it is to develop and deepen its unifying influence upon its adherents wherever they may live, requires a centre. 'While the *Beth Din* endured', said Maimonides, 'there was no dissension in Israel'. Religious disintegration is the inevitable outcome of the lack of a Jewish centre and this is the reason why Jewish religion, more than any other aspect of Jewry, kept the desire and hope for such a centre alive throughout the ages. Here again, as it is hoped, the new Sanhedrin will arise as the guiding and unifying factor of Jewish religion. Thus, as we have shown, it was Jewish religion that primarily kept the idea of the final return to Eretz Israel alive in Jewry, through 'living' with the Bible, with the Talmud, in the daily prayers, in a host of customs and practices. This also becomes no less clear from the one practical example that Toynbee put forward to prove that this was not so. I refer to the role which he attributed to the Agudath Israel. He maintained that this organisation pursued certain thoughts which we have proved were not those of Agudath Israel. Others, however, do pursue this concept—*i.e.* the idea that[369]

> an ultimate restoration is God's will, and that He is certain to accomplish this purpose of His in His own time.

This idea was born in times of great despair, when it was inconceivable to Jews living in an unhappy reality, especially if one considered the powerful forces in possession of the Land in those various periods, that it might be possible through one's own endeavours to regain Palestine. But the Jew did not allow even this despair to deter him from the idea and hope of a return, and in his deep trust in God and in His promise he turned from the hopeless-seeming reality to the supernatural expectation. How could he, in those dark ages, confronted by a hateful world, have expected its realisation to come to pass through Jewry's own endeavours without a miracle? Meanwhile, he strengthened his hope for the miraculous return through God's own Hand with the help of references from the Bible, the Talmud, and other holy works. They gave him strength to believe; and he continued to live and to hope. There are some extremely Orthodox individuals who still believe so and therefore take a hostile attitude towards Israel and Zionism.[370]

It seems fitting, at this point, to reveal a significant occurrence with regard to this attitude.[371] The Rabbi of Klausenburg, in Transylvania, one of the foremost spiritual figures of Orthodoxy, in pre-war times used to forbid his adherents to settle in Palestine because, he used to say, this meant presumptuously doing what God will do in His Own Time and with His Own Hand. And then World War II broke out in all its fury. The Rabbi and his family were taken to a concentration camp and there, one day, he was ordered to line up behind his wife and nine of his children in front of a gas-chamber. When the last of his family had gone through the chamber's entrance and the Rabbi's turn to enter arrived, the big door fell down, closed the opening, and the Rabbi was saved. After years of torturing self-examination the Rabbi came to the conclusion that he had had to go through the incredible Job-like ordeal of his family's destruction because of his great sin in having advised Jewish men and women not to settle in Palestine but rather to wait patiently for God's work and who thus, on his advice, had not saved themselves but perished like his own family. And he was saved, miraculously, so he believed, in order to preach this truth to those who still pursued the fallacious assumption. Now settled in Israel, the Rabbi finally found consolation, which resulted from repentance, thus symbolising the fate of his people: to return to the Land through repentance.

The ideological gap between the concepts of those who 'wait' and those who 'act' is not as deep as Toynbee makes out or as may appear on the surface. Those non- or anti-Zionists who still adhere to a belief in the theory of 'God's Own Hand' differ from Zionists only with regard to the time factor, not with regard to belief in the definite achievement and thus in the essence of the certain national restoration. For, can a deeply religious person pray for something which from the outset he regards as unattainable? And a great part of the Jew's prayers is devoted to Jewry's restoration in Palestine. The idea, therefore, is not less 'national' whether its fulfilment is expected today and through one's own endeavours or in a thousand years. The very fact that some individuals believe that at some time, even if in an infinitely distant future, the restoration will take place not by their own hand but by the Hand of God makes them as nationalistic as are Zionists. Saying it, praying for it, hoping for it, teaching it to their children, and, above all, believing that the appointed time may come 'any day', which means possibly even today or tomorrow (observant Jews pray three times a day, 'Your salvation we expect all the day'[372]); that is non-professed Jewish nationalism.[373] It is in its essence nothing other than pure Zionist nationalism. It is the concept, deeply rooted in Judaism, that God's promise will definitely be fulfilled.

Therefore it does not make the slightest difference to the Jews, and to the world at large for that matter, which has accepted the 'historical connection of the Jewish people with Palestine',[374] if Toynbee challenges God's right[375]

> to give Israel possession of a land that was neither his to give nor Israel's to take.

If this is so, why does Toynbee so enthusiastically support those who hope that God will bring his children back to the Land with His own Hands and in His own time if this same God has no right whatever to possess them with the Land? We shall, of course, receive no answer to this question because it is in the realm of logic and does not fit into the chaotic mixture of the witch's 'Einmal-Eins' which occupies the introductory page to this work.

Meanwhile, let Toynbee embark upon his private war against Yahweh, who had categorically said 'The Land is Mine' (*Leviticus*, xxv, 23). Yahweh appears 'repellent'[376] to him in any case, and not only on this count. Let him challenge Yahweh's rights and power; he has anyhow already set himself up as God's rival, sweepingly foretelling what will happen to the Jews 'on the day of Judgment'.[377] Toynbee may feel in this challenge some advantage over his contemporary Yahweh-'clastes', Theodor Fritsch, the pre-Hitlerite Nazi who, thirty years before Toynbee, had already declared his private war against Yahweh in his *The False God. My Evidence Against Yahweh*.[378] For Fritsch handed down his 'evidence' to Hitler and Streicher for further use. Toynbee, obviously, has no followers or epigones. 'Self-centredly prejudiced in his own favour',[379] he prefers to carry on his private crusade with 'his own hands and in his own time'. What a *Gotterdämmerung* duel is foreseen here—Toynbee's 'challenge' and Jehovah's 'response':

Permanent Separateness—A Historical Fact

It has been shown in the sections dealing with religion, the 'community', nationalism, and Palestine, that Jewry's separateness from other peoples is inherent in every one of these important aspects appertaining to the survival and continuous existence of the Jewish people. In Toynbee's writings this separateness appears to be a deliberate endeavour of the Zionists, and the Zionists only. They are presented as if they had created this segregation of Jews from Gentiles for nationalistic purposes and thus emulate other nationaliities. Toynbee further maintains that because of this, Zionism and antisemitism are 'at the bottom expressions of an identical point of view'.[380] On both points he is, of course, wrong. We have shown his fallacious contention regarding the Zionist-antisemitic identity on this point elsewhere. Here we deal with his second fallacy.

Jewish separateness is not a 'Zionist invention'. It is as old a tradition and way of life as the age of Jewry itself. Some four thousand years ago Moses set the pattern when he said to the Lord:[381]

> For wherein will it be known that I have gained Your favour, I and Your people? Is it not that by going with us, so that we may be separated, I and Your people, from every people that is on the face of the earth?

And some two thousand years later Jeremiah, in a turbulent period of Jewish history, delving into the same problem, exclaimed:[382]

> Thus said the Lord who gives sun for light by day, and the fixed order of the moon and of the stars for light by night, who stirs the sea and its waves roar ... If this fixed order departs from before Me, says the Lord, then will also the seed of Israel cease to be a nation before Me forever.

The meaning of this passage is obvious: as long as the cosmic order prevails, Jewry will exist as a separate nation. It is, in fact, identical with the thought expressed in the simile in the *Midrash* which has been quoted previously, and which, over a thousand years ago, maintained that 'just as oil will not mix with other liquids, so Israel will not mix with other nations of the world'.

All this has been to the Jews part and parcel of their existence throughout the ages to this day. But it was not confined only to those who strictly adhered to tradition: so enlightened a man as Spinoza also believed in continuous Jewish separateness, as when pointing out that apart from anything else[383]

> the sign of circumcision is in my opinion . . . so important that . . . it alone would preserve the nation for ever.

And he came to a 'Zionist' conclusion over two hundred years before Zionism, and not in any way as a reaction to antisemitism, when continuing:

> I even regard it as very possible that the Jews, assuming that the foundations of their religion do not soften them up, if once a favourable opportunity presents itself—human conditions are subject to change—will rebuild their former state and God will choose them again.

And a man of Disraeli's eminence, who may be regarded as the prototype of a 'genuine assimilationist', as described above, could do nothing other than recognise the eternity of the Jewish people and their distinctiveness from the others through the 'segregating genius'. And this notwithstanding the fact that his own personal 'Jewish problem' had been solved when he left the fold and was received into Christianity. Yet he had Sidonia reflecting on the Jews:[384]

> When he reflected on what they had endured, it was only marvellous that the face had not disappeared. They had defied exile, massacre, spoliation, the degrading influence of the constant pursuit of gain; they had defied Time. For nearly three thousand years according to Archbishop Usher they have been dispersed over the globe. To the unpolluted current of their Caucasian stricture, and to the segregating genius of their great Lawgiver, Sidonia ascribed the fact that they had not been long ago absorbed among those mixed races, who presume to persecute them, but who periodically wear away and disappear, while their victims still flourish in all the primeval vigour of pure Asian breed.

While thus Jews have been proud of their differences, conscious of a peculiar spiritual heritage and historic culture, and looking forward full of hope to the realisation of their national and religious ideals, it was this fact more than any other that aroused the envy and enmity of their Gentile neighbours. In the Greco-Roman period their offence was that they were nationalist in a cosmopolitan society; in the Dark and Middle Ages, that they were heretics and infidels in a Christian society; in the second and post-emancipation periods that they were cosmopolitan in a national society. But beneath the specific complaint the fundamental ground of dislike was, as it is today, that the Jews were and are different, refusing to be absorbed as numerous other minorities have been in history, and keeping themselves religiously, as well as a community, separate.

As has been pointed out, Jewish separateness has not been confined to literary expression—which would fill a large library itself—or to religious belief. Life itself testifies to its undeniable existence, in the numerous attempts during the Diaspora to 'return' to Palestine, in order to give physical expression also to this distinctiveness. There has not been a single era in Jewish history when Jews, whether few or many, have not returned to Palestine. And those who were unable to do so meanwhile created those fundamental elements which maintained them as a unified people until the moment when the great return might come to pass. This is expressed in the fact that Jewry in every age and in every land has always desired and worked towards social separateness or independence, even if not always consciously. The strongest element in this process, as repeatedly pointed out, has been Jewish religion, which strengthened the separateness through comprehensive regulations connected with the private lives of the Jews, and by that very fact with their relationship to the surrounding peoples.[385] The separateness was emphasised by the instinctive tendency of Jews, when settling in a new land or a new place, to concentrate in specific areas. The authorities' rules regarding the confinement of Jews in concentrated areas, the so-called 'ghettoes', did not precede the settlement of these Jews but followed it. The rules were not the cause but the result of Jews settling first in these enclaves.[386] Even in the absence of these restrictions, and right up to our own day, Jews settle voluntarily in a London Whitechapel, in a New York Lower East Side, or, today, in

certain sections of suburbia. As Bezalel Sherman described it with
regard to American Jewry:[387]

> From a legal standpoint Jews have never lived in a ghetto in America;
> socially, however, they have never as a group stepped out of the ghetto ...
> One thing is certain: there is no less social separation, and in some cases
> even more, between Jews and non-Jews in the suburbs than in the large in-
> dustrial cities. This fact plays no small role in the greater eagerness of subur-
> ban Jewry to join synagogues, build community centres, establish Jewish
> schools and form other Jewish organisations.

And Dr Nathan Glazer arrived at these same conclusions from the fact
that not only has the idea of the 'melting pot' proved unrealisable in the
United States, but 'cultural pluralism', which took its place, has also
not brought 'integration'. He wrote:[388]

> When the great exodus to Queens, Long Island and other suburban areas
> began after the Second World War, many observers assumed that Jews
> would cease to be concentrated. . . . However, before long the mixed
> developments showed a strong tendency to become almost entirely Jewish
> or non-Jewish.

This separateness, accompanied by an intensified Jewish consciousness,
is, for instance, clearly discernible in the contrast between city and
suburbia in the field of Jewish education. Thus, in New York City
'more than a third of the Jewish children attend Jewish schools during
a given year; in the suburbs more than two-thirds attend'. And the
reason for this difference in relative school attendance is that there is
'less anonymity and more cohesion in the suburbs and that Jewish life
there tended to be centred more around the synagogues'.[389]

In addition to religion and an instinctive drawing together, a third
element also arose from the situation in which the Jews found themselves struggling for the preservation of their separate identity: the
emergence of their own economy—*i.e.* of areas of the economy which
were open to Jews and which enabled them to work together, to act
together, and to enjoy together the fruits of their activities.[390] This was
not a dominant element in the past, but an important corollary of their
material existence. It diminished as time went on because Gentiles
gradually took over those economic areas which originally had been
left open to Jews, and because in our day the economy as such is, in

many lands, to a much wider extent open to them, although concentration in certain specific activities or professions is still clearly discernible.[391]

Because of this distinctive separateness, resulting from the various elements described above, Jewry was unable physically to disappear or to merge with other social structures, however many individuals deserted it or vanished for other reasons in the course of history. This separateness was not always demonstrated as a conscious expression of a national will, but the very fact of Jewry's uninterrupted existence made all those who sensed it one people.

Unanswerable Questions

This oneness was felt, and is felt to this day, by great masses, one can say without exaggeration by the majority of Jewry. It makes no difference to the basic issue if some individual Jews are opposed to these ideas or deny the existence of a Jewish people or its national unity. It is quite sufficient as a given fact to those who feel this way. A conscious member of this community does not have the urge to define the existence of the people or to prove it; or to ask all those collectively unanswerable questions 'What is a Jew?', 'Who is a Jew?', 'Am I a Jew?', and so on. As Dr Johnson put it:[392] 'We all know *what* light is; but it is not easy to *tell* what it is'. Questions of this sort are frequently raised these days. To a natural member of the Jewish people they seem strange indeed.

Formulated as they are above, such questions suggest that the questioner wishes to receive a ready-made answer. But there are no ready-made answers. Israel's former Prime Minister, David Ben Gurion, was trapped in that fallacy when, for special reasons relating to the State of Israel, he approached 46 scholars, rabbis, men of affairs, spiritual leaders all over the world to provide such 'answers'. And, sure enough, notwithstanding some basic similarities or identity among some of them, *quot homines tot sententiae*; as many people as were asked, so many opinions were uttered. That is because no definition is possible covering Jewry and every Jew in it. Therefore it is necessary to make it clear that questions of this sort are of a purely individual nature, and emanate from the strictly personal position of

the questioner. In this connection it should be pointed out that the
references are to such questions raised by Jews anywhere and not connected with specific issues in the State of Israel. The reasons for raising
these questions are obviously different, some religious, some national,
others psychological. They are often raised by Jews who feel the
impact of the collective majority culture and do not find their place
in it as Jews; or by those actually uninterested in Judaism yet having a
'Jewish problem'; or by those who consciously or subconsciously wish
themselves out of the Jewish ranks but somehow are unable to escape.
There are still other reasons which lie within these or allied areas. But
they are all individual questions and individual problems. They can
therefore be answered only individually, and primarily by the person
concerned, for it is up to him to find his relationship to his people and
not *vice versa*. If he already has enough desire and interest to raise his
question, he should also have enough desire and interest to find his
answer. And he cannot arrive at his own 'solution' by guesswork,
simply by formulating questions, or by superficial or one-sided reasoning, which is often influenced in advance by a tacit or even unconscious
wish which has already given direction to his questions. There is no
other way, nor can there be, if he wants to know, than that of acquiring
a knowledge of the history, literature, language, customs, and the other
aspects of Jews and Judaism to which he wishes to define his relationship. How can he do otherwise than through study and knowledge,[393]
unless he does not take himself and his own questions seriously and has
no true desire to arrive at an honest conclusion. In this way, as experiences in the past have shown, an inquirer and seeker will soon arrive
at questions not as formulated above ('what', 'who', and 'am I') but at
those resulting from information gathered, namely, 'In what way does
my Jewishness express itself?', 'With whom does this Jewishness of mine
align me?', 'To what extent am I interdependent with other Jews?' At
that point he will not query his belonging and, after thus first having
found his position in Jewry, he will turn to finding his position as a
Jew in the non-Jewish milieu. On the other hand, there are thousands
and thousands of Jews, unconcerned with their Jewishness or their
belonging *per se*, who never even ask questions about themselves. If
life in general does not one day, unexpectedly, throw the issue at them,
Jewish leaders or institutions, lay or religious, could contribute con-

siderably to enabling Jews to find themselves by provoking what at first must needs be a negative reaction, but a reaction that eventually may lead to a positive approach. But whether the questions are generated spontaneously or through external pressure, in both cases the way to understanding is the same: study. But the questioner must do all this himself; no-one can do it for him. The required sources of information lie like an open book before him; and there is no doubt that if instead of asking questions without answers, he were to ask for literature and sources, he would receive them in practically every library or local Jewish institution.

Toynbee's own experience provides us with a similar, even if not identical, problem. When arriving at a critical borderline (like some of his Jewish equivalents) and becoming doubtful about his belonging to the English, to their culture, social structure, and so on, he made an approach different from 'borderline' Jews today. He did not ask himself, 'What is an Englishman?', 'Who is an Englishman?', 'Am I an Englishman?' In this respect he acted like any other national of any other people. These (Frenchmen, Germans, Italians, Spaniards, and so on) never raise questions of this sort; nor has any of these nationalities produced a literature to this effect as is the case with Jewish writers. But when Toynbee felt that for reasons of his own he might not wish to identify himself with his people any more, he did not ask questions but made the statement that if he could he would leave it for one of a number of possible other nations. Alas, he had to confess that he could not do this. 'After all, I am an Englishman,' he exclaimed, and remained one.

There is indeed something natural in being part of one's own people, however much of an inquirer and seeker one may be. That is why the conscious Jew, as mentioned above, does not ask all those questions about the essence of a Jew, or about his being a Jew. He feels it, he is conscious of it, he believes in it, he loves it as it is, he accepts it as one accepts mother and father as one's parents. This 'taking it for granted' is the criterion of any normal uninhibited child of any people, as it is the criterion which Toynbee at one time, when still an unbiased liberal, adopted.[394]

In fact we do not think of nationality, statistically—in terms of square miles or human units, any of which can be balanced, and if necessary

bartered, against any other. For us, nationality is the spiritual experience
and self-expression of a human society. Our nation's existence—its internal
cohesion and its external independence of other groups—is something we
take for granted.

Thoughts like these help us also to understand the meaning of Jewish
separateness. For the most important factor in this understanding lies
in the concrete fact of the Jewish people as a reality, as it lives and moves.
Jews are no phantoms but human beings. One has only to live among
them to understand this. Therefore, no theory of nationalism, racism,
or any other 'ism is required to prove the existence of the Jewish people
or nationality to the Jew conscious of his being a Jew. Nor can any
general theory apply to Jewry, because of its unique structure. Nationalism may be a suitable term for non-Jewish nationalities; racial theories
may or may not be adequate for Gentile people. None of these can
sufficiently express what the Jewish people is. Nor has there ever been
in the Hebrew language one such term denoting it. In Hebrew, Jewry's
own language, we find such terms as *Am, Banim, Bayith, Eda, Goy,
Kahal, Knesset, L'om, Umma.* None of these embraces the full meaning
of Jewry. They all reveal a multitude which forms a unity through
common endeavour, through a common religion as well as common
civic, social, cultural, and every other activity and institution. Numerous
attempts have been made, particularly in the last 150 years or so, by
scholars and writers, by Jews and non-Jews, not only to find the right
term but also the right definition of nationalism *per se.* To this day they
have remained unsuccessful.[395] Toynbee himself does not reveal to us
what the 'nationalism' is which he spoke about and praised in his
pre-bias days, as we have quoted above,[396] or the nationalism which he
now condemns. He did not even attempt to do so in his comprehensive catalogue of terms in which he explains those which he uses in
his writings.[397] Moreover, he adds to the confusion, because in his
works he speaks of 'peoples', 'nations', 'races', 'communities', and other
such terms, almost interchangeably. How can we draw conclusions as
regards Jewish 'nationalism' from a Gentile or any other nationalism
if we do not know what either of them stands for? And how, in these
circumstances, can Toynbee's contention be taken seriously that Jewish
nationalism is an imitation of Western nationalism?[398] Or, finally, his
suggestion that Jews give up their nationalism, if it is thus not clear

what it is that they should actually give up? But this apart, all those who have attempted to define Jewish nationalism have failed because they applied contemporary terminology to Jewish historical existence. Therefore, if we in this analysis employ modern terms, we do so only because they are generally accepted conventions and, after all, some terms must be used; and because these terms are employed by Toynbee in the works with which we deal. But we do so in the absence of a really appropriate vocabulary, for convenience sake, fully aware of their inadequacy. Thus, unable fully to define Jewry in any of these or other single terms, one can only delimit it as that historical community which millennia ago came into existence, has been able to maintain itself through historical tradition, religiously, culturally, socially, economically, through common sufferings and common hopes, has remained a clearly discernible separate unity, and has the will to continue its existence.

Returning now to the Toynbeean denationalised Jewish 'community confined to religion only', we see that life and hope or, to use the modern terms which for convenience sake we have employed, nationality and religion are one whole as far as the Jews are concerned. They are Jewry's inner bond: 'Ye shall be holy unto me: for I the Lord am holy, and have separated you from the peoples, that you should be Mine' (*Leviticus* xx, 26)—a people which lives, as has been so aptly said, through its religion, which in turn lives only through this people.[399]

Misuse of Internal Strife

There is no doubt that with his suggestion for a denationalised Jewry and its confinement solely to religion, Toynbee, hoping for 'suicide' from within Jewry, has not only blindly copied the ideas of old Jewish Liberals, but has also made use of a contemporary internal Jewish controversy in which Jews, sheltering behind a claim to be adhering to Jewish religion, oppose Zionism and the national aspect of Jewish peoplehood upon which Zionism is based.

The most vehement protest that one hears from this anti-Zionist camp is the emphatic denial that Jews are a people or a nationality or an ethnic group. 'We have separated ourselves from "the Jewish people",' exclaimed a leader of those who think in this way.[400] A Zionist or

Jewish nationalist cannot object to a Jew or to a group of Jews who state that they do not believe in the existence of the Jewish people or in the possibility of an all-embracing Judaism. The most vociferous section of those Jews who do not believe in the existence of a Jewish people and declare that they do not belong to a 'non-existing people' is the organised group in America already mentioned. Others, less aggressive in local and international fields, are, for instance, the Canaanites,[401] who also do not regard themselves as members of the Jewish people; and there are a number of other organised groups or unorganised individuals all over the world who feel likewise.[402] From the point of view of this study it would, however, be futile to enumerate those Jews who adhere to what might be called this 'negative' way and analyse their various reasons. More important is the positive aspect of the issue, *i.e.* the fact that there are great masses of Jews who believe in and feel part and parcel of the Jewish people. No one, either Jew or non-Jew, can in honesty deny or even disregard what these Jews feel. And in fairness to all concerned, only those who believe in and regard themselves as part of the Jewish people are justly entitled to speak as members of the Jewish people, as was so aptly stated by Theodor Herzl:[403]

> If someone wishes to turn away from the Jewish nationality from which he hails, and wishes to go over to another nationality, let him do so. Zionists will not stop him. But he then becomes a stranger to us. His affairs in the new nationality do not interest us, nor do our affairs interest him. He has no say in our circle, and if he is wise, he will not even try, because it may cast suspicion upon him in the eyes of the Germans, Frenchmen, and Anglo-Saxons, if he still remains concerned with internal Jewish affairs. If he wishes to win converts to his brand of assimilationist solution of the Jewish question, his best means to attain this will be to show how full recognition has been given to him and how happy he feels there.
>
> But to belong to the Jewish people, to practise Judaism, so to speak, professionally, yet simultaneously to fight against it, that is something that arouses the rebellion of every just feeling.

It is therefore preposterous for those who do not believe in a 'Jewish people' and are not members of it to roam the world, as they all, apart from the 'Canaanites', do, and deny something that actually exists but does not concern them. It is worthy of note in this connection that public denials of the existence of a Jewish people come exclusively from groups or individuals who think of themselves as Jews by religion while ethnically regarding themselves as members of the French, German, Italian, or English nationalities, or of the American people (whatever that term may stand for). They react publicly on every occasion whenever anything is stated or done by members of the Jewish people in matters connected with the Jewish people. This reaction betrays a nervousness on the part of the protestors which, by its very nature, indicates uncertainty about their own status. Their 'concern' may in a negative way even testify to the impossibility of dividing the religion and ethnicity of the Jew, as mentioned before. But anyhow, why be 'concerned' at all?—particularly if one does not belong to the 'Jewish people'. It only provokes doubts about the genuineness of the professed ethnicity of these protestors. For it must be stated in truthfulness that no such protests or denials come forth from any of the other religious groups to which members of these same respective ethnic peoples adhere, for instance, the Catholics of America, or the German Lutherans, or Greek Orthodox. One never hears protests from these quarters against Jews speaking as members of the Jewish people, or against the existence of an ethnic Jewish people. This totally different attitude of the non-Jewish members of a nationality and its Jewish members is worth noting. This, however, is an internal moral issue of the various nationalities; it does not concern the Jewish people.

The international community of nations and nationalities, including those of whom the above-mentioned Jewish 'protestors' regard themselves as members, have taken cognisance of the fact of the Jewish people's existence and have accorded recognition to this fact in a number of statements and international agreements. The 'Jewish people' has thus been given recognition in international law.

The 'Jewish People' in International Law

The initiative in this direction was taken by Theodor Herzl in his analysis of Jewry's condition and in his programme for the solution of the Jewish problem when he concluded:[404] 'We are a people, *one* people'. The Zionist Organisation adopted this concept and laid down in its Basle Programme (1897) as its aim[405] 'the establishment in

Palestine of a Home for the *Jewish people* . . .' Six years later (1903) the British Government, in an official communication to the Zionist Organisation,[406] offered to establish a Jewish settlement in East Africa on a *national* basis, which, as that document states, His Majesty's Government regarded as a step towards 'the amelioration of the position of the Jewish Race' (in Anglo-Saxon terminology 'race' stands for 'people').[407]

Fourteen years later (1917) the British Government adopted the term 'Jewish people' in its meaning as a national entity for world Jewry, when it stated in the Balfour Declaration:[408]

> His Majesty's Government view with favour the establishment in Palestine of a *national* home for the *Jewish people* . . .

In its realistic appraisal of the complexities within British and world Jewry the British Government, when issuing this Declaration, endeavoured to meet the situation of both those Jews who regarded themselves as belonging to the collective 'Jewish people' and those who denied the existence of such a collective, and/or regarded themselves as not belonging to it. Among those in the latter category were some whose spokesmen presented to the British Government their viewpoint in this respect, headed by Edwin Montagu, Claude Goldsmid Montefiore, Sir Leonard Cohen, and Sir Philip Magnus.[409] When subsequently the Declaration was issued the Government retained the terms *national* and *Jewish people* after receiving full information about their arguments, repeated today without change by those who deny the existence of the 'Jewish people'. The position of these men, who in British public life played a far more important role than any of the Zionist leaders, was taken seriously into consideration. Their rights, like the rights enjoyed by all Jews—Zionists and non-Zionists alike—in their respective countries, were not to be prejudiced through the official introduction of the term 'Jewish people' in international usage or through the creation of a Jewish National Home in Palestine. Every Jew was to have a free choice. Accordingly a safeguarding clause was inserted in the Balfour Declaration making it clear that the establishment of the Jewish National Home shall not prejudice

> the rights and political status enjoyed by Jews in any other country.

The different terminology used in this Declaration ('Jewish people' for attaining a national home and 'Jews' wherever they may live) was well chosen after 'careful consideration' to show that the latter term applied to all individual Jews wherever they were, both those who regarded themselves as belonging to the Jewish people and those who did not so regard themselves. These rights were thus derived not from any 'ethnic', 'religious', or other similar basis, but from the citizen-ship and political status which Jews as individuals enjoyed according to the conditions in the countries of which they were citizens. In the final analysis this also confirms the Herzlian concept, referred to above: those Jews who do not regard themselves as belonging to the 'Jewish people' will not only not be summarily declared as belonging to it but they are completely free to remain what they are or want to be. Having received this confirmation of their individual status, they are thus, like any other outsiders, not entitled to a say in matters appertaining to the affairs and interests of the 'Jewish people'.

It must be pointed out in this connection that the Balfour Declaration did not 'invent' the term 'Jewish people' nor did the British Govern-ment, through its issuance, only then, accord recognition of the term's existence. As already mentioned, an official British document referred fourteen years previously to the 'Jewish race' in whose interests the British Government was willing to enter into an undertaking. We know also that the Jewish people has never ceased to exist and has throughout history been known, designated, and recognised as a separate community, not confined to one specific country. The Balfour Declaration accepted this uninterrupted existence as a given fact when it promised to establish a National Home for that Jewish people. It goes without saying that such a 'National' Home (whatever meaning or interpretation may be put on this term) can only be established for and by a people or nationality that exists and whose existence is accepted as a given fact. The Jewish people has all along been such a 'people' and would also have remained one without the Balfour Declaration. This Declaration was, therefore, not issued in order to recognise the 'Jewish people'. It was a 'contract'[410] between Great Britain and the existing Jewish people, represented by its spokesmen, primarily Zionists,[411] on a *quid pro quo* basis: Britain issued the Balfour Declara-tion as her part of the agreement, and the Jews fulfilled their part of the contract through assistance in World War I.[412]

The importance of the term 'Jewish people' in the Balfour Declaration does not lie therefore in a recognition of the Jewish people, for which there was no necessity, but in its introduction in international usage. This is confirmed and considerably strengthened by the fact that the Balfour Declaration did not remain a bilateral 'contract' or 'agreement' between the two contracting parties, although an agreement couched in international terminology between two international bodies suffices for acceptance. A number of Allied Powers in World War I, such as the United States, France, Italy, Japan, Greece, Serbia, and Siam, 'approved of the terms of the Balfour Declaration'.[413] Its text was, finally, incorporated *in toto* in the Palestine Mandate, adopted in 1922 by the League of Nations,[414] which at that time comprised fifty-two member States.[415] But in addition to the inclusion of the Balfour Declaration in the Mandate, the term 'Jewish people' was further emphasised and interpreted in the Mandate's Preamble:

> Whereas recognition has thereby been given to the historical connection of the *Jewish people* with Palestine and to the grounds of reconstituting their National Home in that country.

And so as to avoid any misunderstanding as regards the terms 'National Home' and 'Jewish people', the British Government, before submitting the text of the Mandate to the League of Nations, made its understanding of them clear in the following paragraph of an official statement:[416]

> When it is asked what is meant by the development of the Jewish National Home in Palestine, it may be answered that it is ... the further development of the existing Jewish community, with the assistance of Jews in other parts of the world, in order that it may become a centre in which the *Jewish people* as a whole may take, on grounds of *religion and race*, an interest and a pride. That is the reason why it is necessary that the existence of the Jewish National Home in Palestine should be internationally guaranteed, and that it should be formally recognised to rest upon ancient historic connection.

Seventeen years later (1939), Winston Churchill, who was responsible for the document of 1922 just quoted and who was Colonial Secretary when the building up of the Jewish National Home in Palestine began and when the Mandate was submitted to and subsequently approved by the League of Nations, stated in retrospect:[417]

To whom was the pledge of the Balfour Declaration made? It was not made to the Jews of Palestine, it was not made to those who were actually living in Palestine. It was made to world Jewry and in particular to the Zionist association. . . . This pledge of a home of refuge, of an asylum, was not made to the Jews in Palestine but to the Jews outside Palestine . . . whose unchanging, unconquerable desire has been for a National Home—to quote the words to which my right hon. Friend the Prime Minister (Mr Neville Chamberlain) subscribed in the Memorial[418] which he and others sent to us: 'The *Jewish people* who have through centuries of dispersion and persecution patiently awaited the hour of its restoration to its ancestral home'. Those are the words. They are the people outside, not the people in. It is not with the Jews in Palestine that we have now or at any future time to deal, but with *world Jewry*, with Jews all over the world. That is the pledge that was given.

One could go on quoting official documents of the time, besides statements by those responsible for the political affairs of Britain as well as of other countries, confirming what has been said hitherto. None of these statements is of more interest for this study than the one made by Toynbee at a time when his bias had not yet dimmed his objectivity in affairs of Zionism and Jewry. He then described the Jewish position as follows:[419]

The Jewish party to the conflict [*i.e.* the Arab-Jewish conflict] is not simply the Jewish population, amounting just now to something like 162,000 souls, which happens to be resident in Palestine at this moment. The Jewish community which is concerned in Palestine is the Jewish community throughout the world. A national home in Palestine has been guaranteed by Great Britain and by the League of Nations, to the Jews in general. And this Jewish national home in Palestine is the legitimate concern of any Jew, anywhere, who cares to concern himself about it, even if he lives in China or Peru and even if there is not any likelihood that either he or his descendants will ever go to live in Palestine themselves. That is a very important point, so I will try to drive it home with an analogy which I believe to be almost exact. Palestine concerns every Jew in the world in the sense in which Rome concerns every Roman Catholic. It is obvious that your Chinese Roman Catholic or your Peruvian Roman Catholic is most unlikely to become an inhabitant of the Vatican City. At the same time, it is obvious that his legitimate concern in the 'Roman Question' is a moral and political [*sic!*] fact of capital importance in international affairs. No one would suggest that the only Catholics concerned in the 'Roman Question' were the Catholic population of Vatican City, or even the much larger Catholic population of the Papal State at its widest extent in the past. One of the parties to the 'Roman Question' is the Catholic Church through all the world. One of its two parties to the 'Palestine Question' is the Jewish community through all the world . . .

But the Jewish national home of the Balfour Declaration and the Mandate means more than that. . . . The City of the Vatican which was created the year before last, might fairly well be described as a cultural home, established on the soil of Rome, for the Roman Catholic Church throughout the world. If the Jewish city of Zion could be built on the pattern of the Catholic City of the Vatican, how easy the solution of the 'Palestine Question' would be! And undoubtedly the Jewish national home in Palestine does mean for Jews everything that the Vatican City in Rome means for Roman Catholics. But of course it means something else besides a cultural home. It means land and population—'close settlement by Jews on the land';[420] the facilities of Jewish immigration . . .[421] Well then . . . The Jews could not be expected to be content with a national home in Palestine which was confined to cultural elements and which was not expressed in terms of land and population as well.

From this description two conclusions of importance emerge: in the first place, one which interests us in another connection, namely, that Toynbee does not see the problem as a purely religious issue but as one of world Jewry 'legitimately concerned' with Palestine beyond the religious and cultural aspects. His 'Jewish community based on religion only' would thus head into considerable trouble. The second conclusion, and this interests us at this point, is that world Jewry as a collective is recognised as one party to the Palestine issue. This is in full accord with what was stated in the official British interpretation quoted above and confirmed in the other international documents, through which the term 'Jewish people' was introduced into international usage and thus became a fact in international law.[422] Prof. Ernst Frankenstein, of The Hague Academy of International Law, stated this clearly:[423]

Thanks to these documents [*i.e.* the Balfour Declaration and the Palestine Mandate] the existence of the Jewish people is an indisputable fact in international law.

This is not only the opinion of a private, although important, expert, but also that of the distinguished Vice-Chairman of the Permanent Mandates Commission of the League of Nations, whose authority in the Palestine issue throughout the Mandatory period Toynbee also acknowledges.[424] At one of the meetings M. Van Rees noted,[425] in connection with the MacDonald letter which the British Government had officially transmitted in 1930 to the League,[426]

> that in paragraph 3 of the Prime Minister's letter he found that 'His Majesty's Government . . . *recognises that the undertaking of the mandate is an undertaking to the Jewish people and not only to the Jewish population in Palestine*'. The White Paper, on the contrary, nowhere gave the impression that any special importance was attached to this essential distinction. Judging, for example, from the last sub-paragraph of paragraph 3, it rather appeared that the British Government had only assumed responsibility as regards the Jews established in Palestine, whereas the preamble of the mandate referred expressly to the *Jewish people* in general.

In the course of his reply Dr Drummond Shields, in the name of the Mandatory Power (Britain), said[427]

> that the policy of His Majesty's Government must be taken as a whole, as formulated, explained and amplified in the Parliamentary Debate, in the White Paper and as interpreted, in certain points, in the Prime Minister's letter.

In the subsequent debate on the question of nationality Dr Shields suggested, *en passant*, that[428]

> when a Jew came to Palestine, he came, not as a Jew, but as a foreign national of one kind or another.

> *Mr Van Rees* agreed, but pointed out that such a person was still a Jew, whether of French or any other nationality. He did not enter the country without being in possession of a certificate giving him the right so to enter, in accordance with the regulations for Jewish immigration. He came, therefore, in his capacity as a Jew and not as a national of any particular country.

> *Dr Drummond Shields* concurred, but suggested that in international law there was no such thing as a Jew from the standpoint of nationality.

> *Mr Van Rees* agreed that Dr Drummond Shields would be perfectly

correct from the point of view of international law, were it not for the existence of the Balfour Declaration, the Mandate and the White Paper, which had introduced a new element into this law in favour of the Jewish people.

The evidence could be multiplied, but I believe we have sufficiently confirmed the fact of the 'Jewish people' as a concept in international law: not as a political entity, not as a supra-nation in the meaning of Statehood, but as an 'international personality' to be given and to receive undertakings of an international nature, *i.e.* for those who regard themselves as members of the Jewish people; undertakings made by States which those 'States consider binding upon them'.[429] This is in full accord with the general principles of international law, by which the system is constituted which not only governs the relations between sovereign States but which 'also applies to other bodies to which such states attribute international personality'.[430] And this is precisely the meaning of the terminology used in the above-quoted official British documents where they refer to a 'definite contract between Britain and the Jewish people' and to 'the mandate as an undertaking to the Jewish people'; documents which were adopted by a host of sovereign States.

With this clarification in mind, we now can turn to the relationship between the Jewish people and the State of Israel.

5
Israel and the Diaspora

The relationship between Zionists or other members of the Jewish people in the Diaspora to the State of Israel is based on one common denominator: the maintenance, continuous development, and strengthening of Jewry. Israel's Jews are part of Jewry, and Jews in the Diaspora lands are parts of Jewry; together they are the Jewish people. It is, therefore, natural for all these to join in efforts to share the responsibility for the future of the Jewish people, to share in the fulfilment of the destiny which history has in store for it, and to share in every effort to strengthen this self-chosen obligation. In doing this, Zionists, national Jews outside and inside Israel, believe that the Jewish people is and will continue to be unified by that indefinable bond that makes it one, a bond, as we have been able to show in the section dealing with Jewish nationalism, that is rooted in the Jews' consciousness of the existence of this unity, a consciousness which results from the inner experience of each individual Jew who feels he belongs to the Jewish people. And this structure of one people is based on two pillars: Israel and the Diaspora, which separately are two geographical terms but together, as stated, constitute the Jewish people. But geography by itself is not the criterion, for England's Jewry, South African Jewry, American Jewry, and Israel's Jewry would separately also represent only four geographical terms; only jointly, and including all other Jewries, do they constitute the Jewish people. However, the Jewish people does not rest on four or ten or fifty pillars, but, as emphasised above, on only two, because there is a fundamental difference between the sections of the Jewish people living in the Diaspora and the one living in Israel. The former is transitory throughout (however long or short a time this transitory quality has periodically lasted in the past or will last in the future), as has been shown; but Eretz Israel is the permanent national centre. None of the past or present Jewish Diaspora communities was created through the conscious desire, will, or effort of the world-wide Jewish people; these Diaspora communities came into existence when, with the permission of the local non-Jewish authorities, a sufficient number of Jewish individuals was enabled to settle in the respective areas and to organise itself. The duration of these settlements has always depended on local conditions. The State of Israel, on the other hand, apart from its other aspects (divine, religious, historical, cultural, etc.) dealt with before, is the conscious creation of world Jewry, of the Jewish people, and it remains an integral part of it. On this basic position no external factor can have any bearing whatsoever. Therefore it does not matter if only a minority of Jewry lives there today. Palestine (Israel), as has been shown, has always been the national centre in the consciousness of the Jew in every age, however few Jews lived there. It would have been that centre even if no Jew happened to live in the land. No other country, no other Jewish community has or can have this central position in Jewish life. Therefore the State of Israel is more than a geographical area occupied by few or by many Jews. Therein lies the deep fundamental difference between Israel and the Diaspora *per se* or any sectional Diaspora community. In this difference, simultaneously, is also inherent the relationship between the two.

It is important that in any evaluation and understanding of the position this distinction and relationship should be recognised in its true setting. This will not least also help in understanding the issue of 'loyalty' and 'allegiance' with which we deal further on in this study.

And from all that has been said above it may be concluded that in essence Israel is, apart from its spiritual centrality, also, thanks to its sovereignty, today an instrument of the Jewish people, the paramount instrument, because of its twofold practical importance in the life of Jews; it means, first, an end to physical insecurity in that it is open to every Jew to settle there freely by right, if the circumstances of his life in the world at large make it necessary,[431] or if by choice he wishes to live there so as to participate personally in the building up of the State and making it secure. Secondly, the State possesses all the pre-conditions for the development of what the genius of Judaism is capable of developing; for it is free from the minority system under which Jewries all over the world live, and this means that in its own system matters of culture, religion, literature, art, and so on, are not subject to any overpowering influence by the majority—working in different spiritual aspects and concepts—and can thus develop under the distinctive impact of Jewish spiritual strength. Thus, the State, as this important instrument, is not a purpose in itself; it is not the people's master, it is their servant. It is the beginning, a first step, in a millennia-old dream and hope which has accompanied Jewry throughout history, as had been shown, a hope that will only be fulfilled, as the great prophets of Israel have foretold, after the physical return of the Jews to Palestine. It is not an escape into mythos or mysticism if one observes with an incredulous astonishment that so many nations and peoples and States have disappeared during the march of time and yet the Jewish people is still here, a concrete fact, alive, in undiminished vigour. We have put the question of the meaning of Jewry's continuing existence before but it is not inappropriate to present it again, though in a different context. Can one really pretend to believe that the Almighty has kept Jewry alive, through so many generations and lands, through so many tragedies and vicissitudes, for no other purpose than that they simply become citizens of a State called Israel, or of any other country for that matter? Surely there is a higher purpose in that preservation, reaching far beyond the duties which every person has naturally towards his country or State. Citizenship, political allegiance, patriotism, and whatever other comparative terms may be selected, are self-evident in the case of every other citizen worthy of that name. But the conscientious Jew is aware of the additional great obligation for which he has been kept alive, and he endeavours to fulfil it not only for the sake of the Jewish people but to no less a degree for the country of which he is a citizen, and indeed for mankind. He hopes, therefore, to be able to make such a contribution through either living in or supporting Israel as a first step on the way to a prophetic fulfilment, as has been described elsewhere in this study. As it was once put by Ormsby-Gore, Britain's spokesman at the Permanent Mandates Commission.[432]

> Our original advocacy of Zionism had, no doubt, other causes. It was not conceived as a refugee problem; it was conceived as a spiritual problem. In the mind of Balfour, his adherence to Zionism was due to his belief that if the Jews were enabled to build up their civilisation in Palestine once again, it had something of real constructive value to the world, and that the Jews in their old home would again produce, as they did in the past, and release great spiritual forces.

Dual Loyalties and Single Allegiance

This brings us to an issue which has been repeatedly raised in connection with the relationship of Zionists or other national Jews and the State of Israel: to whom do these Jews living outside Israel owe and give loyalty and political allegiance? It might be thought that this question has been clarified by an objective understanding of what has been described in the preceding pages and what has so often in Zionist history been stated to the same effect. But in the controversy against Zionism and ethnic Judaism the question of 'dual loyalties' turns out to have acquired so much importance because of its psychological impact that it continues to be used notwithstanding all the logic and truth that reduces it to nonsense, and it therefore has to be dealt with here.

As a starting-point we can take his statement[433] that only after the surrender of the ethnic basis of his Jewishness

> a member of the Jewish Diaspora would be a citizen of some political territorial state to which he would pay political allegiance without any political reservation. At the same time, he would continue to be a member of a 'Jewish' community which would be a religious body . . .

If this is the Diaspora that is expected to arise (we doubt it, of course, in the light of Toynbee's other statements regarding the future of the Jewish Diaspora), and for argument's sake we accept that it is, then it must be made unequivocally clear that such a Diaspora would not have to emerge only after Jews had dispensed with their 'ethnic basis', for it already exists in spite of the fact that Jews have not dispensed with that basis. Jews all over the world are a 'distinct community' and loyal citizens of their respective countries, to which they pay sole 'political allegiance without any political reservation', whether they regard themselves as Jews by religion, by birth, or by ethnic or any other characteristics. Toynbee has not submitted a single piece of proof in his *Study of History* or anywhere else in his writings that this is not so. In fact, if he were to be called upon to submit such evidence he would be unable to. On the other hand, one could with ease supply evidence in such quantities that it would grow into a small library containing statements, articles, and pronouncements by Royalty, statesmen, and leaders from all walks of life, praising the unreserved allegiance of Jews, and not only political allegiance, towards the States all over the globe of which they are citizens. This applies to Zionists and to all those who regard themselves as members of the Jewish people to no less a degree than to assimilationists or to those who regard themselves as Jews only by religion or any other distinguishing mark.

An Old Accusation

As in so many other instances, as we have been able to show, in this connection also Toynbee is of course not original. He simply copies what for centuries has been said time and again against the Jews *per se* by those who, because of lack of any other arguments in their crusades of hatred, blamed the Jews for 'dual loyalties' and for the 'inability of faithful allegiance to the countries where they lived'. The model teacher of that school, Haman, started the ball rolling when he advised King Ahasuerus:[434]

> There is a certain people scattered abroad and dispersed among the peoples in all the provinces of thy kingdom; and their laws are diverse from those of every people; neither keep they the king's laws; therefore it is not for the king's profit to suffer them.

Some nine hundred years later, although Jews were fighting on the side of the Romans—as the example of Tella in the struggle against the Sassanian armies shows—they were nevertheless suspected of and were still blamed for lack of loyalty towards the State. An historian of the period, taking this event as an example, stresses:[435]

We shall see how these suspicions of Jewish loyalty during the barbarian invasions were to swell into a chorus during the centuries of Muslim-Christian struggles in western Europe, to become almost a literary cliché among medieval chronicles.

But these suspicions did not end in the Middle Ages. They were 're-discovered' in the seventeenth century by that notorious Jew-hater Eisenmenger, and he hastened to declare that[436]

> even if the Jews say that they are obliged to pray for the welfare of the rulers of the world and of their citizens, it does not excuse them, because the question is not whether they are obliged to pray for the welfare of the authorities and their inhabitants in the lands in which they dwell, but whether in real life they also act accordingly. They are supposed to do so in accordance with the order of Jeremiah,[437] but they do not do it. Otherwise this would be visible in the many prayer-books which they use in their houses of worship and in their homes. But in every book of this kind, I do not find anything other than a . . . prayer which they say for the rulers. This prayer is there only for pretence, and not to be adhered to and practised. How very little interest they have in the welfare of a Christian sovereign is shown at the end of that prayer very clearly: 'In His days and in ours Judah shall be saved, and Israel shall dwell safely, and the Redeemer will come unto Zion'.[438]

Eisenmenger's work, although disproved and based on glaring misquotations, remains to this day the source-book of antisemitic writers.

The argument of Jewish disloyalty towards the rulers, the authorities, and the Governments of the lands in which the Jews dwelt stayed uninterruptedly on the agenda of all the Jew-haters. It was even heard in the British Parliament, when the great debate about Jewish emancipation took place on April 17, 1833. In reply to such accusations, Sir Robert Grant, the Whig stalwart who had moved the resolution to remove Jewish disabilities, said:[439]

> The opponents of the measure have, however, attempted to find certain special grounds of disqualification. They contend that, even conceding the rule of general admissability, our Jewish fellow-subjects ought, for certain peculiar reasons, to be debarred from the benefit of that rule. These reasons may be reduced to two heads: the first, political; the second, religious; and I am willing to bestow a few words on each.
> First, in the political view, it is said that there is, in the doctrine and disposition of this class of religionist, something which unfits them for the

rights of citizenship in the countries in which they may chance to be located. They are exclusive in spirit, and anti-social in manners. They are preoccupied with an ardent feeling of patriotism—a feeling, however, not towards the country of their casual residence, but towards the country, however distant, of their original descent and ultimate hopes. They look for a restoration to the land of their fathers, at some period undefined and hidden in the mysteries of futurity; and, absorbed in this vision, they have no attachment to the soil on which they may temporarily be cast . . .

It is not true that the doctrines, either moral or religious, of the Jews, are such as to disqualify them for political identity with those among whom they dwell, or to induce them to segregate themselves from the rest of the community, or to unfit them from becoming good citizens. The objection is founded on complete ignorance of all past history . . . In the most sacred of their books the Jews are told, when in a state of captivity, to act on this rule: 'Build ye houses, and dwell in them, plant ye gardens, and eat the fruit of them; and seek ye the peace of the city whether I have caused you to be carried away captives, and pray unto the Lord for it; for in the peace thereof shall ye have peace'.[440]

But these, it may be said, are the precepts they inculcate; what is their practice? I answer, that the experience of ages proves that, with these precepts, their practice is in conformity. They are to be found in every nation; and in every nation they have been conspicuous for their civil and political virtues. The very circumstance of their wide dispersion has supplied a copious field of experiment on this point. Wherever they have been protected, they have for all practical purposes become part of the people among whom they dwell. This is not merely the case in modern times, but instances of it are to be found in the earliest period of their history.[441]

I believe that this classic answer, given nearly one hundred and forty years ago to those who doubted the loyalty and allegiance of the Jews towards the State because they formed a separate nationality, adhered to a religion different from the majority religion, and hoped for the return to Palestine, should be read by all those who, to this day, repeat these outdated and incorrect contentions. And it is particularly fitting reading for those who try to adapt these old, outdated arguments to every new movement that arises within the Jewish people. They were used, as Sir Robert pointed out, on many occasions in Jewish history. It was the easiest and cheapest form of antisemitism—to cast doubt on the Jews' loyalty and allegiance to the State. From attacks such as these not only were pre-emancipation Jews not spared but also those Jews who as a result of being emancipated hoped to prevent such 'accusations' by doing their utmost to surrender everything Jewish in them. In the end, they were accused of the same 'disloyalty' as were the Jews who had not surrendered any of their national elements or religious principles. It is pathetic to read the great number of books and articles of Jewish writers of the emancipation period, who had honestly believed in full equality and were probably more patriotic than many non-Jewish nationals of these various countries, defending themselves against accusations of doubtful allegiance.[442] As these books and articles were mainly replies to antisemitic onslaughts, it goes without saying that the antisemitic literature of the emancipation period is replete with these accusations, and Hitler's Nazism made full use of spadework prepared by its predecessors.[443] Of course, this old anti-Jewish 'recipe' was used against Zionism as soon as that movement appeared on the scene, and was exposed by Max Nordau in his hard-hitting article 'Patriotism and Zionism'.[444] It was not at that time, in 1903, raised by non-Jews or by antisemites in particular. Those Gentiles who indulged in 'dual allegiance' accusations blamed all the Jews and not just the Zionists or any other particular section of Jewry. Decent non-Jews, indeed the great majority of nations all over the world, have never stirred up such suspicions and do not utter such accusations at all. They know them to be unfounded. But accusations of 'dual loyalties' were made against the Zionists since the emergence of modern Zionism by anti-Zionist Jews, who thus wrote one of the darkest chapters of internal Jewish strife. Anti-Zionist Jews then looked upon the Zionists and Jewish national brethren as disturbers of their peace and, accordingly, used every opportunity to emphasise their own patriotism towards the countries where they lived. They often exaggerated it to such a degree that they naturally invited doubts about their own sincerity, because constant protestations of loyalty made them look ridiculous in the eyes of those who take their nationalism and loyalty as natural and self-understood attributes and accordingly despise that kind of flattery and clinging. In these efforts assimilationists did not hesitate to switch over the (unfounded) accusations against themselves and all other Jews to the Jewish nationalists only. They thus hoped to accentuate their own patriotism to their countries by denouncing other Jews. One of assimilationism's leaders, Professor Ludwig Geiger, went so far as to suggest publicly in 1906 that 'Zionists be deprived of their German citizenship'.[445] It is of no consequence for the basic attitude of persons of this conviction that such attempts ended in utter failure. They are characteristics of a mentality which one would have hoped had died out as a result of Jewry's experiences since those days. But the curious climax of Geiger's efforts came in World War I, when he had to give confirmation in his book:[446]

> The *Vaterland* called and all its sons came. Neither Zionists nor Social Democrats kept away. Those whom one blamed, not without justification, in that, though dreaming of a Jewish State for others, they regarded themselves as sons of another than German nationality and who saw us, who adhered to that nationality, as shameful assimilationists . . . they seem to have forgotten their view. They too, with enthusiasm and a ready-to-die attitude, like the non-Zionists, joined the ranks of the volunteers.

Thus reality taught the professor what Zionists all along regarded as their self-evident position in the State. But, as the quotation shows, even in the moment of retraction Geiger could not resist letting the embers of his bitterness glow and he still clung stubbornly to his old 'suspicions'. He talked himself into a 'justification' of his former accusations, although truth and facts had proved the reverse. This by now insignificant incident reveals a characteristic which should not remain unnoticed when questions on this aspect are dealt with today. The conclusion is a simple one: if Jews up to that time had not learnt from history the lesson of the futility and immorality of denouncing other Jews with so baseless a 'crime', there is no excuse for subsequent generations, right up to our own day, to plead ignorance. As has been already stated, there are no Jews *qua* Jews, whether Zionists, nationalists, assimilationists, religious or a-religious, who do not give unequivocal political allegiance to their countries. The leaders as well as all the other citizens of those countries know this very well. And in their eyes, those of the non-Jews, a Jew remains a Jew whatever reason or definition of Jewishness he may advance. The effects of the continual denunciation by Jews of other Jews for 'disloyalty' thus may, and, as experience tells us, will through historical necessity, not remain confined to the abused section only. As a matter of fact, over fifty years ago that great American Jew and Zionist, Justice Brandeis, gave an unequivocal answer to any such accusation against the Zionists, which, one would have expected, would have disposed of this sort of talk once and for all. He then said:[447]

> Let no American imagine that Zionism is inconsistent with Patriotism. Multiple loyalties are objectionable only if they are inconsistent. A man is a better citizen of the United States for being also a loyal citizen of his state, and of his city; for being loyal to his family, and to his profession or trade; for being loyal to his college or his lodge. Every Irish American who contributed towards advancing home rule was a better man and a better American for the sacrifice he made. Every American Jew who aids in advancing the Jewish settlement in Palestine, though he feels that neither he nor his descendants will ever live there, will likewise be a better man and a better American for doing so.
>
> Note what Seton-Watson says:[448] 'America is full of nationalities which, while accepting with enthusiasm their new American citizenship, nevertheless look to some centre in the old world as the source and inspiration of their national culture and traditions. The most typical instance is the feeling of the American Jew for Palestine which may well become a focus for his déclassé kinsmen in other parts of the world.'
>
> Indeed, loyalty to America demands that each American Jew become a Zionist. For only through the ennobling effect of its striving can we develop the best that is in us and give to this country the full benefit of our great inheritance.

This was also the position of another member of the U.S. Supreme Court, Justice Felix Frankfurter, who actively participated in Zionist work.[449] And a third member of the U.S. Supreme Court, Justice Arthur Goldberg, publicly declared his being a Zionist and 'that in his Zionist conviction he continues in the ways of Justices Brandeis and Frankfurter'.[450] And shortly after this declaration Justice Goldberg was appointed by President Johnson to represent America at the United Nations, symbolising America's 'faith and the commitment to the United Nations'.[451] This appointment of a proud, upright Jew was hailed by American public opinion, in the words of the *New York Times*,[452] as a 'personification of the continuous opportunity afforded by American democracy to its ablest sons'. Can anyone dare to raise his voice in doubt of the loyalty and allegiance of these Zionists?

I believe it would be tantamount to insulting the intelligence of honest citizens if I were to quote even a selection from the innumerable declarations in various lands by heads of Governments and national leaders, before and since the establishment of the State of Israel, in praise and support of Zionism and of Zionists, recognising fully the compatibility between being a Zionist and a good citizen and an honest national Jew. The numerous Zionist young men who, in every land where they lived, came to the defence of their country, fought with vigour and bravery, gave their lives for it, speak a clearer language than thousands of speeches or articles could do. Everywhere in the civilised world Zionism carries on its work in the clear light of day, complying fully with the laws and principles of these States. And, after all, these Governments, their leaders, their Parliaments, and so on, do not require any lessons from Toynbee on who is loyal or disloyal to their country. 'All my life I have been an unfaltering Zionist', exclaimed Winston Churchill,[453] who understood the meaning and essence of Zionism and surely does not require any confirmation of his British patriotism. And the two moving forces within the British Cabinet for the issuance of the Balfour Declaration (1917), the Prime Minister, David Lloyd George, and the Foreign Secretary, Arthur James Balfour, understood probably better than many other persons, then or today, the absurdity of a 'dual loyalties' challenge against a Zionist because he is a proud son of his Jewish people and a proud citizen of the country where he happens to live. For Lloyd George was a proud Welshman and Balfour a proud Scotsman, both unyielding in their opinion of their own peoples and of the English, yet admired, respected, and loved as patriots of Britain. Only in areas ruled by antisemites is Jewish loyalty doubted, for the purpose of 'justifying' Jew-hatred. There, the doubt is raised not only with regard to Zionists or Orthodox Jews or atheists, but about all Jews without distinction. Toynbee identifies Zionists with 'disloyalty' because of the importance that the State of Israel plays in the Zionist ideology. He maintains that this close relationship must necessarily lead to a conflict of loyalties, particularly as a situation[454]

> has been created by the establishment of the state of Israel, followed up by Israel's claim on the political allegiance of Jews who are not Israelis.

Out of this premise he then concludes that[455]

> one cannot be a loyal citizen of two local states simultaneously. One can be

a loyal citizen of only one local state at a time. One cannot have two local citizenships, any more than one can have two local domiciles . . . Any citizen, anywhere, who puts a foreign country's interests before his own country's interests, will incur his fellow countrymen's censure and hostility.

These are very serious words, but they have no substance in fact, and they are based on a false premise: his emphasis on 'Israel's claim on the political allegiance of Jews who are not Israelis'. Toynbee would be unable to submit one single piece of evidence of such a claim made by the State or Government of Israel, or by any of her responsible leaders. It would not be difficult, on the other hand, to quote dozens of statements by Israel authorities to the contrary, *i.e.* that Jews outside Israel do not owe any political allegiance to the State of Israel. We may select just one from among a host of possibles made by the then Prime Minister of Israel, David Ben Gurion:[456]

> Israel is like all States: sovereign within its confines and to those confines limited. Its governing authority reaches out to all its inhabitants, and to them only. Only its citizens determine its course and elect its Government; the laws of the Land are binding only on those who dwell in it, and all who dwell in it, be they Jews, or not, have equal rights. The Jews who live in other countries are their citizens, subject to their laws and policies: the State of Israel has no authority to speak in the name of those Jews or to direct their actions. Touching the relation and link between Jews overseas and the countries where they live, Jewish citizens are no different from non-Jewish, any more than Jew differs from non-Jew in Israel.

Although Toynbee maintains (incorrectly, as we have shown) that Israel supposedly claims the 'political allegiance' of Jews outside the country, one could quote countless statements by Zionist leaders outside Israel declaring no political allegiance to that State. As we have quoted one representative statement from an Israeli leader, it may be right to quote one from among a host of many other possibles from the pen of the then head of the American Zionists and a prominent leader of the World Zionist Organisation, Dr Abba Hillel Silver. He said:[457]

> Israel will come to be again the non-political centre of world Jewry. Pilgrims will go there as of old—and not merely the pious. There will be a free flow of manifold communications, of mutual stimulation, of give and

take. Israel will again come to exercise a unifying and sustaining influence in Jewish life everywhere.

We shall remain one people, one historic community, as of old. But the Jews of Israel will be Israeli citizens and the Jews of the United States will be citizens of the United States, and similarly with Jews in other lands.

They will owe undivided allegiance to their respective countries and they will discharge loyally their full duties as citizens, as Jews have always done. But they will retain a special attachment to the land of Israel which will in no way interfere with their duties and obligations as citizens of their respective countries.

It was Voltaire who said that every cultured man should have two fatherlands—his own and France. In an even more profound sense, but equally non-political, it may be applied to the Jew and Israel. Israel will be the Shabbath in the life of our people when, according to a beautiful tradition, an additional soul is vouchsafed unto man.

That is how responsible leaders of Israel and the Diaspora have spoken. After all, they should know from whom to expect allegiance, or, respectively, to whom they owe it. They are at least as qualified to make their position clear and say what they believe in or not as Toynbee was when, in a debate on the London B.B.C., he repudiated a challenge by Professor Geyl about his beliefs and exclaimed:[458] 'I suppose I must be the last judge of what my own beliefs are'. Zionists have made their position abundantly clear time and again.

Israel today exists and is gradually fulfilling the great purposes for which it was created by the Jewish people. Jews all over the world, in and outside of Israel, who feel part and parcel of the Jewish people, and believe and strive for its future, wish, therefore, in a joint effort not only to secure the existence of the State, but also to enable and assist it to fulfil its important share towards the Jewish future. The Zionist, the national Jew—every conscientious Jew—who feels he belongs to the Jewish people, gives enthusiastic loyalty, therefore, to the State of Israel, as he does to his Jewish People. This loyalty should not be confused, as Toynbee does, with political allegiance. The Zionist or any other Jew outside the State is not subject to any of the rights and duties of Israeli citizens. But he is loyal to his people, and loyal to his people's creation: the State. Like anybody else, the Zionist and the Jew is entitled to indulge in as many loyalties as he chooses.

And in every free society these loyalties are manifold, as was so ably expressed by Justice Brandeis in the statement quoted above.[459] The late President Kennedy, for instance, was loyal to the Catholic Church, whose centre is abroad, in Rome; he was loyal to the autonomous Commonwealth of Massachusetts and to a great many other things such as family, friends, Harvard, and so on. Yet his unequivocal political allegiance to the United States was beyond reproach. Nevertheless, those who attempted to undermine his eligibility for the Presidency sounded the 'wolf-call' of 'dual loyalties' because of his Catholicism, and stated that[460]

> the Catholic Church is a political as well as a religious organization . . . and while [Mr Kennedy] states specifically that he would not be so influenced [by political pressure from the Church], his Church insists that he is duty bound to admit to its direction. This unresolved conflict leaves doubt in the minds of millions of our citizens.

Kennedy regarded this as what it was, namely, a statement by a group (one can almost hear the 'echo' of assimilationist Jews against Zionists[461]) 'that questioned my loyalty to the United States and my ability to fulfil my constitutional oath'.

In his speech of September 12, 1960,[462] for which he chose a hostile arena, a meeting of Protestant ministers in Houston (Texas), Kennedy was able to clarify the issue in a forthright and courageous speech. The arguments of this particular issue do not interest us at this point. The fact is undeniable, however, that the issue of 'dual loyalties' was raised because of bigotry, antagonism, opposition, dislike, or whatever else. This was neither for the first nor the last time. There rarely exists an idealistic, religious, national, or other movement, or its leaders, that at one time or another has not been accused of 'dual loyalties' for the same reasons that such a cry was raised against the late President Kennedy. But in the end it turned out to be the abused ones who were the patriots and their abusers the reverse. No difference whatever exists between these accusations against non-Jews and those against Jews, as we have been able to show. For a citizen, an honest person, will always know where his duty lies and will always fulfil it.

Conflicts can, of course, arise between what an individual believes and what the State authority of the day declares as law, as they have always arisen ever since man began to think independently. The

Huguenots were also accused of 'dual loyalties' because they believed in Protestant Christianity in a Catholic country. And as contemporary history teaches us, men go underground and, when they can, leave their countries to go to war against the rulers who happened to have gained power there, because, in their view, these rulers represent concepts which they have promulgated in the country's laws which clash with the allegiance which the rulers of those countries happen to demand of their citizens. In similar style occurred the 'dilemma' of Jews who, for instance, long before Zionism and the emergence of the State of Israel, lived in countries whose policy was antisemitic or whose authorities did not object to organised pogroms against Jewish citizens. Could one expect these Jews, in allegiance to their country to have stood to attention, as Jabotinsky once put it,[463] when the National Anthem was played—to the tune of which a pogrom against their wives and children took place?[464]

There are also lesser possible conflicts, but conflicts nevertheless. Thus, when a few years ago two Orthodox Jews in Pennsylvania closed their shops on Saturday, as their religious conviction demanded, and opened them on Sunday, they came into conflict with the law of that State, which prohibits this.[465] So did some stores on New York's Lower East Side when, ignoring the law, they opened their shops on Sundays.[466] Or when Rabbis (together with other clergymen), American citizens, giving faithful allegiance to the United States, arrived in its Southern States and joined Negro citizens in waiting-rooms and restaurants. And as this was against the law of these States, they were arrested.[467] Of course it would be absurd to apply the phrase 'disloyalty to the law of the country' in such cases also. Examples such as these could be multiplied from all national or religious denominations. In a quite different area, and of much more significance, for example, lies Dr Martin Luther King's defiance of Judge Johnson's order with regard to the Selma-Montgomery march. Dr King said[468] that there are

> two types of law . . . just and unjust. . . . I think we have moral obligations to obey just laws and disobey unjust laws.

The great majority of the American people was aware of this; they supported the march; there is no record of any accusation of 'dual loyalties' or of lack of patriotism.

Or, to quote one more example, when Ian Smith proclaimed the independence of Rhodesia, the senior Anglican Bishop of Rhodesia Dr Cecil Alderson, opposed its proclamation and stated *inter alia:*[469]

> It cannot be required of a Christian, as a moral duty, to obey laws unlaw-fully enacted. . . . There is a Christian right, and maybe a Christian duty, to disobey.

The Bishop was hailed all over the world for his courage and patriotism. Nor have any cries of 'dual loyalism' been raised against the thousands of American citizens who protested against the war in Vietnam in which the U.S.A. was involved, many of these 'protestors' loudly calling and wishing for a Vietcong victory, *i.e.* a U.S.A. defeat.

From all this the conclusion can be drawn that in matters of loyalty it all depends on what it is that a State can demand of its citizens, and what the political allegiance is that a citizen owes to his country.

Probably no free man would maintain that the population of a country must in every respect be homogenous and unified. This was the ideal Platonic conception of the State, and counterpoint to it stood the totalitarian, deified State of Fascism, Nazism, or Communism. But for the modern and thinking person, the State is the machinery which society employs for its purposes. The State, to mention Masaryk's concept,[470] which 'should be conscious of the fact that the meaning of man's life and of his search for happiness lies in a struggle for increasing spiritual and moral freedom . . . must be an instrument and a means to achieve this end'. Thus the State, as we said before, serves the indi-viduals who live in it and not *vice versa.* It serves these free individuals in their desire to develop their individuality to the fullest extent. And each section of individuals will endeavour to give its best to the com-munity; so will each nationality existing in the land. To no less a degree this applies to the cultural, artistic, economic, and every other aspect of these individuals' endeavours.

The citizens, in order to maintain the State, must, of course, adhere to a minimum of obligations. What are they? The payment of taxes to-wards supporting the State, participation in public affairs, and the defence of the country if it is threatened. There are other obligations also, but these depend on the free will or the selection of the citizens. They are selected by them voluntarily and additionally and thus to do their best for the common good. This presupposes different interests among the individuals, which will be expressed in spiritual matters such as religion, cultural activities, literature; in political affairs, forming or joining political parties; or in other forms. Every stratum of human endeavour thus performed leads to better citizenship.

This is the point where the Zionist, beyond his minimum obligation as a citizen, would endeavour to make his contribution. Zionism is based on the principles of Judaism—on which non-Zionist Jews also base their creed. Both can thus contribute to the common good of all the citizens particularly if they reach back conscientiously into the storehouse of Jewry's ideals and thoughts. The Zionist is also a nationalist who is deeply concerned with nationalism and thus as an observer of the national scene in general, has been able to study and learn throughout his national history the transgressions which nationalism, when brutally expressed, can commit; and it is the Zionist and the national Jew who can bring home to his country those ideals out of which modern nationalism has arisen and which, as we have shown, are rooted in the Jewish Bible. He, better than anyone, can contribute towards the purification of the air that has been poisoned by the various forms of barbarian nationalism in all peoples, the Jewish included, and a host of Zionist literature on the subject of nationalism, past and present, bears testimony to that important contribution. World issues such as minority rights, the independence of small nations, the problems of refugees, for instance, show the clear impact of Zionist and Jewish national thinking.

The Zionist will also do many other things in the way of endeavouring to educate better citizens, for instance. (See in this connection the impact that Zionism has had on the development of schools of all categories up to the highest level.) But all this does not mean that he must surrender every one of his loyalties to the State. This would be a renewal of the very barbarism for which the free world has now fought two world wars. The Zionist living in a free country feels free to fulfil every one of the minimum obligations as well as those others which he chooses to add towards the State of which he is a citizen; and he also wishes to remain loyal to Jewry at large and to the State of Israel, where his brethren live and whence, he hopes, a great contribution will come forth towards the progress of mankind and by that fact therefore also to the country where he lives. And however unique Jewish nationalism is, and however much it differs from what is commonly regarded as 'nationalism', the Zionist and the national Jew is at the very least in no different position from the Irishman who lives in England or America, or the Pole or Greek who resides in the Chicago area, or the Swiss who lives in other lands. While all these conduct their allegiance in exemplary fashion to the State where they live, they maintain deep love and enthusiasm and sincere loyalty for the country where their people created their own Statehood.

A Concrete Case

In the light of what has been said, it is therefore futile to indulge in a study of 'dual loyalties' and 'dual allegiances' unless a concrete case is presented. Nor should or could one draw conclusions from remote contingencies or hypothetical clashes in the future. It is impossible to enumerate all the hypothetical possibilities of such clashes; nor would such enumeration solve the deeper problem of the relations of the individual to the State. But in every civilised society a first assumption must be accepted: that a citizen will honestly fulfil his obligations towards his country. Only if it is proved otherwise must he be punished. Simple decency and humanity dictate this position. It cannot, therefore, be regarded as other than an act of 'malice and all uncharitableness'—as the *Book of Common Prayer* characterises[471] this sort of fomenting of suspicion—when Toynbee, because of his inability to submit a single piece of evidence of a clash between a Zionist's loyalty to the State of Israel and his allegiance to his country, selected a hypothetical case. He took his cue from the Suez War of 1956, about which he had this to say in 1960:[472]

> Let us suppose that he—*i.e.* the Jew—is a citizen of the United States, and that some serious difference of interest and policy has arisen between the United States and Israel. The supposition is not at all fanciful. This did happen in 1956, and it might happen again at any moment and any number of times. In such a situation, will American Jews feel and act politically as the American citizens that they are and have chosen to be?

He replied to this question in the affirmative. He believed they would act in accordance with their duties towards the United States. But he had some doubts as regards the Zionists, although he was not clear about these doubts. A year later (1961) he was less doubtful. When again reverting to this 'example', he stated:[473]

> In the fall of 1956, for instance, there was a head-on collision between the United States and Israel. Obviously, any Jewish American who, in such circumstances, worked for Israel against America would be a traitor in the eyes of his American fellow-countrymen.

While we see from the first quotation above that in 1960 Toynbee still spoke only of 'some serious differences of interest and policy' and only asked how American Jews would feel and act in such a situation, in 1961, as the second quotation shows, the 'difference' is already a 'head-on collision' and he already knew the answer: they would act as 'traitors'.

Toynbee, of course, knew in 1960 and 1961 that four and five years previously there was no 'head-on collision between the United States and Israel', for there was no war. He must also have known that the pressure that was exercised on Israel in those days was (a) that of the President of the United States, in support of a move in the General Assembly to have Israel condemned, and (b) in correspondence with the Israel authorities; and (c) that there was talk even of a 'boycott of Israel' by the United Nations to which the United States was to give its consent. But it never even came to the thought of a war, not least because the United States authorities were convinced that Israel's war against Nasser was justified self-defence against aggression. As Robert Murphy, the President's personal representative, wrote:[474]

> We in the State Department were painfully aware of the Egyptian military build-up in the spring and summer of 1956, and a Watch Dog Committee has been organised accordingly. We knew that substantial acquisitions of Soviet heavy equipment, including about fifty bombers, were stored on the edge of the Gaza Strip, the disputed truce-line between Egypt and Israel on the Mediterranean shore. In view of this aggressive Egyptian attitude, it did not appear surprising that the Israel Government might have decided it would be safer to attack than wait to be attacked.

With such beliefs, one does not go to war against the defender. Besides this, the fact that from the outset the United States Government did not think in terms of a 'head-on collision', *i.e.* war, at all is clear from President Eisenhower's

> warning to the Soviet Union that the U.S. would oppose any effort by the U.S.S.R. to intervene by force in the Middle East and . . . it is unthinkable that the U.S. join the Soviet Union, as Premier Bulganin proposed, 'in a bipartite employment of their military forces to stop the fighting in Egypt'.[475]

There was also strong Congressional opposition to any eventual anti-Israel steps, and meanwhile public opinion in the U.S.A. was appalled at the way this affair was handled by President Eisenhower and his Secretary of State, John Foster Dulles. And here is the point where the question has to be put: where is the evidence that a Jew in America, if he opposed a certain policy of the Government of the day, was working against America? Or that he loved America less than those who supported the Government's policy? Does one love one's father less if one disagrees with him on certain ideas or steps? There were millions of non-Jewish Americans who then condemned the American Administration's stand in the Suez matter, and they did so not as 'traitors' to America but as American patriots who believed that their Government had betrayed the country's ideals in supporting Colonel Nasser, a dictatorial 'Führer' backed by Communist Russia, instead of living up to its ideals and supporting proved friends of America such as the democracies of England, France, and Israel. The American press of the time is full of comments similar to the stand taken by the *New York Times:*[476]

> It would be ridiculous to permit Colonel Nasser to pose before the United Nations or the world as the innocent victim of aggression, or to hold a protecting hand over him. On the contrary, in so far as there is any one man guilty of aggression it is the Egyptian President, for he has waged war against Israel, Britain, and France by propaganda, by gun-running, by infiltration of murderous bands, by stirring up rebellion in French North Africa, by seizing the Suez Canal by force, by scrapping a treaty in the same manner in which Hitler marched into the Rhineland, by blocking the canal for Israeli shipping in defiance of United Nations orders—finally, by his whole loudly proclaimed programme of throwing Israel into the sea in alliance with other Arab states and creating an Arab empire under his own

hegemony which would expand his influence in concentric circles to all Africa and the whole Muslim world.

At that very time (November 1956), the late Adlai Stevenson, candidate for the U.S. Presidency, speaking for his party for which, five days later, 26,028,887 American citizens (Jewish and non-Jewish) gave their votes,[477] said with regard to the Suez affair:[478]

> ... the hostilities going on tonight in which Israel, Egypt, Britain, and France are involved reflect the bankruptcy of our policy; and they have given the Soviet Union two great victories. The first Communist victory is the establishment in the Middle East of Russian influence. The second Communist victory is the breakdown of the Western alliance. This has been a supreme objective of Soviet policy since the end of the Second World War.
>
> As the climax, the United States finds itself arrayed in the United Nations with Soviet Russia and the dictator of Egypt against the democracies of Britain, France, and Israel.

And Lyndon B. (afterwards President) Johnson, who at the time was leader of the Democrats in the House, together with the then leader of the Republicans (Eisenhower's own party) in the Senate, William F. Knowland, made it clear to President Eisenhower that they would not pass his Middle Eastern legislation ('Eisenhower Doctrine') should he take any drastic steps against Israel, particularly sanctions.

> Washington was particularly desirous of avoiding a vote on this ticklish question, because influential members of Congress flatly opposed sanctions and were threatening to withhold their approval of the Middle East resolution if the administration supported them.[479]

And separately these leaders, on behalf of their parties, took a strong stand against the Administration, also in public. Senator Knowland threatened to resign his membership of the U.S. delegation at the United Nations if the United States approved sanctions[480] and in a public statement he 'denounced as "immoral" and "insupportable" any punitive action against Israelis'.[481] And Johnson in a letter to Dulles stressed[482] that 'the merits, the justice and the morality in this situation are clear against such imposition of economic sanctions' and he emphasised that the Democrats in the House (who had a majority) would not only abstain but 'resist them with all skill'. This letter was subsequently formally endorsed by the Senate Democratic Policy Committee.[483] And the New York Board of Rabbis (a purely religious body), representing over 700 Orthodox, Conservative, and Reform rabbis, thanked Johnson publicly for his 'forthright stand' in opposition to any plan of sanctions against Israel.[484] The Democrats, however, went even further and demanded the establishment of a special committee to investigate the Middle East policy of the Administration, which they regarded as disastrous. They also rejected a request to give Eisenhower unconditional authorisation for the use of military force,[485] and without such authorisation there could never have been what Toynbee termed a 'head-on collision' between the United States and Israel.

Toynbee furthermore writes:[486]

> The Israelis had been compelled to withdraw [from the Gaza strip, which in the course of the Suez war they had occupied] by President Eisenhower, and this had been one of the most courageous acts in his political career. He had taken this firm stand on the eve of an election, without stooping, as so many American politicians do stoop, to woo the Jewish vote. His uprightness had been rewarded in his re-election by a large majority.

We know of course, as Toynbee does, that elections in the U.S.A. take place in November. There was no exception to this fixed election date in 1956. Eisenhower was then elected by a large majority to the Presidency. As President he requested the withdrawal of Israeli troops in February 1957—four months after his election. It is to be hoped that Toynbee will not now cut down Eisenhower's 'courageous acts' or his 'uprightness'.

And as to the 'stooping . . . to woo the Jewish vote', it can be pointed out that Eisenhower, like all other upright American candidates for office, cared very much about receiving the votes of Jews, as of any other ethnic or religious minority in the U.S.A., as their speeches in areas of Polish, Czech, Italian, and other such minorities testify. But they all pursue American political interests and nothing else. Nor do these minorities want or expect anything else. American ideals are sufficiently deep and great to induce her leaders to stand up for justice and truth, and do not require marks for behaviour from Toynbee. It therefore goes without saying that the leaders referred to above, in their steps in favour of Israel, had America's interests at heart and no other, apart from the fact also that all this took place months after the elections of November 1956, as shown.

Did all these leaders of both Parties, the members of Congress, the millions of voters, the religious leadership of American Jewry (not the Zionist leadership alone) know less about patriotism and loyalty to America than Professor Toynbee? Today it is, of course, generally accepted that the official American stand in 1956 and 1957 during the Suez crisis was a first-rate blunder. Even Richard Nixon, who at that time was Vice-President of the United States, and thus co-responsible for the Eisenhower policy, had to confess[487] that, though the decision in 1956 'seemed right at the time',

> it had never been the United States' habit to contend that we make the right decision all the time.

If Toynbee's thesis, which he applied to Jewish opposition to the Eisenhower-Dulles stand in the Suez affair, is thus also to be applied to those who then openly opposed or condemned that policy, non-Jewish American patriots like Stevenson, Johnson, Knowland, Kennedy, numerous other leaders inside and outside the Senate and Congress, the most influential press, and millions of ordinary citizens (all condemning that policy)—would have to be regarded as 'traitor[s] in the eyes of . . . [their] American fellow-countrymen', as Toynbee put it.

The very fact that Toynbee used these events as the only example which he could find to show Zionist 'dual loyalties' at a time, four or five years after the event, when it was clear beyond a doubt even to him that the whole thing had been a first-rate fiasco, which did not lead to any 'collision' with Israel and was very detrimental to the democracies, shows that there is no basis in the accusation of 'dual loyalties'. But he was not satisfied with implanting this accusation alone in his readers' minds, for he concluded his statement as follows:[488]

> The American people has shown, ever since the First World War, that it is acutely sensitive to the menace of the 'hyphen' and the 'fifth column' . . . [and] to the dangers of a dual allegiance . . .

In other words, unrelated stigmas ('hyphen' and 'fifth column') are juxtaposed to strengthen the indictment.

And one postscript to all this which may fill a little gap in Toynbee's autobiographical section *ad hominem*:[489] it ill becomes a person to insinuate, even hypothetically, disloyalty or treason by a considerable group of Jews who are loyal, law-abiding citizens and who, whenever called upon by America (and the same applies to any other country of which Jews happen to be citizens), have always been ready for any, including the supreme, sacrifice. This particularly ill becomes an accuser who, as is the case with Toynbee, has exhibited astonishing disloyalty to his own national civilisation ('what a bore one's own civilisation is'),[490] language ('a barbarous substitute for Latin'),[491] culture ('the distorting effect of one's relativity to one's cultural milieu' and 'the bias implanted in me by the accident that I am a Westerner and an English one'),[492] history ('Sir Ernest Barker is right in reporting that I do not know English history and do not love it'),[493] and country ('compared to Egypt what is England after all? . . . She has never played a part of first-class importance in the world as a whole . . .').[494] And, as mentioned before,[495] he did not hesitate to express his willingness to 'barter my Anglo-Danish birthright' for a host of others 'if it were possible . . . as it is to change one's name'. For in fact he is really not interested at all in 'loyalties' or 'allegiances' of people to their respective countries, nor to his own, as the following passage shows:[496]

> While the state of which we happen to be citizens makes more concrete and more imperious claims on our allegiance, especially in the present age, the civilisation of which we are members really counts for more in our lives. And this civilisation of which we are members includes—at most stages in its history—the citizens of other states besides our own. It is older than our own state: the Western civilisation is about thirteen hundred years old, whereas the Kingdom of England is only one thousand years old, the United Kingdom of England and Scotland less than two hundred and fifty, the United States not much more than one hundred and fifty. States are apt to have short lives and sudden deaths: the Western civilization of which you and I are members may be alive centuries after the United Kingdom and the United States have disappeared from the political map of the world like their contemporaries, the Republic of Venice and the Dual Monarchy of Austria-Hungary. This is one of the reasons why I have been asking you to look at history in terms of civilisations, and not in terms of states, and to think of states as rather subordinate and ephemeral political phenomena in the lives of the civilisations in whose bosom they appear and disappear.

And for the preservation of this meta-national civilisation he preaches[497] the formation of a world-state where

> the people's paramount political allegiance [*sic!*] will be their loyalty to the world-community

and not to 'the local states—Britain', etc. And he knows of course that once such a universal State were established, even if only for a short period, the national States would anyhow completely disappear:[498]

> Thus normally the establishment of a universal state, even for no longer than a single spell, has resulted in a permanent obliteration of the identities of the local states and peoples that have been incorporated in it.

He is quite prepared to offer that 'sacrifice' of his own country even for a 'single spell'. This is, in fact, an illuminating example of what Toynbee once termed the destruction of one's own people 'through suicide from within'.

6

Antisemitism and Zionism

Assimilationism was not the only negative response with which Toynbee attempted to connect Zionism. In his endeavours to fortify his assessment of the Zionist Movement as a negative concept—*i.e.* only reacting to events and aiming at liberating Jews *from*, but not *for*, something—he rediscovered a supposedly common basis of Zionism and antisemitism. I have written 'rediscovered' because almost from the beginning of modern Zionism this 'identification' has been the slogan of all the anti-Zionists, in whatever camp they stood. 'Antisemites want to get rid of the Jews in their lands, and the Zionists want to remove the Jews from these lands', has been the cry ever since 1897. The cry is completely superficial, based as it is on a complete misunderstanding of the origin and causes of both Zionism and antisemitism. Toynbee has found the following new formula for this old slogan:[499]

> At bottom Zionism and anti-Semitism are expressions of an identical point of view. The assumption underlying both ideologies [*sic!*] is that it is impossible for Jews and non-Jews to grow together into a single community, and that therefore physical separation is the only practical way out.

He found a much closer 'affinity' even when he stated[500] that

> It is perhaps no accident that a nineteenth-century Jewish Zionism and a twentieth-century German Neo-anti-Semitism should have arisen successively in the same geographical zone of the Western World, and that this

locus should have been the German-speaking territories of the Austrian Empire just west of the domains of the Hungarian Crown of St Stephen and the former United Kingdom of Poland-Lithuania.

While the old idea was thus presented in a new form, it did not lack the same characteristic ingredient: superficiality.

Toynbee in his first quotation completely disregarded the fact that antisemitism, while as a term it dates from 1873,[501] did not appear as a phenomenon for the first time during the period of the birth of modern Zionism (1897), but has accompanied the Jews since the dawn of their history, centuries before the rise of Christianity. Throughout long periods of that history, and especially in the longest periods of the Diaspora, antisemitism was nourished by the unavailing thought and effort devoted to forcing the Jews by 'persuasion' or 'persecution' to adopt the 'majority' religion and thus to merge with it. This means that antisemites believed in the possibility and even the desirability of merging, and not in a 'physical separation', as Toynbee wrote. And they became antisemites because they were unable to induce the Jews to merge with them. Toynbee himself, in an analogy[502] between the antisemitism of Western Christianity and that of Nazism, compared the latter with the expulsion of the Jews from Spain in A.D. 1492 and 'their forcible conversion in Castile in A.D. 1391 and in Portugal in A.D. 1497'. This last date was precisely four hundred years before the emergence of the Zionist Organisation (1897). Having established this analogy, Toynbee continued that

> the medieval persecutors in the Iberian Peninsula besought and, in the last resort, compelled the Jews to abandon the ghetto and transform themselves by conversion, into fully enfranchised citizens of the *Respublica Christiana;* and once within the fold, these Jewish converts were allowed a free field to compete with their Christian neighbours for the highest positions in Church and State, as well as for the fleshpots of commerce.

His own example thus refuted his own theory, because fundamentally there is no similarity between the Iberian antisemitism which had offered an alternative—merger through conversion, and the neo-antisemites (*i.e.* Nazis), who rejected such an alternative. As he himself had to confirm later:[503]

. . . the Spaniards and Portuguese did genuinely enfranchise any Jews who conformed to the practice of Western Christianity, whereas the German National Socialists' racial tribalism left a Jew no avenue from being the 'Non-Aryan' that Nature was alleged to have made him.

This means then that even the Iberian antisemitism, which in Toynbee's analogy came nearest to the German neo-antisemitism (*i.e.* Nazi antisemitism), did not regard it as 'impossible for the Jews and non-Jews to grow together in one community' but, on the contrary, believed in its advisability and desirability, and therefore brought the Jews forcibly into it. Mohammed and Luther also believed in the desirability and possibility of a merger; they became violently antisemitic[504] only when they were unable to persuade the Jews to accept the merger, and at that time they had no physical power to force them into the fold (although 'in revenge' Mohammed annihilated a few Jewish communities).

To sum up, we see thus that antisemitism for centuries believed in and aimed at a merger of Jews and non-Jews into one community. It had its condition—baptism—but it meant a merger.

On the other hand, it is not just since 1897, when the Zionist Movement was established, that Jews have refused to accept the conception of a merger with other communities, as has been shown in the section 'Permanent Separateness', and have remained a people apart. This was not a new discovery in the 1890s but was an established and accepted fact for some millennia. Even without knowledge of the appropriate literature and history, the fact could not have escaped Toynbee's observation that the continuous survival of the Jews is a testimony to their will to live as a separate community. Indeed, he said so:[505]

> The survival and vitality of the diaspora has been a *tour de force;* but, just on this account, the diaspora has been, and still is, the supreme and characteristic instrument and monument of the Jewish people's persistent will to maintain its distinctive communal identity.

This statement further confirms the fact that Toynbee knew very well that this will to separateness did not arise only in 1897 but had existed since the dawn of Jewish Diaspora history. Numerous other references in Toynbee's writings also stress national separateness as characteristic of Jewry in every period of history, and not just from 1897 onwards.

In the light of this, it is incomprehensible why Toynbee, disregarding what he has himself repeatedly stated, has singled out Zionism as the sole Jewish force not to believe in a merger with other communities, and thus puts it on an equal level with antisemitism, which was said to aim at the same thing. It is not without interest to recall at this point that the Nazi theoretician, Alfred Rosenberg, also selected the Zionist sector as the sole bearer of 'the counter-racial idea' of Jewry that 'at the end of the nineteenth century assumed definite forms',[506] *i.e.* did not believe in the possibility of a merger with others, and 'decided to return to the Orient'. Significantly 'racial' antisemitism was the only kind of antisemitism which rejected the possibility of Jews and non-Jews growing together. It was based, according to Toynbee[507] himself, on the race theory

> invented by a nineteenth-century Frenchman, de Gobineau,[508] and popularised in pre-war Germany by a *fin-de-siècle* Englishman, Houston Chamberlain.

It maintained that individual races not only differ from each other physically but also spiritually, and therefore should not mix with unequal ones if they want to preserve their own culture. The only pure race in existence was the Aryan race, and especially its Germanic section.[509] This assumption was applied in general with regard to all peoples and races and not only Jews. It was because of this also that Hitler, in accepting Gobineau's theory,[510] applied it to all non-Germanic peoples, when, for instance, he wrote in *Mein Kampf*:[511]

> Repulsive to me was the racial conglomeration which was seen in the Empire's capital [Vienna], repulsive all that mixture of peoples like Czechs, Poles, Hungarians, Ruthenes, Serbs and Croats, etc., among all these the permanent fission-fungus of mankind—Jews and again Jews.

On the basis of their theory, racial antisemites came to their contention that not only was a merger with Jews impossible, but, as an 'inferior race', Jews should be eliminated, in order not to 'endanger' the surrounding 'superior' Germanic race. And wherever Jews had succeeded in assimilating even genuinely, *i.e.* abandoning everything, including their religion, and had become members of the German people, such a merger had to be cancelled in order to keep the race pure. Toynbee has described this in the following way:[512]

It remained for Herr Hitler and his followers in Germany of 1933, to persecute the Jews avowedly and implacably on the ground of physical race. 'The Aryan paragraph' penalised the *ci-devant* Jew who had become a convert to Christianity, together with his brethren who had remained members of the Jewish religious community. Under the Nazi dispensation, salvation and damnation depended neither on works nor on faith, but on physique.

The distinction, however, between the antisemitism that existed before the 'racial' theory and that of 'racialism', no doubt well known to Toynbee, was omitted in his statement quoted earlier,[513] where he identified Zionism with antisemitism on the ground that both believed in the 'impossibility for Jews and non-Jews to grow together in one community'. Yet, if Zionism and antisemitism have 'an identical point of view', and if antisemitism then equals Nazism, the next step inevitably leads to an 'identification' of Zionism with Nazism, for which Toynbee laid the foundation in statements such as the one which we have been analysing.

That this was his aim is proved by the second quotation[514] about the common geographical origin of Zionism and German neo-anti-semitism. Here, Toynbee's pursuit of 'external' similarities, and the consequent superficiality, has provided us with a classic example. Let us, therefore, look at this 'geographical accident of birth'. As Toynbee's statement stands (both 'Zionism and . . . German Neo-anti-Semitism have arisen successively in the . . . German-speaking territories of the pre-1914 Austrian Empire'), it can only mean the following: the Zionist Movement was formed in 1897 as a result of Theodor Herzl's initiative. He himself lived in pre-1914 Austria. German neo-anti-semitism, *i.e.* Nazism, was the result of Hitler's initiative in the 1920s. He was born in pre-1914 Austria. It is Austria, in Toynbee's contention, that was the birthplace of both Zionism and neo-antisemitism. In both cases Toynbee is wrong.

The age-old Zionist concept cannot be pinpointed to any one person, to any one area, or to any one age; and we shall elaborate on this aspect further below. At this point we may, however, call upon him to provide us with his own contradictory statement. And here it is:[515]

The spectacle of anti-Jewish demonstrations in Paris at the time when the battle over the Dreyfus case was being fought out in France was the experience that converted the Austrian Jewish journalist Theodor Herzl from being an ardent assimilationist into becoming the Apostle of Zionism.

This referred to the impact which the Dreyfus affair, with its accompanying antisemitism, is supposed to have had on Herzl in 1894-1895, and finally led to the establishment of the Zionist Organisation.

As is well known, Dreyfus, a Jew, was a French Army Captain, condemned in France for treason but finally rehabilitated; Herzl at that time lived in Paris (1891-1895) as the correspondent of *Die Neue Freie Presse*, of Vienna;[516] the antisemitism which accompanied the Dreyfus affair was French (not Austrian). If, therefore, the part that antisemitism played in Herzl's mind has to be pinpointed with the help of a geographical term then undoubtedly it was French antisemitism which deserves mention, not Austrian. Herzl himself, too, when dealing in his *Judenstaat* with the problem of antisemitism, did not select for his analysis its Austrian brand, but that of France[517]—because a Russian, Hungarian, Bohemian, or Austrian antisemitism would not have had such an impact on him as a French antisemitism—for France was then the epitome of liberalism and enlightenment, the first European country to emancipate Jews; and for Herzl the fate of French Jewry was 'the strongest example' in his case.[518] But as a matter of fact the Dreyfus affair was not the cause of Herzl's awakened Jewish consciousness, and antisemitism not the cause of his Zionism.

It may be of additional interest to note that the First Zionist Congress, at which the modern Zionist Movement was formed, took place in 1897 at Basle, Switzerland (not Austria), and that among its 208 delegates, 163 were from some 18 countries all over the world, and 45 from Austria-Hungary, which then included Polish Galicia, Magyar Hungary, Czech Bohemia, etc.[519]

The 'accident' of the common Austrian birthplace of Zionism and German neo-antisemitism of which Toynbee spoke did not, therefore, take place as far as Zionism is concerned.

Nor was neo-antisemitism of the Hitlerite brand born in Austria, but in Germany. It was the Hamburg journalist Wilhelm Marr who, in his *Judenspiegel* (1862) and *Der Sieg des Judenthums ueber das Germanenthum* (1873), developed the idea, based on Hegel's uni-national State conception and on Gobineau's racial ideas, that the Jews, because of their inability to integrate into other people, should be eliminated. He was the first racial 'nazi' antisemite. He was the first to coin the term 'anti-semitism'. Ten years later, racial antisemitism became widespread all over Germany.[520] From there the movement spread to other countries: 'More serious have been the effects of German anti-Semitic teachings on the political and social life of the countries adjacent to the Empire—Russia, Austria and France.[521] The anti-Jewish pogroms in Russia in 1881 were the direct result of the German example and of its reactionary teachings.[522]

Even in the Austrian-Hungarian Monarchy, these teachings did not at first take root—in what Toynbee terms the 'German-speaking territories of the pre-1914 Austrian Empire west of the domain of the Hungarian Crown of St Stephen'—but in the Hungary of St Stephen, where since the 1870s Marr's pamphlets were translated into Magyar and the 'Association of Non-Jews' was formed in 1880 on the pattern of the 'German Anti-Semitic League'[523] and succeeded in sending six members to the Hungarian Parliament.[524] It was two years later that out of Schoenerer's nationalistic political party, an Anti-Semitic League was formed in Vienna.[525] Gustav Schoenerer's own antisemitism was the result of Heinrich von Treitschke's influence on him.[526] Thus, obviously, 'in Austria-Hungary the anti-Semitic impulses came almost simultaneously from the North (Germany) and the East (Russia)'.[527] It is therefore absurd to maintain, as Toynbee does, that German neo-antisemitism was brought into Germany from Austria. Again, none other than Toynbee himself helps us to refute his own contention. He asserted[528] that Hitlerism had

> found [in Germany], and adopted, an 'ideology' and a faith which already had a long history behind them before Herr Hitler advanced them and took them for his own and expressed them in terms of a crude theory of 'Race' and introduced them in this peptonised form to the German lower middle class.

It is, of course, known that Hitler had lived in Austria until 1912 and had witnessed antisemitic manifestations there. This, however, does not confirm in any way whatever Toynbee's theory that racial neo-anti-semitism was brought from Austria into Germany and there became 'Nazism'. For, while racial antisemitism had been imported from Germany into Austria, and Hitler had become acquainted with it in

Vienna, the Austrian brand of antisemitism was, in Hitler's words, 'immoral' and had therefore to be rejected. He came to this conclusion after becoming aware of antisemitism in Munich and reviewing it retrospectively in 1923. It was wrong, in his opinion, because it had not been based on racialism, which meanwhile he had learned in Germany; the reason for the attitude of the Austrian antisemites was that they were too patriotic and would not accept pure racialism, as this would have led to Austria's dissolution because of the many nationalities which then lived in the Monarchy.[529]

If Toynbee frankly adhered to this theory of common geographical origins, he might have found himself obliged to compose, for instance, the following formulation (patterned on his statements above), which could be adapted to any momentary requirements: 'It is perhaps no accident that Nazism and world-wide influences on mankind caused by such persons as Sigmund Freud, Johann Gregor Mendel, Gustav Mahler, Max Reinhardt, Josef Popper-Lynkens, Franz Brentano, Thomas G. Masaryk, Victor Adler, Karl Renner, and many others, should have arisen successively in the same geographical zone, namely, the German-speaking territories of the pre-1914 Austrian Empire'. And if he were then consequentially to apply this geographical theory to other lands also, he might have found even himself, Arnold J. Toynbee, Oswald Mosley, the Fascist leader, and John Amery, executed in 1945 for high treason, to have arisen successively in the same geographical area of pre-1939 Britain. This makes neither more nor less sense than the absurd contention of the geographical origin of Zionism and neo-antisemitism (apart from the fact that Toynbee does not even have his geography right when promoting Hitler to a 'Sudetenlander'[530] when, in fact, he hailed from Upper Austria).

In pursuit of this argument Toynbee did not even hesitate to sacrifice one of his hotly debated 'articles of faith'—his rejection of determinism. In the course of a debate on whether or not he was a 'determinist', he most strongly objected to Hampl's[531] contention that 'I have no business *not* to be a determinist on my own theory . . . and [to] O.H.K. Spate's contention . . . that I am accordingly a determinist, notwithstanding my disavowal of this'. This was written in 1961, the same year as he made the statement about the not-so-accidental birth of Zionism and neo-antisemitism in one and the same area.[532] Whether, however, the scholars are right or wrong about Toynbee's rejection of determinism, there cannot be any doubt about one of his other theories—that of geographical stimuli. 'We have shaken ourselves free', he wrote in Volume I of his *Study of History* 'from the conception of environmental stimuli peculiar to this or that climate and area, or this or that human background, or this or that combination of the two'.[533] He had not departed from this viewpoint even twenty-seven years later, when in his *Reconsiderations* he emphasised, in a chapter devoted entirely to 'The Relations between Man and His Environment':[534]

> An objectively identical geographical 'set-up' will offer a promising environment to one group of human beings . . . while it will offer only bleak and niggardly environment, or no environment at all, to other groups with other organisations and other equipment.

And he continued:[535]

> In another chapter of the same volume [*i.e.* the quotations above from Volume I of his *Study of History*] I tried to prove my case. I tried to demonstrate, by examples, that the challenge of an identical 'set-up' did not invariably evoke an identical response from identically endowed and equipped human beings to whom this 'set-up' offered a potential environment. If this attempted demonstration of mine had held water, it would, I should say, have proved that, in an encounter, something comes into play that is not present in the previous 'make-up' of either party of the encounter, and that this intervention of something new is the decisive factor in determining the outcome.

I am still convinced that this is the truth. Yet he abandoned this truth, abandoned his own thesis, in the Zionist case, and accepted the great sacrifice of surrendering his diligently and ardently constructed conception when developing his idea of the not-so-accidental emergence of Zionism and neo-antisemitism in the same geographical zone.

7

Zionism as Negative Reaction: Herzl and Weizmann

In the preceding pages we have analysed Toynbee's definition of Zionism as a negative conception, because of its supposed common denominator with assimilationism and because of its supposed equation with antisemitism. In both these comparisons Zionism was described by Toynbee as a kind of reaction to penalisations. We have shown the untenability of these contentions. It remains now to deal with two specific examples which Toynbee has selected in his writings, on the basis of which he has attempted to prove that there were external forces that caused the creation of Zionism and that, therefore, Zionism was a negative concept because it arose as a reaction to these influences. His examples were the lives of Theodor Herzl and Chaim Weizmann, and their paths to Zionism.

(a) *Theodor Herzl*

In the preceding chapter we have dealt[536] with Toynbee's contention that it was 'perhaps no accident' that Zionism and neo-antisemitism successively arose in the pre-1914 Austrian geographical area, because both Herzl and Hitler had lived in the Hapsburg Monarchy. We dismissed this 'geographical' theory as absurd, in the light of known facts and not least with the help of Toynbee's own statement that Herzl had become an Apostle of Zionism in reaction to the Dreyfus affair. This would have meant that it was a reaction to French, not

Austrian, antisemitism. But in dismissing this 'geographical' theory, we were solely concerned with unmasking Toynbee's superficial approach to Zionism. We did not accept his theory that Zionism, nor Herzl's path to it, was born out of a reaction to the Dreyfus affair or out of a reaction to persecutions in themselves. For, in fact, contrary to his suggestion, the Dreyfus affair, which at the time made an impression on the young Toynbee,[537] was not the cause of Herzl's becoming a Zionist or even turning to the Jewish problem.

In fairness it should be pointed out that Toynbee, in attributing to the 'Dreyfusiade' the reason for Herzl's Zionism, accepted a widely prevalent opinion[538] which, in fact, was also mentioned by Herzl in an article written in 1899, four and a half years after the first Dreyfus trial.[539] Although it must be added that in this article Herzl also referred to other motives which led to the emergence of his Zionism, it should, I believe, have been Toynbee's duty to check the facts of an example from which he intended to draw basic conclusions as regards the essence of Zionism. After all, we see that[540] he agrees with 'the legitimate requirement' that his 'theories . . . can be validated only if they are confronted with the relevant facts and are confirmed by them'. But on this occasion, as on many others, he did not apply this sensible rule to his own investigations.

A mere biographical chronology of Herzl's life shows that his Jewish national consciousness had been aroused long before the Dreyfus affair, and that he had already been President of the World Zionist Organisation for two years when he came to evaluate and appreciate the impact that the Dreyfus affair had had upon him and all Jewry.[541]

The first Dreyfus trial began on December 19, 1894, was conducted almost throughout *in camera*, and ended with the Captain's degradation on January 5, 1895.[542] Neither the Jewish nor the non-Jewish contemporary press recorded any antisemitic street outbursts or public demonstrations against Jews, preceding, accompanying, or following this trial and the degradation. Nor had Herzl, who, as already noted,[543] was then Paris correspondent of the Vienna *Neue Freie Presse* and had regularly informed his readers about these events, reported any accompanying anti-Jewish actions.[544] The actual Dreyfus controversy opened only in March 1896 after a retrial had been demanded,[545] as a result of which a raging political storm ensued. But even this storm, which, with intervals, was to last until 1899, was at first not accompanied by those anti-Jewish mob demonstrations in the streets of Paris which are generally said to have so deeply hurt and influenced Herzl. In March, 1896, however, Herzl was no longer the Paris correspondent of his paper; he had left the French capital for good on July 27, 1895.[546] Thus he could not have witnessed any antisemitic demonstrations there even if they had taken place. Moreover, at the time when the public controversy began about the reopening of the Dreyfus trial (March, 1896), Herzl's *Judenstaat* was already conquering Jewish readers all over the world.[547] Accordingly, these events of 1896 could not have made him a Zionist; he was one already. The violent mob demonstrations in the streets of Paris and other French cities, with the cry of 'Death to all the Jews!', were launched only in 1898, the year which a famous historian called 'the saddest year in the newest history of French Jewry'.[548] As Hannah Arendt, in a study on the subject, wrote:[549]

> However much antisemitism expanded in the three years following Dreyfus's arrest and preceding Clemenceau's fight, and however much the antisemitic press exaggerated the number of its readers, the streets remained quiet up to that time.

Herzl's *Diaries*, which he began writing in Paris in May, 1895, five months after the Dreyfus degradation, did not even mention the case in the first thirty pages, in which he described his path to the Zionist solution of the Jewish problem. It is not mentioned in his *Judenstaat* either, although contemporary antisemitic manifestations in general, and in France in particular, are recorded therein.[550] Nor was the 'Dreyfusiade' mentioned in Herzl's correspondence and conversation in 1895 with Baron Hirsch, who then also lived in France and objected to Herzl's plans. A reference to Dreyfus might possibly have helped to convince the Baron; it was not used.[551] In his entire campaign for the propagation of Zionism, beginning with his *Judenstaat* and leading to the calling of the Zionist Congress (1897), Herzl did not mention the Dreyfus case. Nor did he do so in his opening speech to the First Congress.[552] Herzl also participated, through his Zionist paper *Die Welt*, in the debate on the reopening of the Dreyfus trial in 1897[553] and analysed the affair from a 'Zionist' viewpoint, yet nowhere did he refer to its influence on his becoming a Zionist. Soon after, he wrote an 'Autobiography' for the London *Jewish Chronicle* in which, apart from some biographical data, he described his way to Zionism. This was three years almost to the day after Dreyfus's degradation and was in the midst of the renewed violent controversy over Dreyfus mentioned above. However, Herzl did not refer to the case at all.

Only during 1898 did the Dreyfus case assume its wider and deeper Jewish aspect, and then it also became an important factor in Zionist propaganda in the controversy with those Western Jews who had seen in 'emancipation' and assimilationism the solution of the Jewish problem. It was only then for the first time that the 'Dreyfusiade' was mentioned at a Zionist Congress, the Second, which assembled at Basle on August 28, 1898. Max Nordau in his speech set the tone when he proclaimed:[554]

> The Dreyfus case has simply drawn aside veils and exposed modes of thought that had been hidden till then. It projects itself as a warning and a lesson in the face of those Jews who still persist in believing themselves to be received definitely and without reserve into the national comradeship at least of the most advanced Western countries. This makes it momentous in the history of Jewry, and even gives it harsh educational value of a warning, of a sentence, of a punishment; a value which permits us, in our ineradicable Jewish optimism, to cry out even in observing the Dreyfus case: *Gam zu letova!* Even this is for the good!

Zionists and Herzl too from then on came to see the entire case from a different perspective. It now fully exerted its impact on him. There is no other explanation for the fact that it was only after all these last events and protestations that in 1899, in the article referred to above, Herzl repeated Bernard Lazar's by then popularised version (' "Death to the Jews"—I would not let it pass without protest that for the sin of an individual a whole people should be blamed')[555] and, in retrospect, attributed to the Dreyfus case that great influence upon him. The evidence thus shows that, contrary to popular opinion uncritically snatched up by Toynbee, the Dreyfus case was not the cause of Herzl's becoming a Zionist.

Moreover, it was not this trial and its accompanying antisemitism that aroused his Jewish consciousness. This consciousness is known through his own words to have been evident in him some thirteen years earlier, as his entries in a *Youth Diary*[556] of February, 1882, show, although there is no reason to assume that in the absence of written evidence he had not been a conscientious Jew also during the twenty-two years of his life prior to 1882 (he was born in 1860). Thus, for instance, it is nowhere recorded in his *Youth Diary* that he had acquainted himself with Graetz's *History of the Jews*, but in his speech in Vienna on November, 1896,[557] almost a year before the First Zionist Congress, he developed an original interpretation of antisemitism in Jewish history, based on Graetz, which presupposes a rather thorough knowledge and understanding of both. But his concern with the Jewish question obviously grew with his spiritual and physical maturing. Tracing back his path to Zionism, in 1895, he remarked in his *Diaries*:[558]

> When did I actually begin to concern myself with the Jewish Question? Probably ever since it arose; certainly from the time that I read Duehring's book.[559] In one of my old notebooks now packed away somewhere in Vienna are my first observations on Duehring's book and on the Question.

In the phrase 'probably ever since it arose' lies an important revelation of the transition from his Jewish consciousness to the urge to concern himself with the problem which, from then on, was not only his own but also that of all other Jews. As he once put it:[560]

> It was thought that the Jewish people was dead and had disappeared. But we felt dimly, before it stepped into our consciousness, that this was not true.

Therefore Duehring's antisemitic book, which he read in 1882, did not create his Jewishness in him but provided a welcome opportunity to summarize the thoughts on the Jewish Question which he had accumulated over the years and sporadically expressed in remarks in his *Youth Diary*[561] before he read this 'infamous book'.[562]

A similar process can be traced in another assimilated, a religious Jew who, like Herzl, had also not experienced antisemitism, Franz Kafka. The study of Graetz's *History of the Jews* gave him the opportunity to define this development of growing Jewish consciousness, which he had vaguely felt, into a full understanding of its essence as the process 'to allow my Jewishness to collect itself'.[563]

But Herzl's Jewish pride, which connotes one step beyond consciousness, was already clearly discernible in 1882, in his ironic rebuke to Duehring:[564]

> He sees in the Jews . . . only abject and infamous characteristics. This alone rouses suspicions on the clearness of his view. For how would such a low, inactive race[565] have been able to maintain itself through one and a half millennia of inhuman pressure if there had been nothing in it?

But this was only the beginning of Herzl's Jewish consciousness turning towards serious concern with the Jewish problem. He continued with the recollection of his feelings and thoughts of those days:[566]

> As the years went by, the Jewish Question bored into me and gnawed at me, tormented me and made me very miserable. In fact, I kept coming back to it whenever my own personal experiences—joys and sorrows— permitted me to rise to broader considerations.

And, of course, he wanted to do something about it, first for his own satisfaction, but soon also for those whom he believed to be in a similar position. All sorts of ideas cropped up. But even when he played with the thought at one time of solving the problem through organising a mass-conversion to Christianity,[567] he meant it for other Jews, not for himself:

> . . . the leaders of this movement—myself in particular—would remain Jews . . . We, the steadfast men, would have constituted the last generations. We would still have adhered to the faith of our fathers.

He soon recognised the fallacy of such thoughts. For, just as he wanted to remain 'steadfast', so would other Jews too, and the problem would remain. But it continued to occupy his mind. He planned to write about it,[568] and whenever he had a chance he discussed it with friends and thus deepened and broadened his own thoughts and ideas. As these conversations show, he had already in 1894 arrived at the conviction of Jewish distinctiveness as the source of Jewish nationalism.[569] To free himself from the pressure of these thoughts, he wrote a play in seventeen days, *Das Ghetto* (later renamed *Das neue Ghetto*).[570] His dying hero, Jacob Samuel, summarized Herzl's thoughts of these years in his last words:[571]

> Jews, my brethren, you won't be allowed to live again, until you—get out of the ghetto!

The play was completed on November 8, 1894, almost six weeks before the opening of the first Dreyfus trial.[572] With this play, as Herzl's biographer emphasised,[573] 'Herzl completed his inner return to his people'. That meant that now he knew what the problem was. But the play reveals that he did not yet know how to solve it. He was aware of the need for the Jews to leave the ghetto, in order to 'live as Jews again'; they obviously could not do this if they were to assimilate and disappear as Jews. In his search for a practical way to solving the problem, he soon recognised that a play would not do. It did not suffice to think[574]

> that through this eruption of playwriting I had written myself free of the matter. On the contrary, I got more and more deeply involved with it. The thought grew stronger in me that I must do something for the Jews.
>
> For the first time I went to the synagogue in the Rue de la Victoire and once again found the service festive and moving. Many things reminded me of my youth, of the Tabak Street Temple at Pest. I took a look at the Paris Jews and saw a family likeness in their faces . . .

Thus the 'emancipated', assimilated, a-religious Western Jew did not seek reasons and theories in the Gentile surroundings, but went where he hoped for, and indeed found, an atmosphere known to him which had lain dormant in him since his youth—where he would find others in a similar position and would recognise his people. He went 'home', even in Paris notwithstanding all the external differences, and he felt as if he had not been away long from the people he use to see in his boyhood regularly every Friday evening and Saturday morning in his old Budapest Synagogue.[575] He recognised the familiar faces, and felt himself naturally an integral part of the family, a member of the Jewish people. The echo of this experience resounded in his opening speech at the First Zionist Congress, where he said:[576]

> Zionism is the homecoming to the Jewish fold even before the return to the Jews' land.

He spoke of the 'homecoming' to the family, thus indicating that he in fact had never left the fold, however long he had not seen them and however far he had wandered away. From there, the step to Zionism was only a formal matter. Once the 'homecoming' was performed, the 'return' followed of its own accord. For, once the basis of nationality is accepted, every effort at maintaining and strengthening it arises automatically from this premise. Statehood constitutes the formal acknowledgment of a nationality's existence. Zionism is the continuation of this fact, translated into Jewish terminology. (For the purpose of the record, it should be repeated at this point that all these developments took place prior to the Dreyfus trial.)

(b) *Chaim Weizmann*

As the second example in his theory that external factors caused the creation of Zionism, Toynbee selected Chaim Weizmann, who was the President of the Zionist Organisation (1921–1931, 1935–1946) and subsequently First President of the State of Israel. As in Herzl's case, here too Toynbee transposed individual experience on to the whole Zionist Movement. But in the case of Weizmann he went even further and applied this individual's experience to a large section of the Jewish people. Toynbee bases his conclusions on a conversation with Dr Weizmann during the Paris Peace Conference in 1919,[577] in the course of which the Zionist leader is recorded as having told two anecdotes, which made it possible for Toynbee to understand

> why this great statesman and scientist—the most distinguished member of the Ashkenazi community in his generation—had become a convert to Zionism.
>
> The first anecdote was this. In Dr Weizmann's boyhood, at Vilna, there was a young Jewish sculptor of great promise who was expected to become one of the historic exponents of the Jewish culture. The young man's promise was fulfilled, but Jewry's hope was disappointed; for the *chef d'oeuvre* in which this Jewish artist eventually gave expression to his genius was a statue of the Russian Orthodox Christian Czar Ivan the Terrible! Under the duress of 'the Pale', Jewish genius had been perverted to the glorification of Jewry's oppressors. It was as if the *chef d'oeuvre* of Jewish literature in the second century B.C. had not been the Book of Ecclesiastes or the Psalms but some panegyric, in the Isocratean manner, upon Antiochus Epiphanes. Truly, that statue of a Russian Czar by the hand of a Vilna Jew was as great an eyesore for Jewish eyes as the statue of Zeus which the Seleucid once set up in the Temple of Yahweh at Jerusalem: an 'abomination of desolation standing where it ought not' (*Mark* xiii, 14; *Matthew* xxiv, 15; *Luke* xxi, 20; *Daniel* ix, 27).
>
> Dr Weizmann's second anecdote was an incident which had happened to himself as a grown man before his migration from Vilna to Manchester. A piece of urgent business made it indispensable for him to break the

Russian law then in force, under the Czardom, by trespassing beyond the eastern boundary of 'the Pale' in order to have a personal meeting with a friend in Moscow. As a precaution against the vigilance of the Russian police, it was arranged beforehand that Dr Weizmann should travel from Vilna to Moscow in a train arriving at nightfall, do his business in his friend's house during the night, and return to Vilna by a train leaving Moscow before dawn; but this arrangement fell through. For some reason, the friend whom Dr Weizmann had come to see was unable to keep the appointment; and Dr Weizmann found on inquiry that there was no return-train to Vilna earlier than the train which he had been intending to take. How should he pass the night hours? To engage a room in a hotel would be tantamount to delivering himself to the police. Dr Weizmann solved the problem by hiring a cab and driving round and round the streets of Moscow until the hour of his train's departure. 'And that,' he concluded, 'was how I had to pass my time on my one and only visit to the capital of the Empire of which I was supposed to be a citizen!'

Such anecdotes as these sufficiently explain the ethos of the Ashkenazi immigrants from 'the Pale' into the more enlightened countries of the modern Western World.

It is, of course, an extraordinary thing for a responsible writer to regard two anecdotes as a satisfactory basis for a 'sufficient' understanding of the beliefs even of an individual, not to speak of their suitability for understanding the ethos of a large section of a multitudinous people. But the indiscriminate 'selection' which Toynbee has practised in his endeavours to 'prove' his case is already known to readers of this study. The Weizmann example, however, enriches the collection from a different aspect. With regard to Herzl, Toynbee at least tried to deal with historical events, even if he exhibited some lack of knowledge of and research into the correct facts. But in Weizmann's case he dispensed with a serious basis altogether, accepted two stories heard over a luncheon or dinner table, and went on, unperturbed, to draw his conclusions from these. There is no need to stress that, as in the case of Herzl, Toynbee apparently did not trouble to check the facts of the anecdotes which he had heard fifteen years previously.[578] From the literature which is available, he would have found that, in the first place, geography, to which he devoted a whole volume of his *Study of History* (XI), again played its tricks on him. For from the reading of any biography of Weizmann it would have come to light that the

Zionist leader did not spend his youth in Vilna but in Motol and Pinsk;[579] did not move to Manchester from Vilna but from Geneva;[580] and did not travel to Moscow from Vilna but from Berlin, where he was then studying.[581] In the second place, through a study of the literature Toynbee would also have found that the sculptor in question was Mark Antokolski,[582] born in Vilna in 1842, who, by the time of Weizmann's boyhood (Weizmann was born in 1874), was not 'a young Jewish sculptor of great promise' but a man in his thirties, of world fame, and for over ten years already a member of the Russian Academy of Arts. The statue of 'Ivan the Terrible'—'Jewry's oppressor', in Toynbee's words—was completed by Antokolski in 1870, four years before Weizmann's birth, and is regarded in art circles as the culmination of a trend which began with his bas-relief 'The Inquisition' (1867), in which he depicted a Jewish family in Spain at the Passover table, invaded by the soldiers of 'Jewry's oppressors'. Nor were oppressors of Jews the subjects of Antokolski's only or foremost statues. Indeed, his works were so manifold that his critics called him a 'cosmopolitan'. His 'Socrates' is no less important, nor his 'Mephisto', nor his 'Christ', whom he depicted in a *yarmulka* (a skullcap) such as Orthodox Jews wear, by doing which he aroused violent anti-Jewish attacks against himself in the reactionary press. Nor can his 'Jewish' works, such as his 'Jewish tailor' or 'Talmudic discussion', be minimised because they aroused less controversy in public. He was cited at the Fifth Zionist Congress in 1901 by Martin Buber, the spokesman of the 'Democratic Faction', of which Dr Weismann was one of the founders and leaders,[583] as 'our greatest sculptor . . . of whose works of Jewish content the most interesting is his Spinoza'.[584]

It would, of course, be pure academic speculation to investigate the question of what Jewish art is, and whether a Jewish artist should depict only Jewish types and scenes, and above all, solely pleasant ones. In our context this question does not arise, for we are concerned at this point with a story which was turned into an event of historical importance. And from this viewpoint the entire story as told by Toynbee appears as a mixture of bad memory, wrong history, and false conclusions. The last-named particularly deserves stressing, because Toynbee emphasised that factors such as those which he enumerated in the anecdotes had 'converted Weizmann to Zionism'. This is almost the identical phraseology used in connection with Herzl's becoming a Zionist because of the Dreyfus trial, as mentioned above. However, while with regard to Herzl the external event is made to elevate him to the position of 'Apostle of Zionism', with Weizmann a similar external influence only makes him a 'convert' to Zionism. This is characteristic of Toynbee's complete ignorance of Weizmann's life and, indeed, of Jewish life altogether. To begin with, the term 'converted' connotes a spiritual and moral change combined with a personal change from one belief to another; one becomes 'converted' to a Church, for instance, to which one did not belong before. This certainly did not apply to Weizmann. With Herzl and with Weizmann, no particular single external experience in their lives was the cause of their becoming Zionists. We have chosen passages above from Herzl's writings which refer to his development towards Zionism. Dr Weizmann, in his autobigraphy,[585] has also dealt at length with his path to Zionism; neither in it nor in any other of his writings or speeches has he referred to the influence upon him of his visit to Moscow or of Antokolski's work in the meaning ascribed by Toynbee. For he did not have to be 'converted' or to 'join' Zionism; he was a Zionist all his life. It was taken for granted that even during his earliest youth, at school or in his free time, he would be together with other Jewish boys, thinking like them, feeling like them, and dreaming of a future free Palestine. Recalling those days, he wrote that to him all this was a matter of faith:[586]

> This faith was part of our make-up; our Jewishness and our Zionism were interchangeable; you could not destroy the second without destroying the first. We did not need to listen to propaganda. When Zvi Hirsch Masliansky, the famous folk orator, came to preach Zionism to us, he addressed the convinced. Of course we loved listening to him, for he spoke so beautifully, and he invariably drew on texts from the book of Isaiah[587] which all of us knew by heart. But we heard in his moving oration only the echo of our innermost feelings.

It was with this very consciousness that he had lived from his infancy in his father's house; unlike Herzl, he did not have to 'come home'—he was at home:[588]

> . . . the house was steeped in rich Jewish tradition, and Palestine was the centre of the ritual, a longing for it implicit in our life . . . the 'Return' was in the air, a vague, deep-rooted Messianism, a hope which would not die.

Who, in the circumstances, cared about those Jews who attempted to assimilate and find their way into Russian society, be it in commerce, literature, or art? The children brought up in the same spirit and climate as Weizmann did not require any external evidence of their Jewishness, or any external experience to make them Jewish nationalists. After all, right from their early childhood they were aware of the fact that they lived in a world of restrictions and disabilities on Jews. They grew up in them, with them, and knew precisely and in every detail the regulations appertaining to the 'Pale' and their implications for Jewish citizens within and outside that area. Therefore, the incident outside 'the Pale' (which, by the way, was a frequent occurrence among Russian Jews), as told in the second anecdote by Dr Weizmann to Toynbee in Paris, 1919, does not have at all the significance which the latter attributes to it: as so impressive an event that it led Weizmann to become a Zionist and enabled Toynbee to understand the ethos of Ashkenazi Jews.

It would not be worth while to deal with the second story as well were it not for the fact that here we become acquainted with another of Toynbee's superficialities in his treatment of Jewish matters. Compare, for instance, Toynbee's narrative with Dr Weizmann's own story about these events as he related them in his memoirs. He went to Moscow in 1897—according to these reminiscences—on the advice of his professor in Berlin, Von Knorre, to sell a chemical invention to Ilyinsky, a friend of the professor (and not 'to have a personal meeting with a friend', as Toynbee wrote). Referring to the special danger of such a journey, Weizmann continued:[589]

> Going to Moscow was not a simple business. I had no right to travel outside the Pale without a special permit, which I could not get. In Moscow I would not be able to register at a hotel; and anyone who put me up privately without reporting me to the police would himself be liable to arrest. So I had to make my arrangements carefully in advance. I found it necessary to stay in Moscow two days. The first night I slept at Ilyinsky's place, the second at Naiditch's . . .[590] I did not sell my chemical discovery.

A glance at Toynbee's and Weizmann's versions of the same event shows up, of course, the inaccuracy in Toynbee's rendition, even in such minor items as the difference between sleeping in private homes for two nights instead of the supposed one night trotting around the streets of Moscow. Moreover, Toynbee also omitted to date the event. The year of Weizmann's visit to Moscow (1897) shows that this could not have influenced him at all with regard to Zionism, because by then he had already been an active member of the Zionist students' group in Berlin for some years and was, in fact, preparing for his journey to the First Zionist Congress when, owing to the delay in Moscow, he had to abandon that journey.[591] Thus, he was a full-fledged Zionist before going to Moscow; as he had been a national Jew since his childhood.

We have thus seen that Toynbee's assessments of both Herzl and Weizmann were based on completely false premises, and for this reason alone his evaluation becomes void. Moreover, it would have become void even if he had been able to prove that his statements about Herzl and Weizmann had been true in every detail. No world-wide movement, no ideology adhered to by an uncountable multitude can —as Toynbee himself has stated[592]—be assessed by the same motives which induced two or three or more individuals, however important, to accept it. For he knows that[593] the most unsatisfactory usage of all is to ascribe political events to the personal act of one individual human being. Finally, apart from the fact that occurrences such as the Dreyfusiade or Antokolski's portraying of Jewish oppressors, or the restrictive measures outside the 'Pale', have been experienced by Jews throughout the centuries to a greater or lesser degree, yet they did not lead to the emergence of political Zionism. The reasons for the creation of Zionism, therefore, must, also on this count, lie somewhere else; they do, as will be shown further below.

In the light of this, there is no sense in analysing Toynbee's sweeping statement that the two Weizmann anecdotes 'sufficiently explain the ethos of Ashkenazi Jews' from the 'Pale'. After all, there is a limit to how far even superficiality should be permitted to go.

Surrender—with a purpose

There is another aspect of this issue. In his theories Toynbee has emphatically rejected, on principle, the method of forming a judgment from one or two external events. For instance, on the occasion of his discussing the bridging of the gap between human beings and social phenomena, he wrote:[594]

> Even where one is dealing with a small and more or less closed circle of *dramatis personae*, and where also the accessible information about each of them is comparatively copious, what remains undiscovered will still far exceed what has been brought to light, even if we have conducted our researches with the utmost possible skill and industry.

It does not require new evidence to show that in the selection of his two examples Toynbee did not 'conduct researches with the utmost possible skill and industry', and he did not seek out the 'accessible information', although it was available to him—as the sources which he used in his biased writings on the Zionist issue show. He thus defied his own credo:[595]

> I have a greater respect for the historical evidence than I have for a particular hypothesis that I happen to have picked out of my tool-bag.

But this is not the only 'sacrifice' Toynbee made for the sake of his two examples. As in a number of other cases, we find here too a readiness to surrender or 'forget' his own general theories once they do not fit into his requirements with regard to Jewish matters. In this instance we encounter two such 'surrenders'. The first is his attempt to link antisemitism with Zionism through the experience of two individuals. This stands in direct contradiction to his principles concerning historiography in general, to which he devoted a special chapter.[596] He there presented the following summary of the particular question which concerns us at this point.[597]

> In giving an account of social phenomena, an historian or a sociologist is constantly slipping into treating them as if they were persons, instead of rigorously treating them all the time as the enormously complex relations between an enormous number of persons which is what institutions really are, but which is also something beyond the human mind's present capacity to comprehend.
>
> This procedure is as misleading as it is difficult to avoid. It is misleading because there is not, I believe, really an illuminating analogy between the psycho-somatic organism that we call human being and the network of relations between human beings that we call a social phenomenon. If they have any points of likeness at all, they certainly have many more points of difference.

The second 'surrender' concerns his conception of what he termed the 'panoramic view'.[598] According to this, while regarding detailed historical studies as useful and important, he does not regard them as sufficient to make larger developments comprehensible. In contrast, he defends and practises the universal, *i.e.* panoramic approach, viewing 'some landscape where the horizon is not restricted to the boundaries'[599] of a single nation, country, event, or age, but covers the global field of history or of the components of its civilisation. Yet he emphasised:[600]

> there is no escape from the formidable requirement that we must each of us attempt to take the panoramic view of the whole field; and, considering how vast this is by comparison with our intellectual powers, we have to face the truth that our panoramic view is bound to be a superficial one. Superficiality is a defect about which we cannot afford to be complacent, because it exposes us to the risk of misconstruing Reality, and the whole purpose of intellectual inquiry is to come as near as possible to seeing Reality as it is. How are we to correct our superficiality? The defeatist remedy is to avoid it by renouncing the panoramic view that exposes us to it; but this means renouncing the endeavour to arrive at any understanding of human affairs. A more constructive remedy is, not to seek to avoid superficiality at this prohibitive price, but to try to counterbalance it by aiming at thoroughness in some fraction of the total field. This fraction must be small enough for us to be able to achieve thoroughness here without having to devote so much of our energies to this that we have not enough left for taking even the most superficial panoramic view as well.

From our analysis it is obvious that with regard to the 'panoramic view' of Zionism derived from the 'fraction' of Herzl's and Weizmann's personal experiences, Toynbee did not practise what he preached. The required 'thoroughness' of research and study was completely absent. While he thus defied his own principle of historiography, he can nevertheless derive satisfaction from the fact that his supplementary statement that 'our panoramic view is bound to be a superficial one' has been fully confirmed in the examples under investigation.

The Influence of Antisemitism

It would, of course, be preposterous to deny the fact that antisemitism had its influence on both Herzl and Weizmann, as it has had on every Jew throughout Diaspora history. And there is nothing unusual in that. As far as this particular aspect of the issue is concerned, Jews are in a situation similar to that of many other individuals in general history. These, too, encountered their own form of 'antisemitism' and sought possibilities of living in freedom in new territories if their situation became unbearable in their homelands. The Pilgrim Fathers arrived on the American shore because of an English form of 'antisemitism'—the suppression of freedom of conscience. The Huguenots left France for Switzerland, Holland, England, America, and other lands, after the revocation of the Edict of Nantes, which gave rise, in France, to that form of 'antisemitism' which deprived them of equality of rights. A similar fate befell the Moravian Brethren, who, because of the prevailing 'antisemitism' in Bohemia and Moravia, were prohibited from pursuing their ideals of universal equality and brotherhood and left the country under the leadership of Amos Comenius. Many a State and country in history that later became a leader of civilisation and liberty was created in the pursuit of ideals which individuals were unable to foster in their fatherlands because of the oppressive methods there which, for convenience sake, I have collectively and equivalently named 'antisemitism'. None of these oppressed people surrendered their ideals; they preferred an uncertain fate to submission or compromise.

But the paramount conclusions as regards the essence of Zionism and of the appearance of the Pilgrim Fathers, the Huguenots, the Moravian Brethren, and so on, cannot be drawn from the fact of the oppression, but from an understanding of the ideals which dominated these people long before 'antisemitism' made its appearance. 'Antisemitism' was a reaction to their existence, not *vice versa*. In the same way, Jewish distinctiveness from the others, Jewish religion, Jewish nationalism, with all their ideas and hopes, Jews *per se* were in existence long before they drew hatred and jealousy upon themselves in the form of historical or contemporary antisemitism. For antisemitism everywhere arose *after* Jews had settled in a country, and not before, as Toynbee himself well understood when he wrote:[601]

Anti-Semitism arose in the Western World wherever there was an appreciably rapid increase in the numerical ratio of the Jewish to the Gentile ingredient in the local population.

He was thus in full agreement with one of Zionism's basic tenets, which Herzl had formulated thus:[602]

> The Jewish question exists wherever Jews live in appreciable numbers. Wherever it does not exist, it is carried in by immigrating Jews. We are naturally drawn into those places where they do not persecute us; through our appearance the persecution arises.

Fundamentally, and seen from the classic Zionist observation post, 'antisemitism' is that external force with which every living organism is confronted, as we have said before,[603] and it derives great strength from the preparedness to meet it and the defence against it. 'Fear of punishment by God' in most religions is of great concern to the faithful ('serve the Lord with fear'[604]; 'the fear of the Lord is the beginning of knowledge'[605]; etc.), and while it is not the positive basis or cause of creed and religion, it results in a more intensified observance of moral precepts.[606] So does the citizens' fear of punishment by the judiciary for not complying with the law. Without that fear one wonders how society could organise itself. 'Fear of the enemy' is to this day one of the strongest unifying factors in the world—stronger, unfortunately, than the positive desire for brotherhood and good-neighbourly relations. One has only to follow the denunciations in the West of the 'Communist danger', or in the East of the 'capitalist danger', or of the Chinese danger which frightens India, and so on, to find confirmation of the importance of external perils as a rallying cry to unify people. Toynbee has termed this phenomenon 'The Stimulus of Pressures'[607] applying to cases where the exercise of external pressure causes appropriate rallying and reaction. But often such pressure does not have to be used; it is sufficient for people to become aware of its possible emergence. This awareness encourages preventive countermeasures and the unification of those 'afraid', and it thus becomes a kind of what might be termed 'Stimulus of "Potential" Pressures'.

Herzl recognised the importance of this external factor and attributed to it an appropriate role in the life of all nations and nationalities. He believed that every normal people lives with an awareness of itself but without any emphatic consciousness as long as its existence is not threatened from external sources. But as soon as that danger appears, the first act of self-defence is self-consciousness. A people is not created suddenly at that moment because of this enlivened consciousness, it existed, as stated, all along. But this aroused consciousness becomes a strong stimulus to the recognition by this people of its own Ego, of its essence as a people, and thus strengthens its cohesiveness. It invigorates it to meet the external danger. 'The enemy is the iron hoop of a nation', Herzl once said.[608] And from his writings we see that he laid the greater stress on the 'enemy' in the life of every people on earth, for he felt unable to believe that the high ideals of equal rights, equal opportunities, brotherhood, and universal peace for all men were at hand, which would allow one to disregard the potential enemy from without. Therefore he did not preach beautiful but unrealistic dreams of the future for his brethren. The Zionism which he preached was a movement of *today*, which had to deal with people living *today* and, therefore, however high and lofty the prophetic ideals and those of mankind, and however much everyone strove towards them, they were in Herzl's day neither nearer to nor further from realisation than they are today. Herzl saw all nationalities, the Jewish included, as we see them today: from the realistic viewpoint that they lived and had the will to continue to live, notwithstanding all the difficulties, pressures, fears, and dangers. He therefore regarded every nationality as[609]

an historical group of people, who visibly belong together, and are kept together by a common enemy.

When turning from this general description to the Jewish nationality, he did not attempt to define the term 'Jewish people', for, as we said before, this would have been impossible with the insufficient modern vocabulary. He accepted the existence of the Jewish people as a given fact, as he accepted the existence of all other people, and applied the general principle above also to Jewry:[610]

We thus are and shall remain, whether we want it or not, an historic group of recognisable cohesiveness. We are a people—the enemy makes us *one* without our consent, as has always been the case in history. In affliction we stand together and then we suddenly discover our strength.

In this conception, therefore, the Jewish people has existed and continues to exist as a cohesive and recognisable group of people. In the past it has lived and in the present it continues to live under the threat of danger or under actual attack. The time factor is unimportant. The enemy has always arisen whenever Jews hoped for or tried to find a basis for coexistence with other nationalities or faiths, or adapted themselves to prevailing conditions. They were not permitted to do so by the non-Jewish majority. The attack began at the point of saturation. The Jews were pushed back again to their original position; they remained an historic group of recognisable cohesiveness and were thus strengthened again by the common enemy by holding together in unity, to become, from 'a' people, '*one*' people (a terminology which some translators of Herzl's German have not perceived[611]). It is from this viewpoint that Herzl evaluated antisemitism as[612]

a reminder that we must stand loyally together.

This same kind of external force has exercised and still exercises its influence on every people on earth, 'as has always been the case in history', and not only in Jewish history. If at this point we recall Toynbee's 'penalisation' theory[613] we shall understand why continual suffering as a 'stimulus of survival' is contrary to everything that Judaism and Zionism stands for.

'Antisemitism' is thus a purely external factor. It did not create the Jewish nationality or the Jewish people. But it strengthened it to continue its existence because it induced the Jews not only in the centre but also on the fringe to unite in defence against the common danger. It was therefore natural that it should have been made full use of in Zionist propaganda. Because of this, the opponents of Zionism indulged themselves in linking it with antisemitism. We have seen that the idea also slipped into Toynbee's anti-Zionist arsenal. But it is totally unfounded. Zionism, as a political movement based on reality, saw before it the age-old Jewish people as an existing factor, and the age-old antisemitism as equally so. Contrary to every previous Jewish attempt at containing this enemy, Zionism, instead of dealing with each brutal or mild manifestation of antisemitism, went to the roots of the problem and recognised that neither defence nor fighting against it would bring about its downfall. It was necessary to remove its basic cause: the fact of the existence of a distinctive minority within the majority. The customary running from one country to another only extended the problem; it did not solve it. The ancient, never-absent ideal of the Jewish people returning to their Land thus became a practical objective for today. And again it must be stressed: the ideal and the hope of the return to Eretz Israel had been there ever since the beginning of the Diaspora, as we have shown.

The external enemy had an importance for the Zionists' propaganda from the fact that it was visible for all to see and for large sections of Jewry to feel. Thus antisemitism became a corollary of *Judennot*, as Jewish misery has been called in German. And Herzl proposed to make full use of this. He wrote:[614]

> It all depends on the propelling force. And what is this force? The misery of the Jews ...
>
> Who would dare to deny that this force exists?
>
> The force of steam is also known, a force generated in a tea-kettle by boiling water, which raises the lid. These tea-kettle phenomena are the attempts by Zionists and many other forms of association 'to ward off antisemitism'.
>
> But I say that this force, if properly utilised, is powerful enough to propel a large engine, to move people and goods. Let the engine have whatever appearance it may.

According to this thesis, the utilisation of this propelling force rested on the two not necessarily interrelated pillars of Jewish reality: Jewish misery and antisemitism. They therefore constituted the twin pincers of Zionist propaganda: internally towards the Jews in every land, and internationally towards the world. At this point it must be emphasised that these propaganda aspects were only part of the vast area of the overall Zionist propaganda and other activities. They are specifically emphasised and dealt with here because they form part of the question of antisemitism with which this chapter is concerned.

As stated, Zionist propaganda was based to an important extent on the *Judennot*, under which both Jewry and the Gentiles suffered in one way or another. In this connection it is of no consequence whether the situation arose out of economic pressure, out of the desire for self-preservation, or out of downright hatred. Or, as Herzl once formulated these various phenomena:[615]

> I believe I understand antisemitism, which is an extremely complicated movement. I examine this movement as a Jew, without hate and without

fear. I believe I recognise in it those elements which are merely brutish humour, mean economic envy, inherited prejudice, religious intolerance; but I also recognise the element of unconscious self-protection.

From the standpoint of this analysis we take for granted the existence of both the misery and antisemitism, without further regard to their natures; as it is also undeniable that they were perceptible to everybody (a) in the urge of Jews to leave their countries and (b) in the actual stream of Jewish migration. Zionist propaganda utilised these facts, as stated internally and externally.

The internal Jewish picture was approximately as follows: Jewish communities the world over were sought out by those brethren who, because of economic pressure or because of threatening or actual antisemitism, left their countries in search of 'havens of refuge'. This meant, in the first place, the importing of the Jewish problem into countries where hitherto it did not exist, because the migrating Jew sought first for those countries where existing Jewish communities lived in safety. And they lived so because of their small numbers in relation to the rest of the population. The arrival of refugees meant, in Toynbee's words,[616] a 'rapid increase in the numerical ratio of the Jewish to the Gentile ingredient'. It thus meant that in the almost foreseeable future antisemitism would arise, threatening not only the newcomers but also the old Jewish settlers. In its propaganda efforts Zionism accordingly turned to those 'old settlers' to enlist their co-operation towards the realisation of the Zionist aim, for purely utilitarian reasons: the preservation of their own *status quo* through assisting in diverting the migration stream away from their countries and towards the one country, Palestine. As Herzl told English Jewry in 1900 from the Congress platform:[617]

> No-one may draw false conclusions from the fact that Jews in glorious England enjoy full freedom and human rights. He would be a poor friend of the Jews in this country as well as of the Jews residing in other countries who would advise the persecuted Jews to flee hither. Our brethren here would tremble in the midst of their joy if their position meant the attraction to these shores of our desperate brethren in other lands. Such an immigration would mean disaster equally for the Jews here and for those who would come here. For the latter, with their miserable bundles, would bring with them that from which they were fleeing—I mean antisemitism.

On the other hand, antisemitism presented itself in that very same aspect to the nations of the world. In some lands brutal antisemitism caused internal unrest and economic difficulties. Zionism believed that most of these States were as interested in a solution of the problem as were Jews themselves.[618] Through an offer to organise the exodus of large groups from these lands, to the joy of the suffering and to the satisfaction and probably relief of the States, Zionist diplomacy would look forward to feasible collaboration.

Other States were in a more delicate situation. They had officially proclaimed equal rights, emancipation, freedom, and democracy, yet found themselves confronted with the fact of an existing discrimination against Jews. One cannot preach lofty ideals to the world while over-looking them at home. But the mild, sometimes almost invisible anti-semitism in those lands was in danger of becoming visible and growing rapidly into a difficult problem once the stream of migration, caused by antisemitism elsewhere, found its way into those lands—drawn there by the loud pronouncements of high human ideals by their leaders. Zionists therefore concluded that their solution of the Jewish problem would also find sympathy and co-operation in these States, as a kind of preventive measure for the future.

Antisemitism thus played an important part internally and externally. To a large degree, as stated, the propaganda of the Zionists was based on these considerations. They were to help the Jews, but they were also to help the Gentiles, who did not know how to cope with the problem. It was with this concept in mind that Herzl, in his *Judenstaat*, fore-told:[619]

> they will pray for the success of the work in the synagogues. And also in the churches. It is the relief of an old burden under which all have suffered.

But this also led to another important aspect of the problem. As a result of the Zionists disseminating propaganda all over the world, the Jewish question no longer remained a local affair, of local Jews and local Governments, but became a world-wide issue. Through the propaganda directed towards an understanding of antisemitism as a non-Jewish issue also, Zionism forced world-wide public opinion to come to re-cognise the Gentiles' own interest in the Jewish problem. On the basis of this common interest, then, Zionism went beyond its 'educational' efforts, and endeavoured to enrol the assistance and co-operation of all nations in helping to solve the Jewish problem by recognising and accepting it also as their own.

Basically, the negotiations of Zionist leaders with the various Governments were the same, whatever form antisemitism had assumed in their respective countries. There was always the common interest just referred to. It thus enabled Zionism to raise the Jewish problem to the level of one with which many nations were concerned; and following this, to an international co-operation with them in the fulfilment of the Zionist programme. On this, one axiom of Zionism was built: international co-operation in the solution of the Jewish problem. As Herzl put it in his *Judenstaat*:[620]

> The Jews' State is a world necessity; therefore it will arise.

And therein lies the meaning of the term 'secured by public law' of the Basle Programme.

In this is shown one of the fundamental differences between every other attempt at solving what is generally termed the 'Jewish problem' and Zionism. The latter rejected the philanthropic method practised by individuals or individual groups to assist persecuted Jews to escape from one land and settle in another. This method disregarded the essence of Judaism and the meaning of Jewish survival. On the contrary, as repeatedly mentioned, it only transplanted the 'Jewish problem' into lands where hitherto it did not exist. Zionism, however, rooted in Jewish historical aspirations, aimed at realising the return to Palestine through applying the modern method of organising the Jewish people on a national basis and through the application of modern political and propaganda methods for attaining its goal. Raising the problem to an international level, which then necessitated official negotiations between the Zionist leadership and the Governments of the world, has, in the end, through the rise of Israel, proved the correctness of the procedure.

From what has been said above, it is obvious that antisemitism played an important role in the Zionist doctrine, tactics, and methods. But, as the French nation was not born out of a negative process, such as, say, out of German Francophobia, and as the English nation was not created out of a reaction to the hatred or jealousy of Continental European nations, so Jewish nationalism was in existence long before it drew hatred and jealousy upon itself in the form of historical or contemporary antisemitism. And therein lies Toynbee's fundamental misjudgment and lack of understanding of the issue as exemplified in his statement[621] of an 'identical point of view' or even a common geographical origin of Zionism and antisemitism.

Antisemitism had its share in strengthening the Jewish people internally, just as Francophobia strengthened the inner feelings of Frenchmen and kept them alert to defend their existence. As Judah Magnes once put it:[622]

> Antisemitism cannot be the guiding negative principle of Jewish life. Only freedom and service can be the guiding principles of the living Jewish people.

Antisemitic manifestations, appearing with clockwork regularity at all times, in so many lands, strengthened the consciousness of the Jews and caused them to band together for decisive resistance in the struggle for survival. But antisemitism did not arise out of a common ideology with Zionism or with any other aspect of Judaism; it was and is a non-Jewish reaction to Jewish existence. This is a sufficient reason for its remaining an important factor in the Zionist philosophy.

Some may take issue with this last remark that antisemitism still "remains" an important factor in the Zionist philosophy. But a glance at the situation of world Jewry today makes it clear that the considerations above cannot be confined to history alone, however much we have treated them as historical. Large masses of Jews are still confronted with brutal as well as cunning antisemitism, as is seen in a number of European, American, and Arab countries; and it still involves millions of Jewish people in many areas. Even if conditions in many lands have fundamentally changed, equal rights and individual freedom today form integral parts of legislation, brutal Hitlerite antisemitism has disappeared, while, on the other hand, the State of Israel has become a reality—notwithstanding all this, the basic problem of antisemitism continues to exist. For it is inherent in the reality of the Jewish Diaspora and in its transitory character. No Jew anywhere in the Diaspora can say today that 'it cannot happen here' or 'it will not happen here'; and no serious non-Jew can honestly object. In fact, Toynbee said as much himself when he warned his fellow-Westerners of the possibility of a repetition of Nazi-like methods, or of their adaptation to conditions that prevail at the moment when they reappear in the future. Antisemitism is a corollary of Jewish existence within the non-Jewish society. It has always been a wrong assumption, frequently heard, that Zionism preached the expectation that through the establishment of a State of and for the Jews antisemitism would disappear by that fact. And now, after the establishment of that State, Israel, this has been proved a wrong assumption. Statehood in isolation, without the Jews, was never a tenet of Zionism. Antisemitism was not to disappear through a simple proclamation of the Palestine territory as a State. It was to disappear with the Jewish exodus from the Diaspora into that State. This has not taken place and Zionism has thus so far not been given the chance to prove its case in this respect. This is not the place to investigate the reasons and to outline future developments in this direction. We are concerned with the facts of today: Israel houses only about 15 per cent of world Jewry; and this cannot mean an end to antisemitism, as it confronts the other 85 per cent living with minority status. Jews staying in the Diaspora must accept the unavoidability of antisemitism as long as they are Jews and intend to remain Jews. This is not meant to create fear or a threat of today or tomorrow. It is said as a simple fact corroborated by 3,000 years of Jewish experience, just as it is also honest to say that nobody can foretell the forms and methods of the antisemitism of tomorrow. It can be bloody, visible, insignificant, or perceived out of sensitivity. In Jewish history it has always appeared in a different form adapted to the conditions of the time. What and how it will be tomorrow we cannot tell, for it will show its face only in the moment of 'crisis', and it would be folly to guess either the form or the moment of that 'crisis'. But once it appears and this external pressure sets in, it will strengthen Jewish consciousness and thus Jewish togetherness. This remains the course of Jewish history, which has seen uncountable similar developments in one form or another.

It is, of course, a fact that many Jews turned to Zionism because of their encounter with antisemitism, as it is also a fact that hundreds or thousands of Jews have settled in Palestine or Israel not out of Zionism but because of the necessity to escape from antisemitism or from other dangers. They have not necessarily become Zionists even after settling in Israel. They are the benefactors of what Zionists, under most difficult and heroic conditions, had been able to prepare for such eventualities as an integral part of their overall ideology in renewing Jewish Statehood.

Antisemitism is thus an important factor in Zionist philosophy and in practical life. Its lesson can help many a Jew, wherever he lives, to understand the problems with which he or his children are or may one day be confronted. But it is not the only factor. There are also other external factors, of lesser overall importance than antisemitism, but nevertheless factors or, rather, motivations towards coming from an 'outside world' into the Zionist ranks. None of these would fall into the category of brutal antisemitism. All of them come under the different heading of the relationship of the Jew in non-Jewish society rather than what is usually regarded or accepted as antisemitism. It is the non-Jew's defence of his own position, which expresses itself in discrimination against Jews, in the impossibility for a Jew to make progress in those areas, in hurt feelings, isolation, and so on. There are other individual factors also. Martin Buber once devoted an illuminating article[623] to these other external motivations, describing their nature and their influence on individual Jews: the social philosopher, for instance, who hopes to fulfil his ideas of a new society in a new land; the industrialist who may wish to expand his wealth into new branches; the architect seeking to experiment with new forms and their practical application; the archaeologist in pursuit of new discoveries; or the man who is simply trying to escape from a civilisation which he believes to be in decay; and many other examples. Such men became Zionists because they believed that Zionism created the *terra firma* upon which they could and would fulfil their hopes and interests. In none of these kinds of decisions by individuals is antisemitism the original cause. Yet all these factors are also external. And just as antisemitism is not the cause of the belief in the Jewish future, so would it be equally wrong to select any or all of these motives together and elevate them into being the reason for the emergence of a world-wide Zionist movement. They are reasons for individuals eventually to join the movement. They cause their decisions, but they have a bearing only on them individually, not on the essence of Zionism.

In contrast to all those influenced by such external factors, there is that great mass of Jewish people who are Zionists as a matter of natural self-evident identification with their nationality or people. They feel themselves part of the people which has existed throughout the centuries and of which they are just the present-day generation, ready and willing to pass on the heritage to the next generation. Chaim Weizmann, mentioned above, is a case in point. His example could be multiplied *ad infinitum*. For these Jews possess, as Herzl once described it:[624]

> the inner unity which many other European Jews have lost. Their feeling is as national Jews, but without the restricted or impatient national conceit which in the present situation of the Jews could hardly be understood. They are not plagued by the idea of assimilating, their existence is simple and uninterrupted. . . . These people are on the right track almost without argument, possibly without even noticing any difficulties. They do not assimilate themselves to any other nation, but they endeavour to learn everything good from all other peoples. In this way they manage to be upright and genuine.

In this way they are Zionists. They are simple Jews, people of our time. They want to lead their lives in a Jewish way, in their own sense and meaning, like other human beings who have the right to live according to their own wishes. They believe that they are a part of the vital link between past generations and the future; and they have the will to preserve Jewish continuity in and through a State of their own, in pursuit of their religion, culture, and so on, so as to preserve the heritage of the great values which they have inherited. And in the will to continuity is also incorporated the will to strive towards those great ideals which the Jewish prophets foresaw for Israel. Therein rests the immense positive power of Zionism, not only true for past generations but also for ours. That it is a positive movement not only emerges from its work and ideals, but also from the analysis of the negative elements which Toynbee brought into the picture. For we have been able to show that these external factors could arise only because a Jewish people existed whose members pursue the positive aim of continuity. After all, it was Toynbee himself who, in an analysis of external factors appertaining in particular to danger of the sort inherent in antisemitism, came to the conclusion that its importance was in fact almost nil in creating the will to do what is necessary for resistance. He has thus given the best answer to his attribution of so important a role to 'penalisations' and antisemitism in the survival process of the Jewish people and in the emergence of Zionism. He wrote:[625]

> Danger, even when it is as extreme as ours is today, is never a sufficient stimulus in itself to make men do what is necessary for their salvation. It is a poor stimulus because it is a negative one. A cold-blooded calculation of expediency will not inspire us with the spiritual power to save ourselves. This power can only come from the disinterested pursuit of a positive aim that will outrange the negative one of trying to avoid self-destruction; and this positive aim can be given to me by nothing but love.

This is a correct rendition of the positive inner image of Zionism, the concept of love of the Jewish people, what a Jew in his own language calls '*Ahavath Israel*'. And if, after all this, there is still a need to confirm that this positive aspect applies to Zionism, Toynbee again provides us with a formulation which is now over fifty years old, yet is still true and right:[626]

> . . . if the Jewish migration to Palestine had remained nothing more than a stream of refugees, he[627] might possibly have succeeded in his purpose. But in these last twenty years this Jewish movement [Zionism] has become a positive thing—no longer a flight from the Pale but a remembrance of Zion—and Zionism has already challenged and defeated the policy which Dr Trietsch represents.[628] 'The object of Zionism', it was announced in the *Basle Programme* drawn up by the first Zionist Congress in 1897, 'is to establish for the Jewish people a publicly and legally secured home in Palestine'.

Part II
Zionist Reality

When Trevor-Roper goes on to say that my theories are not tested by the facts either, he is laying down a legitimate requirement, and my claim to be using an empirical method of inquiry does stand or fall according to the verdict of this count. I agree that my claim cannot be sustained if I have not tried to test my theories and hypotheses by the facts, or if I have tried but have not done the job properly or successfully. For, while it is true that theories and hypotheses can never be deduced from facts, it is also true that they can be validated only if they are confronted with the relevant facts and are confirmed by them.

—Toynbee, *Reconsiderations*, p. 245

1

Toynbee v. Toynbee

After the analysis in Part I, we can now attend to specific matters, to the challenge which Toynbee has issued against Zionism in its task of realising its ideals.

In a fairly recent article[1] Toynbee laid down two principles upon which he based his approach to all the concrete problems of Zionism, whether it be the subject of Jewish rights to Palestine, or Zionist political, economic, and other activities in Palestine, or Zionist relationship to the Arabs, to Britain, and to the world, or any other element of its work. These principles are:[2]

> (a) Rights may perhaps be defined as claims which are recognised as being valid not merely by the claimants themselves but by a general consensus of disinterested parties.

> (b) The case must be argued in terms of human rights that are more or less universally recognised as being valid.

Both these principles have one thing in common: they stress the necessity of a universal consensus of disinterested parties. Applied to the issue before us, this in itself eliminates, as interested parties, the Arabs, the Jews, and the British, although Toynbee names only the former two as included in his formula:[3]

> All the Arabs and all the Jews in the world, added together, amount to no more than a small minority of the human race.

Although we accept Toynbee's two principles for this analysis in order to prove that also on his own latest ground his conclusions are wrong, it should be pointed out that they constitute a departure from his old method in this matter. He himself had adhered in his writings to the old method until it now became a hindrance in his new crusade. Throughout the Mandatory period, his position, and that of Britain, was: 'No settlement should be imposed from outside on the inhabitants of Palestine not agreed upon previously by Jews and Arabs'. This gave 'the claimants' the decisive say and did not leave it to the 'consensus of disinterested parties'. We shall show that it was precisely on Toynbee's new basis which Toynbee now advanced that the 'disinterested majority', the United Nations, made their decision with regard to the area, a decision which he now advanced on principle but rejected on practical realisation.

For an understanding of his latest method, it is worthwhile following his reasoning. He maintains that because of the different interests of Jews and Arabs and because of their direct concern with the country, not they but the majority outside should be the decisive judge with regard to their respective rights and claims. Who is this majority? Toynbee's only reference to it reads as follows:

> The majority, to which I happen to belong, is also concerned in the Palestine dispute, though it is disinterested in the sense that it has no local claims. Nevertheless, its concern is legitimate and a most respectable one.

But he does not define this majority nor does he name its constituents. No evidence, of course, is submitted to show that he has been authorised by any or all of these disinterested parties to speak in their name, nor does he show documentary or literary proof that this 'disinterested majority' has at any time uttered sentiments which he appears to present in their name or that it has agreed with him on all or at least on one or more of his contentions. Finally, by emphasising disinterest as identical only with the absence of a local claim, he obviously leaves the door open for his own wished-for right to have a say in the matter. But objectivity arising out of disinterest must not be confined to a local geographical claim. Economic interests (oil, for instance), or ideological (Communism, for instance), and many others, show to no less a degree than a direct local claim an interest in an area, and particularly the Middle Eastern area. And from this viewpoint, it cannot be forgotten, after what we have already proved in Part I (and what will further be shown in the present Part II) of this study, that Toynbee cannot be regarded by any stretch of the imagination as a 'disinterested party'. He is the victim of what he himself once described more convincingly than any list of examples of such self-appointment could prove:[4]

> Self-centredness . . . is a vice which is capable of visiting any feelings and judgments and which therefore renders all feelings and judgments suspect . . . It is a sound working rule to presume, *unless and until convincing evidence has been produced to the contrary*, that a human being is self-centredly prejudiced in his own favour. But self-centredness in the singular is not the only form of vice. There is also self-centredness in the plural . . . [This] is perhaps even more difficult to cope with in its plural form than it is in the singular, because in the plural it is more insidious and potent.
>
> It is more insidious because, when a human being is acting self-centredly, not solely on his individual account, but in the name of his family, parish, nation, or church, he can delude himself into imagining that he is acting on behalf of something that is not only greater than himself but is outside himself.

Reading Toynbee's works, one is bound to suspect that almost his every theory, hypothesis, statement, or argument on any topic would begin with a capital 'I'. He is therefore the classic example of his own theory of self-centredness, of a person's prejudice in his own favour both in the singular and in the plural. This will probably be better understood if it is considered in conjunction with the general prejudice against Jews that permeates Toynbee's work, as we have been able to show.

The matter goes deeper, however. Toynbee, assuming for himself the right to a say in the Palestine-Israel matter, has conveniently overlooked his own bias and prejudice. And had he tested his right to speak on behalf of the majority of the human race by the means which he himself suggested for such tests, *i.e.* the facts, in our case, in the light of international decisions arrived at by preceding debates and votes at international forums, he would have had to confess that both his claim to a say and his anti-Zionist arguments are not those of the majority of the human race. The ideas which he unfolds are no other than those which the Arabs have repeatedly advanced and for which they never attained a general consensus in these forums. In this way, while eliminating officiously Arab and Jewish viewpoints as those of the 'directly concerned parties', Toynbee brings the 'directly concerned' Arabs into the picture by the back door. There is in his more recent writings, since the publication in 1935 of Volume IV of his *Study*, rarely a single point concerning Zionism, Palestine, Israel, and the Arabs which at one time or another has not been raised in the works of Steuart Erskine,[5] George Antonius,[6] J. M. N. Jeffries,[7] Clare Hollingsworth,[8] Ilene Beatty,[9] Elie Kedourie,[10] George Kirk,[11] and others; or which has not appeared in the memoranda and statements of Arab spokesmen in the last forty and more years before various Palestine commissions, the League of Nations, and the United Nations. Without difficulty, anybody reading this literature, which includes the Arab viewpoint, could pinpoint chapter and verse which correspond to the statements in Toynbee's writings. Thus, contrary to the innocent-sounding but clearly implied pretence to speak as part of or as spokesman of the majority of the human race, Toynbee does nothing more than restate the Arab position. In this way he actually excludes himself from a say in the matter, if he takes his own principle seriously, that the viewpoints of the parties directly concerned should be subjugated to those of the 'general consensus of disinterested parties' when judging their claims.

The 'general consensus of disinterested parties'—represented numerically and morally in the League of Nations and in the United Nations —has openly and repeatedly voiced its opinion in these matters in blatant contrast to everything which Toynbee appears to convey in their name. And it was Toynbee himself who helped to guide the consensus of the majority of 'disinterested parties' towards the recognition of Zionist principles and Zionist aims. His was an important share in the favourable decisions leading to the Balfour Declaration and to the Palestine Mandate. He was in those days not a 'disinterested party' because he then favoured Zionism, as he is not a 'disinterested party' today when favouring the Arab anti-Zionist arguments.

This attitude becomes more amazing and significant when it is revealed, as it will be, that in his serious and scholarly treatment of these same problems in the past, Toynbee repeatedly refuted, with great skill and with the help of convincing evidence, documentary, literary, and factual, precisely those Arab arguments which he now restates. It will be my endeavour to concentrate on this evidence and to quote as frequently as possible from his own writings. In this way I shall present the case of Toynbee v. Toynbee.

One may, of course, raise the point that a man is entitled to change his mind. I agree. That is the right and privilege of every person. A serious historian of Toynbee's reputation would have in such a case to state clearly his reasons for his change of mind, as he did repeatedly with regard to other issues.[12] But, astonishingly, with regard to Zionism he wishes to maintain that he 'had not changed his view'. We will show in the following pages the precise opposite. And to prove this contention I have accepted Toynbee's principle and put it as a maxim for this whole section, that his statements

> can be validated only if they are confronted with relevant facts and are confirmed by them.

2

A Friend of Zionism

Toynbee's interest in contemporary Near Eastern affairs dates back to the Turkish revolution in 1908.[13] But when, in the first year of World War I, in the midst of his academic career at Oxford (1912– 1915), he entered Government service for war work,[14] he concentrated on propaganda activities in the cause of the war in general, including the Turkish scene.

In the same year as he took on his war work he published among other writings two books that have a direct bearing on our issue: *Nationality and the War*[15] and *Armenian Atrocities, The Murder of a Nation*.[16] In both these books, Turkey's present and future occupied important sections. And through these sections ran the idea that the Turkish frontiers of the time were illogical and untenable. The people living within her borders would have to attain independence or, in any case, become free if the moral principles for which the war was fought were to be realised after the conclusion of hostilities.

These were still only the general outlines of the problems and it was to be about a year and a half before the issues became clearer and the proposals more specific. By 1917 Toynbee was able to present two more books on these very same Near Eastern problems and outline in them the future of the area and of the peoples as he visualised them. These books were: *The Murderous Tyranny of the Turks*[17] and *Turkey: A Past and a Future*.[18]

In these he did not confine himself to stating only the principles of the break-up of the Ottoman Empire, but also outlined how this should be done. He then suggested the establishment of four independent territorial units in the area: (1) Turkey proper; (2) Arabia, centred on Damascus; (3) A national home for the Armenians; (4) A national home for the Jews.

The part in *Turkey: A Past and a Future* appertaining to Zionism and the future of the Jewish homeland in Palestine was of such importance to him that he sought an approach to Dr Weizmann, the Zionist leader, to have it read before publication. Obviously this was done not only so that Dr Weizmann could read it but also approve of it. This part about Zionism was originally to appear in a somewhat shortened version in a magazine. One day in May, 1917, Dr Weizmann received out of the blue the following letter:[19]

> 14 Great Russell Mansions,
> Great Russell Street, W.C.
> 16.5.1917
>
> Dear Weizmann,
> Would you cast your eye over enclosed proof of part of Toynbee's first Round Table article. It will be abridged for the Magazine but will be published as a pamphlet also. Perhaps you will let me have it on Friday. We look forward to coming at 8. My sister will do her best not to fail.
> Toynbee is anxious to meet you—will you be at the B'nai Brith on Sunday?
>
> Yours,
> A. Zimmern

The article actually appeared in the London *Round Table* almost simultaneously with the book itself.[20] It is a concise, factual, and positive appraisal of the Zionists work and was written with warm support for the Zionist aim.

Subsequently, the Acting Editor of the *Round Table*, Reginald (later Sir Reginald) Coupland, wrote to Vladimir Jabotinsky:[21]

> 22 May 1917
> Please convey my compliments to Dr Weizmann and thank him for having been so kind as to read the proofs of the article for the *Round Table* dealing with Palestine.

The importance of the letter to Dr Weizmann can be better appreciated if we consider the background against which it was sent to him.

At the end of 1916 a new Government was formed in Britain headed by Lloyd George. As an innovation he instituted a small five-member War Cabinet which was to be entrusted with the whole control of the war and decisions on questions of high policy.[22] Balfour, though Foreign Secretary, was not a member of this Cabinet, but he frequently participated in its deliberations.[23] Next to the Prime Minister, Lord Milner exercised the strongest influence within the Cabinet.[24] These three, as we know, became the decisive instruments in the issuance of the Balfour Declaration.

Lloyd George also provided for the War Cabinet a special Secretariat, headed by Sir Maurice Hankey,[25] which, apart from its other objective, assisted the War Cabinet largely in formulating policies.[26] From the Zionist viewpoint the most prominent members or advisers of the Secretariat were Leopold Amery, Sir Mark Sykes, and Major Ormsby-Gore (later Lord Harlech). The specialist on foreign and imperial affairs in the Prime Minister's own Secretariat was Philip Kerr (later the Marquis of Lothian), the Editor of the *Round Table*.[27]

Toynbee's article appeared in the June, 1917, issue of the *Round Table*. The entire issue was devoted to post-war problems and had been discussed at a *Round Table* committee meeting in March of that year.[28] Toynbee, employed then in the Near Eastern section of the Foreign Office, was asked to write the article on Palestine. Thus his article became a major contribution to shaping and propagating the pro-Zionist policy of the War Cabinet, as Stein so aptly described:[29]

> All this might have been of no particular significance if *The Round Table* had not been what it was—the organ of a group of liberal-minded Imperialists, having Milner as its presiding genius and Philip Kerr and Amery among its members. Though Milner had joined the War Cabinet and both Kerr and Amery were, at a lower level, associated with the Government, all three had continued to take an active interest in *The Round Table*. The *Round Table* article, therefore, with its strong hint in the direction of a pro-Zionist policy, was more than an abstract expression of opinion; it meant that by March 1917, when its publication was approved, the case for British sponsorship of Zionism had made a serious impression on a group which had before the change of Government commanded more respect

than influence but was now represented in key-positions in, or on the fringe of, the inner circle.

That Toynbee's article constituted an important step towards the Balfour Declaration can also be believed from the fact that *The Times History of the War*, when explaining to its readers the essence of British policy in Palestine, patterned its description on the central part of this article,[30] including, for instance, the arguments against Trietsch[31] and the references to the Zionist Mule corps.[32] The *Times* survey was published after the issuance of the Balfour Declration and after the conquest (December, 1917) of Jerusalem[33] under the title: 'Palestine For the Jews', and concluded with the following words:[34] 'The future of Western Asia was shaping itself in the form of an entente between Arab, Armenian, and Jew'. Apart from this what I would call 'internal aspect', the general military and political situation also help us to understand the background of Toynbee's article and the approach to Dr Weizmann.

The year 1917 began and continued for a large part a bad year for the Allies in their war against the Central Powers. In its global effort to gather every friend, British propaganda was heavily concentrated on the United States in general and on American Jewry in particular. Leonard Stein has described these efforts in his comprehensive work on the Balfour Declaration.[35] At the time a gigantic struggle was waged by both belligerent camps to gain the help of world Jewry, primarily in America, which only in 1917 joined the war. Toynbee refers to these efforts as follows:[36]

> Another political factor which the First World War brought into play was a competition between the belligerents in courting the sympathy of Jewry. To win Jewish support—and, still more, to avert Jewish hostility—was an object of great moment to both sides. . . . The Jews were now an appreciable force in the domestic political life of Central and the Western European Powers alike, and of the United States to a still greater degree; and the feelings of the American Jewish community loomed large in the calculations of European belligerents who had come to realise that the United States would have the last word to speak in a European conflict and that this American last word might be influenced appreciably by the views of Jewish American citizens.

Reviewing the situation at this critical period, the official *History of the Peace Conference* stresses that in that year (1917)[37]

> The German General Staff desired to attach Jewish support yet more closely to the German side. . . . In fact in September 1917 the German Government were making the most serious efforts to capture the Zionist movement.

At long last the serious danger of this began to alarm official British Government circles, as is seen from the Foreign Office *Handbook*'s statement[38] that

> the Zionist movement is openly advocated in Germany as a means of spreading Teutonic influences—an aspect of the question which in this country is not sufficiently appreciated.

The urgency and seriousness of this situation is also confirmed by Toynbee himself. In this connection he then particularly stressed the necessity of not overlooking the anti-Russian feeling prevailing among Jews because of Russia's antisemitic record. And as Russia up to the Bolshevik Revolution in November, 1917, was part of the Allied camp, the Germans had an advantage on this point. Toynbee wrote:[39]

> In the course of the thirty-six years ending in A.D. 1917 the Jews throughout the World had come, with good reason, to look upon Russia as being Jewry's 'Enemy Number One', and, in the First World War, Germany, as the protagonist on the anti-Russian side whose victorious arms had liberated a large part of 'the Pale' from an Anti-semitic Russian rule, stood to gain those world-wide Jewish sympathies which the West European powers stood to lose as Russia's allies. After the German Army had pushed the Russian Army back in A.D. 1915 to a line approximating the Russo–Polish political frontier of A.D. 1793, the German General staff gave American Jewish journalists opportunities of seeing with their own eyes how the Russians had found vent for their rage at their shattering defeat at German hands by discharging it on an innocent and defenceless Jewish population in the territory that they had been forced to evacuate. For the West European Powers—and for the United States likewise, as soon as she became their co-belligerent—it was a matter of urgency to outmatch this card which Germany had acquired through conquering 'the Pale', and a trump card had been placed in their hands by the British conquest of Palestine which put it in their power to offer satisfaction to Zionist aspirations.

But this conquest of Palestine came only over a year later. Meanwhile the United States were not yet in the war and the situation was grim as the year 1917 set in. The British Government awoke at last to this urgent task.[40] It decided to embark in the first place upon a propaganda counter-offensive through the department concerned with propaganda relating to the Near Eastern areas. And so it came about that Toynbee was then chosen by the *Round Table* committee to write his article[41] and, in fact, was instructed, as he wrote,[42] 'by the United Kingdom Government' to get going. In describing the agitation of the British Government and the urgency of the counter-measures with which Toynbee dealt in the above-quoted sections of his *Study*, he omitted through his modesty to point out there and also later in his lengthy personal statement[43] his own important role in that counter-offensive against Germany's 'trump card'. His book *Turkey: A Past and A Future*, which he then put together, dealt in its Palestine section with this very important propaganda issue. In his efforts to stem the anti-Russian and perhaps pro-German tide among Jewry, particularly American Jewry, Toynbee selected a brochure to serve as a basis for his counter-stroke. This brochure, *Die Juden in der Tuerkei*,[44] was written by Davis Trietsch, a Zionist writer then living in Germany, who in it set out all the arguments in favour of close collaboration between world Jewry, and particularly the Zionists, and Germany. As this brochure contained all the arguments favouring a pro-Zionist orientation for Germany, it enabled Toynbee to deal with these arguments point by point and present the case to the contrary. We now quote some characteristic passages from Toynbee's answer:[45]

> . . . the Pale has been ravaged as well as liberated during the war[46] and the Jews of Germany have based an ingenious policy on this prospect, which is expounded thus by Dr Davis Trietsch, of Berlin:[47]
>
>> 'According to the most recent statistics about 12,900,000 out of the 14,300,000 Jews in the world speak German or Yiddish (*juedisch-deutsch*) as their mother-tongue. . . . But in its language, cultural orientation, and business relations the Jewish element from Eastern Europe (the Pale) is an asset to German influence. . . . In a certain sense the Jews are a Near Eastern element in Germany and a German element in Turkey.'

> Germany may not relish her kinship with these lost Teutonic tribes, but Dr Davis Trietsch makes a satirical exposure of such scruples:

'It used to be a stock argument against the Jews that "all nations" regarded them with hostility, but the War has brought upon the Germans such a superabundance of almost universal execration that the question which is the most despised of all nations—if one goes, not by justice and equity, but by the violence and extensiveness of the prejudice—might well now be altered to the Germans' disadvantage.

'In this unenviable competition for the prize of hate, Turkey, too, has a word to say, for the "unspeakable Turk" is a rhetorical commonplace of English politics.'

Having thus isolated the Jews from humanity and pilloried them with the German and the Turk, the writer expounds their function in the Turco-German system:

'Hitherto Germany has bothered herself very little about the Jewish emigration from Eastern Europe. People in Germany hardly realised that, through the annual exodus of about 100,000 German-speaking Jews to the United States and England, the empire of the English language and the economic system that goes with it is being enlarged, while a German asset is being proportionately depreciated. The War found the Jewry of Eastern Europe in process of being uprooted, and has enormously accelerated the catastrophe. Galicia and the western provinces of Russia, which between them contain many more than half the Jews in the world, have suffered more from the War than any other region. Jewish homes have been broken up by hundreds of thousands, and there is no doubt whatever that, as a result of the War, there will be an emigration of East European Jews on an unprecedented scale. . . . The disposal of the East European Jews will be a problem for Germany. . . . It will no longer do simply to close the German frontiers to them, and in view of the difficulties which would result from a wholesale migration of Eastern Jews into Germany itself, Germans will only be too glad to find a way out in the emigration of these Jews to Turkey—a solution extraordinarily favourable to the interests of all three parties concerned . . .'

And from this he passes to a wider vision:

'The German-speaking Jews abroad are a kind of German-speaking province which is well worth cultivation. Nine-tenths of the Jewish world speak German, and a good part of the remainder live in the Islamic world, which is Germany's friend, so that there are grounds for talking of a German protectorate over the whole of Jewry.'

By this exploitation of aversions, Dr Trietsch expects to deposit the Jews of the Pale over Western Asia as 'culture-manure' for a German harvest; and if the Jewish migration to Palestine had remained nothing more than a stream of refugees, he might possibly have succeeded in his purpose.

Toynbee then described the essence and aims of the Zionist Organisation in establishing 'a nation' in 'its Motherland' and showed that the Zionist programme was not a negative[48] concern for 'a stream of refugees' but a positive striving for a national home—in contrast to Trietsch's suggestion.[49] We reproduce this important statement on Zionism elsewhere. But Toynbee in his further analysis of the brochure also denied Trietsch's contention of the importance of the German language in the effort to win over Jewry for German plans in Turkey. He proved his case by referring to the 'language struggle in Palestine' of the Zionists before the outbreak of World War I:

> . . . the revival of Hebrew as the living language of the Palestinian Jews . . . brought them [*i.e.* the Zionists] in conflict with the Germanising tendency.

After giving some details of the struggle between German-speaking and Hebrew-speaking schools, supported by Zionists, he continues:

> the Germanising party was compelled to accept a compromise which was in effect a victory for the Hebrew language.
>
> Dr Trietsch himself accepts this settlement, but does not abandon his idea:

> 'It was certainly impossible to expect Spanish and Arabic speaking Jews[50] to submit in their own Jewish country to the hegemony of the German language . . . Only Hebrew could become the common vernacular language of the scattered fragments of Jewry drifting back to Palestine from all the countries of the world. But . . . in addition to Hebrew, to which they are more and more inclined, the Jews must have a world-language (*Weltsprache*) and this can only be German.'

Anyone acquainted with the language-ordinances of Central Europe will feel that this suggestion veils a threat. . . . What is the outlook for Palestine after the War? If the Ottoman pretension survives, the menace from Turkish Nationalism and German resentment is grave.

In order to strengthen his case against Trietsch and against German-Turkish influence in Palestine, Toynbee then made two significant references. In the first he wrote:[51]

> Dr Trietsch admits that Jewish colonisation in Palestine was retarded because 'the leading French and British Jews remained under the impression of the Armenian massacres' (of 1885–7) 'as presented by the anti-Turkish, French and British Press. . . . In reality, the butcheries of Armenians in Constantinople were a convincing proof that the Jews in the Ottoman Empire were safe, for . . . not a hair on a Jewish head was touched.' One wonders how he will exorcise the 'impression' of 1915.[52]

And the second reference reads:

> As early as 1912 the German Vice-Consul at Jaffa betrayed his annoyance at the progress which Zionism was making. He admits indeed that 'the falling off in trade last year would have been greater still than it was, if the economic penetration of Palestine were not reinforced by an idealistic factor in the shape of Zionism'; but he is piqued at the 'Jewish national vanity' which makes it advisable for German firms to display their advertisements in Palestine in the Hebrew language and character.

There cannot be any doubt that Toynbee in these pages takes a pro-Zionist stand and is outspoken in Zionism's defence, injecting in the process quite a dose of cynicism. But he not only remained critical of the German orientation and rejected it, he also tried to persuade his readers, primarily in America, of the importance of supporting the Allies, who alone would be able and willing to fulfil the Zionist aims. And it was his thesis—Allied support of Zionism, as against German attempts to capture it—which finally prevailed, as he himself confirmed long after the event.[53] As at the time of writing his book, in the middle of 1917, Toynbee was not yet sure that the Allies would heed this advice, he concluded this part of his argument as follows:[54]

> As for the British side of the question, we may consult Dr Trietsch.

> 'There are possibilities,' he urges, 'in a German protectorate over the Jews as well as over Islam. Smaller national units than the 14 1/3 million Jews have been able to do Germany vital injury or service, and, while the Jews have no national state, their dispersion over the whole world, their high standard of culture, and their peculiar abilities lend them a weight that is worth more in the balance than many larger national masses which occupy a compact area of their own.'

Other Powers than Germany may take these possibilities to heart.

And they did take them to heart, precisely as Toynbee suggested. The Balfour Declaration, issued some four months later, was the first outcome of this policy, and the subsequent Palestine Mandate, incorporating this declaration, the second.

We have seen that Toynbee helped to create the atmosphere in England and the free world during World War I which led to the issuance of these important decisions. But this was not all. In 1919, when the vital question of the future of Palestine came before the victorious Powers, Toynbee was one of the experts on the Orient in the British delegation at the Paris Peace Conference.[55] While there, he met Dr Weizmann.[56] And while so far no record has been made available of any previous meeting or of their conversations in Paris, it can be assumed that it was to no small degree the presentation of the Zionist issue by Dr Weizmann which caused Toynbee's ensuing admiration for the Zionist leader.[57] Also in Paris, he wrote the following letter to Nahum Sokolow, another leading Zionist spokesman before the Peace Conference, on receipt of the first volume of his *History of Zionism*:[58]

> 7.3.1919
> British Delegation
> Paris

Dear Dr Sokolow,

It is extremely kind of you to give me a copy of your book, and I shall look forward to the second volume which you tell me is to follow.

I hope there will be a third—unless 'Zionism' ends with the accomplishment of its aim and you give a new name to the work of national reconstruction in liberated Palestine.

The next stage should be the most interesting, as I hope it will be the most prosperous of all—though I cannot help thinking that, on looking back, Jewry will be most proud of the first stage of Zionism in which, in the face of so many obstacles, it reached the point it has come to now.

With very many thanks once more for your kindness in sending me the book.

> Yours sincerely,
> Arnold J. Toynbee

This letter shows, of course, more than 'diplomatic' sympathy, it shows satisfaction not only over the work done by the Zionists but also, and in the first place, with the Zionists' aims. The hope for 'the accomplishment of its aim', which was the national reconstruction' (one should not overlook the prefix 're', which Toynbee uses here and which is of great importance for the issue) 'in liberated Palestine', leaves no doubt about this. Moreover, Providence permitted Toynbee to see his hope of almost half a century ago fulfilled: 'a new name' was given to the work of 'national reconstruction in liberated Palestine'—the State of Israel.

And although his sympathetic assistance towards their attainment helped the Zionist aims to become established as facts, it should be pointed out that even subsequently, when the actual work in Palestine was about to begin, Toynbee still rendered service to the Zionist cause. For instance, he attended the fifth meeting of the 'Advisory Committee to the Palestine Office', which was held on May 10, 1919, at the residence of Herbert (later Lord) Samuel,[59] in the course of which his colleague Commander Hogarth declared:

> There might have been a certain objection to himself and Mr Toynbee being present today, since they were to form part of the Commission to Palestine. He was told, however, by Paris that there was no objection, but he thought that it was in the interest of the Committee and obviously necessary not to allow it to be known that they were here.

The Future of Palestine and Zionism

Having touched on Toynbee's help to Zionism during World War I and afterwards, it now seems pertinent to investigate what he understood to be Zionism in those years when propagating the idea and suggesting its implementation. It has been mentioned[60] that already in 1915 he published a book, *Nationality and the War*, in which he dealt with post-war problems as they would apply, *inter alia*, also to the Near East. It was his first study on this issue. In it he laid down the principle that the peoples within the Ottoman Empire would have to attain independence or, in any case, become free, if the moral principles for which the war was fought were to be realised after its conclusion. But were all the constituent parts of Turkey ripe for freedom or independence? Toynbee wrote:[61]

There are some units, however, so raw in their growth or so deeply sunk in decay as to lack the attribute of sovereignty altogether—units which through want of population, wealth, spiritual energy, or all three together are unable to keep the spark of vitality aglow. Such dead units are the worst danger that threatens the peace of the world: in conflict, a vacuum into which the current of life swirls like a maelstrom. In these 'no-man's-lands' where no sovereignty exists, our international organ[62] can and must assert its own sovereignty against the sovereign states outside . . .

(a) In every such area the standing international executive should regulate immigration from over-populated sovereign units—

(b) It should likewise regulate the influx of capital . . .

(c) In areas where the pressure of spiritual energy is so low that the population cannot save itself by its own efforts from political anarchy, the international executive should be prepared to step in and organise 'strong government'.

Into which of these categories did the Palestine area fall? Was it ripe for freedom, self-government, and independence, or was it one of the 'no-man's-lands'?

At that time the term 'Palestine' was politically and administratively not in use; the area was identified only as Southern Syria, although even the popular term 'Syria' was no more than a vague designation of a territory which neither physically not politically constituted an entity.[63] Consequently, the only way to determine the pertinent facts about 'Palestine' of that time, its population, its economic strength, its ethnic and religious divergences, and its most suitable form of government, was by way of a selection from general description of Syria. Only then was it possible to assign the Palestine area to one of the categories into which Toynbee divided post-war Turkey. His writings at this period (1915), together with the later crop of his Near Eastern studies (1917), offer sufficient evidence that 'Palestine' fell clearly into the 'no-man's-land' category. This conclusion was in full accord with the opinion then prevailing in British official circles, to whom Toynbee belonged as an employee of the Foreign Office. As is known, the Government during World War I prepared *Handbooks*[64] which subsequently became guide-books for the British delegation at the Paris Peace Conference. In many respects the similarity between Toynbee's writing of those years and that of the official *Handbooks* is striking.[65]

These latter were compiled by the Historical Commission of the Foreign Office, of which Toynbee was not a member.[66] I therefore inquired of Toynbee about the meaning of these similarities and he suggests[67] as

> the most likely explanation . . . that these similarities derive from a common stock of general ideas that were current, before and during the World War I, in liberal circles in Britain.

But, apart from these current general ideas, Toynbee, no doubt, also expressed the understanding and attitude towards Turkey, the Arabs, and Zionism then prevailing in official circles. And so we see that with regard to the Palestine area one of these Government *Handbooks* offered for the period before World War I the following description:[68]

> There are no statistics by which birth- and death-rates, with the rate of increase of the population, may be determined, but the death-rate is known to be high. Emigration has seriously drained the country for many years, although, on the contrary, some towns of western Palestine have lately increased rapidly (Jerusalem, Jaffa, Haifa, Nazareth). Since 1880 the population of the coast towns generally has constantly increased in population. . . . The most numerous immigrants since 1880 have been Jews (between 60,000 and 70,000), who have settled in Palestine and are the chief cause of the modern growth of Jerusalem and Jaffa.
>
> The people west of the Jordan are not Arabs, but only Arab-speaking. The bulk of the population are *fellahin*; that is to say, agricultural workers owning land as a village community or working land for the Syrian effendi. In the Gaza district they are mostly of Egyptian origin; elsewhere they are of the most mixed race. They have for centuries been ground down, overtaxed, and bullied by the Turk, and still more by the Arab-speaking Turkish minor official and the Syrian and Levantine landowner.

It will be noted with interest that the two principal statements in this official *Handbook* are repeated almost verbatim in Toynbee's book of the same period:[69]

> There are Arabs in name who have nothing Arabic about them but their language—most of the peasants in Syria are such . . .
>
> Syrians and Armenians have been emigrating for the last quarter of a century, and during the same period the Jews, whose birthright in Western Asia is as ancient as theirs, have been returning to their native land . . .

The description quoted in the *Handbook* contains all the elements of Toynbee's 'no-man's-land' territories: these Arabic-speaking people in Palestine were obviously 'dead units', 'unable to keep the spark of vitality aglow', and definitely 'lacked the attribute of sovereignty'. A vast contemporary literature exists describing the abandonment of the country to the desert by its Arab inhabitants. It would be futile even to attempt to quote; any book of the period, chosen at random, could be consulted for this description.[70]

Nothing shows the poor state of the Arabs' position in Palestine clearer than the bare figures. At the time when the Balfour Declaration was issued (November, 1917) there lived only 10 to 15 people per square kilometre in the Palestine area; in the most densely populated Jerusalem district, 25 people per square kilometre, in contrast, for instance, to neighbouring Lebanon, where at that time 159 people lived on a square kilometre.[71] And, most characteristically, in the same period less than 12 per cent of the total Palestine area was brought under agricultural development.[72] In quoting these figures of people and land it should not be forgotten that they already include the new Jewish immigration and colonisation, which had proceeded for about three decades before that time (1880), and by 1917 formed a considerable part of the increase in the total percentage.[73]

This was the state of affairs in the Arab sector of Palestine not only in the decades before World War I, but as a pattern which for centuries before that period had characterised the attitude of the Arabic-speaking Palestinian inhabitants towards their soil.[74] This obviously shows on the Arab side an absence of love of the land which is the precondition of caring for it and cultivating it; not to mention the pride which the people of a place in general have for their native soil. This is a point to which, years later, Winston Churchill, as Colonial Secretary, drew the attention of Parliament:[75]

> I am told that the Arabs would have done it themselves. Who is going to believe that? Left to themselves, the Arabs of Palestine would not in a thousand years have taken effective steps towards irrigation and electrification of Palestine. They would have been quite content to dwell—a handful of philosophic people—in the wasted sun-scorched plains, letting the waters of the Jordan continue to flow unbridled and unharassed into the Dead Sea.

If moral values and human rights are not to remain wishful verbiage —and together with Toynbee we have accepted them as basic principles of our analysis—then somewhere from these humanitarian and moral laws conclusions must be drawn about the neglect of a country which prevents it from becoming useful to mankind. It was E. G. Hirsch who over seventy years ago laid down a principle now generally accepted:[76]

> Wherever the right of property clashes with a duty toward humanity, the former has no credentials that are entitled to consideration.

And it was Toynbee himself, as we have seen, who warned us that this sort of neglect of one's country's soil creates a vacuum and thus constitutes

> the worst danger that threatens the peace of the world.

It is in order to prevent this very same danger that Toynbee claims the right for 'disinterested parties'[77] to have a say in the Palestine issue, to prevent the outbreak of

> a world war that might destroy the human race.

In view of the great importance in general of the cultivation and development of the soil in the interest of people's well-being, and by that fact of peace, and in particular, in view of the land problem which Toynbee comes to stress in connection with the Arab refugee problem, it is imperative to emphasise these basic facts about the conditions in Palestine as they existed when the Zionist work began and which Toynbee himself made full use of when, basing himself on them, he advanced his support for Zionism. The utter neglect by the Arab population of the land (not only with regard to cultivation) can be compared to a mother's neglect of her own children, a problem that greatly concerns civilised society. In a report of the United States Children's Bureau we read:[78]

> Abandonment, substantial and continuous neglect, and parental incapacity to discharge parental responsibility should be sufficient grounds for the rights of neglectful parents to be terminated for the welfare of the child.

No doubt such were the considerations, or similar, which in those years induced Toynbee to devise his 'no-man's-land' theory. They

made him hope for an improvement of these conditions for the sake
of world peace. With this in mind, he therefore made his suggestions
pertaining to the regulation from outside of 'immigration' and 'the
influx of capital' into such areas. Once these poured into a country,
the 'dead units' would be helped to improve their lot. From this basic
concept Toynbee assessed the Zionist work in Palestine. It was found
that it improved the Arab's lot while building up the Jewish National
Home there. Through this, he hoped,[79]

> the Arabs should receive a sufficient share of any additional material re-
> sources of the country, which might be produced by development, to
> enable them to provide for their natural increase . . . even with an
> improvement in the standard, if the existing standard were lower than what
> might be regarded as reasonable minimum.

We shall see that, like all the objective observers of the development
in Palestine in subsequent years, Toynbee expressed every satisfaction
that this great material improvement of the Arabs in the country had
taken place to an unexpectedly successful degree.

But it was not only the neglect of the land that led Toynbee to his
conclusions as regards the importance of the Jewish National Home for
the interests of the Arabs themselves, weighty though such a material
consideration may have been. One might advance the argument that
the Arabs' needs could have been alleviated, without establishing a
Jewish National Home, by simply providing material support and
capital for an underdeveloped area. But this obviously did not apply
in this case. For, as Toynbee makes it clear in his outline of the 'no-
man's-land' theory, there were more basic problems involved than the
material aspect, and more fundamental reasons attached to it for these
units to have become 'dead relics'. One of these, probably the most important, according to him, is the absence in these people of any 'spiritual
energy'. This, he believes, becomes a vital factor[80]

> where the pressure of spiritual energy is so low that the population cannot
> save itself by its own efforts from political anarchy.

The combination of lack of spiritual energy and the great poverty of
Toynbee's 'no-man's-land' inhabitants appeared two years later in the
following version of the Government *Handbook*, according to which,[81]

These Arabs in Palestine . . . have little, if any, national sentiment, and would probably welcome any stable form of government which would guarantee to them reasonable security and enjoyment of fruits of their labour.

This formulation has a striking resemblance to a statement made by Toynbee some two years previously when he laid down as one of the preconditions of qualifying for independence the active expression of the 'spiritual energy', which ranked as another term for a 'national will', the 'spirit of nationality', or 'national sentiment'. He wrote:[82]

We want to break up Turkey but we assure them that peace can only be secured by giving free play to every manifestation of the spirit of nationality.

When surveying the situation in the Ottoman Empire from this point of view, he had to confess that the spirit of nationality was absent, not only from the Arabs in Palestine but from other groups as well. He wrote:[83]

The area within her [Turkey's] frontiers is a veritable cockpit of nationalities so mutilated that they have never even achieved that unity which is the essential preliminary to a national life.

And in this situation he did not see any advantage in the fact that these people spoke one language. He stressed[84] that the common use of Arabic did not carry with it a corresponding sense of national solidarity.

3
Turkey's Break-up: Four New States

It was, therefore, a most difficult task for him to delineate the areas which, according to his own definition, he regarded as suitable for independence. As pointed out,[85] he saw only four units possessed of the national will and capable of establishing their own nations: the Turks proper in Anatolia, the Armenians in their region, the Arabs in the 'New Arabia' centred on Syria, and the Jews in Palestine. He was also certain about the Jews' ability to establish their National Home in Palestine. He wrote in 1917:[86]

> Syrians and Armenians have been emigrating for the last quarter of a century, and during the same period the Jews, whose birthright in Western Asia is as Ancient as theirs, have been returning to their native land. . . .
>
> The most remarkable result of this movement has been the foundation of flourishing agricultural colonies. Their struggle for existence has been hard; the pioneers were students or tradesfolk of the Ghetto, unused to outdoor life and ignorant of Near Eastern conditions. . . . As a result of this enlightened policy the number of colonies has risen to about forty, with 15,000 inhabitants in all and 110,000 acres of land, and these figures do not do full justice to the importance of the colonising movement. The 15,000 Jewish agriculturists are only 12½ per cent of the Jewish population in Palestine, and 2 per cent of the total population of the country; but they are the most active, intelligent element, and the only element which is rapidly increasing. Again, the land they own is only 2 per cent of the total area of Palestine; but it is between 8 and 14 per cent of the area under cultivation, and there are vast uncultivated tracts which the Jews can and will

reclaim, as their numbers grow—both by further colonisation and by natural increase, for the first generation of colonists have already proved their ability to multiply in the Promised Land. Under this new Jewish husbandry Palestine has begun to recover its ancient prosperity . . . there is no fear that, as immigration increases, the Arab element will be crowded to the wall. There are still only two Jewish colonies beyond the Jordan.

But will immigration continue now that the Jew of the Pale has been turned at a stroke into the free citizen of a democratic country.[87] Probably it will actually increase, for the Pale has been ravaged as well as liberated during the war. . . . But in the last twenty years this Jewish movement has become a positive thing—no longer a flight from the Pale but a remembrance of Zion—and Zionism has already challenged and defeated the policy which Dr Trietsch represents.[88] 'The object of Zionism,' it was announced in the *Basle Programme* drawn up by the first Zionist Congress in 1897, 'is to establish for the Jewish people a publicly and legally assured home in Palestine.' For the Zionists Jewry is a nation, and to become like other nations it needs a Motherland. In the Jewish colonies in Palestine they see not merely a successful social enterprise but the visible symbol of a body politic. . . .

Here, then, are peoples risen from the past to do what the Turks cannot and the Germans will not in Western Asia. There is much to be done. . . . But the Jews, Syrians, Armenians are equal to their task, and, with the aid of the foreign nations on whom they can count, they will certainly accomplish it. The future of Palestine, Syria, and Armenia is thus assured.

No Independence for Palestine Arabs

In his analysis of the situation and in the outline of the future of the diverse fragments of the Ottoman Empire Toynbee did not mention one word about the Palestine Arabs as a possible element, unit, or group, to be considered for autonomy, self-determination, or independence. In the above-quoted lengthy reference to the past and future Jewish National Home, Toynbee showed that he was not only aware of the existence of Arabs in Palestine but that he also expected them to live within the area of the Jewish National Home. He even comforted these Arabs with the assurance that

there is no fear that, as [Jewish] immigration increases, the Arab element will be crowded to the wall. There are still only two Jewish colonies beyond the Jordan, where the Hauran—under the Roman Empire a cornland with a dozen cities—has been opened up by the railway and is waiting again for the plough.

Reading this last statement with due care, one can discern two important facets which to this day play an important part in the controversy over the extent of the Jewish National Home and the position of the Arabs in it. In the first place, it appears that when Toynbee spoke about the emptiness of the Hauran and its suitability for colonisation, he took it for granted that Transjordan forms part of Palestine and would be part of the Jewish National Home. He thus accepted the borders of the historic Palestine territory, as later laid down in the Palestine Mandate;[89] and which, after the surrender of the Mandate by Britain, was unequivocally claimed by the Zionist-Revisionists as embracing the area on 'both banks of the Jordan', *i.e.* including Transjordan.[90]

Toynbee's statement may also have had another meaning. In the context in which it appears in the quotation above, it may tend to imply a transfer of the Arab population from one part of Palestine to another, *i.e.* into the eastern sector, should Jewish immigration increase in the western part to such an extent that Arabs living there become 'crowded to the wall'. In this case, Toynbee would appear more radical and extreme than any Zionist. For no responsible Zionist ever thought of the establishment of the Jewish National Home and of the Jewish State on any other basis than in terms of the existing Arab population in Palestine remaining where it was. There was only one person, Toynbee's countryman and well-known author, Israel Zangwill, not a member of the Zionist Organisation, who at the same time, 1917, suggested a similar transfer of Arabs from Palestine, although in a much more radical way.[91]

The solution of intricate problems through resettlement or population exchange is not so far-fetched as far as Toynbee is concerned. We still remember his warm welcome of the arrangements regarding the resettlement of Near Eastern Greeks after their defeat at the hands of the Turks.[92] 'The success of the scheme for settling refugees in Greece', he wrote at the time,[93] 'showed what could be done'. And he also praised in similar terms the resettlement of Bulgarian refugees.[94]

It is anyhow not without irony to find the likelihood or possibility of such a concept in Toynbee's works as regards Palestine Arabs, especially if it is kept in mind how bitterly he fairly recently crusaded against the realisation of this idea by the force of circumstances.

Whatever interpretation, however, is put on this particular aspect in Toynbee's outline of the Zionist plans in 1917, it is undeniable that he thought in terms of a Jewish National Home in Palestine and not of an Arab National Home. It is, therefore, hard to understand how, in the light of this, Toynbee can say, thirty years later, that[95]

> if the local Arabs had been allowed to exercise the human right of choosing a political regime themselves they would have voted for immediate independence.

This sounds as if Toynbee had not only forgotten his own earlier statements and the role which he then played, but also the literature and the facts of life which without doubt he cannot claim not to know. Have new facts now been discovered that would show that the Palestine area of Syria was in 1917 a flourishing Arab land, Arab national sentiment was aglow, and, far from being 'no-man's-land' types, the Arabic-speaking people there were ready, capable and willing to vote and to proclaim their independence? If such new facts exist, Toynbee does not reveal them to his readers. How is it, therefore, that he suddenly knows, because it happens to fit in with his contemporary requirements, what he did not know at the time? Or what he did not know in 1927, ten years after he had written his long, above-quoted statement, when he declared:[96]

> The [Arab] people . . . would have preferred, apparently, that no mandate regime at all should be imposed upon them or, as a second choice, that a single mandate for the whole of 'Syria' (in the popular sense) should be conferred upon some Power other than France.

This could even imply that the Arabs would have wanted Syria to be incorporated in the Palestine Mandate. But, anyhow, there is no trace of a desire for independence by the Palestinian Arabs in 1917. Nor for that matter in 1927, other than statements made in those later years by anti-Zionist propagandists, Arab, British, Fascist, and Communist. But obviously Toynbee wrote these lines in 1927 retrospectively in the light of the events which he followed from the end of World War I and right up to that year, when resentment against the French in Syria had grown[97] and when Arab propaganda had pursued the line which he then recorded. But there is no doubt that he was fully aware of the fact that this was primarily a propaganda effort by which the Arabs attempted to prevent the establishment of the Jewish National Home rather than create something of their own. As he then wrote:[98]

> The Palestinian Arabs were seeking self-government as a means to prevent the establishment of a Jewish National Home in Palestine and to re-entering into a political union with their own countrymen in other ex-Ottoman territories.

Even if these statements are taken at their face value, it is clear that not even in 1929, twelve years after the Balfour Declaration, were the Arabs, in Toynbee's words, ready to proclaim their independence, as almost forty years later he wished us to believe. On the contrary, all the indications point to the fact that even if Arab opposition had prevented the establishment of the Jewish National Home, and Palestine had remained as it had been throughout all those centuries in the past, the local Arabs would never have proclaimed or even 'voted' for independence. At best, in Toynbee's own formula, they would have become part of another Arab entity.

It may suffice to refer to one out of a host of possible other statements made at the time to show the Arab stand in those years, above all a statement from a source unfriendly to Zionism. It is known that British military circles in the Middle East were during and soon after World War I the main opponents on the spot of the Jewish National Home.[99] Yet one of their top men, the then (1919) Chief Political Officer of the Egyptian Expeditionary Force in Palestine, General G. F. Clayton, participated in a meeting with leaders of the Jewish Agency in London[100] and reported that a

> declaration of the *fait accompli* [of the Balfour Declaration] would probably be accepted peaceably by at least 75 per cent of the Arab population.

This confirms the assertion of the Government *Handbook*[101] that 'the Arabs would accept any stable form of government', and also confirms Toynbee's original statement of 1917 and, above all, his basic theory of the 'no-man's-land' people, who were unable to express their will because they were neither nationally unified nor did they exhibit any

sign of national consciousness and were therefore incapable of directing
their own affairs.

The Absent National Consciousness

The absence of any sign of national consciousness in the Palestine Arabs
is not a phenomenon confined to those years gone by. It continued.
Jon Kimche pointed to this remarkable aspect among Arabs in general,
recalling[102] that in 1956, during the Suez War, ordinary fellahin who
were captured, when asked to give their nationality, replied: 'I am an
Arab'. This looked like the emergence of national consciousness. But
Kimche wondered what the simple fellah soldiering in the mountains
of Yemen would reply when taken prisoner by either the Yemen Royal
or the Yemen Republican forces, or by the Egyptian occupying forces.
Would he still say to these Arabs, 'I am an Arab'? He obviously would
not. For, as Kimche concluded,

> Arab national consciousness is only strong when it faces the Zionist and
> Israeli, it grows weaker as it turns towards the aggressive Western and
> Soviet Powers, and weakest when it is confronted with fellow Arabs.

This doubt about the national consciousness of Arabs in general, in
World War I, is reflected in Toynbee's plan quoted above for creating
four independent units after the break-up of Turkey. But in this ill-
favoured picture one should in all fairness point out the contrast between
Arab and Arab. It is the Palestine Arab who as a matter of course
emerges at the bottom of the ladder. Thus even in World War I a
leader arose in Hedjaz, King Hussein, capable of concluding an important political and military agreement with Britain;[103] as there arose
another leader in Saudi Arabia, Ibn Saud, representing his Wahabite
people, equally capable of concluding an important political and military agreement with Britain.[104] And in Syria proper, a National Committee was created in Damascus which[105]

> had made overtures to the British Government, employing as their inter-
> mediary the Amir Husayn of the Hidjaz[106] in the hope of throwing off
> Turkish rule by force and winning national independence for all the Arab
> provinces of the Ottoman Empire with the assistance of the Allies.

At that time, as stated, Palestine was still part of Syria, and Syrian leaders used to make statements and claim rights of a political, cultural, and other nature on behalf of the whole of the Syrian area, Palestine included. As the *Report* of the Royal Commission confirms:[107]

> ... the Arabs ... regarded Syria as one country and in Syria the Emir's leadership had been accepted.

At the Paris Peace Conference then the Arabs were represented by the son of the Emir Hussein referred to, Emir Feisal, their wartime revolutionary leader, and by a rival Syrian delegation, headed by Chakri Ganem. When Feisal appeared before the Council of Five at Pichon's room at the Quai d'Orsay, on February 6, 1919, he referred to Palestine as follows:[108]

> Palestine for its universal character he left on one side for the mutual consideration of all parties interested. With this exception he asked for the independence of the Arabic areas enumerated in his memorandum.

The minutes of this meeting record Toynbee's presence in his capacity as adviser to the British Delegation.[109]

Three weeks later, Feisal wrote in a letter to Felix Frankfurter:[110]

> The Arabs, especially the educated among us, look with deepest sympathy on the Zionist Movement. Our Deputation here in Paris is fully acquainted with the proposals submitted yesterday by the Zionist Organisation to the Peace Conference, and we regard them as moderate and proper. We will do our best, in so far as we are concerned, to help them through; we will wish the Jews a hearty welcome home.

On his return home from the Paris Peace Conference, Feisal addressed a conference of Syrian notables in Damascus (May 9, 1919), among them also representatives from Palestine areas. He put questions to them, and they replied:[111]

> Q. Do you approve of all that we have done?
> A. Yes, good. (Great applause).
> Q. Are these deeds satisfactory to the people?
> A. Quite satisfactory. (Great acclamation.)
> Q. Is what we have done in conformity with the wishes of the nation?
> A. Quite so; exactly. (Great applause.)

In the end they elected him with great enthusiasm to remain their leader also in the future.

This attitude was in full conformity with the sentiments expressed too by the native Syrian delegation, which appeared a week later before the Peace Conference. Although they opposed the incorporation of Syria into Feisal's unified Arab State, with regard to Palestine their spokesman stated (February 13, 1919):[112]

> Palestine is incontestably the Southern portion of our country. The Zionists claim it. We have suffered too much from sufferings resembling theirs, not to throw open wide to them the doors of Palestine. All those among them who are opposed in certain retrograde countries are welcome. Let them settle in Palestine but in an autonomous Palestine connected with Syria by the sole bond of federation. Will not a Palestine enjoying wide internal autonomy be for them a sufficient guarantee?
>
> If they form a majority there, they will be the rulers. If they are in the minority, they will be represented in the government in proportion to their numbers.

As during the Feisal statement, so also during the statement read by Chakri Ganem on behalf of the native Syrian representation, Toynbee was present in his capacity as expert in the British Delegation.[113] There is, therefore, no room for any possible misunderstanding on his part about the position of the Palestine Arabs at this decisive time. Beyond any doubt, the delegations and spokesmen of the Arabs who appeared before the Peace Conference did not mention in their memoranda and statements Arab independence in Palestine, or Arab autonomy, or even their entering into a union with any other Arab State. On the contrary, these Arab representatives showed themselves more than willing to accept the prevailing situation in the area and to accept the justice of Jewish rights in Palestine. Moreover, as their statements here quoted show, they promised to help in this direction, Toynbee's assertion to the contrary notwithstanding.

They Refused to Fight

There is a further aspect of the issue arising out of the absence of 'any manifestation of the spirit of nationality', which Toynbee has defined as a minimum required for the right to independence. As stated, the Arabs of Palestine showed no signs of interest in their own national existence, never mind a land of their own, and extended this lack of interest to their native soil by neglecting it. They also refused to take part in any struggle for the improvement of their lot, both as individuals and collectively. As a result of the authorisation of the above-mentioned 'Arab National Committees', King Hussein in 1915 entered into a correspondence[114] with Britain, represented by Sir Henry MacMahon. In subsequent years these letters became the subject of heated discussions which have not yet died down. The chief interest in the debate surrounding them concentrated on the delineation of the borders: whether Palestine was or was not included in the area allocated to the Arabs for their independent State. It is now an accepted fact that, notwithstanding the vague vocabulary, Palestine was not included.[115] But in the controversy about 'certain fine-drawn points of phraseology and terminology'[116] concerned with geographical lines, national frontiers, and the old Turkish administration, it is generally overlooked that the MacMahon-Hussein correspondence also contains clauses which are not less important than those on the geographical area. Some of these clauses, moreover, are preconditions for validating the agreement. Thus, one of the documents, constituting an integral part of the agreement, stipulated active Arab participation and assistance in the war as a precondition of British support for future Arab independence:[117]

> . . . it is most essential that you [King Hussein] should spare no effort to attach all the Arab peoples to our united cause and urge them to afford no assistance to our enemies.
>
> It is on the success of these efforts and on the more active measures which the Arabs may hereafter take in support of our cause, when the time for action comes, that the permanence and strength of our agreement must depend.[118]

Hussein promised to live up to these conditions and later reported the steps he had taken to fulfil them. Nowhere in this whole correspondence, or in all the reports on the subsequent military uprising of the Arabs under Hussein's son, Feisal, or in the entire literature concerned with the history of that venture, are Palestine Arabs referred to as participants or even as desirous of taking part in the struggle for their liberation. The late Governor of Sinai, C. S. Jarvis, wrote with reference to this phenomenon:[119]

> The Syrians as a people did nothing whatever towards the Arab cause . . .

beyond holding secret meetings and talks. The inhabitants of Palestine did rather less than this.

And a participant in the operations in the Near Eastern theatre of war, Philip Graves, was astonished to find that[120]

the Palestinians confined themselves to deserting in large numbers to the British, who fed and clothed them and paid for the maintenance of many thousands of such prisoners of war, few indeed of whom could be induced to obtain their liberty by serving in the Sherifian Army.

On the other hand, as Toynbee wrote:[121]

the Amir Husayn of the Hidjaz . . . revolted against the Ottoman Government, with British aid, in the name of Arab Nationalism against Ottoman Imperialism and also in the name of Islam against the impiety of Young Turk Free Masons and Free-thinkers.

In the years following World War I the claims of Arab groups outside Palestine for independence and Statehood were in the main based on the argument that they had fulfilled the condition laid down in the MacMahon-Hussein correspondence with respect to their military assistance against the common enemy, the Turk.[122] 'After having taken part in this war against the Caliphate itself,' Feisal wrote to Lloyd George on September 21, 1919,[123] 'the Arabs at least expect that their rights should be taken into consideration.' And on a number of other occasions he repeated these claims during the negotiations for the establishment of Arab Statehood.[124] Also his brother, Emir (later King) Abdullah of Transjordan, cabled Lloyd George on October 4, 1919:[125]

King Hussein and Arabs only joined Allies to secure their independence relying on *bona fides* of Allied nations and their rulers.

Summarising this aspect of the question, Toynbee pointed out:[126]

Like Hussein, the other Arab rulers in the Ottoman sphere in the Peninsula *who revolted against the Turks during War 1914–1918* all gained their independence.

Speaking on the same theme, Winston Churchill once pointed out:[127]

I cannot feel that we have accorded to the Arab race unfair treatment after the support which they gave us in the late War. The Palestinian Arabs, of course, were for the most part fighting against us, but elsewhere over vast

regions inhabited by the Arabs, independent Arab kingdoms and princi-
palities have come into being such as had never been known in Arab history
before.

On this count, too, the Palestine Arabs forfeited any claim, even if
they had had one. The MacMahon-Hussein agreement clearly stipulated the participation of 'all the Arab peoples to our united cause',
as a precondition for independence. Moreover, that correspondence
also stipulated that 'no assistance to our enemies [the Turks]' be
rendered. And yet the Palestine Arabs did not lift a finger for their
liberation, but those led by Hussein, Feisal, Abdullah, and the other
rulers were able to establish their independence after the Allied victories.
On that basis they subsequently proclaimed nine independent Arab
States. As Toynbee had put it,[128]

> Here nationalism, assisted by politics of West European Powers, seemed to
> be achieving at one stroke the results which had demanded a century of
> effort in the Balkan Peninsula; nine independent or potentially indepen-
> dent Arab states were now arising in the area, and the political map was
> visibly transformed.

At this point, while concerning ourselves with the elements of Toynbee's 'no-man's-land' theory, we are not viewing these political successes from a military point of view. After all, the military value of the
Arab rising is still problematical[129] and is overshadowed by the monet-
ary considerations of these individual princes and rulers[130] and by their
playing it shrewdly against both sides and against each other, as Toynbee himself made clear with regard to both these aspects:[131]

> The militant peoples of Islam obtained political concessions out of pro-
> portion to their military achievements.
> The Arab chiefs, whose adherence to this side or that was largely decided
> by the fact that their local Arab rivals were taking service with the opposite
> party, employed their subsidies in conducting, at their respective patrons'
> expense, those operations which in any case they would have undertaken
> against one another under the ordinary conditions of inter-Arab warfare.

In the light of all this, we do not, as stated, consider the military aspect
or its moral side, but simply view it, with Toynbee, as the given fact of
a 'revolt' and thus as some sort of evidence of a national consciousness.
Even this bare minimum, however, was completely absent from the

Palestine Arab, as we have been able to show. Never in their history having had a State of their own in the Palestine area, they had nothing to remember from the past nor to dream about with regard to a future in freedom. No wonder, therefore, that they remained unconcerned and did not rise in revolt, even when called upon to do so by their brethren in other areas. They did not possess, and were therefore not willing to fight for, national ideals which, at the time and still today, are regarded as an important element, an understood precondition, leading to national self-determination. They did not evince any such sentiments up to the end of the Mandatory period. Even then the Anglo-American Enquiry Committee was obliged to conclude from investigations made on the spot and after hearing the Arab case that[132]

> their divisions have not been overcome and a formally organised community developed is in part the result of a less acutely self-conscious nationalism.

In addition to the references above about the Palestine Arab attitude during World War I, it should be said that the only conclusion it is open to draw from them is that the Palestine Arabs were quite content to remain for ever under what to everyone else meant Turkish oppression. This was not a phenomenon discovered at some later period; its import was, on the contrary, conveyed to the Palestine Arabs themselves by the then Colonial Secretary, when facing one of their delegations in Jerusalem in 1921. That delegation handed to him a memorandum in which they demanded the abolition of the Balfour Declaration. Churchill replied *inter alia:*[133]

> The paper which you have just read painted a golden picture of the delightful state of affairs in Palestine under the Turkish rule. Every man did everything he pleased; taxation was light; justice was prompt and impartial; trade, commerce, education, the arts flourished. It was a wonderful picture. But it had no relation whatever to the truth, for otherwise why did the Arabs rebel against this heavenly condition?
>
> Your statements sounded as if you overthrew the Turks. This is not so. Glance at the British war cemeteries! Many British lives were sacrificed for Palestine. . . .
>
> The Balfour Declaration was made when war was in progress and when victory or defeat was hanging in the balance. Therefore, it must be regarded as definitely established by the victory.

Toynbee's generous apologetic explanation of the phenomenon of Arab unconcern with their own future is most illuminating with regard to the Palestine Arabs' national character:[134]

> Their leaders are too prudent and the people too peaceable, their stake is too great, their forces are too scattered to allow them for a moment to contemplate the rising in arms.

But such a term as 'prudence' cannot be applied to a people not concerned enough with its future at least to rise against tyranny when there is no danger in doing so, as was the case in Palestine at the time. The Palestine Arabs did not assist the Allies, and thus their own cause, even within the areas which the British had already liberated from the Turks, so obviating any eventual 'risk' or 'stake'. They remained unconcerned. Therefore, in addition to the absence of any spirit of nationality and of love for their native soil, on this count also they forfeited any claim, even if they had been specifically included in the MacMahon-Hussein agreement, because this correspondence, as is shown above, made it clear that those Arabs who could not or would not join the Arab rebellion would still become beneficiaries of the agreement if they only fulfilled the other condition: 'not to afford assistance to our enemies'.[135] And on the contrary, as stated, the Palestine Arabs did just this, as Churchill emphasised in Parliament,[136] as emerges from the remarks of Jarvis and Graves,[137] and as one of their leaders, reviewing the situation in retrospect, confessed:[138]

> the 'prudence' of the Arabs in Palestine, Arabs who were more loyal to the Turks than were other subjects, resulting from national apathy, may have been of some advantage to individuals, demonstrating thus that their material interests of 'today' were for them more important than freedom in the 'future', to use Toynbee's description of the basic war aim.

They thus acted as would a spineless unit, or, as Toynbee phrased it, a 'dead unit'. Accordingly—recalling Toynbee's principle of the right of a claim to independence—the Palestine Arabs showed themselves unfit for self-government or nationhood. One can say without injuring objectivity that this situation continues to this day. Palestine Arabs are still divided: they have not been able to select their own fully accepted spokesmen from within their own fold, and/or to organise themselves in a form even resembling a single unit. As in the olden

days, when Syrian notables and political leaders used to speak automatically for the Palestine sector also, so the Palestine Arabs continued
to have other Arabs speak for them and tell them what their actual
wishes were or ought to be. This is exemplified, for instance, by the
activities of the leaders of the Arab States when they embarked in 1947–
1948 upon a war against Israel. Most local Palestine Arabs did not want
that war nor did they provide a single military unit worth mentioning. And the same picture was presented in the political arena, when,
for instance, the United Nations Committee dealt with the Palestine
problem and a Palestine 'Arab Higher Committee' appeared before it.
But this committee represented, in fact, only itself, because its members
were self-appointed, by permission of the Egyptian authorities, resided
in Cairo and not in Palestine, and the Mufti of Jerusalem and his en-
tourage, although also in Cairo, refused to recognise even these few individuals. It was therefore no surprise to anyone that, after looking into
this situation, the Polish representative, Mr Wieniewicz, who had
raised the issue in the U.N. Committee, had to come to the conclusion
that the Palestine Arabs were 'represented by the five Arab States which
are taking part in the deliberations'.[139] They were the bosses and not
the people concerned, and, in fact, these Arab States were not interested at all in the Palestine Arabs, for they had obviously the worst
possible opinion about their brethren's national consciousness. As Toynbee's *Survey* so aptly quoted from the pen of a leading Palestinian
Arab:[140]

> . . . What concerned them [the Arab States] was not to win the war and
> save Palestine from the enemy, but what would happen after the struggle,
> who would be dominant in Palestine or annex it to themselves and how
> they could achieve their ambitions. Their announced aim was the salvation
> of Palestine, and they said that afterwards its destiny should be left to its
> people. This was said with the tongue only. In their hearts all wished it
> for themselves; and most of them were hurrying to prevent their neigh-
> bours from being predominant, even though nothing remained except the
> offal and bones.

No wonder that, in these circumstances, a Moslem thinker, Mohamed
Wabi, lamented a few years ago[141] that the situation had not been re-
medied and that 'the Arab people lacks real national consciousness'.

The Great Contrast

At the same time the national spirit of preparedness for sacrifice was clearly demonstrated by the Palestine Jews, by Zionists, and by Jews all over the world when the historic moment came in World War I. Toynbee, in his description of the Palestine situation in 1917, stressed that[142]

> one significant consequence [of Zionism] was the appearance in Egypt of Palestinian refugees, who raised the Zion Mule Corps there and fought through the Gallipoli campaign.

The significance of this unit lies not in its military nature or value but in the fact that it was voluntarily and spontaneously formed six months after Turkey had entered the war. It was not created as the result of an agreement with Britain or the Allied Powers containing all the *quid pro quos* (like the MacMahon-Hussein correspondence, for instance),[143] nor did the initiators or leaders of this Jewish unit, such as Joseph Trumpeldor, receive any consideration in return, as did all the Arab leaders, who accepted vast amounts of gold for siding with the Allies.[144] The Jewish military unit was formed out of a desire to fight against the Turks so as to assist in their defeat, which would bring about the liberation of Palestine.

When Toynbee, in the paragraph quoted above, referred to the Jewish unit in Gallipoli, the Jewish Legion was not yet completed. It was officially established in August, 1917, as a result of the activities of Vladimir Jabotinsky.[145] The Jewish Legion, too, was not formed on any prearranged *quid pro quo* basis, but was a unit of Jewish volunteers from the world over, including Palestinian Jews, to take part in the war. Its main object was to fight as a distinct national military unit, under its own national flag, on the Palestine front against the Turks. To these soldiers this was a war of liberation of the old Jewish National Home from foreign domination. When these Jewish soldiers entered Palestine, as part of the victorious British armies, the Jewish youth did not hesitate to join up (compare the Arab attitude),[146] as the official British *Handbook* confirms:[147]

> The most important event which has taken place, so far as the Jewish community in Palestine is concerned, since our occupation, has been the recruiting

of Palestine Jews, whatever their national states, into the British army; and practically the whole available Jewish youth of the colonies and many of the townsmen of military age came forward for voluntary enlistment in the Jewish battalions, took the oath to King George V and were clad in British uniforms. The initiative in favour of the recruiting movement took place as the result of the demand of the Jewish population itself, rather than from any desire or even encouragement from the British authorities. The campaign in Palestine is regarded by the Jews as a campaign for the liberation of the country from the thraldom of Turkish misrule, and the return of even Turkish suzerainty would be regarded by them as betrayal.

It was not only by this desire to join the military forces against the Turks that the Jewish national spirit was characterised. At the time (1915) when the Zion Mule Corps was formed in Egypt, a group of Zionist youth formed Nili, a spy ring, in the Palestine area, then held by the Turks. They supplied the British Army with valuable information. Like their soldier-brethren outside the country, so also these youngsters inside risked their lives. Many of them, including the heroic Sarah Aaronsohn, were tortured to death by the Turks for their activities.[148]

The Gallipoli units, the soldiers of the Jewish Legion, the young Jewish men and women in Nili were certainly not 'prudent' in Toynbee's apologetic terminology for Palestine Arab unconcern with their and their country's future;[149] and although the Jewish 'stake was too great and their forces too scattered',[150] they did 'rise in arms' for their future.

And even the Jewish population *per se*, which was largely non-Zionist, welcomed the victorious troops, in marked contrast to the Arab population. This welcome gave great encouragement to the soldiers. The *Official History* of the war recorded[151] that the Jewish

> settlements, and the warm welcome received from their inhabitants, were to represent to the troops the pleasantest aspect of the operations in the Philistine Plain. Even fair-sized Arab towns like Majdal and Yibna made to them no such appeal as the Jewish villages. . . . The Jews for their part were delighted to be rid of the Turks.

The British, in conquering Palestine, were of course conscious of the fact that the warm welcome given by the Jews was their expression of joy over the removal of the Turks from the Land, as we learn from the

Handbook.[152] But, on the other hand, they also understood that liberation from Turkish tyranny had a meaning only if it was accompanied by practical assistance on the part of Britain and the other Allies towards Jewish nationhood in Palestine. As the official *Handbook* confirms:[153]

> The whole secret of Britain's popularity in Palestine depends upon our willingness to give the Jewish people freedom to develop their own national consciousness in their own way.

Important as this warm reception of the invading troops by the Jewish population was, there is no doubt that the contribution of the Jewish Battalions through combat to final victory was of no less importance. Their Commander-in-Chief, General Chaytor, on presenting decorations to those who won them, addressed the Jewish troops and said, among other things:[154]

> I am pleased to be able to tell you, however, that I was particularly struck with your good work on the Mellahah front, and by your gallant capture of the Umm esh Shert Fort and defeat of the Turkish rearguard when I gave you the order to go, for I was then enabled to push my mounted men over the Jordan at that crossing, and so you contributed materially to the capture of Es Salt and of the guns and other material which fell to our share; to the capture of Amman; the cutting of the Hedjaz Railway, and the destruction of the 4th Turkish Army, which helped considerably towards the great victory at Damascus.

This important military contribution by the Jewish battalions and the references to the Zion Mule Corps and the Nili spies testify to what Toynbee called the 'manifestations of the spirit of nationality', which in this 'language of war' also asserted in unequivocal terms its claim to nationhood. Even from a purely military standpoint, just as the Arabs outside Palestine secured their independence because of their fighting the Turks, so Jews, through helping to fight the enemy, secured for themselves the right to make their claims. These are the rights for which the war had been fought in the first place, as Toynbee so markedly pointed out:[155]

> We have to carry this war to a successful issue, because on that depends our freedom to govern our own life after the war is over, and the preservation

of this freedom itself is more important for us than the whole sum of concrete gains its possession has so far brought us. Thus we are sacrificing our
present to our future, and therein obeying the civilised men's ideal to the
utmost.

What a glorious war song by the Toynbee of 1915! Although it was
written in the midst of propaganda which Toynbee happened to be
promoting on behalf of war in those years, this basic philosophy for the
purpose of the war was also regarded by him as valid in peacetime.
When looking at this retrospectively ten years later, he wrote:[156]

> It was significant that almost all these apparently reckless appeals to force
> were eventually more or less *justified* by their political results, and this
> whether they were successful or not from the military point of view.

At this point we may recall[157] the statement made by Churchill to
the Arab Delegation in Jerusalem in 1921 emphasising the fact that the
Balfour Declaration 'must be regarded as definitely established by
the victory'.

But now follows an example of the amazing method employed so
frequently, as we have shown, by Toynbee. Over forty years after
the event, he now moralises, with regard to Jewish rights in Palestine,
about[158] the

> barbaric claim that a valid legal claim can be derived from an act of military
> conquest.

As an historian, he knows of course that every territoiral gain, barbaric
and civilised, in the history of mankind has been made in the course of
wars and their aftermath. As a prominent Arab has written with regard to his own people,[159]

> Sovereignty and the right to rule cannot be conferred on no matter whom,
> by the first comer, as a result of an academic discussion. Sovereignty is
> acquired by force and power and by violence. It was by violence that the
> sons of Osman seized power, reigned over the Turkish nation, and main-
> tained their domination for six centuries.

As we have seen from the references[160] above, Toynbee had praised the
consequences and results of World War I with regard to the Near
Eastern area, including Palestine. Yet it would not be fair to say that it
is only prejudice all along that induces him now to 'forget' all this and

disapprove of Jewish rights to Palestine if they are claimed on military achievements (which anyhow is not the case). The extenuating circumstances which he may put forward on his own behalf result from his personal spiritual development. After years of indulging unperturbed in war-propaganda, he now, under the impact of atomic destructive power and with the progress of age, turned pacifist[161] and by 1961 arrived at the conclusion that[162]

> I hate war . . . War is an impersonal use of collective human force for the purpose of imposing the will of rulers and people of one state on those of another. . . . In any case, since the rise of civilisation, war has been one of its two chief scandals and scourges—the other being the system of social and economic inequality and injustice. . . .

This reads, of course, differently from the glorification quoted earlier of the aims of World War I,[163] which he had preached to an attentive world, and differently also from the 'justification' of war in view of its 'political achievements'.[164] Other analysts of Toynbee's contradictory statements and attitudes towards war and peace have also drawn attention to these significant discrepancies. E. I. Watkin, for instance, writes:[165]

> In this vision and probably forecast we fear he is right. But it has, we think, led him to an inconsistent and hesitant view of the part actually played by war in human civilisations. At times he distinguishes between justifiable and unjustifiable wars, between wars which preserve a growing civilisation from barbarians without, and anarchy within, the pale, the wars of militarist aggression. . . . This confusion . . . has, we think, damaged his historical picture. For it is abundantly clear that civilisation could not have arisen and developed without the employment of war, however destructive its unbridled indulgence proved later.

Toynbee feels that this is the crux of the problem and deduces therefrom that[166]

> Watkin suggests that my consciousness of the present potentialities of war may have coloured retrospectively my estimate of the actual effects of war in the past.

And, heeding this criticism, he concedes:

> I agree that one must try to distinguish between the different purposes for

which wars have been fought, and the different degrees of material and spiritual devastation that they have inflicted. . . . I acknowledge that I have been guilty of 'wishful thinking' in pushing my denial of the efficacy of the use of force as far as I have pushed it. If one believes, as I do, that war has had an important effect on the course of human affairs, it is inconsistent to maintain that the use of force has not been efficacious.

And this brings us back from the Toynbee of 1961 (a 'barbaric claim . . . derived from an act of war'[167]) to the original statements of the Toynbee of 1915 ('we are sacrificing our present to our future'), which he made[168] when World War I was being fought and when he became one of its important figures in the field of public enlightenment.

Where, however, the extenuating circumstances end and prejudice again sets in can be gathered from the fact that at the very same time (1961) when, in *Reconsiderations*, Toynbee retracted his absolute pacifism and recognised definite values arising out of wars, he wrote the statement quoted above about the 'barbaric' nature of such values if applied to Jews. This becomes still more incongruous if one takes into account the establishment of nine independent Arab States, which came into existence, according to him, solely as the result of the Allied victory in World War I.[169] Why then should these Arab successes be praised and welcomed even if they were 'out of proportion to their military achievement', as Toynbee put it,[170] while the Jewish rights are regarded as 'barbaric' although, apart from numerous more important factors, they derive from the same war (if for argument's sake we confine ourselves strictly to the business of the war)? This means, in other words, that as a result of the agreement between Britain and the Zionists in a dark moment of the military situation in World War I[171] the latter were helpful in weighting the scales in favour of Britain, and thus helped to defeat Turkey, and enabled the Arabs to establish nine States. It is pathetic to read between the lines of the Royal Commission's *Report* a regretful hint that these Arab States should, instead of waging war and campaigns of hatred, rather remember Jewry gratefully for assisting in their emergence. Here a man of Toynbee's standing in the Arab world could have helped towards peace. But instead he encouraged these Arabs towards war. Toynbee obviously operates on a double morality: Arab claims should be validated by military victory, Jewish claims must not. As if to make clearer this Toynbeean discrimination, the Royal Commission on Palestine emphasised in its review of the situation:[172]

> The Arabs do not appear to realise in the first place that the present position of the Arab world as a whole is mainly due to the great sacrifices made by the Allied and Associated Powers in the War and, secondly, that in so far as the Balfour Declaration helped to bring about the Allies' victory, it helped to bring about the emancipation of all the Arab countries from Turkish rule.

It must, however, be stressed that, while nations and States throughout history have derived their claims solely from conquests, and most of them still rest on the laurels of ancestral conquerors, the Jews' claim to Palestine was not put forward by the Zionists at the time or subsequently on the basis of the Jews' participation in World War I and their share in military victory. These military contributions were natural corollaries of Jewish nationalism. Jews, like any other national unit in the war, showed their willingness to 'obey civilised man's ideal to the utmost', as Toynbee put it.[173] The Jews' claim to Palestine did not have to be advanced only after the victory of 1918; it existed long before the war. Victory only confirmed its existence and enabled its realisation. In fact, Jewish claims and rights in Palestine remained uninterruptedly alive from the first day of the Diaspora. These ancient claims have been recognised by the great 'majority of the human race' as represented in the League of Nations, which, as also did Toynbee, we accepted as sole judges in respect of the validity of either claimant in Palestine.[174]

4

'Statute of Limitations'

In this connection it may be advisable also to dispose of another 'argument' which Toynbee more recently began to raise with the same object in mind of denying Jewish claims and rights to Palestine. We mentioned before that among his various reasons for such a denial he also intended the long period that had elapsed between the Roman conquest of Palestine and the establishment of the State of Israel. Based on this assumption, he then concluded that[175]

> when the Jewish historical claim to a special position for Jews in Palestine is carried to the point at which its implementation inflicts wrongs and sufferings on the present-day Arab inhabitants, the Jewish claim runs up against the statute of limitations. This is an almost universally accepted principle of law. . . . The principle is that ancient rights, even if valid originally, lose their validity in course of time if they have fallen into desuetude and have consequently been superseded by other rights that have been validated by a long period of usage. It is rightly held that the hardship and injustice that would be caused by the annulment of long-since-established subsequent rights is bound to outweigh the satisfaction that would be produced by a revalidation of the ancient rights for the benefit of remote descendants of the people, dead many generations ago, by whom those ancient rights were once possessed.

With this argument Toynbee entered into the area of legalism. It is therefore within that area that his challenge can and should be dealt with.

He obviously intermingles private and international law. The 'statute of limitations' in Toynbee's description above is clearly one of private law. The Limitation Act, 1939, of His Majesty's Government could have enlightened him on this. By this law the legislator can determine the duration of possession by individuals and the time of expiration of such rights. If one were to accept Toynbee's thesis and apply what he defines as a 'statute of limitations' on a Palestine issue, it could only be through a fantasy in which an individual Jew would have to be invented to claim a house or a piece of land now used or possessed by an Arab, on the grounds that two thousand years ago this particular house or piece of land had been owned and occupied by that Jew's ancestor. But such a simple claim would not suffice; it would have to be proved:[176]

> In the strongest language that our law knows the demandant has to assert ownership of the land. He says that he, or his ancestor, has been seized of the land as of fee 'and of right' and, if he relies on the seisin of an ancestor, he must trace the descent of 'the right' from heir to heir into his own person.

The law, as Toynbee correctly mentions, always protects the present occupant or possessor of specific properties, although even this protection is not absolute, for the law stipulates that[177]

> the ownership is valid until an older is proved. No one is ever called upon to demonstrate an ownership good against all men: he does enough even in a proprietary action if he proves the older right than that of the person whom he attacks.

In theory, therefore, the older claim would have to be proved by the Jew with regard to the house or land in Palestine. And as it is not even conceivable that a single Jew could be found anywhere in the world able to prove ownership by his remote ancestor of these specific properties in Palestine or to prove that these properties had been forcibly taken from his ancestor, and that throughout the two thousand years they had been claimed from heir to heir and had never been sold or otherwise disposed of, the 'statute of limitations' would leave the properties without doubt to the Arab. But this is fiction. In fact, modern legislation sets precise time limits for the right of private claims. The term 'statute of limitations' conveys just this and nothing else. We see therefore from the fictitious example above the absurdity of Toynbee's attempt at using the term for matters other than private law.

If further evidence of this absurdity is required, Toynbee has given it in stressing that if the United Nations had a right to decree that a Jewish State be established in Palestine it is conceivable that[178]

> if . . . the Government of Continental China were one day to expel the Kuomintang Chinese from Taiwan . . . the United Nations [could] then decree that the state of Delaware should be detached from the United States and should be placed at the disposal of the Kuomintang Chinese refugees.

This is revealing and confirms our contention that Toynbee completely lacks understanding of the legal aspect of the 'statue of limitations' and the problem of sovereignty in international law. The same is true with regard to the comparison he suggests between Jewish rights in Palestine (which he definitely recognises[179]) and Kuomintang Chinese 'rights' to Delaware; or with regard to the absurd implication that as the United Nations had decreed, without regard to facts and rights, a State for the Jews, they are therefore capable of doing the same for the Chinese in Delaware. After all, it was Toynbee himself who, when criticised for the fancy analogies which he uses in his writings for proving much that he wants to prove, said:[180]

> The weakness of analogy as a method of thought seems to lie, not in the nature of the method itself, but in the nature of most of the phenomena to which it is applied.

> No doubt, each time that we resort to the method of analogy, we are courting the risk of misapplying it. I plead guilty to having carried my use of analogy to excessive lengths. I should have guessed that I might have made this mistake, even if I had not been accused of it by a convincing consensus of critics. I am conscious that 'going too far' is a standing temptation for me, and that too often I have succumbed to it. I agree that analogies are not explanation, but are heuristic [exploratory] devices for seeking explanations.

This was written in 1961. Six months later (July, 1961) he forgot his confession of guilt and returned to his good old 'standing temptation'.

How disrespectful to history the historian Toynbee is, and how disrespectful to his own beliefs, can be judged from the following example appertaining to matters of sovereignty, rights, and his sort of 'statue of limitations'. It was after World War I that the question of the inter-nationalisation of Constantinople (Stambul) became a hotly discussed theme. Toynbee was then strongly in favour of this internationalisation, and when the British Prime Minister, Lloyd George, who originally supported it, changed his mind and came out against internationalisa-tion, Toynbee, in a bitter attack, blamed him for having 'broken the spirit of promise', and emphasised[181] that

> Greek emperors ruled in the imperial palace for eleven centuries before a Turkish sultan set foot there, and the Caliphs of Islam (or, rather, of one sector of Islam) have sojourned there only for four centuries—since 1517 A.D. Sentiment and history would assign Stambul to Greece, and though Mr Venizelos,[182] with rare statesmanship, forbore to claim it when he laid the Greek case before the Conference[183] last year, he waived his title [sic!] in favour of an international administration, and on the understanding that the city would in no circumstances be left to the Turk. Greek sentiment would justly [sic!] be wounded to the quick by the perpetuation of Turkish sovereignty over Stambul . . . and if, for the convenience of the Govern-ment of India, Stambul is left to the Turk after all[184] Greece ought to be compensated by the full satisfaction of her legitimate national claims [sic!] in other parts of Turkey.

Here we see clearly Toynbee's double standards: although the Turks had sovereignty over Constantinople since 1517, Greeks, he claims, have a right to the city because Greek emperors ruled there for eleven centuries before 1517. On the other hand, although the Jews ruled Palestine and had their Kings, Judges, and rulers for many centuries (before the Babylonian conquest and under the Maccabees) before the settlement of Arabs (even supposing that these are the ancestors of the present-day Arabs[185]), and moreover, although—unlike the Turks——these Arabs at no time possessed sovereignty, he decrees that the Arabs and not the Jews have legitimate 'national claims' to the country.

Another example of Toynbee's appropriation of the 'statute of limitations' to his personal whim is provided in his handling of the Goa question. In his *Study*, published in 1954, he wrote:[186]

> The contemporary population of Portuguese India was hardly distinguish-able in race from the inhabitants of the rest of the sub-continent, since the Portuguese blood that had been infused into the veins of the Goanese in the course of some four and a half centuries was no more than a tincture. This

tincture, however, was significant, not in virtue of its physical strength, but because it was an outward visible sign of an inward spiritual union which the Portuguese conquerors of Goa had consummated with a conquered native Indian population that had embraced the conquerors' religion. In A.D. 1952 it remained to be seen whether the community of religion that was a voluntary act between Goa and Portugal might not prove morally stronger than the community of race and the geographical contiguity that would tend to attract the tiny territory of Goa towards the mighty mass of encompassing India.

He thus hoped and expected that Portuguese sovereignty over Goa, based on a 'religious community', would prevail and continue to flourish. Nine years later Nehru's India invaded Goa, occupied the area, incorporated it in the Indian State, and proclaimed Portuguese sovereignty at an end. And at that moment Toynbee could not refrain from making a public statement in which he regretted the use of force by India, 'but he added that Portugal should have given up her enclaves in India long ago'.[187] Thus the 'morally stronger . . . community of religion' was blown to the winds by Toynbee to make room for 'the community of race'.[188] It might also be noted that Toynbee made his statement in Cairo. In such circumstances it does not matter what the 'statute of limitations' stands for. It also does not matter that the example of Goa, if applied to Palestine, must lead to the conclusion that the Arabs, like the Portuguese in Goa, who for centuries lived in those lands, are racially no Arabs but only a sort of mixed religious community which, after the conquest of the country by Britain and the instituting of the Mandate, 'should have given up long ago' any claim to sovereignty and accept the new sovereign.

The Greek and Goan examples show that the *Hexeneinmaleins* accompanies Toynbee in his great art of confusing his own theories and analogies. Instead of 'statute of limitations', the term 'extinctive prescription', the principle of time-limits, is known in international usage. 'In the international sphere, however,' writes Professor Schwarzenberger,[189] 'there is no general agreement as to the exact time limit which will bring the principle of "extinctive prescription" into operation.'

From everything said above it is quite evident that one cannot apply the term and principle of 'statute of limitations' to the problem of

Palestine. It is not applicable to the question of Jewish historical rights or claims in Palestine because these are matters of international law and not of private law. And the 'statute of limitations' is not known in international law. It does not exist there for the simple reason that no law or legislation has been or can be internationally promulgated which could define or prescribe a period in which action could be taken. The beautifully phrased and nice-sounding definition of 'statute of limitations' which Toynbee applied in his argument against Zionism is, therefore, nothing but invalid verbiage.

Zionists, like Jews before the emergence of the Zionist Organisation, have never based Jewish rights to Palestine on claims for particular houses, properties, or land areas under the title of ancestral ownership. Zionism claimed sovereignty over the territory. And sovereignty does not depend on the question of who owns or occupies this or that particular house or piece of property, however large, in the State. As Herzl once put it very clearly:[190]

> We can acquire pieces of land at any time anywhere in the world. But the Zionists are not interested in this at all. Private law in our case is completely irrelevant; it will come later, once the land speculators join us after our successes. The eyes of the Zionists are turned only towards public law. There they are seeking the solution of the old evil. If I am permitted to express a paradox, I should say: A land which according to public law belongs to the Jewish people, even which down to the last lot is registered in the official land registry in the name of non-Jews, means the solution of the Jewish problem for ever.

It is for this reason that the Basle Programme of the Zionist Organisation stipulated the establishment of a National Home for the Jewish people in Palestine 'secured by public law'. And it was secured 'by public law' (the term at that time stood for 'international law') when the Palestine Mandate, as mentioned above,[191] recognised the uninterrupted bond between Jewry and Eretz Israel in 'the historical connection of the Jewish people with Palestine', on which was based the Jewish people's desire to 're-establish' its National Home there as a first step towards Statehood, i.e. its former sovereignty. No other people on earth has any such claim and right of previous sovereignty than the Jewish people, because, bearing in mind the two periods referred to above of Jewish sovereignty in Palestine, only one non-Jewish sovereignty has existence in the country, *i.e.* the Latin Kingdom established by the Crusades in 1099, which lasted 88 years till 1187, when Saladin conquered Jerusalem. At no time before or since the Arab conquest has any State sovereignty existed in Palestine. Throughout, sovereignty has been exercised from outside and Palestine was occupied territory. In thirteen centuries the Land has passed 14 times from one foreign domination to another, apart from the numerous short periods of change during wars.[192]

The Mandate stipulated the wider term 'historical connection' and not 'historical rights' because connection through history makes any reference or claim to national rights unnecessary. Within the terms of an uninterrupted connection such rights are of themselves inherent in it. The term 'rights' was reserved in the Balfour Declaration, and through its insertion in the Mandate, for the status of the then existing non-Jewish population in Palestine ('Nothing should be done to pre-judice the civil and religious *rights* of the existing non-Jewish communities there')[193] and of the Jews living outside Palestine ('the rights . . . enjoyed by Jews in any other country').[194] It is, therefore, clear that the term 'rights' is used here for individual rights, and not for collective national or international ones.

The text of the Mandate leaves us in no doubt that the recognised 'historical connection' was stipulated for the purpose of basing on it and regarding it as 'grounds for reconstituting their national home in the country'. Thus the striving of the Zionists for sovereignty on the basis of the historical connection, which includes the right to former sovereignty, was recognised in international law.

This was made possible without rancour by the fact that Turkey, the Power exercising sovereignty before the end of World War I, officially surrendered it. This sovereignty by the Ottoman Empire had lasted for five hundred years. It was never exercised by Arabs in Palestine over the Palestine area, as Toynbee himself confirms when he states that the Arabs never had their own 'independent territory' in Palestine,[195] or even self-government,[196]

a political luxury which, after all, they had never yet effectively enjoyed.

That sovereignty over Palestine was surrendered by Turkey to the victorious Allies. As Toynbee once put it:[197]

The rights of Turkey, the former sovereign over both mandated territories [Syria and Palestine], were extinguished by the Treaty of Lausanne, which was signed on the 24th July, 1923, and came into force on the 6th August.

Anticipating any possible challenge about the legal position on the basis that the surrender was signed in the Treaty of Lausanne only in 1923, *i.e.* four years after the establishment of the new Administration in Palestine, Toynbee emphasised:[198]

> Technically, the Occupying Powers were bound to apply the previous administrative regime[199] in the occupied territories until the juridical status of these territories had been changed by the coming into force of a peace treaty with Turkey, and by the assignment and approval of the two mandates under which the territories were to be placed. Actually, the French and the British Governments did not (and, indeed could not) wait for these events before introducing administrative innovations.

A similar conclusion couched in more definite terms was formulated by M. van Rees, Vice-President of the Mandates Commission:[200]

> The Arabs maintained that their country belonged to themselves and that they had been masters in it for fourteen centuries. Great Britain, in authorising the establishment of a National Home, had disposed of a country which did not belong to it.[201] This claim was particularly open to refutation. It was not in accordance with most elementary facts of ancient history in Palestine. It would be enough to point out that Palestine had belonged before the war to the Ottoman Empire. The country had been conquered, not by Arabs of Palestine, but by the Allies, and had finally been ceded to the Allies, and not to the Arabs. Since 1517, Palestine had been under the rule of the Turks. There could be no reference, therefore, of an Arab nation in Palestine, nor could it be claimed that the territory formed part of an Arab nation.

There is, therefore, no question in international law that the rights to the re-establishment of sovereignty by the Jewish people in Palestine are legitimate and have been recognised as such by the majority of the human race, which, together with Toynbee, we have accepted as the sole determining factor in the Palestine issue.[202]

It is, therefore, erroneous for the Arabs, and, following them, Toynbee, to claim that because the Arabs had a majority of the population in the land when these decisions (Balfour Declaration, Mandate, and

Statehood) were made, the land was 'theirs'. The land was never theirs, for they never ruled it. Large properties which they possessed were certainly theirs, although we have shown above[203] what they had done with the properties and how they neglected them to an incredible degree. Apart from this, if figures of large or small property-holdings by Arabs in Palestine are to be applied, and they are introduced by Toynbee on every occasion, then it must be said unequivocally that the larger portions of the Palestine area were unoccupied, uncultivated, and completely desolate when the international community decided to accept the claim of Jewish rights in Palestine. Toynbee himself made this clear when he wrote in 1917[204] that 'there are vast uncultivated tracts which the Jews can and will reclaim'.

When the decisions about Palestine were made (1917–18) the area known then as Southern Syria had a total of 10,540 square miles (27,315 square kilometres),[205] with a population of 700,000 with no more than about 650 square miles, or $6\frac{1}{4}$ per cent, of land under agricultural cultivation. In the light of these figures a discussion even from the point of view of private and individual law becomes meaningless, because the Arabs had cultivated an insignificant part of the total area, leaving the overwhelmingly larger part as a prey to deterioration. Any serious discussion about the Arabs' private rights becomes superfluous also in the light of the fact that in the Zionist concept the aim of Jewish sovereignty in Palestine was not based on any infringement of the individual rights and possessions of these Arabs.

5
'Human Rights'

Apparently aware of the weakness of his arguments from the historical and legal viewpoints, Toynbee later began to interpolate 'human rights' as the criterion for attributing rights or wrongs to the narrower and the wider participants in the Palestine venture. It is hard to ascertain why he chose such a vague term. Ever since the proclamation in 1948 by the United Nations of the 'Declaration of Human Rights', the international body has been trying to formulate the 'Covenants of Human Rights' which were to be binding upon all members of the U.N. But no formula has so far been found.[206] Toynbee, too, does not define 'human rights' in his article. Instead, he lays down a basic premise which, for the purpose of this analysis, I have accepted.[207] It is the principle that we regard as 'human rights' those which 'are more or less universally recognised as valid'. How can we, however, ascertain whether or not they are universally recognised as valid in a given case? Is it not a fact that despite great efforts the nations on earth found the utmost difficulty in drafting the first few articles of a Covenant to define the meaning and to guide the understanding of 'human rights'? In view of this complexity, I propose to accept as the most convenient and democratic forums of world opinion the League of Nations and its successor the United Nations. This seems fair not only because these forums have been respectively the only ones through which the overwhelming majority of the human race has voiced its opinion, but also primarily because the issue of Palestine, Zionism, and the Arabs has been repeatedly presented to them in all its aspects, not least in that of 'human rights'.

The Balfour Declaration, having been approved by 'a large number of Allied Powers',[208] was subsequently incorporated in the Palestine Mandate under the terms described in the previous chapter. The Mandate was approved by the League of Nations on July 24, 1922.[209] At the time when this decision was taken the League represented some 1,250,000,000 people,[210] including Toynbee's favoured communities of 'Hindus, Buddhists, Confucians, and Shintoists'. As Toynbee himself has stated,[211]

> . . . by December, 1920, the League had already embraced the great majority of the self-governing nations, including two ex-enemy states (Austria and Bulgaria), and forty-four out of those fifty-seven intermediate and minor states which, collectively, were so prominent a feature in the new map of the world. Moreover, this majority was united in support of the international order which the League represented. . . .

Before any of these decisions were taken (Balfour Declaration and Mandate), the problems of Arabs and Jews were carefully considered in the light of any possible implications. *A History of the Peace Conference*, in which Toynbee was one of the collaborators, confirms[212] that the Balfour Declaration was

> not a project of sudden origin, or hastily embraced, it was carefully considered in all its bearings and implications.

Also Winston Churchill emphasised in a speech in the Commons:[213]

> It is often supposed that the Balfour Declaration was an ill-considered sentimental act . . . and that . . . it was a thing done in the tumult of the War. But hardly any step was taken with greater deliberation and responsibility.

Finally, Professor Felix Frankfurter, at the time an important figure at the Paris Peace Conference, later a member of the Supreme Court of the U.S.A., confirmed this in an article:[214]

> The presence of the existing Arab population, of course, made the establishment of a Jewish National Home more difficult than if Palestine had been wholly empty. The difficulties of the undertaking were, however, fully canvassed before the Declaration was made and the Mandate issued; the undertaking was assumed with full knowledge of its implications.

Throughout the Mandatory period the Permanent Mandates Commission of the League and the League's Council watched meticulously over the conditions and developments in Palestine.[215] As the published official *Minutes* and *Reports* of both these League instruments show, every single basic argument now recapitulated by Toynbee in his writings was presented by the Arabs and their spokesmen time and again to these forums which time and again upheld the justice of Jewish rights to build a National Home in Palestine. Thus for over forty years of the Mandatory period, while the Jewish National Home progressed, and while these international institutions functioned, the overwhelming majority of the human race spoke through their decisions and resolutions in favour of these Jewish rights.

Toynbee's arguments of today were also aired by the Arabs and their spokesmen before the various committees and commissions which the British Government set up itself[216] or jointly with the Government of the U.S.A.[217] They were also fully dealt with by the U.N. Special Committee for Palestine (Unscop),[218] the proposals of which led to the recommendations by the General Assembly on November 29, 1947, for the establishment of the State of Israel.[219] They were, finally, recapitulated during the intense investigation by the *Ad Hoc* Political Committee of the General Assembly[220] before Israel's admission as an independent State to the family of nations.[221] On all these occasions the general consensus expressed itself in favour of Jewish rights in Palestine. Let it not be forgotten that when the actual functions of the League of Nations (1939) came to an end, it represented 1,500,000,000 people all over the globe,[222] and the U.N., when making its decision regarding Jewish independence in Palestine (1947), over 2,000,000,000 people.[223] Rarely has any other national or international problem been so often and over so long a period scrutinised from every possible angle; historical, moral, religious, legal, political, economic, and not least from the aspect of 'human rights'. Toynbee raises the cry for 'human rights' retrospectively, looking at the issue from his present-day 'concern' for Arab refugees. He is so blind on this point that he loses every consideration for the general aspect of 'human rights' of others than his pet child. After all, he personally bears as much responsibility as any other person, statesman, diplomat, or man of affairs, who made the issuance of the Balfour Declaration possible, as a result of which hundreds

of thousands of Jews settled in Palestine and Jewry all over the world
contributed thousands of millions of dollars to build up the country so
badly neglected up to then. Have these Jews, in their belief in the
pledged word of the civilised human race, no 'human rights'? Are
these 'human rights' to be sacrificed for suddenly discovered new
'human rights' of Arab refugees who are financially supported by the
international community and who *do* have a way out, which Jews
never had? There is also the fact that the Jews were attacked by the
Arabs, and have they not, what Toynbee applies to himself,[224] 'My
human right of self-defence'? Rarely, moreover, has any other issue
been approved subsequently so consistently by the democratic process
of a vote by representatives of the majority of the human race as was
the case with regard to Jewish rights in Palestine. Thus the 'majority
of disinterested parties', which I, together with Toynbee, have accepted
as one of the basic principles of this analysis, has spoken clearly and
unequivocally.

The Balfour Declaration

Toynbee's survey of the contemporary Zionist-Israel-Arab scene was
summarised in an article which he published after the appearance of
the last volume of his *Study*.[225] He set out in this survey a short analysis
of the Balfour Declaration of November 2, 1917. And it is characteristic
that this analysis was to fit his requirements for the rest of his articles
and his conclusions. Thus, instead of quoting the central part of that
Declaration verbatim, he presented it in the following form:[226]

> . . . the British Government recognised, and undertook to uphold, the
> Jews' right to a 'national home' in Palestine, subject to the stipulation that
> this undertaking was to be implemented without injury to the rights and
> interests of the existing inhabitants of the country.

In order to comprehend the ambiguity of this statement and to discern
the adaptation by Toynbee of established facts to momentary requirements, the full Balfour Declaration might appropriately be quoted:[227]

> Dear Lord Rothschild,
> I have much pleasure in conveying to you, on behalf of His Majesty's
> Government, the following declaration of sympathy with Jewish

Zionist aspirations which has been submitted and approved by the Cabinet:

> 'His Majesty's Government view with favour the establishment in Palestine of a national home for the Jewish people, and will use their best endeavours to facilitate the achievement of this object, it being clearly understood that nothing shall be done which may prejudice the civil and religious rights of existing non-Jewish communities in Palestine, or the rights and political status enjoyed by Jews in any other country.'

I should be grateful if you would bring this declaration to the knowledge of the Zionist Federation.

Yours sincerely,
Arthur James Balfour

Even a superficial glance at these two texts shows the inaccuracies in Toynbee's version. Britain undertook more than just 'to uphold the Jews' right to a "national home" in Palestine'. She undertook to act positively, to 'use her best endeavours to facilitate the achievement of this object'. On the other hand, the rights of 'existing non-Jewish communities' which were not to be prejudiced (the term 'injured' does not occur in the original) referred to 'civil and religious rights', and not to the 'rights and interests' as expanded by Toynbee.

Having given his description of the Balfour Declaration, Toynbee went on to say:[228]

> This would entitle the Jews, as well as the native Arab majority, to be at home in Palestine, and would also entitle the Jewish community in Palestine, to increase its previous numbers by immigration; but this Jewish right of immigration would still be limited by the overriding stipulation that the rights and interests of the existing inhabitants must not be injured. This would mean that Jewish immigration must not be admitted in so great a volume that it would overwhelm the native population of Palestine and would reduce them to the unfavourable position of becoming a minority in their own country.

In the course of the twenty-seven lines that lie between the first and second quotations above in Toynbee's original article, the word 'national' has been dropped from the 'Jewish national home' and superseded by 'Jews . . . to be at home in Palestine'; and the phrase in his first quotation, 'subject to the stipulation', has been elevated, in the second quotation, to an all-important 'overriding stipulation'. It is obvious that Toynbee used this terminology to show that the Arabs, having in 1917 had a numerical majority of population in Palestine, were not to be deprived of this majority in any circumstances, because the 'overriding stipulation' precluded them from becoming a minority. Toynbee's main purpose in this analysis was, then, to arrive at the conclusion he did, that

> the rights of the native Arab majority in Palestine that were recognised and guaranteed in the Balfour Declaration and mandate, have been violated . . . by the establishment of the Jewish State of Israel in Palestine.

Through this form of presentation, the reader is thus led to believe that the Balfour Declaration and the Palestine Mandate had nothing whatever to do with the emergence of a Jewish National Home, but were concerned solely with recognising and guaranteeing an Arab majority for all time in the country.

As the comparison between the original text and Toynbee's version shows, his was an incorrect account of the Balfour Declaration. No wonder that the interpretation and the conclusion based on that presentation were equally incorrect. They simply interfused the two principles of which the Declaration consists: (a) the positive undertaking—to use the best endeavours to facilitate the achievement of the Jewish National Home; and (b) the negative undertaking—to do nothing to prejudice the civil and religious rights of the non-Jewish communities. Had the authors of the Declaration intended what Toynbee now suggested, to make the second principle the 'overriding' one, *i.e.* that the structure of balance of Palestine's society (Arab majority and Jewish minority) was to remain as it existed in 1917, there was no need for Britain to issue a declaration to the Jews at all, for the Allied Powers to approve of it, and for the international forums to go to all their trouble, issue a Mandate and select a Mandatory Power. It would have sufficed to promise assistance to Arabs in the development of an 'Arab National Home', or to encourage the Arabs to proclaim a State of their own immediately, subject to some stipulation that Jews be permitted to immigrate on the basis of some vague historic-religious rights which not even Toynbee denied.[229] Such stipulation of Jewish immigration would, of course, have become obsolete once an Arab authority or Government began functioning, for it would have the right to decide upon 'the maximum amount of Jewish immigration', a right which Toynbee wishes to see given to the Arabs in any case. Where would all this lead to? Who could or would prevent the Arab authority from stating after the arrival of a few thousand Jews that immigration had to stop? After all, much more enlightened Governments and nations, even with ample space at their disposal, before that time and since, restricted Jewish immigration. This was indeed what an official report, published in 1921, after the arrival in Palestine of some 10,000 Jewish immigrants in the preceding two years, indicated:

> ... but ... particularly since they [Jews] have come in relatively large numbers, has aroused the same feeling of hostility and alarm that alien immigration has excited in other communities with which we are familiar. It would be useless to argue with the Arab that they are not aliens because they are returning to their ancient home. In any case he [the Arab] complains that they take the bread out of his mouth.[230]

This would also have been the consequence had the Balfour Declaration, as Toynbee now imputed, endowed the 'civil and religious rights of the non-Jewish communities' with 'overriding' power. Winston Churchill, who as British Colonial Secretary was responsible for beginning the implementation of the Balfour Declaration, stated with reference to this question:[231]

> The two obligations are indeed of equal weight but they are different in character. The first obligation is positive and creative, the second obligation is safeguarding and conciliatory. Our Mandatory obligation towards the Jews throughout the world who helped us, and towards the Palestinian Arabs who were the conscript soldiers of our Turkish enemy, are both binding and we are bound to persevere in the establishment of the Jewish National Home and in safeguarding the civil and religious rights of Arabs. Merely to sit still and avoid friction with Arabs and safeguard their civil and religious rights and to abandon the positive exertion for the establishment of the Jewish National Home would not be a faithful interpretation of the Mandate.

That such was the intention and understanding of the Palestine Mandate appears from its text, in which these two principles were three times repeated: in the preamble, in which the text of the Balfour Declaration (quoted above) was incorporated as an integral part of the Mandate, and in Articles 2 and 6.[232]

Article 2 laid down:

> The Mandatory shall be responsible for placing the country under such political, administrative and economic conditions as will secure the establishment of the Jewish National Home, as laid down in the preamble, and the development of self-governing institutions, and also for safeguarding the civil and religious rights of all inhabitants of Palestine, irrespective of race and religion.

Article 6 stated:

> The Administration of Palestine, while ensuring that the rights and position of other sections of the population are not prejudiced, shall facilitate Jewish immigration under suitable conditions and shall encourage, in co-operation with the Jewish Agency, referred to in Article 4, close settlement by Jews on the land including statelands and waste lands not required for public purposes.

There can be no question of misunderstanding the meaning of the 'stipulation' adopted in the Mandate from the Balfour Declaration; and I can do no better than invite Toynbee of 1930 to reply to Toynbee of 1961. He then wrote:[233]

> In these two articles [2 and 6] of the Mandate, the Mandatory Power was required to do three things. First, it was to promote the numerical increase in Palestine of a Jewish population which was to be established in Palestine as of right and not on sufferance—and this in both its aspects as a number of individual Palestinian citizens and as an organised Jewish national community. In the second place, the Mandatory Power was to ensure that the rights and position of other sections of the population in Palestine—that is, the Muslim and Christian Arabs—were not prejudiced by the measures taken for the development of the Jewish National Home in the country. In the third place, the Mandatory Power was eventually to make its own activities and its own presence in Palestine superfluous by developing a self-governing body politic out of the population of Palestine with its Jewish and Arab constituents.

In this objective description there is, of course, no word or indication about an 'overriding stipulation' in favour of Arabs or about any Arab rights controlling Jewish immigration. Moreover Toynbee himself has shown that not only is his latest interpretation wrong, but also that the role of the Arabs in Palestine under the Mandate was subordinated to the primary object: the Jewish National Home. He wrote:[234]

> The juxtaposition of these three obligations without any indication of their relation to one another left two open questions: first, were the three obligations mutually compatible, and second, if they were, what would be the outcome if and when they were fulfilled. The answer to both these questions depended on the unknown quantity: the amount of population which Palestine could be made to support on standards of living adequate for the diverse elements out of which the population was to be constituted. . . . The quantity would be complex and difficult to calculate because it would be governed in the last resort by the general economic capacity of Palestine within the framework of the general economic capacity of the world at the time. . . . In the nature of things, there was bound to be a maximum figure; and the numerical value of this maximum, whatever it turned out to be, might be of profound importance for the social and perhaps for the political destinies of Palestine because it would make the whole difference to the relative strengths of the Arab and Jewish constituents of the population. The absolute future strength of the Arab element could be forecast more or less accurately by calculating the natural increase of the existing Arab population. The condition, laid down in the Mandate, that the rights and position of this element should not be prejudiced might be taken to imply that the Arabs should receive a sufficient share of any additional material resources of the country, which might be produced by development, to enable them to provide for their natural increase without lowering their existing standard of living, or even with an improvement in the standard, if the existing standard were lower than what might be regarded as a reasonable minimum.

This elucidation of Articles 2 and 6 of the Mandate pertaining to the rights and the position of the non-Jews in Palestine shows clearly that Toynbee understood it to possess no 'overriding stipulation', that there was no question of any Arab increase by immigration, and no guarantee of the permanence of an Arab majority. After all, the insertion of the safeguarding clauses would have no meaning if the Arabs were expected to remain numerically in the majority. For then there would have been no necessity to 'safeguard' their rights; on the contrary, the Mandate would have stipulated that they be asked to guarantee such 'safeguards' to the non-Arab minorities. Therefore the insertion of the safeguarding clauses could only have been necessitated by the author's expectation that in the event of the Jews, as a result of immigration, which was stipulated in the Mandate as a positive obligation,[235] attaining a population majority in Palestine, the civil and religious rights and the existing position of the then Arab minority should be safeguarded. This was in the spirit of the provisions regarding similar rights of other minorities which were inserted in the various peace treaties at the Paris Peace Conference. Safeguarding clauses such as these were then generally expected to put an end to the oppression of minorities. One of their staunchest advocates was Toynbee himself, who, as far back as 1915, demanded definite 'guarantees of alien minorities within the national state', after the war:[236]

> When we guarantee a national minority we have of course to define certain liberties which it is to enjoy—liberties, for instance, of religion, education, local self-government—and all the parties at the Peace Conference must contract responsibility for the observance of such stipulation.

It is in the spirit of the minority rights stipulations of the post-World War I period that Toynbee, in the statement of 1930, quoted above, interpreted the term 'civil and religious rights' as meaning the enabling of the Arabs, particularly after the attainment of a Jewish majority in Palestine with all its consequences, to enjoy their rights and position freely as hitherto and, in addition, to maintain and, if possible, improve their standard of living. In his words, again, '. . . the Arabs should receive a sufficient share of any additional material resources . . . to enable them to provide for their natural increase without lowering their existing standard of living'. The same interpretation of these principles was made by the British Government, and it was approved by the Permanent Mandates Commission.[237]

In the course of this analysis I shall submit evidence, again primarily from Toynbee's own writings, that, in accordance with the premise which he outlined in 1930, through the expansion of the economic capacity of the country, (1) additional space has been created for a great multiplication of the number of inhabitants who at the time of the Balfour Declaration and of the Mandate lived in Palestine; (2) the living standard of these elements has greatly increased in every direction;

and (3) all this was the result of the development by Jewish immigrants of Palestine.

In his interpretation of the meaning of the Jewish National Home and of the clauses safeguarding civil and religious rights as outlined above, Toynbee precisely foresaw the likelihood, thanks to Jewish endeavour, of such a prosperous future for the country accompanied by an improvement in the general standards of all the inhabitants. But he expected more. He hoped for a larger surplus of the benefits than the inhabitants, Jews and non-Jews, could utilise. He was sure that such a surplus of benefits would encourage additional Jewish immigration, because these newcomers would not only be no burden on the country but would be able to share in these benefits and increase them further through their labour; and this, finally, might lead to the fulfilment of the Zionist aim: a Jewish majority population as a prerequisite of Statehood. He wrote:[238]

> The margin of additional material resources, arising from development, would be available for the maintenance of an increased Jewish population; and it was certain that the whole available margin would be used for this purpose, since, according to the terms of the Mandate, the Jewish population in Palestine was to be recruited, not only through the natural increase of the Jews already settled in the country, but through immigration; and the number of Jews throughout the world who desired to migrate to Palestine was certainly sufficient to fill the largest practicable annual immigration quotas many times over. Thus, in the matter of population, the eventual strength of the Jewish, not the Arab, population in Palestine was the ultimate unknown quantity. If the maximum possible total population turned out to be low, the Jews might be destined to remain for ever a minority vis-à-vis the Arabs; if the maximum turned out to be high, they might find themselves in a majority before the final aggregate figure was reached.

We see from this that it did not even occur to Toynbee (thirteen years after the Balfour Declaration!) to doubt the right of Jews to immigrate into Palestine and eventually to become a majority there. Nor did he then pretend his deep concern with 'human rights' which he suddenly seems to have discovered more lately[239] with regard to Arabs. On the contrary, he understood and foresaw the great blessing for all the people in the Land of the Jewish minority growing into a majority, as he had applied this minority-majority relationship also with regard to other areas. For instance, elsewhere in this study it has been shown[240] that Toynbee suggested for the territory of the Ottoman Empire, after the break-up, the establishment of four sovereign States, among them the Jewish National Home in Palestine and the 'Armenian National Home' in a certain section east of Anatolia.[241] It is worthy of note in this connection that Toynbee strongly supported the establishment of the Armenian National Home, emphasising[242] that 'the Armenians, next to the Jews, were the most scattered nation in the world', and that they deserved it notwithstanding the fact that they were a minority in the area of Armenia ('no portion of the Ottoman territory was exclusively inhabited by them'[243]). Significantly, the title of his chapter referring to this proposal reads as follows:[244] 'The Armenian Minority in the Area and the Establishment of an Armenian "National Home".'

From this example it also becomes clear that there was no doubt in Toynbee's mind at the time about the possible or probable development of a minority through a national home into a majority population; as is also clearly stated in the quotation above from 1930. The conclusion from this is clear: not only was a permanent Arab majority in Palestine not guaranteed, but if Jews were to respond to the call of Palestine they might in time become a majority in the country. And when, finally, a 'self-governing body out of the population of Palestine with its Jewish and Arab constituents', to use Toynbee's words, had developed, as it might, then a Palestinian State ('body politic') might be proclaimed. In this case the State would be what was once termed a binational State consisting of the two constituents, an Arab minority and a Jewish majority.

That this was the meaning of the Balfour Declaration was confirmed by its authors,[245] who, after all, should have known what they issued, and by its designation as a 'declaration of sympathy with Jewish Zionist aspirations', as stated in the Declaration itself. As to the meaning of these 'Zionist aspirations', there surely could never be any doubt. They certainly never aimed at safeguarding and guaranteeing a permanent Arab majority in Palestine. They were at the time defined by a commission of the British Foreign Office, in two guide-books for the British Delegation to the Paris Peace Conference,[246] as follows:

Jewish opinion would prefer Palestine to be controlled for the present as a part, or at any rate a dependency, of the British Empire; but its administration should be largely entrusted to Jews of the colonial type, who have already made such notable improvements in the cultivation of the soil, notwithstanding the almost hopeless difficulties imposed upon them by their former corrupt Turkish rulers. Zionists of this way of thinking believe that, under such conditions, the Jewish population would rapidly increase until the Jew became the predominant partner in the combination.[247]

The essence of the Zionist ideal is the desire to found upon the soil of Palestine a revised Hebrew nation based upon an agricultural life and the use of the Hebrew language.[248]

As in many other instances, in this respect also Toynbee provided us with an appropriate description of 'Zionist aspirations', which he wrote in the year of the issuance of the Balfour Declaration:[249]

> For the Zionists Jewry is a nation, and to become like other nations it needs a motherland. In the Jewish colonies in Palestine they see not merely a successful social enterprise but the visible symbol of a body politic. . . . The foundation of a national university in Jerusalem is as ultimate a goal for them as the economic development of the land, and their greatest achievement has been the revival of Hebrew as the living language of the Palestinian Jews. . . .
>
> What is the outlook for Palestine after the War? If the Ottoman pretension survives, the menace from Turkish Nationalism and German resentment is grave. But if Turk and German go, there are Zionists who would like to see Palestine a British Protectorate, with the prospect of growing into a British Dominion.

The first thing that comes out prominently when reading this quotation from Toynbee's book of 1917 is that he refers there to the emergence 'of a body politic' in Palestine in the same sense as he used the phrase again in the passage quoted earlier from his writings in 1930. This shows a consistency, 'a unity of outlook, aim and idea', of which he spoke with some pride in connection with another consistency in his ideas during a period of over twenty years.[250] Primarily it shows, however, that there was no way of misunderstanding or misinterpreting the meaning of Zionism and its aspirations either when it was first considered for realisation (1917) or during the process of realisation (1930).

It is in the same sense that the League of Nations, incorporating the Balfour Declaration into the Palestine Mandate, emphasised that[251]

> recognition has thereby been given to the historical connection of the Jewish people with Palestine and to the ground of reconstituting their National Home there.

The prefix 're' in the word 'reconstituting' is of vital importance. It refers to something that had existed in Palestine in the past, and this something was neither vague nor unknown; it was the last sovereign rule of Jews in Palestine. It is equally important in the formulation above of the Mandate to find the term 'their' National Home and not 'a' National Home, emphasising that it is to be 'theirs' and nobody else's. And it does not matter, despite Toynbee's great efforts to complicate the point, whether in history that sovereignty was exercised all the time over all the Palestine territory, or at times over parts of the country only, or even beyond its borders. What matters is the fact that Jews had been sovereign rulers in Palestine and, in fact, the only native sovereign rulers—discounting the Latin Kingdom—and it was the intention of the Mandate to assist them to attain such sovereignty again within borders to be agreed upon by the deciding parties concerned. And there can be no sovereignty without a majority population. Zionists aspired to attain this majority. They did not conceal these aspirations when presenting them to the nations of the world in the decisive years. Dr Weizmann, their principal spokesman before the Paris Peace Conference, when asked by the American representative Robert Lansing whether the term 'Jewish National Home' meant an 'autonomous Jewish Government', replied that[252]

> The Zionist Organisation did not want an autonomous Jewish Government, but merely to establish in Palestine, under a mandatory Power, an administration, not necessarily Jewish, which would render it possible to send into Palestine 70,000–80,000 Jews annually. The Association would require to have permission at the same time to build Jewish schools, where Hebrew would be taught, and in that way to build up gradually a nationality which would be as Jewish as the French nation was French and the British nation British. Later on, when the Jews formed a large majority, they would be ripe to establish such a Government as would answer to the state of development of the country and to their ideals.

We know, of course, that the British authorities later repudiated the phrase 'as Jewish . . . as Britain is British', because it could have been interpreted as implying the imposition of Judaism and of the Jewish ethnic nationality upon the Arabs,[253] which would transgress the safeguards of their civil and religious rights. The Zionists unequivocally accepted this repudiation.[254] But the Zionist aspiration of attaining in Palestine a majority population and subsequently possible Statehood has remained unaltered, as Churchill, after whom that *White Paper* containing the 'repudiation' is named, confirmed to the Royal Commission,[255] and as Toynbee himself pointed out, in an otherwise unfriendly article, soon after the acceptance of that document by the Zionists:[256]

> The Zionist Organisation has now officially accepted the British government's programme of procedure. This shows very praiseworthy strength of mind and moderation on their part, when the pressure of extremists is taken into account. But after all, the Jews have everything to gain by a régime under which they will be able to raise from being a small minority to becoming equal to or even stronger than the Arabs.

In fact, Toynbee should have derived great satisfaction from his own original support of the establishment of a Jewish National Home in Palestine,[257] and should have taken pride in the fact that, as his letter to the late Nahum Sokolow of 1919 shows,[258] he hoped for the re-establishment of Jewry in liberated Palestine at that early moment, and was able to witness its realisation twenty-nine years later. And even beyond this, having carefully studied the conditions as they developed after World War I and having observed the emerging difficulties in the Jewish-Arab relationship, it was he of all people who foretold precisely what actually was adopted eighteen years later in the resolution of the United Nations in 1947.[259] Speaking at a meeting in London in 1930, he said:[260]

> I prophesy[261] that, on the ultimate map of population and landholding in Palestine, the Jewish population and the land in Jewish hands will be separated geographically from the Arab population and from the land in Arab hands. The two communities in Palestine will be segregated into two separate blocks.

But the enigmatic Toynbee went a different way. Disregarding all these past sentiments and beliefs, over forty years later, and through an incorrect rendition of the texts and an incorrect interpretation of their meaning, he turns iconoclast in order to assist the enemies of Zionism and Israel in their attempts to undo the work resulting from the Balfour Declaration, the Mandate, and the subsequent developments in Palestine. This is not a question of whether these attempts succeed or not; it is a moral question of the spirit and manner in which support is given to these attempts. In comparison with his writings, replete with appeals to morals, ethics, and human rights, this deep contrast cannot be missed. It is not only a contrast between correct and incorrect texts but also, and primarily, between the two Toynbees whom we have met in the previous pages and will encounter again, with regard to both learning and intentions. This antipodal aspect is to no small degree apparent also in its human features. For instance, in contrast to his militantly negative attitude towards the vital documents which have been dealt with in this section, and towards their implementation in their original meaning, Toynbee advised his readers forty-odd years ago, with regard to this very theme, as follows:[262]

> ... there were thus some Near-Eastern people who were deeply aggrieved by their lot. The difference was that, the aggrieved parties no longer seriously expected to alter it. ... *In the interest of the defeated peoples themselves, as well as for the general good,* it was better that this should be so and that even justifiable claims should be abandoned in despair, for only this turning of the back upon the past could release the remaining energies of each nation for the urgent task of putting its own house in order and repairing the economic waste of a hundred and fifty years of conflict.

Instead of heeding his own advice, Toynbee, in his article as well as elsewhere in lectures and writings, reopens the discussion. Fifty-odd years ago the *History of the Peace Conference*, in which Toynbee was one of the collaborators, offered the following explanation:[263]

> The policy of the [Balfour] Declaration may be justifiable or unjustifiable, the adoption of that policy wise or unwise. But conceding that the policy must now be executed, the terms of the Mandate are difficult to criticise except in a spirit of factiousness.

But, in fact, Toynbee, blinded by prejudice, later went far beyond factiousness. For none but a bellicose meaning can be given to his words:[264]

It was only ninety years after the conquest of Palestine by the Crusaders that the Muslims won the disputed Holy Land back again. So what are the nine years during which the present-day Palestinian Arab exiles have been waiting so far?

Or to the question which he asked in a later work:[265]

> But what about Israel? Did nineteenth-century Italy have any thorn in her flesh like that? Well, yes, she did. She had the Papal States. The maintenance of the Papacy's temporal power was backed by World Catholicism, and this is as formidable a force as World Jewry. Yet in 1870 the union of Italy was completed by the incorporation of Rome.

And in such allusive yet clearly understandable terms writes the prophet of a new age who roams the world preaching peace and humanitarianism to others, advancing the idea of one world in the sense of Deutero-Isaiah and Jesus Christ, and warns us of the danger of future wars.

Part III

Nazism—Zionism—Toynbeeism

... the first stage in an historian's spiritual pilgrimage is the experience of a communion on the mundane plane with persons and events from which, in his usual state of consciousness, he is sundered by a great gulf of Time and Space that, in ordinary circumstances, is impassable for all his faculties except his intellect.

—Toynbee, *Study of History*, X, 129/130.

Pharaoh never died in the waters of the sea; and will never die. He stands at the portals of Gehinom and, when those who oppress or hurt Jews enter, he greets them with the words: 'Why have you not profited by my example?'

—An old Jewish legend.

1

The First Phase: Deir Yassin and Expulsions

In connection with the Arab refugee problem, Toynbee has repeatedly identified Zionism with Nazism. Since making a statement to that effect publicly for the first time in 1954, he has changed his basic argument about the reasons which, in his opinion, justified him in making this identification. It is interesting to follow the two phases of his argumentation, which are not only diametrically opposite in character and scope, but also shed light on Toynbee's method of writing history.

The first phase can be summarised by the term 'Deir Yassin and Expulsions'; the second phase by the term 'Seizures and Expropriations'.

His first published statement about Zionist-Nazi identification, as remarked above, was made in 1954, when he wrote:[1]

> The evil deeds committed by the Zionist Jews against the Palestinian Arabs that were comparable to crimes committed against the Jews by Nazis were the massacre of men, women and children at Dayr Yassin on the 9th April 1948, which precipitated a flight of the Arab population, in large numbers, from districts within range of Jewish armed forces, and the subsequent deliberate expulsion of the Arab population from districts conquered by the Jewish armed forces between the 15th May 1948, and the end of the year. . . .
>
> The Arab bloodshed on the 9th April, 1948, at Dayr Yassin was on the heads of Irgun; the expulsions after 15th May, 1948, were on the heads of all Israel.

Throughout his *Study* and his other works, Toynbee always showed himself most anxious to quote chapter and verse in corroboration of statements he made, or of events to which he referred, even if those sources were one-sided or biased. But he usually had some source to refer to. However, in this case no literature was quoted. Nor was the wider background of the happenings around and in Deir Yassin mentioned; above all, it was nowhere stated that the tragic struggle for Deir Yassin was one of the many battles in a war that, with interruptions, had lasted for many months before April 9, 1948. Toynbee seemed to disregard even the one reference to Deir Yassin which appeared in the same year (1954) under his editorship—in the *Survey for 1939–1946*. Therein he could have found the following description:[2]

> Deir Yassin was attacked and it was asserted that an Arab band had seized the village for an attack on Jerusalem, that it was an important point in the movements of Arab guerrillas in this sector, or even that the Haganah's regional commander in Jerusalem had authorised the attack in order to further a plan to establish a Jewish airfield there.[3] The I.Z.L.[4] attackers shouted over a loud-speaker from an armoured car orders in Arabic to the inhabitants to leave their houses and take shelter within fifteen minutes. Some obeyed. The I.Z.L. afterwards claimed to have suffered appreciable casualties in the house-to-house fighting that followed.[5]

A serious historian would also have looked for further literature and evidence, to have his assumptions 'confronted with relevant facts and . . . confirmed by them', a principle which he himself had laid down and we accepted as a guide for this investigation. In the memoirs of the chief commander of the Irgun, the body responsible for the Deir Yassin tragedy, which his *Survey* had quoted, we read:[6]

> Through Deir Yassin Arab forces from Ein Kerem and Bethlehem crossed to the Kastel front, whence they attacked Jewish convoys along the only road from Jerusalem to the coast. . . . it had to be captured . . . both sides suffered casualties. We had four killed and nearly forty wounded. The number of casualties was nearly forty per cent of the total number of attackers. The Arab troops suffered casualties three times as heavy. The fighting was thus very severe. Yet hostile propaganda, disseminated throughout the world, deliberately ignored the fact that the civilian population of Deir Yassin was actually given a warning by us before the battle began. One of our tenders carrying a loud-speaker was stationed at the

entrance to the village and it exhorted in Arabic all women, children and aged to leave their houses and to take shelter on the slope of the hill. By giving this humane warning our fighters threw away the element of complete surprise, and thus increased their own risk in the ensuing battle. A substantial number of the inhabitants obeyed the warning and they were unhurt. A few did not leave their stone houses—perhaps because of the confusion. The fire of the enemy was murderous—to which the number of casualties bears eloquent testimony. Our men were compelled to fight for every house; to overcome the enemy they used large numbers of hand-grenades. And the civilians who had disregarded our warnings suffered inevitable casualties.

There was, of course, bloodshed in Deir Yassin and many Arab people, old and young, lost their lives. No Jew, no Zionist, approved of such tragic events, and the Jewish Agency as well as the Chief Rabbinate made this clear in unequivocal terms.[7] Toynbee would not have had to look far for the Zionists' reaction to Deir Yassin, for the *Survey* under his editorship also emphasised that[8] the Zionist authorities expressed 'horror and disgust' over them. The Headquarters of the Irgun also expressed deep regret over the death of innocent people in its official statement about Deir Yassin:[9]

> We express our great sorrow that women and children were also among the dead, but our fighters are not guilty. They did more than their human duty (*i.e.* the warning preceding the attack, thus endangering their own lives).

In addition, the Irgun chief commander himself stated in his memoirs:[10]

> The education which we gave our soldiers throughout the years of revolt was based on the observance of the traditional laws of war. We never broke them unless the enemy first did so and thus forced us, in accordance with accepted custom of war, to apply reprisals. I am convinced, too, that our officers and men wished to avoid a single unnecessary casualty in the Deir Yassin battle.

And, as Toynbee in his attitude towards Zionism has adopted the Arab viewpoint in recent years, it may be appropriate to refer also to a description of the Deir Yassin tragedy by one of the surviving Arab inhabitants of the village, who, in an account of the battle, wrote:[11]

The Jews never intended to hurt the population of the village but were forced to do so after they encountered enemy fire from the village populace, who also killed the Irgun commander.

All this was not mentioned in Toynbee's story. The only hints which the reader may find in his volume (*Study*, VIII) at some fighting, apart from the Deir Yassin event, were couched in uncorroborated generalisations such as 'the territory of Palestine which the Zionist Jews conquered by force of arms',[12] or 'the Zionist Jews who seized the *Lebensraum* for themselves in Palestine by force of arms'.[13] Thus formulated they continued the method he employed with regard to Deir Yassin, *i.e.* to show that suddenly, for no other reason presumably than a lust for conquest, the Jewish armed forces were sent against the unaware, innocent, and undefended Arabs in Palestine and deprived them, in the Nazi terminology, of their *Lebensraum*. Only one phrase in this whole book can be interpreted as indicating that, after all, there was a war on in Palestine, namely, where Toynbee speaks of 'military operations between the outbreak of hostilities in Palestine in December 1947 and the massacre of the 9th April, 1948'.[14] But in the context of the description of this period, this phrase can mean nothing else than a summary of Jewish aggression, for, in the three pages of his *Study* where Toynbee described these events,[15] there is not one word about the participation of Arabs in the hostilities; they were the 'victims' only. Nor is any word to be found about the fact of which President Truman was already informed[16] on October 9, 1947—six weeks even before the U.N. made the Palestine decision—that the Arab Governments had then already sent troops to the borders of Palestine, ready for action when, in their opinion, the time was ripe. Nor does Toynbee mention the war which the Arabs themselves had initiated in December, 1947, against the Jews, and to which the U.N. Palestine Commission had called attention two months before Deir Yassin:[17]

> Powerful Arab interests, both inside and outside Palestine, are defying the resolution of the General Assembly—*i.e.* the resolution of November 29, 1947, for the partition of the land into a Jewish and Arab state—and are engaged in a deliberate effort to alter by force the settlement envisaged therein.

Describing the battles of this war, in the course of which hundreds of Jews and Arabs were killed, Toynbee's own *Survey* stated that[18]

> the attacks were bloody affairs in which neither side was accustomed to
> give quarter or return prisoners.

In the days of Deir Yassin (April, 1948), the war had already lasted five
months, and its scope, to quote Toynbee's *Survey* again, had assumed
wide proportions:[19]

> At the beginning of April the Zionists were still seriously challenged by the
> 'Arab Liberation Army' which had by this time publicly received the
> blessing of the Governments of Arab states and had been reinforced to a
> strength of between 6,000 and 7,500 men, preponderantly Syrians and
> Iraqis with an Egyptian contingent at Gaza. The Arab forces were based,
> with a large measure of British tolerance, on localities within the territory
> assigned to the Arab state by the resolution of partition.

Toynbee omitted all reference to these events, not only in Volume
VIII of his *Study* but also in all subsequent writings which touched on
that period. It may suffice as a comment on this omission, to quote a
statement made by the late Dr Mordecai Eliash, representative of the
Jewish Agency, a strictly Orthodox gentleman, known and generally
recognised as a gentle, 'saintly' person, in the Security Council on May
15, 1948, which was neither denied nor contradicted by any subsequent
Arab speaker:[20]

> Atrocities which have been invented—I say it quite deliberately—have been
> enumerated in the telegram read before this Council,[21] but the facts which
> have occurred—such as when some seventy members of the Hebrew
> University and Hospital, including professors, doctors, and nurses, were
> brutally murdered on the way to the University on a peaceful mission—
> are never mentioned. Nor is mention made when, within the sacred walls
> of the Old City of Jerusalem, passions were let loose to such an extent that
> in an ecstacy of war the heads of beheaded Jews have been used in dancing
> within the sacred walls. They are not mentioned as things that have
> happened in Palestine.

Indeed they were never mentioned, as Dr Eliash said, nor has even one
Arab leader ever found it necessary to express 'horror or disgust' over
them, as did Jewish and Zionist leaders in the Deir Yassin tragedy, or
regret about the inevitability of such heavy sacrifices, as did the leader

of the attacking force. In none of Toynbee's writings is reference to these Arab atrocities found.

To take just one example, one might recall the Jewish settlement of Kfar Etzion, where a wholesale massacre of Jewish men, women, children, and the aged by the Arabs took place on May 14, 1948. This massacre was not only not condemned or regretted by Arab leaders, but was hailed in the Arab sector of Jerusalem by Nazi-like fanfares and church bells. Kfar Etzion was a village, one of four Jewish settlements, inhabited by strictly Orthodox Jews, *i.e.* Jews of a religious observance which Toynbee has endeavoured in his writings to set against Zionism and national aspirations.[22] If for no other reason than that, his oft-declared admiration for and acceptance of traditional Judaism should have induced him to pay tribute to these martyrs, who, even if only fleetingly, had been mentioned in the *Survey* under his editorship.[23] When Kfar Etzion was attacked

> the Legionnaires of [Transjordan] were joined by hundreds of local Arabs who swarmed into the village in their wake; the battle was turned into a massacre.
>
> An officer of the Legion called on the defenders to surrender, and some fifteen men came out and gave up their arms. As they stood in a row at the command of the officer, who wished to photograph them, a local Arab stepped forward with a sub-machine gun and mowed down the line of men, despite the protests of the officer. Altogether, of the whole population of the village, only three men and a girl succeeded in getting out; the rest were all killed. It was the end of Kfar Etzion.
>
> Meanwhile, in near-by Jerusalem, the fall of Etzion was the cause of jubilation among the Arabs. Church bells in the old city rang out the victory tidings . . .[24]

Many more examples of Arab brutalities could be quoted, a great number of which can be found in the works, referred to above, with which Toynbee was so closely connected.[25] But in his own writings, no word about these brutalities or the war is mentioned. In an objective description of the Arab-Israel war it would have had to come out, through correct documentation, that the Arabs launched the war and that the Jews had only defended their lives, their rights, and the decision of the United Nations approving of the establishment of the State of Israel.

Jews Should Not Defend Themselves

In the light of Toynbee's attitude towards Jewry *per se*, this last point goes deeper than just serving as an additional reason for his silence on the war. For in his view, Jews, unlike other human beings, if attacked, are not supposed to defend themselves. As we have shown in a previous section, Toynbee has designated quite a different role for Jewry— namely, to continue its existence in the Diaspora:[26]

> As an historian, peering into the future in the light of the past, I spy the wave of the future in the Jewish Diaspora.

We have dealt elsewhere with the various objects which Toynbee has set out for the Diaspora, with its meaning in the past and in the future. At this point one more characteristic can be added (it is, indeed, one of the principal characteristics of the Jewish Diaspora in Toynbee's structure). According to this,[27] it was

> quietism . . . that has been Jewry's consistent practice for some sixty generations . . .

which to no small degree is said to have helped it to survive. This is nothing other than his 'penalisation' theory in another guise.

Webster defines the term 'quietism': 'A system of religious mysticism, teaching that perfection and spiritual peace are attained by self-annihilation and passive absorption in contemplation of God and divine things'.

In order to fit the eighteen centuries of the Jewish Diaspora into this quietist concept, Toynbee, in his *Study of History*, 'adjusted' events in Jewish history to serve his purpose. One of the many examples which he enumerates suffices to make this clear. Thus he says,[28]

> the Jewish Martyrs who gave their lives for Judaism in its three-hundred-year-long struggle with Hellenism, all suffered and died without offering any physical resistance.

There is no doubt that this suicidal martyr's way arouses his admiration. Anything defying quietism in Jewish history therefore meets with his emphatic rejection; as did the defiance of quietism by the armed in- surrection of Judas Maccabaeus. Describing this event, Toynbee, as he did with regard to the fighting in the Arab-Israel war of 1948, omitted reference to the fact that the Maccabees had fought a desperate battle in defence of their lives, of Jewish independence, of national, cultural, and religious survival; a defensive war against Antiochus Epiphanes, who had massacred the Jewish population of Jerusalem, stolen all the treasures of the Temple, and enthroned the Olympian Zeus in the Holiest of Holies. Yet Toynbee himself had once described the Maccabaean battle, when he wrote[29] that

> they turned the swords that had first been drawn in self-defence, in order to save the Jewish religion from extinction.

Although he thus understood the religio-national aspect of this defensive war, without regard to these facts, he indulged in a description of the Maccabees' defence with such phrases as

> the Satanic Jewish émeutes[30] . . . and the demonic reaction of the Maccabees,[31]

a terminology which he used in this same work and another for the description of Nazism, when he referred to

> Hitler's satanic spirit[32] . . . and the demonic German Neobarbarism.[33]

This reveals an unfortunate identity of terminology which illustrates Toynbee's efforts to confuse desperate defence with murderous attack when Jews, in the past and in the present, were involved. He had to embark on this line, for otherwise he could not maintain his amazing theory of Judaism and the Diaspora as he had laid it down in his theory of 'penalisations', of 'pioneering through sufferings', and the passive endurance of persecution.[34] This is, as we have shown, an imitation of Christian teachings; they are not Jewish tenets and have never been accepted by Jews. Judaism teaches resistance against evil and the duty to overcome it. 'Hate the evil, and love the good, and establish justice in the gate', admonished the great Amos (v. 15).

Quietism in the Diaspora was not a voluntary act; it was forced on the Jews by the overwhelming physical power of a merciless world. Wherever the Jews had a chance, they resisted it—from Moses, when destroying the Egyptian oppressor, and the Maccabees, when fighting Syria to regain freedom, to the revolt in the Warsaw Ghetto against the Nazi tyranny, and to the defence in Palestine against Arab efforts at annihilation. This was in full conformity with the teaching of the Jewish Sages which forms part of the Jewish oral tradition (Talmud):

If someone comes to kill you, get up and kill him.[35]

Rabbi Akiba, who himself, to quote Toynbee,[36] was one of the 'martyrs who gave their lives for Judaism', interpreted the words (*Leviticus*, xxv, 36) 'that thy brother may live *with* thee' as meaning[37]

that your life comes before the life of your neighbour.

To defend oneself is, however, not only a Jewish teaching but has been accepted by all peoples on earth who refuse to be annihilated—whatever the purpose of that annihilation may be. The great philosopher of humanism, and statesman, Thomas G. Masaryk, whom Toynbee held in such high esteem,[38] expressed the above-quoted Talmudic thought (unconsciously, of course) in a conversation with Count Tolstoy in Yasna Polyana in 1910, as follows:[39]

If someone attacks me with the intention of killing me, I shall defend myself, and if I cannot avoid it, I shall kill the attacker. If one of us two must be killed, let the one be killed who has the bad intentions.

This is, of course, Toynbee's attitude where he himself or the non-Jews are concerned. Challenged by his critics on the matter of defence, he agreed:[40]

The first step towards conquering a dangerous enemy or keeping at bay a dangerous disease is to take danger seriously. This is one of the elementary rules of self-defence. The most fatal of all possible reactions to an opponent is to try to get rid of him by ignoring his existence. This is, surely childishly irrational, and, if so, any student of human affairs in the Age of Civilisations up to date ought to give far more attention to war than to all the arts of peace put together.

But what applies to all other peoples does not apply, in Toynbee's world, to the Jews. They are anyhow 'debris' and therefore not worthy of further existence. As he said in 1934(!)[41]

The debris of this devoted Syriac people . . . is a splendid failure.

Jews therefore are not entitled to the considerations expounded by Toynbee, who elsewhere[42] points out the perils of pacifism in practical life. They are not to refuse 'submission' to an enemy who had announced in unequivocal terms, through the mouth of the Secretary General of the Arab League:[43]

> This will be a war of extermination and a momentous massacre which will be spoken of like the Mongolian massacres and the Crusades.

In the moral distinction between the pattern of aggression and the act of resistance lies the fundamental difference between the Nazi-like crime and Deir Yassin. The Nazis were seeking conquest and expansion; and because they could not attain these by threats and blackmail, they plunged the world into a terrible war, in the course of which millions of innocent people lost their lives and/or homes. These innocent people were killed by both the Nazi aggressors and by what Toynbee termed the 'unaggressive peoples' who fought back in self-defence. Likewise Palestine Jews and world Jewry did not seek conquest or expansion, nor did they try to attain their aims through initiating a war. By peaceful means of persuasion in presenting their case to the civilised world they raised their claim for a State of their own, and after a long and thorough consideration by the nations of the world, this claim was found to be justified. The Jews accepted the resolution of the world community as represented in the United Nations. They were, however, attacked by Arabs primarily from outside even before they set out to implement the resolution. This aggressive attack by foreign Arab States forced the Jews to defend themselves and thus automatically also the decision of the United Nations. Like the 'unaggressive people' of the world who won their defensive war against Nazi tyranny and thus 'bought for our society an opportunity to get rid of War by a better way than submission', as Toynbee so wisely stated, so the unaggressive Jews, too, won their defensive war by not accepting surrender and submission.

The Double Standard

Toynbee's writings, as we have seen, apply two different standards to Jews and non-Jews. The former are always to be different, to be the exception. The refrain frequently recurs in his works: 'Jews should not do this or that', or 'to see any Jews, however few', doing what others are doing, is repulsive, etc. . . .[44] This device enables him to eliminate at pleasure any comparison between Jews and non-Jews in history and in the present when acts of a similar nature are to be judged from either a moral or a simple comparative point of view. By saying 'you are finer people, this is not becoming to Jews', he creates an opportunity for himself to avoid such comparisons and always to blame the Jews. Two examples may be noted from his writings and will suffice to prove this point: one concerning the Greeks he admires and the other the Muslims.

After the Greek debacle in Anatolia (1922), Greek residents escaped to their old homeland, and, in order to make room for them, the Greek authorities expelled the Bulgarian inhabitants who for generations had lived in Western Thrace. In the course of these expulsions the Greeks seized the Bulgarians' houses, lands, and properties. The returning Greeks, as Toynbee then wrote,[45] 'were lodged in these Bulgarian deportees' vacant houses'. In many instances the Bulgarians had to be forcibly expelled, as, for instance, in the peaceful border village of Tarlis. One morning all the men of the village, some sixty to seventy Bulgarians, were arrested by the Greek police and, as Toynbee describes it,[46]

> on the following day twenty-seven Bulgars were tied together and dispatched to a neighbouring village . . . On the way Lieutenant Doxakis opened fire on the Bulgarians. Thirteen appear to have been killed on the spot, and others wounded.

The Mixed Emigration Commission, in investigating this event, called it 'a massacre without justification or provocation'.[47]

One may pause and inquire whether Toynbee's conscience compelled him to condemn these massacres in strong terms. Nothing of the kind. He blandly noted that[48]

> they [i.e. the Emigration Commission] exonerated the Greek Government from responsibility but censured the local authorities, apart from the question of the massacre itself, for grave negligence. . . .

And, in effect further exonerating the Greeks from the guilt of creating that tragic refugeedom, he added an equally bland footnote in which he stated:[49]

See, however, a letter from Colonel Proctor . . . in which the assertion that Bulgarians had been forced to leave Western Thrace to make room for Greek refugees was categorically denied.

What a convincing piece of 'evidence'!

There seems to me no need to draw a contrast with Toynbee's treatment of Deir Yassin or to speculate on what vocabulary Toynbee would have used had the Greeks in Tarlis been Zionists. But Greeks apparently were permitted to be 'lodged in . . . deportees' vacant houses', their Government was exonerated from the guilt of a massacre, and only the local authorities were 'censured', etc. . . .

It may be said that the Greek episode is not a valid example of his double standards, because Toynbee's attitude towards massacres may have undergone a profound change since 1925, when he wrote the description above. Although I do not accept the correctness and justification of such an argument, for massacres are massacres and remain morally condemnable throughout every phase of a person's life (Toynbee in 1925 was already 36 years old and had been a University teacher for 13 years), nevertheless I submit another example from his writings, published in 1954, quoted from the very volume in which he compared the Deir Yassin tragedy with Nazi crimes. This example confirms not only the double standards, but also his unchanged moral stand towards massacres when perpetuated by those whom he favours.

Referring to Mohammed's treatment of the Jews, Toynbee could not avoid mentioning the Prophet's and his gang's military raids against the Jews in the Medina area,[50] the massacres they committed, and their distribution of the spoils among themselves. He wrote:[51]

> . . . this militant prophet had provided for his landless Meccan followers at Medina by instigating the massacre and spoliation of the Jewish husbandmen in the Medina oasis.

As a great admirer of Mohammed and[52] Islam, Toynbee is without doubt familiar with the special Sura incorporated in the *Koran* in praise of this massacre. His memory may, however, be refreshed with the first two verses from that Sura:[53]

> 1. What is in heaven and on earth praises Allah. . . .
> 2. He it is who forced the infidels of the people of the Book to leave their

homes[54] and to join those who emigrated before them.[55] You did not think that their fortifications would save them against Allah. But Allah came from an entirely unexpected side and cast fear into their hearts. Thus when were their houses laid waste at their own hands as well as through those of the believers. Take this as an example, you men who have eyes!

One would think that Toynbee, who only six pages after mentioning Mohammed's massacre wrote about the Deir Yassin tragedy and compared it with Nazi crimes, would have found some harsh words of condemnation for the massacre and plunder of innocent people whose only 'crime' was that they did not accept Mohammed's teachings. Did Toynbee condemn this act? Did he compare the massacre of these villagers by the Muslims with the butchery in Lidice or in concentration camps by the Nazis? Nothing of the kind. This is how he excused the Muslims:[56]

> ... after all, had not Mohammed made some considerable amends to the rest of Jewry for a crime committed by him against a single Jewish community of the Banu Qurayzah in the single oasis of Yathrib (*trucidati* A.D. 627) when, on the occasion of his subsequent conquest of the North Arabian Jewish oasis of Khaybar (*captum* A.D. 629), he had given Judaism an abiding legal guarantee of toleration under Muslim rule by a less maleficent exercise of the same political power that he had misused in dooming the Medinese Jews to destruction?

Apart from the fact that this description is not correct,[57] it is very illuminating and characteristic in the context of the study of Toynbee's double standards. The paragraph above shows that Toynbee found it compatible with the moral and ethical principles which he does not fail to proclaim on every occasion to excuse the murder of men, women, children, and the aged in one village as the price of permission for other people to live peacefully in another village. No less characteristic is it that in the defensive war of the Maccabees, he applies to *the soldiers*, as we have seen, the same epithets as he applies to the Nazis, such as 'demonic' and 'satanic', although the Maccabean uprising took place almost 800 years before Mohammed, while the two or three Lidice-like crimes planned and executed by the prophet and founder of one of 'the higher religions'[58] described in a volume where Nazi crimes do not play an unimportant role in comparison with massacres of this kind, did not induce Toynbee to find even one word of condemnation of the Muslims.

All these considerations seem to me relevant in the investigation of the question of why Toynbee did not mention that the 1947–1948 war was initiated by the Arabs against Palestinian Jews, and why he selected Deir Yassin as the only tragic event in the Arab-Israeli strife. Next to his one-sided interpretation, and his unfounded condemnation of the Jews, one can but juxtapose his own views, the sole criterion for arriving at the truth: that statements 'can be validated only if they are confronted with relevant facts and are confirmed by them'.

Expulsions

We have earlier noted that Toynbee advanced the conclusion that Deir Yassin precipitated a flight of large numbers of Arabs, while mass expulsions of Arabs from areas occupied by the Israel armed forces followed the establishment of the State of Israel on May 14, 1948.

There is no doubt that Deir Yassin precipitated flights of Arabs if 'precipitated' here means 'accelerated', and not 'caused to happen suddenly'.[59] Deir Yassin did not begin the flights, and it almost goes without saying that this fact was not made clear by Toynbee. Actually, the Arab exodus began very shortly after the adoption by the U.N. of the partition resolution of November 29, 1947, which, as stated above, was followed by ever-increasing attacks by Arabs on Jews all over the country, and by Jewish countermeasures. On December 18, 1947, the Arabic press reported that already some two thousand Arab families from Palestine had been evacuated from 'danger zones' there and housed in temporary camps in Lebanon.[60]

This was a significant development, because it was the first instance of a new policy pursued by the Palestinian Arab Higher Executive: to evacuate Palestinian Arabs and take them to 'safer' places in adjacent Arab States. This new policy was to play an important role in the course of the Arab-Israel war, and in the creation of Arab refugeedom. It was without doubt arrived at either on the advice of the neighbour-ing Arab States, or in conjunction with them, because the evacuees could not have been brought to the neighbouring States without the consent of those countries. That already at that early date the adjacent

Arab States had considerable strategic influence on internal Arab affairs in Palestine is also confirmed by the fact, emphasised in Toynbee's *Survey*[61] that

> from December 1947 onwards . . . reinforcements from the Arab states came to the support of the Palestine Arabs,

and were soon followed by

> further bands of trained and well-equipped Syrians, their officers drawn from the Syrian army.[62]

They were sent to Palestine 'to stiffen the less effectual local Arab fighters',[63] which clearly indicated that these local Palestinian Arabs were not at all as bellicose towards the emergence of a Jewish State as were their exiled leaders and the leaders of the various Arab States. This was corroborated by the same *Survey*, which further emphasised that[64]

> the more moderate and pacific elements of the Arab community were less enthusiastic, however, about the presence of these non-Palestinian Arab troops . . .

for the simple reason that their presence could only mean fighting and bloodshed. They preferred, therefore, to seek 'safety' in time. This applied primarily to the middle-class portion of the country's Arab population.

This situation, as it developed in the period December, 1947, to April 9, 1948 (Deir Yassin), was described in Toynbee's *Survey* as follows:[65]

> The beginning of the mass Arab flight went back to an early stage of the Arab-Jewish fighting. As early as 27 January 1948 the High Commissioner (United Nations Palestine Commission: First Special Report to the Security Council, A/AC 21/9 [16 February 1948]; cf. *Zionist Review*, 26 December 1947, p. 1; and Channing B. Richardson, in 'International Tensions in the Middle East, A Series of Addresses and Papers . . .,' *Proceedings of the Academy of Political Science*, January 1952, XXIV, 384) had confirmed a 'steady exodus' of Arab middle-class families who could afford to leave the country, taking with them cars and considerable quantities of household goods. In March Zionist sources estimated that 20,000–25,000 Arabs had already left Haifa and 15,000–20,000 Jaffa; and the Arab irregulars' use of conveniently situated Arab villages as bases for attacks on Jewish localities, and the consequent Jewish reprisals against such villages, had caused a substantial flight of Arabs from villages on the fringe of Jewish territory to

safer places. (See *Zionist Review*, 19 March 1948, p. 7, and 2 April 1948, p. 3; [Harry] Sacher [*Israel, the Establishment of a State*, London, 1952], *op. cit.*, p. 149.) That British officials in some cases advised Arabs to seek safety may have been the basis of later Zionist assertions that the British had stimulated the Arabic panic and created the refugee problem (See [Harry] Levin, *op. cit.* [*Jerusalem Embattled*, London, 1950], p. 104, reporting the Hebrew press; Begin, *The Revolt*, p. 179).

From what has now been said, we can discern the first three important factors which led to Arab refugeedom: (1) the evacuation of Arabs from 'danger zones' in Palestine on the advice of Arab leaders; (2) the voluntary flight of Arab middle-class inhabitants to escape from eventual hostilities; and (3) the evacuation of Arabs on the advice of the British authorities. If one looks very carefully into Toynbee's description of the events of those days in Vol. VIII of his *Study*, one might even be able to find a reference to all these three factors in a passage where he mentioned Arabs[66]

> who had already been evacuated by the British mandatory authorities or had already fled on their own initiative or had already lost their home as a result of military operations between the outbreak of hostilities in Palestine in December 1947 and the massacre of the 9th April, 1948.

But the incidental way in which Toynbee mentioned these three important factors underlying the Arab exodus indicated an avoidance of anything that might have weakened his main thesis; Jewish brutalities as the primary cause of Arab refugeedom. One has only to look at the context of this quotation in his book to find confirmation of this. These four lines were placed in the midst of a lengthy paragraph, covering almost a whole page, replete with references to Nazi 'genocide', to the tragedy of Deir Yassin, and to the expulsion of Arabs from Palestine. These four lines do not even constitute a sentence on their own, but form a subordinate part within a sentence of which the first half speaks of hundreds and thousands of expelled Arabs. The sentence following this quotation (quoted earlier) points to the Irgun as the guilty party in Deir Yassin, and all Israel in the expulsions.

This minimising of the events in Palestine preceding Deir Yassin by relegating them to an *en passant* mention is, of course, in line with Toynbee's basic tendency to make the Jews guilty of the Arab refugee problem, and to liken them to Nazis. However, even if the reader of the four lines quoted above were able, with the aid of imagination, to interpret them as referring to events preceding April 9, 1948, he definitely could not conclude from them that by that time, *i.e.* before Deir Yassin, the Arab refugee problem had already assumed enormous proportions, that many villages and towns had been abandoned, and that hundreds of thousands of Arabs had already run away or been evacuated. And this seems to me one of the most serious and also characteristic omissions in Toynbee's narrative.

His *Survey* was in this respect more cautious. Unable to omit any reference to the great numbers of Arab refugees before Deir Yassin, because of the nature of the *Survey* series, it mentioned them as follows:[67]

> A subsequent Zionist assertion (in a pamphlet published by the American Zionist Council in December 1951, quoted by Edward Lathan, ed., in *Crisis in the Middle East*, New York, H. W. Wilson, 1952, p. 136) that 'many weeks' before the Deir Yassin massacre the Arab Higher Committee had 'called on the Arab population to leave the country en masse', should be treated with reserve in the absence of positive evidence to corroborate it. . . .

Toynbee's phraseology seems to point to its author's intention of minimising the assertion of the Arab leader's guilt over Arab refugee-dom by hiding behind demands for corroboration through 'positive evidence'. Had the author adhered to this principle throughout and demanded 'positive evidence' for every statement he referred to, the larger part of this volume could never have been published. It appears, however, that, apart from uttering this warning, the author took no steps to find evidence; and this in itself adds strength to the Zionist contention besides the fact that the writer of the volume is well known for his anti-Zionist attitude. For corroborative evidence exists that Arab leaders induced Arabs to leave the country and seek refuge in neighbouring lands in the time before Deir Yassin and before the estab-lishment of the State of Israel. One statement to that effect was quoted above; another is derived from an Arabic newspaper in which it was stated:[68]

> As soon as the British had publicly announced the time for their relinquish-ment of the Mandate and their withdrawal from Palestine, the Arab League

began holding meetings and calling conferences, and its General Secretary, Abdul-Rahman Azzam Pasha, published numerous reports and declarations in which he assured the Arab peoples and all others that the occupation of Palestine and of Tel Aviv (the Jewish capital) would be as simple as a military promenade for the Arab armies.

Brotherly advice was given to the Arabs of Palestine, urging them to leave their land, homes and property and go to stay temporarily in neighbouring, brotherly states, lest guns of the invading Arab armies mow them down. The Palestine Arabs had no choice but to obey the 'advice' of the League and to believe what Azzam Pasha and other responsible men in the League told them—that their withdrawal from their lands and their country was only temporary and would end in a few days with the successful termination of the Arab punitive action against Israel.

And a neutral international body that carefully investigated the situation in Palestine, also in the period before Deir Yassin (April 9, 1948), came to the conclusion that[69]

> as early as the first months of 1948 the Arab League issued orders exhorting the people to seek temporary refuge in the neighbouring countries, later to return to their abodes in the wake of the victorious Arab armies and obtain their share of abandoned Jewish property . . .

Innumerable similar statements could be quoted from Arab and other non-Jewish sources which confirm the Arab leaders' responsibility for creating large numbers of Arab refugees in the period before and after Deir Yassin.

How many such Arab refugees there were between December, 1947, and April, 1948, will probably never be ascertained, because of the nature of these flights, the chaotic conditions under which the exodus took place, and the usual over- or under-estimates (as the case may be) of figures that occur even in normal orderly conditions. Note, for instance, how substantially different are police estimates of a demonstrating crowd compared with the figures given by the organisers of the demonstration and with those of their opponents.

There is, as stated, no doubt that Deir Yassin constituted a turning-point because it gave an accelerated impetus to the flight of Arabs from Palestinian towns and villages, often even when the fighting was still far from their homes. 'Villages were frequently abandoned,' wrote Glubb Pasha, Commander of the Arab Legion, soon after,[70] 'even before they were threatened by the progress of war.' Glubb spoke of 'abandonment', not 'expulsion'. Toynbee's description implied that it may have been a Jewish device planned to create fear among the Arabs in Palestine, lest they too become 'Deir Yassin' victims as soon as Jews conquered their home places. It is erroneous to assume Jewish premeditation, because neither at the time of the tragedy nor later did the Jews, in their propaganda or in any other way, make use of Deir Yassin to frighten Arabs into flight. Not even Toynbee found it possible to make such a direct accusation. This must be said in fairness to him, because he wisely omitted to repeat a hint to that effect in his own *Survey*, where we read:[71]

> At this stage of the fighting the Jewish attitude to the Arab flight was ambiguous, since, while there is clear evidence that the civil authorities at Haifa tried to tranquillize the Arab population, the Jewish combatants there and elsewhere made skilful use of psychological warfare to break their opponents' morale, and the effect upon the civilians was only what was to be expected.

However, the fact is that the Palestine Jewish authorities, after expressing their horror and disgust over the fatal April 9, 1948, avoided mentioning Deir Yassin, as the contemporary literature and documents show, even in other spheres than that of propaganda against the Palestine Arabs.

But something else happened that is no strange phenomenon in those areas of the world. It shows that there was no need for the Jews to utilise Deir Yassin for propaganda purposes. The Arabs themselves took care of this. The memoirs of the Irgun commander, which Toynbee's *Survey* repeatedly quoted, presented the following explanation of the Deir Yassin aftermath:[72]

> To counteract the loss of Deir Yassin, a village of strategic importance, Arab headquarters at Ramalla broadcast a crude atrocity story, alleging massacres by Irgun troops of women and children in the village . . . This Arab propaganda spread like a legend of terror among Arabs and Arab troops, who were seized with panic at the mention of Irgun soldiers. The legend was worth half a dozen battalions to the forces of Israel . . .
>
> The enemy propaganda was designed to besmirch our name. In the result it helped us. Panic overwhelmed the Arabs of Eretz Israel . . . the Arabs

began to flee in terror, even before they clashed with Jewish forces. Not what happened in Deir Yassin, but what was invented about Deir Yassin, helped to carve the way to our decisive victories on the battle-field.

And an Arab survivor of Deir Yassin, Yunes Ahmed Asaad, confirmed this point in a newspaper article:[73]

> The Arab exodus from other villages was not caused by the actual battle of Deir Yassin but by the exaggerated description spread by the Arab leaders for the purpose of inciting the Arabs to fight against the Jews.

Arabs Encouraged, Jews Discouraged, Arab Flights

At this point, accordingly, we can summarise by stating that, contrary to Toynbee's implication, it was Arab exaggeration of the Deir Yassin tragedy that accelerated the flight of Arabs from other areas in Palestine. It was not Jewish propaganda which made use of Deir Yassin to cause panic. This is not only confirmed by the absence of any evidence to the contrary, it is strengthened in a positive way by the fact that Jewish leaders, throughout the entire period of fighting before and after Deir Yassin, endeavoured to persuade the Arabs to remain in Palestine, to accept and abide by the U.N. decision of November 29, 1947, and to share in the responsibility of building up the country.

Thus as soon as the Arab riots broke out, a day after the U.N. decision, the National Council of Jews in Palestine (Va'ad Le'umi) issued the following call:[74]

> Arabs! The National Council of Jews in Palestine sends you words of peace and calls on you not to follow those who invite you to riots and bloodshed ... The Jews plan to build their state ... through complete co-operation and friendship. They have no interest in destruction but in construction. The Jewish effort developed and enriched all of the country in the past—and it will continue to be in the future a perpetual source of blessing to Jews and Arabs alike.
>
> Do not hearken to those who incite dissensions. Remove the inciters from your public forums and take the hand which is stretched out to you in peace.

Three days after Deir Yassin, on April 12, 1948, the Zionist General Council issued the following declaration:[75]

At this hour, when bloodshed and strife have been forced upon us, we turn to the Arabs in the Jewish State and to our neighbours in adjacent territories with an appeal for brotherhood and peace.

But pleas of this sort were of no avail. Because of the collapse of the morale of the Palestine Arabs and the absence of any local leader, there was nobody to accept or decline such appeals. Isolated in their villages and other localities, the Arabs became prey to the leaders of Arab bands from abroad and who had established themselves there, or of military units of the 'Liberation Army' who had taken control of the Arab areas and acted in obedience to orders received from higher military authorities. War strategy thus dominated the relationship between commanders and the Arab population. And in its course, this led to the results which have been here described.

All the events above pertain to the period preceding Deir Yassin and the establishment of the State of Israel. They were multiplied by a considerable number of further tragedies once the State came into being and the Arab States 'officially' invaded Palestine.

On the day of the establishment of the State of Israel, the Proclamation of Independence contained the following paragraph:[76]

> In the midst of wanton aggression, we yet call upon the Arab inhabitants of the State of Israel to return to the ways of peace and to play their part in the development of the State, with full and equal citizenship and due representation in all its bodies and institutions, provisions and permanent.

But like the pleas before the Proclamation of the State, this plea too was of no avail. The Arabs, having been initially encouraged by their leaders to evacuate their homes and places of living during the fighting, obeyed their leaders' call and rejected the friendly hand stretched out to them by Jewish leaders. That this was the main cause of their flight, and not their expulsion by Jewish leaders, has been bitterly demonstrated by many Arabs. Here are just a few of such statements:

Edward Atiyah, Director of the Arab League's propaganda office in London, 1944–1949, wrote in his book, *The Arabs:*[77]

> This wholesale exodus was partly due to the belief of the Arabs, encouraged by the boasting of an unrealistic Arabic press and the irresponsible utterances of some of the Arab leaders, that it could be only a matter of some weeks before the Jews were defeated by the armies of the Arab States and the

Palestinian Arabs enabled to re-enter and retake possession of their country . . .

And it may be most useful for our analysis to quote a statement by Emil Ghoury, at the time Secretary-General of the Palestine Arab Higher Committee, made in 1948, and compare it with a statement made by him in 1960. This is of particular interest for an understanding of Toynbee's stand in matters of this kind—where he blindly and un-critically presents the Arab viewpoint.

Ghoury's statement in 1948:[78]	*Ghoury's statement in 1960:*[79]
The fact that there are these re-fugees is the direct consequence of the action of the Arab States in opposing partition and the Jewish State. The Arab States agreed upon this policy unani-mously, and they must share in the solution of the problems.	It has been those [Zionist] acts of terror, accompanied by whole-sale depredations, which had caused the exodus of the Pales-tinian Arabs. . . .

Also, in 1948, after the State of Israel had been established, Mahmoud Bey Fawzi, Egypt's representative, spoke at the Security Council, and did not attach importance to the flight of the Arabs in Palestine because he then still awaited an Arab victory any day. In his speech (five weeks after Deir Yassin!) he therefore said[80]

Some Arabs might have been chased away from their homes, and some Jews equally so.

A few days later, when the Security Council had submitted a question-naire to all countries involved in the Palestine struggle on their stand on the various issues, the same Egyptian representative replied in the name of his Government[81] that Egypt intervened in the Palestine war in order to save their Arab brethren who were in danger of annihilation by the Jews. That this danger existed, he said,

is borne out by the continuous flow of thousands of Arabs, men, women, and children, who sought refuge in all neighbouring Arab countries in quest of safety and to escape from Zionist tyranny and oppression.

This, of course, sounds quite different from such a term as 'expulsion', particularly if it is considered in the light of Toynbee's statement that expulsion commenced after May 14, 1948; while this statement was made a week later.

A refugee from Palestine, one of the 'victims', had this to say on the matter:[82]

> We refugees, who have brothers and friends among the Arabs of Israel, we have the right to turn to the members of the Arab League Council and to declare that these our brethren did not opt to stay under the rule of the Jews because they loved the Jews and hated the Arabs. They were cleverer than we, and understood how much they preferred to die in their Palestine rather than in tented camps and in the desert. We left our country because of the deceitful promises by fraudulent Arab commanders; they promised that our exodus would not exceed two weeks and would be a kind of 'trip' at the end of which we would return.

Also, Habib Issa, editor of *Al-Hoda*, wrote:[83]

> Brotherly advice was given to the Arabs of Palestine, urging them to leave their land, homes, and property, and to stay temporarily in neighbouring brotherly States, lest the guns of the invading Arab armies mow them down.

Quotations such as these could be multiplied from Arab sources, for they are frequently recorded in the literature,[84] but these few should suffice.

Soon after the event, when the refugees were able to review their own situation, bitterness had grown against their own leaders. *Falastin*, as early as February 19, 1949, stated:

> The Arab States, which had encouraged the Palestine Arabs to leave their homes temporarily in order to be out of the way of the Arab invasion armies, have failed to keep their promises to help these refugees. . . .

2

The Second Phase: Seizures, Expropriations and Arbritrary Parallels

In subsequent writings Toynbee retained the identification of Zionism with Nazism, but gave up the two original reasons mentioned, Deir Yassin and Expulsion. However, in order to retain this identification he selected his parallels arbitrarily from time to time and advanced new ones, forgetting the previous ones. Needless to say, these new reasons were as groundless as the first. Thus in the last volume of his *Study* he said in a mood of reflection:[85]

On reconsideration, I do not find that I have changed my view of Zionism. I think that, in the Zionist movement, Western Jews have assimilated gentile Western civilisation in the most unfortunate possible form. The seizure of houses, lands, and property of the 900,000 Palestinian Arabs who are now refugees is on a moral level with the worst crimes and injustices committed, during the last four or five centuries, by gentile Western European conquerors and colonists overseas. This is still my judgment on the Zionists' record in Palestine since it first began to resort to violence there. At the same time, on second thought, I do think it may be true that the vehemence of my condemnation of Zionism has been out of proportion to the magnitude of Zionism's guilt; and I also think that, if I have exaggerated, the psychological explanation of this exaggeration that has been suggested by Berkovitz[86] may be the right one. In the German Nazis, and in the English 'Black-and-Tans', I see the detestable dark side of the countenance of Western Civilisation in which I myself am an involuntary participant, and in the Jewish Zionists I see disciples of the Nazis. The Jews are, of course, not the only persecuted people that has reacted to persecution by doing as it has been done by; and, of course, too, the Jews who have reacted in this tragically perverse way are only one section of Jewry. Yet the spectacle of any Jews, however few, following in the Nazis' footsteps is enough to drive a sensitive gentile or Jewish spectator almost to despair. That any Jews should inflict on a third party some of the very wrongs that Jews have suffered at Western hands is a portent that makes one wonder whether there may not be something irredeemably evil, not in Jewish human nature in particular, nor again just in Western human nature, but in the human nature common to all men.

This paragraph reminds us at once of the question which we answered in another connection, of whether Toynbee's self-critical declaration that 'I have not changed my view of Zionism' can stand scrutiny. If this refers to his attitude towards Zionism as expounded by him since the establishment of Israel (particularly in Volume VIII of his *Study of History*, pp. 270–273 . . .), then he is right. If, however, this reflects a general statement, then I do not think there is any doubt, after what has been said in the preceding sections about Toynbee's original understanding of and assistance to Zionism, that he has changed his view considerably. One wonders why (through such general statements as quoted above) he seeks to make the reader believe in his continuous, sequential stand with regard to Zionism, when in fact he could simply confess the truth, acknowledge his altered views, and give his reasons. In some other respects, appertaining to philosophical or historical issues, he almost rushes to be honest with himself and with his readers, sometimes apologising for his mistakes, at others explaining and correcting them.[87] This is a phenomenon which probably only Toynbee himself could explain. I record it as a characteristic glimpse of the individual passions with which Toynbee has failed to deal.

The third sentence in the above-quoted paragraph, mentioning 900,000 Arab refugees, contrasts with his earlier figure, given nearer to the event, of 648,000 refugees.[88] To make the 'crime' more criminal, he thus increases the number of refugees by not far short of 40 per cent, a rise that not even the most fantastic demographic growth would have accomplished during the six years until 1954 when Toynbee's book appeared. Moreover, the number of houses and properties which belonged to 648,000 Arabs in 1948 has of course remained the same to this day, and only a very small percentage of wealthy landowners had such properties, while the masses were poor and possessed nothing. Ignoring such facts, however, Toynbee speaks of the seizure of the lands and properties as morally on the same level as the worst crimes committed against the Jews by the Western world in the five hundred years between 1460 and 1960. In this sweeping identification of crimes, he accepts not only a figure of his own choosing as a basis for his attacks, but he also treats his own statements on the seizure of houses, land, and property as given facts and bases his definite conclusions on them. But what if these 'given facts' are not given facts at all? Indeed they are not.

To begin with, it seems appropriate to repeat that no such act of seizure was committed during the Mandatory period. And what happened to the lands owned and occupied by Arabs before their flight? 'Expropriation' is the depriving of a person of his property through an act of State. No Act of expropriation was passed by the Israel Government or Parliament with regard to these Arab properties; nor could it have been promulgated, because, by the time the Israel Government began orderly functioning, the masses of Palestine Arabs had already become refugees and had abandoned their homes and possessions. During the period of chaos, while fighting and fleeing continued, whole Arab areas were abandoned and had to be dealt with almost everywhere by improvisations devised by local commanders in accordance with their individual judgment on the spot. A thorough study of the administrative and organisational preparations which the Jewish leaders had made in anticipation of establishing a Government reveals that no provision was made for possible abandoned Arab properties of refugees. The Jews never expected nor counted on such a development, as the relevant literature shows.[89] It was therefore six weeks after the proclamation of Statehood before the Provisional Government of Israel published the 'Abandoned Areas Ordinance',[90] and another two weeks before a 'Custodian of Abandoned Property' was appointed,[91] whose functions were gradually elaborated and defined by way of ordinances until they attained their present status in the 'Absentees' Property Law, 5710—1950'.[92] The Custodian became the responsible authority for the abandoned Arab properties, in whom all rights pertaining to them were vested, including their sale. But in

that case the funds obtained were to remain in the Custodian's possession, *i.e.* in safe keeping.

Through the establishment of this custodial authority, the Israel
Government acted like any other responsible Government does in
similar cases; such as, for instance, the British authorities when they
passed the Trading with the Enemy Acts in 1914 and 1939,[93] or like
the system of the Custodian of Enemy Property practised in the U.S.A.
This is no 'expropriation' by any stretch of the imagination. It is the
generally recognised legal way of preserving and safeguarding the
rights of absentee or enemy owners. To confirm this still more emphatically, one can point to the fact that Israel accepted the principle
of sharing in the responsibility for compensation for abandoned
Arab properties,[94] as decided by the U.N. in its resolution of December 11, 1948.[95]

Payment of compensation was accepted in principle as an integral
part of the provisions of this resolution. These foresaw also that 'refugees wishing to return to their homes and live at peace with their
neighbours should be permitted to do so at the earliest practicable
date',[96] and that 'the Conciliation Commission [was] to take steps to
assist the Governments and authorities concerned to achieve a final
settlement of all questions outstanding between them'.[97] As the text
of this resolution shows, the conditions for a return were based on the
assumption that the returning people would wish 'to live in peace'
within Israel, and should return when 'practicable'. Where else could
these vague terms be clarified than at a peace conference, and it was
for this reason that this same resolution anticipated such a conference,
which would meet and 'achieve the final settlement of all the questions'.
Among these questions would be that of compensation, which, as
described in the resolution,[98] was to 'be paid for property of those
choosing not to return and for loss of or damage to property which,
under principles of international law or in equity, should be made
good by the Governments or authorities responsible'. Only, therefore,
round the table at a peace conference could a decision be taken and
agreement arrived at on who was and who was not responsible and,
accordingly, liable to participate in the payment of compensation. As
pointed out, Israel agreed in principle to take part in paying compensation and in solving the other matters connected with these problems.

And therefore, ever since the establishment of the State, she persisted in demanding the convocation of a peace conference, as contemplated in the U.N. resolution. But Arab statesmen have consistently refused; and, although they started all the ruin through their war of aggression, there was no word from them that they too would share in the payment of that compensation. The U.N. resolution speaks clearly of 'governments and authorities' in the plural, and can therefore not be misunderstood. Indeed, it was not misunderstood, as the *Survey*, edited by Toynbee, confirmed.[99]

An authoritative Arab source, King Hussein of Jordan, emphasised the irresponsible attitude of the Arab States in 1960:[100]

> [The Arab leaders were] using the Palestine Arab refugees as pawns for selfish political objectives. In saying this, I am not talking about the Arab people, but Arab leadership. Since 1948 Arab leaders have approached the Palestine problem in an irresponsible manner. They have not looked into the future. They have no plan or approach. They have used the Palestine people for selfish purposes. This is ridiculous and, I could say, even criminal.

However, the fate of the refugees and their abandoned properties hinges on whether the Arab States will or will not agree to a peace. For,

> failing a political settlement between the Arabs and Israel (and failing the adoption by the Arabs of progressive social policies), the future for the refugees was black indeed.[101]

A vast existing literature, documentary, Governmental, and in book and newspaper form, could enlighten Toynbee about the falsity of his contentions. I observe from the literature quoted in his *Reconsiderations* connected with this period and with these events[102] that he has not used a single work for corroborative purposes. After all, if a man of Toynbee's calibre hurls the gravest accusations against a not negligible group of the human race for deeds which they are said to have perpetrated, the least one can expect of him as a responsible historian, as indeed of any responsible person, is to live up to what he himself regards as the basis of any conclusions: 'to be confronted with the relevant facts and be corroborated by them'.[103] Again one wonders why Toynbee lays himself open to the challenge of such obvious superficiality and almost blind disregard for a sound and truthful foundation before launching his attack against Zionism. Once more, this may be understood only from his basic approach: prejudice.

'Interchange' with a Purpose

In the description of 'expropriations' Toynbee interchanges Zionism and the State of Israel whenever it suits him, *i.e.* whenever the one can be criticised or attacked for the ideas or deeds of the other, even if such ideas had never been uttered nor any such deed committed. I have explained above that the responsibility for the laws of Israel is borne by the Israeli Government and Parliament; and even Toynbee should know that not all Israelis are Zionists, that, is, members of the Zionist Organisation. That he knows the difference is obvious from the statement in which he blamed neither Israel nor the Zionists for the tragic events, but the Irgun and Stern Group. And he knows of course that Irgun and Stern, like many other Israeli citizens, were not members of the Zionist Organisation.

At the last Zionist Congress before the establishment of the State of Israel, there were, out of a total of 385 delegates, 79 from Palestine and 121 from the U.S.A., the rest from other countries.[104] At the Zionist Congress held in 1960 1961, Israel had 38 per cent of all delegates, the U.S.A. 29 per cent, and the rest were from other countries.[105]

It is also beyond doubt that 'seizure', 'expropriation', and similar steps can only be Governmental acts, not those of private citizens. Before the State of Israel came into being, Palestine was governed by Britain as Mandatory Power. Under British rule, no Zionist could or would (and there is an absence of any evidence that he would) have dared to 'seize' property belonging to the Arabs or any other inhabitants in Palestine. He would have come into conflict with the law and been put in jail and the 'seizure' would be declared invalid. Nor could a Zionist legally have enforced a 'seizure', because he would not have obtained Government consent to it. I have shown above that, throughout the Mandatory period, no Arab or other non-Jew had been deprived of his properties. It is, therefore, nonsensical to write about 'the seizure' of Arab houses, lands, and property by Zionists. On the other hand, as was also fully explained, these houses were abandoned, the land and property deserted, and their inhabitants gone when the State of Israel came into being. There was therefore nothing to 'seize' by the Israel Government. Consequently this Government found itself confronted unexpectedly with this newly arisen situation. It improvised at first, and then promulgated final laws which I quoted, and vested all lands and properties in the Custodian. They are subject to the compensation also established by law.

If this then is the 'crime' of Zionism or of the State of Israel which deserves to be called 'Nazism', and be identified with the worst crimes of Western civilisation against Jewry in the last five centuries, then Toynbee has not only failed badly in his contention, but he also reveals himself as unjustifiably insulting an entire people and simultaneously misleading the uninformed public.

Suppose for a moment that it were true that the houses, lands, and properties of the Arab refugees had been 'seized' by the Israeli Government. Would this make that Government 'Nazi'-like or murderers and torturers, like those perpetrators of crimes that the last five centuries have produced? Certainly not. 'Seizure' has become a method of governing throughout the world, and can be handled in a decent way with compensation, as Israel has decided; or the other way, without compensation, as in Nasser's seizures. It is instructive that Toynbee once philosophised,[106] 'Freedom of some king of somebody inevitably means a restriction of freedom of somebody else', and in his defence of Nasser's property measures he exlaimed:[107] 'The state, not the tax-payer, decides how a large part of the tax-payer's property is to be used'.

Toynbee, when identifying Zionism with 'Nazism', did not make any other accusation in a later volume than that of 'seizure', as quoted above, and believed this to suffice for the crime-identity. He did not refer, as previously,[108] to 'eviction' and 'deliberate expulsion of the Arab population'.[109] All this disappeared in his *Reconsiderations*, and in his more recent articles and speeches. He probably recognised that in exaggerating and overemphasising supposed Jewish 'cruelties', he fell victim to cold, calculated Arab propaganda which even he could not swallow any more. It is more noteworthy that, although he now confined himself to the 'seizure of houses and properties' as the 'great crime', he nevertheless retained the identification of Zionism and Nazism which he originally formulated for those other crimes. 'Seizure' and 'expropriation' of properties by Jews have been promoted to the 'greatest crimes in civilisation'. I wish, and millions of Jews (for that matter, also millions of non-Jews) wish, that all that Western civilisation and the Nazis had done to the Jews in these past centuries had just been 'seizure' or 'expropriation' of their possessions, even without compensation. The millions of murdered and tortured Jews of these last five hundred years testify to a much grimmer reality. Their possessions were 'seized', not after they had abandoned them in flight, but while they still owned them; and because they still owned them, their lives were also 'seized'. Arab refugees live, and their possessions are vested in the Custodian, awaiting final settlement, including compensation.[110] They lived, in many respects, a considerably better life than before, financially supported by the entire world, primarily the United Nations, including Jews, whose tax-payments are also used towards this purpose. They have been supported by everyone except their own brethren, the Arab States and peoples. In this direction, then, lies the 'great crime' if Toynbee insists on using this terminology; for these Arab States initiated the war against the decision of the U.N., induced their brethren in many cases to leave their homes, and then, when those following their advice became refugees, let them down badly in a way that no other nation, Western or Eastern, had ever let down their own.

A further example of Toynbee's peculiar method in the above-quoted paragraph can be found in his generalisation of the term Zionism. By not distinguishing between those who, he maintains, have committed the 'crimes' and those who have not, he leaves no doubt in the reader's mind that all Zionists are guilty of the seizure of the Arab houses, properties, and lands. From this, the conclusion is unavoidable that all Zionists are bad and that Zionism is a sinister movement, comparable to Nazism. However, at this point we are not concerned with the 'crime' but with the sweeping identification of a world movement with the deeds of one section, even supposing that it were true that this section had done what Toynbee accuses it of. 'I see in the Jewish Zionists disciples of Nazis', he emphasised in the paragraph quoted. That means: all Zionists. There are, as is well known to Toynbee, hundreds of thousands of Zionists all over the world who have never been to Palestine or Israel (Toynbee even poked fun at them for not intending to go there),[111] who did not take part in the war that the

Arabs initiated in 1947 and 1948 in Palestine, and who have never participated in any 'seizures' of other people's land, houses, and properties, and do not have these in their possession now or under their control. Yet Toynbee accuses them all of the 'worst crimes and injustices', which they are said to have committed in Palestine.

It has been shown that he greatly increased his own number of Arab refugees to make the tragedy seem bigger than it is. He applies the same method again. Originally he blamed a small section of Palestine Jewry for crimes against the Arabs, the Irgun.[112] And there cannot be any doubt that Toynbee was fully aware that the Irgun was a 'small but efficient extremist organisation', for that is how the *Survey*, published under his editorship, described them.[113] And he also knew that of the few thousand men which the Irgun numbered at its height,[114] many, if not most, were not members of the Zionist Organisation. Anyhow, they were numerically a tiny fraction of the 300,000 Zionists then (1948) in Palestine,[115] not to mention the World Zionist Movement, which then counted 1,879,875 paying members.[116] Toynbee forgot the 'small . . . organisation' and, instead superseded it by the world-wide Zionist Movement.

The Zionist community the world over can rightly feel itself to have been libelled by these accusations, and to be surprised that such sweeping generalisations and defamatory statements are used by a man who prides himself on having risen far above the moral decay of intolerant past generations.

The intermingling of Zionists, Jews, and Nazis, which constitutes his gravest injustice to Jewry, first appeared in Volume VIII of his *Study of History*, where he set out to describe the guilt of Zionism over the fate of Arab refugees. He then wrote,[117] to repeat what we have noted before, that

> the direct responsibility for this calamity that overtook the Palestinian Arabs in A.D. 1948 was on the heads of the Zionist Jews who seized the *Lebensraum* for themselves in Palestine by force of arms in that year . . .

And with reference to the Nazi-Zionist identification he pointed out[118] that

> the evil deeds committed by the Zionist Jews against the Palestinian Arabs that were comparable to crimes committed against the Jews by the Nazis ·

were the massacre of men, women and children in Dayr Yassin on the 9th April, 1948. . . .

It is in connection with this massacre that, a few lines further on, Toynbee omitted the 'Zionist Jews' as responsible and stated,[119] as already quoted earlier:

> The Arab blood shed on the 9th April, 1948, at Dayr Yassin was on the heads of Irgun.

But instead of deducing therefore that the Zionists are not Nazis, Toynbee unhesitatingly concluded this part of his identification with Nazism by pointing out:[120]

> On the Day of Judgment the gravest crime standing to the German National Socialists' account might be, not that they had exterminated a majority of Western Jews, but that they had caused the surviving remnant of Jewry to stumble. The Jews in Europe in A.D. 1933–1945 had been the vicarious victims of the Germans' resentment over their military defeat at the hands of their Western fellow Gentiles in the war of A.D. 1914–1918; the Arabs in Palestine in A.D. 1948 became in their turn the vicarious victims of the European Jews' indignation over the 'genocide' committed upon them by their Gentile fellow Westerners in A.D. 1933–1945.

As we see here, Toynbee gradually brings 'the Jews' into the picture and in the end omits altogether to mention the Irgunists or the Zionists, but simply puts the onus on Jewry as such:[121]

> In A.D. 1948 the Jews knew, from personal experience, what they were doing; and it was their supreme tragedy that the lesson learnt by them from their encounter with Nazi German Gentiles should have been not to eschew but to imitate some of the evil deeds that the Nazis had committed against the Jews.

There it is then: all Jews are guilty; all Jews have copied the Nazis; all Jews are Nazis. It is this thesis which, in his *Reconsiderations*,[122] he claims he has not changed. He even uses in the latest volume the same method of argumentation, as was pointed out above, by starting with Zionists and ending with the condemnation of Jewry.

To illustrate this it will suffice to repeat the relevant part from the quotation under analysis:

> . . . in the Jewish Zionists I see disciples of the Nazis. The Jews are, of

course, not the only persecuted people that has reacted to persecution by doing as it has been done by; and, of course, too, the Jews who have reacted in this tragically perverse way are only one section of Jewry. . . .

and he then goes on to speak of Jews and the Jewish people without mentioning anything further about Zionists and Zionism. It should not be overlooked that in this paragraph Toynbee sets out, as the first sentence in the quotation emphasises, to restate his 'view of Zionism', not of Jewry or the Jews; yet he suddenly brings in 'Zionist Jews', 'Jews', 'Jewry', and just at the point where he launches his bitterest attack. If he had Zionists in mind, why not say so and use this term to the end? Why formulate a whole theory about the Jewish people, and their reaction to persecution, when, in fact, 'only one section' is meant? Another example of this blurring of vital distinctions, and spreading of supposed guilt by association, appears in a recent article in which Toynbee wrote:[123]

> Paradoxically, a one-hundred-percent genuine 'emancipation' of the Jewish Diaspora in western countries is denounced by Israeli politicians of this school, as being an even greater threat to the Diaspora's survival than the Nazis' policy of genocide. If one thought in these paradoxical terms, one would have to canonise Hitler as the founding step-father of present-day Israel. He has as good a claim to this title as Nebuchadnezzar has to that of being the founding step-father of the Diaspora. But such a paradox is too far-fetched.

Depending upon anonymous 'Israeli politicians', Toynbee projects the peculiar device of saying something and withdrawing it again—in his terminology this may even be characterised as 'challenge' and 'withdrawal'. Thus he makes a statement containing a Nebuchadnezzar-Hitler parallel, yet confesses right away that it is 'too far-fetched'. If that is so, why use it at all? The intention is obvious: the reader has again received an injection of a Hitler-Zionism-Israel combination. And this is, for the propaganda-minded Toynbee, of the utmost importance.

As early as 1933, in the year of Hitler's access to power—and this is, as is shown elsewhere, a most important year in his spiritual *volte face* —he wrote the following:[124]

> Captain Goering found his next opening three days later in the abortive attempt to burn the Reichstag Building—a providential 'act of God', on

the eve of the elections, which Captain Goering took as a mandate to smite the Communists, as Moses had girt himself to smite the Egyptians after hearing the voice in the burning bush.

And into that category also falls the remark quoted a few pages on in that volume:[125]

> Herr Hitler did not borrow anti-Semitism from the Italian Fascist movement, which was free from this barbarity . . . In working out the positive side of his new creed, Herr Hitler acted (no doubt, unwittingly) on the principle that *fas est ab hoste doceri;* for, as a Jewish scholar has pointed out to the writer of this *Survey*, Hitler's main idea—the fanatical worship of a jealous tribal god, at the bidding of a prophetic leader—is the original (though not ultimate) *Leitmotiv* of the Old Testament.

That is a quite remarkable statement, and one can only pause in wonderment at Toynbee's recourse to an anonymous—and Jewish—source (a lack of documentations which is almost unique in Toynbee's scholarship) when propounding an interpretation with such serious implications. Moses and Goering, the Reichstag fire and the burning bush, the fanatical worship, the jealous tribal god, Hitler, the prophet—what is left in the mind of the reader is a distorted intermingling of Judaism and Nazism.

In more recent times, Toynbee has not emphasised Hitler's and Goering's emulations of Judaism and Nazism's anonymousness with historical Judaism, for the simple reason that this may destroy his main argument in his crusade against Zionism and Israel. If he employed such a paradox he could not then conclude that Zionists acted like Nazis if they acted like their ancestors in Palestine in Biblical times, in the days of Moses and of the prophets. In other words, this would mean that Zionists are not Nazis but good Jews, who, faithful to the ever repeated admonishments to recall history, 'to consider the days of old', had remembered and returned to the historical basis of their own people in their historical land. Toynbee's entire, loudly propagated condemnation of Zionism and Israel would thus collapse.

Why the term 'Nazism'? Toynbee is usually choosy about his words, and in the latest book we are considering he devotes ninety-one pages to the 'Explanations and Revisions of Usages of Terms'.[126] Therefore, his stubborn advancement of the identification with 'Nazism' must be deliberate, stemming from the quotation at the beginning of this chapter about the identity of Zionism and Nazism. As we have seen, Toynbee stresses that 'the Jews are not the only persecuted people that has reacted to persecution by doing as it has been done by'. In other words, people react to the actions of the evil-doers whom they detest by adopting these evil-doers' methods. The implications of that statement for the present study need not be pursued any further.

Notes

1. pp. 252–4.

2. Toynbee's footnote at this point: 'This passage was written before the "Aryan" outbreak against the Jews in Germany which accompanied the German National-Socialist Revolution of 1933 . . .' (The situation is today, of course, completely changed owing to the destruction of East European Jewry outside Soviet Russia.—O.K.R.)

3. Toynbee's footnote: 'See the ancient Greek proverb in the *Odyssey*, XVII, 11. 322–3'.

4. Toynbee's footnote: 'Samuel [I], VIII, 5 and 20'.

5. Toynbee's footnote: 'Luke XVIII, 11'.

6. See, for instance, Vol VI, pp. 70n, 216n; Vol VIII, pp. 275, 400, and 600–1, where he reproduces the substance of this summary.

7. Toynbee, *Reconsiderations*, p. 627.

Part I

Note: In his original manuscript, the author included numerous footnotes of cross-reference to his own book. But as a detailed index has now been provided most of these cross-reference notes have been deleted. Moreover, because of the author's death, before the manuscript went to press, two of his footnote references could not be traced. These are indicated by the symbol ‡: numbers 267 and 623 both in Section I of the notes. The footnotes are divided into three sections to correspond to Parts I, II and III of the book.

8. An interesting study on this aspect was made by Professor Salo Baron in 'World Dimensions of Jewish History', in *Simon Dubnow—The Man and His Work*, ed by Aaron Steinberg, Paris 1963, pp. 26–40. The influence of *endogenous* and *exogenous* forces on the growth and essence of nations, communities, and, particularly, the Jewish people is dealt with with great insight by Oskar Wolfsberg, *Zur Zeit-und Geistesgeschichte des Judentums*, Zürich (Gestaltung), 1938, pp. 15ff.

9. *Reconsiderations*, p. 298. He tried to 'soften' the total fossilisation theory (maintained in his *Study*, Vols I–X) by using the ambiguous term 'coelacanthus' (*Reconsiderations*, p. 299), which in fact means that the Jews are dead and alive at the same time (*ibid.*, p. 296).

10. *Study*, Vol. II, pp. 208–59.

11. *Study*, Vol. II, *loc. cit.*—This is not the place to deal with this theory *per se*. We are concerned with the Jewish aspect alone. The conclusions at which we arrive, however, from this particular case, fully confirm Geyl's devastating criticism of Toynbee's 'penalisation' theory as such in his 'Toynbee Once More', in *Debates with Historians*, Cleveland–N. York (Meridian), 1962, pp. 169ff.

12. *Ibid.*, p. 209.

13. For the Diaspora as evidence of his theory see *ibid.*, pp. 234–48, 252–4. The quotation which follows is *ibid.*, p. 248.

14. *Ibid.*, p. 252.
15. see p. 204.
16. Toynbee, *Reconsiderations*, p. 484.
17. Theodor Fritsch, *Mein Streit mit dem Hause Warburg* (Leipzig), 1925, pp. 149–50 (statement in court by his lawyer, Alfred Jacobsen). (Author's translation.)
18. See Hitler, *Mein Kampf*, p. 331; Rosenberg, *Der Mythos*, p. 464.
19. This is the title of one of his articles.
20. *Pioneer Destiny*, p. 14.
21. *Ibid.*, p. 13.—See also *Reconsiderations*, pp. 215–16.
22. Heinrich Graetz, *Geschichte der Juden*, Vol. VI (1894 ed.), pp. 88–9. For an understanding of the background of this Mainz Tragedy see the frightening fictional description in Christopher Davis, *Belmarch* (London, Cassell), 1964.
23. *Reconsiderations*, p. 484.
24. A description of this interview is in Michael Dov Weissmandel, *Min Hamezar* ('Out of Distress', ref. to Psalm cxviii, 5) (Brooklyn, Emunah), 1960, p. 24. Rabbi Weissmandel was the saintly *perpetuum mobile* of efforts to save Slovakian Jewry during World War II. This work is a description of these efforts and at the same time a bitter indictment by this extremely Orthodox figure against the Western world which permitted the massacres of Jewry. See an appraisal of his work in Jirmejahu Oskar Neumann, *Im Schatten des Todes* (Tel-Aviv, Olamenu), 1956, pp. 111f.
25. *Reconsiderations*, p. 617. See also, *Study*, Vol. VI, p. 132 (quoting E. Bevan, *Jerusalem under the High Priests*, London, 1904, pp. 158, 162); *Reconsiderations*, p. 609n (quoting E. Berkovitz, *Judaism, Fossil or Ferment*, New York, 1956, p. 36).
26. See about these distortions Harry M. Orlinsky, *The So-called 'Suffering Servant' in Isaiah 53*, Cincinnati, Ohio (Hebrew Union College), 1964. He proves there convincingly that the 'suffering servant' is not a collective but an individual person, none other than Isaiah himself.
27. See, for instance, what he says about the 'power of creative suffering' in *Reconsiderations*, p. 617.
28. *The Voice of Jerusalem*, London (Heinemann), 1920, p. 9.
29. This and the following quotations are in *Reconsiderations*, p. 478.
30. 'Declaration on the Relations of the Church to Non-Christian Religions' promulgated by Pope Paul VI. See *New York Times*, 29 October 1965, p. 24.
31. *Midrash Rabba to Shir Hashirim* (a popular interpretation of the Song of Song of Songs), i, 3, 2; also *Midrash Rabba to Exodus*, xxxv, 1.
32. *Sabbath*, 55a.
33. *Deuteronomy*, xxx, 19.
34. The term *Kiddush ha-Hayyim* was coined in the darkest hours of World War II by Rabbi Isaac Nissenbaum, in the Warsaw Ghetto (see Nathan Eck, *Wandering on the Roads of Death* [Hebrew], Jerusalem, 1960, p. 37).
35. It is not without a bearing on this belief that Jewish prayers are never individually self-centred. The Jew does not pray just for himself, but always in the plural, for the entire people.
36. *Leviticus*, xxvi, 44–5.
37. This individualism and atomisation are the hallmarks of assimilationism, which accordingly is always a characteristic of the foremost advocates of the Diaspora's permanency.
38. The literature on the issue of Diaspora–Eretz Israel is so vast that it is impossible to refer even to the most important works dealing with it. In an indiscriminate selection mention should be made of Jechezkel Kaufmann, *Gola Vanechar* ('Exile and Strangeness'), two volumes (Tel-Aviv, Dvir), 1954; Jakob Klatzkin, *Probleme des modernen Judentums* (Berlin, Lambert Schneider), 1930;

Ahad Ha-Am, *Al Parashat Derahim* (Berlin, Judischer Verlag), 1921, Vol. II, pp. 57–66, Vol. IV, pp. 62–4; Max Dienemann, 'Galuth', in *Der Morgen*, Vol. IV, No. 4, October 1928, pp. 325–34 (Berlin), 1928; V. Jabotinsky, 'Weshalb wir die Diaspora nicht wollen', in *Der Judenstaat* (Vienna, Glanz), 1936, pp. 7–12; Simon Dubnov, *Die Grundlagen des Nationaljudentums* (Berlin) (1905), 1936, pp. 7–12; *idem.*: 'Die Bejahung des Galuth', (Russ. in) *Jewrejski Mir*, 1909, No. 5; (Heb. in) *Hashiloah*, 1914, xxx, 206–10; Simon Rawidowicz, *Babel Viyerushalayim*, two vols (London and Waltham, Massachusetts, Ararat), 1957; Adolf Böhm, 'Zioni und Galuthnationalismus', in *Jüd. Zeitung*, (Vienna), No. 26, September 1918; Oskar Wolfsberg, *Zur Zeit-und Geistesgeschichte des Judentums* (Zurich, Gestaltung), 1938; Hugo Bergmann, *Jawne und Jerusalem* (Berlin, Jüd.-Verlag), 1919; Martin Buber, *Die jüdische Bewegung*, two vols. (Berlin, Jüd.-Verlag), 1920.

39. *Pioneer Destiny*, pp. 2–3. This idea is more extensively described in *Study*, Vol. VIII, p. 298.

40. This aspect is discussed further below in the section *A Natural Corollary* on p. 128.

41. Toynbee, *Study*, Vol. VIII, pp. 274–5.

42. *Ibid.*, Vol. VII, p. 693.

43. *Ibid.*

44. Toynbee, Study, Vol. II, pp. 271, 272.

45. *Reconsiderations*, p. 516.

46. See, for instance, his admiration of 'the creative power of suffering', (*Reconsiderations*, p. 617), or the extraordinary joy that he derives from criticism of his work and even from personal abuse: 'Here, I think, I was committing the sin of pride . . . I stand convicted, I am afraid; and this is, I also fear, presumptive evidence of conceitedness' (*ibid.*, p. 85n). 'Kroeber finds my mind old-fashioned' (*ibid.*, p. 54n). 'Crossman calls my presentation of the idea a pastiche; Hanson calls the idea itself "mystic nonsense"' (*ibid.*, p. 264n). 'Frequently the point is made at the price of a radical distortion of facts' (P. Bagby). 'He distorts some parts of history' (A. Nevins) (*ibid.*, p. 247n). These examples could be multiplied. Toynbee in his writings appears to gain some inner satisfaction from personal attacks upon him when we discover that he mentions so many of them without even attempting to 'explain' or contradict them.

47. Charles Renouvier, *Psychologie rationelle*, chapter 12, quoted in William James, *The Principles of Psychology*, Vol. II, New York, 1950, p. 309, defined it as a 'belief of a thing for no other reason than that we conceive it with passion'.

48. Nahum Goldmann, 'The Vital Partnership', in *Forum* (Jerusalem, World Zionist Organisation), Vol. IV, 1959, p. 129.

49. Toynbee, *Study*, Vol. VIII, p. 279n. ('Anti-semitism had been rife in a pre-Christian Hellenic world').

50. Carl G. Jung, *Allgemeines zur Komplex Theorie*, Zürich, 1934. For Toynbee's admiration of Jung, see Note 60 below.

51. *Ibid.*

52. Toynbee, *Study*, Vol. IX, pp. 238, 337.

53. *Ibid.*, Vol. II, p. 240. See also for similar descriptions of the 'Jewish ethos' *ibid.*, pp. 241, 242.

54. Philip Toynbee, 'The Situation of the Jews' (book review) in *Observer* (London), 12 May 1963. Toynbee also denies being an antisemite by stating (*Reconsiderations*, p. 597) that some of his close friends are Jews. Which Jew does not recognise this age-old classical antisemitic phrase? (See in this connection the revealing book: Benjamin R. Epstein and Arnold Forster, *Some of My Best Friends* . . . (New York, 1962).

55. Toynbee, *Study* (abridged edition by D. C. Sommerville), Vol. I, p. 304.

56. Jean-Paul Sartre, *Portrait of the Antisemite* (translated by Erik de Mauny), London, 1948, pp. 78–80.

57. Thus also not through 'penalisations'.

58. How does Toynbee express it?—'the well-known ethos commonly called "Jewish"'.

59. A similar thought was expressed by a Negro author when he wrote about the old Negro who 'was defeated long before he died because, at the bottom of his heart, he really believed what the white people said about him' (James Baldwin, *The Fire Next Time*, N.Y., 1963, p. 18).

60. Arnold and Philip Toynbee, *Comparing Notes*, pp. 106–7; also for the quotations which follow. He became an adherent of the school of psychology of Carl G. Jung (*ibid.*, p. 107). See also Toynbee, Study, Vol. IX, pp. 326f, where he devotes a whole section to the 'Laws of the Subconscious Human Nature', which is *inter alia* also interesting from their relationship to the Jewish problem.

61. *Reconsiderations*, p. 108.

62. *Ibid.*, pp. 596–7.

63. See for this Salo Baron, 'Ghetto and Emancipation', in *Menorah Journal* (New York), June, 1928, Vol. XIV, No. 6, pp. 515–26.

64. See long quotations in *Author's Note* in above.

65. This would thus affect their existence in the Diaspora.

66. See *Author's Note* in above.

67. *Ibid.*

68. *Ibid.*

69. Named so after Israel Zangwill's play *The Melting Pot* (New York, Macmillan), 1909, performed in Washington 5 October 1908.

70. Milton Gordon, *Assimilation in American Life* (Oxford), 1965, pp. 24–5.

71. Title of a book by Nathan Glazer and Daniel Patrick Moynihan (Cambridge, Mass., MIT and Harvard Presses), 1957, p. 93. The fallacy of the melting-pot conception was predicted in *The Melting Pot Mistake*, by Henry Pratt Fairchild, as far back as 1926 (Boston).

72. Max Lerner, *America as a Civilization* (New York, Simon & Schuster), 1957, p. 93. See Horace Kallen, *Culture and Democracy in the United States* (New York), 1924, p. 121.

73. See about this, for instance, the report in *New York Times*, 29 May 1965, pp. 1 and 10, by Austin C. Wehrwein.

74. Benjamin Akzin, State and Nation (London, Hutchinson), 1964, pp. 100–1.

75. 'In 1818 Leopold Zunz [the founding father of "Juedische Wissenschaft"] was firmly convinced that, by 1919, a Hebrew book would be hard to obtain. Zunz's discouragement concerning the Jewish cause was characteristic of his friends' and his own way of thinking. In their imagination they had anticipated the future, and found it non-existent. They thus made a remembrance of what should have been a hope for them; moreover, their hope lay behind them, their remembrance ahead. Thus Zunz's life in particular was not only turned backwards, but was, as it were, doubly reversed'. (Luitpold Wallach, *Liberty and Letters: The Thoughts of Leopold Zunz* [New York, Leo Baeck Instit.], 1959, p. 18.)

76. *Weltgeschichte*, Vol. X, § 1.

77. Ahad Ha'am's dictum is still *the* key: 'Learn, learn, and learn; this is the secret of our people's survival' (*Iggeret Ahad Ha'am*, Vol. IV [Jerusalem–Berlin, Yavneh and Moriah], 1924, p. 148).

78. see p. 39.

79. Toynbee, 'Future of Judaism', p. 69.

80. A case in point in our day is the obviously assimilationist American Council of Judaism, which comprises only Jews in its organisations.

81. 'Can Jews Survive?', in *Council News*, 3 May 1963, p. 14. Bettelheim here confuses citizenship with nationality, but it is clear that he has ethnic nationality in mind, otherwise his argument would be meaningless.

82. Toynbee, 'Pioneer Destiny of Judaism', pp. 9–10.

83. See *Author's Note* in above.

84. *Reconsiderations*, p. 414.

85. *Reconsiderations*, pp. 515–16.

86. Two characteristic examples may suffice to prove this point: Sigmund Freud wrote in the preface to the Hebrew edition of *Totem and Taboo*: 'No reader of the Hebrew version of this book will find it easy to put himself in the emotional position of an author who is ignorant of the language of Holy Writ, who is completely estranged from the religion of his fathers—as well as from every other religion—and who cannot take a share in nationalist ideals, but who has never repudiated his people, who feels that he is in his essential nature a Jew and who has no desire to alter that nature. If the question were put to him: "Since you have abandoned all these common characteristics of your countrymen, what is there left to you that is Jewish?" he would reply: "A very great deal, and probably its very essence." He could not now express that essence clearly in words but some day, no doubt, it will become accessible to the scientific mind.' (Quoted from Ernst Simon, 'Sigmund Freud, the Jew', in *Yearbook II* published by the Leo Baeck Institute, London, 1957, p. 290, quoting the preface, dated December 1930.)

The second example is a statement by Justice Felix Frankfurter: 'I remember leaving the synagogue in the middle of the service saying to myself, "It's a wrong thing for me to be present in a room in a holy service, to share these ceremonies, these prayers, these chants, with people for whom they have inner meaning as against me for whom they have ceased to have inner meaning." I left the service in the middle of it, never to return to this day. By leaving the synagogue, I did not, of course, cease to be a Jew or cease to be concerned with whatever affects the fates of Jews.' (*Reminiscences*, Recorded in Talks with Dr Harlan B. Phillips (New York, Reynal), 1960, p. 290.)

87. Toynbee, *Study*, Vol. II, p. 252; quoted above, *Author's Note*.

88. Quoted in Bentwich, *Magnes*, p. 290.

89. In Great Britain and Ireland, for instance, 4,400 children attended Jewish schools in 1950; in 1963, there were nearly 9,000 children in 48 of these schools, apart from the Hebrew classes attached to every synagogue in the country, and apart from *Yeshivoth* and other institutions of higher learning, where the increase of students was equally considerable. In comparison with these increases, the Jewish population figures between 1950 and 1963 have remained the same at about 450,000 souls. (Dr J. Braude in *Jewish Chronicle*, 3 May 1963, p. 18; *The Jewish Year Book*, London, 1950, p. 310, and 1963, p. 190.)

The U.S.A. also shows striking increases in this field. There, in the spring of 1962, 588,955 children were enrolled in all types of Jewish schools (day schools, afternoon weekday schools, and Sunday schools—day schools provide secular and religious instruction; afternoon weekday schools offer religious education for children who attend public and private schools, one-day-a-week (Sunday) or two-day-a-week (Tuesday or Wednesday) schools provide basic religious instruction), in contrast to 1950, when 268,253 children were enrolled. While thus the enrolment increased in Jewish schools over 120 per cent in 12 years, the Jewish population in the U.S.A. grew by 11·2 per cent in this same period, or from 5 million to 5,531,500 (*American Jewish Year Book*, Philadelphia, 1950, pp. 71–3, and 1963, pp. 151–2; see also Oscar I. Janowsky, *Jewish Education in Crisis*, offprint from B'nai B'rith *Monthly*, New York, 1962, p. 2).

In 1964 there were in the U.S.A. 320 joint day schools in 130 counties in 32 States (Joseph Kaminsky, National Director, National Society for Hebrew Day Schools, in *New York Times*, 29 January 1965, p. 28). Of these, 301 were Orthodox and their statistical charts show that in 1945 there were 24 such schools with an enrolment of 7,000; in 1965 there were 301 with an enrolment of 65,000. *New York Times*, 16 May 1965, p. 83).

This is not the place to evaluate the depth of Hebraic study and knowledge of Judaism provided at these schools, which, as is natural, often comes under criticism from people concerned about Jewry's spiritual future. Jews in every land are concerned with the education of their youth as the basis of their future existence. The facts above are mentioned here to show that many thousands of parents are concerned with their youth and with the perpetuation of their Jewish knowledge.

The increases in both England and the U.S.A. (as in many other free countries) are therefore rightly attributed to a strengthening of Jewish consciousness, as is also confirmed by the greatly increased enrolment in all Jewish religious bodies (see, for instance, *American Jewish Year Book*, 1963, pp. 145–50).

90. Thus in 1940 there were 47 Jewish theological seminaries in the U.S.A.; in 1957 there were 112. (Salo Baron, 'Inaugural Speech of the Hebrew Department at Rutger's University', quoted in *Reconstructionist*, New York, 17 May 1963, p. 4.) Still more striking is the increase in the strictly Orthodox religious *Yeshivoth* in the U.S.A. from 14 in three cities in 1939, with a few thousand students, to 80 in 20 cities, with 50,000 students, in 1963 (Dr Isaac Margolis, Director of the National Council for Torah Education, quoted in *Day-Jewish Journal*, 27 May 1963, p. 5). In the New York Yeshivah University alone, 3,000 students attended Torah studies every day in 1963. This makes the University 'the greatest religious institute in Jewish history' (Dr Menahem Rackman, Assistant to the Yeshivah University President, quoted in *Day-Jewish Journal*, 23 October 1963, p. 1).

91. Hebrew is used in services and taught in schools of all Jewish religious denominations.

92. Even the Reform movement, which in the first phase of its development abolished most of the customs, has come to recognise that as a religious movement it could not exist without them. Thus one of its spiritual leaders, Dr Maurice Eisendrath, President of the Union of American Hebrew Congregations, recently had to confess ('Reform Judaism', in *The National Jewish Monthly*, Washington, April 1965, p. 7): 'It is just that we Reform Jews have indeed sinned in our emasculation of too many of our traditionally rich and beautiful ceremonials. We cast aside many precious gems together with some of their admittedly tarnished settings. These symbols and forms which still do have significance today must be recaptured and refurbished, others must be created anew, not because dogmatically we believe they were all everlastingly ordained at Sinai, but because many of them have added dignity and beauty and have breathed loyalty and heightened morale into Jewish living. . . . Only that synagogue which hews to at least a minimum code of practice in Jewish knowledge, in ritual and ceremonial observance, and in moral conduct and social action. . . .'

93. Rabbi Marc Tannenbaum in an address in New Rochelle (N.Y.), quoted in *New York Times*, 22 April 1965, p. 35. Such continuous co-operation appertains primarily to common goals such as improvement of schools, more playgrounds and parks, P.T.A., etc. (see the interesting study by Dr Benjamin B. Ringe, 'Lakeville' Basic Books, 1965).

94. Charles Singer, *The Christian Failure* (London, Gollancz), 1943, pp. 116–17.

95. See, for instance, the 'Prayer for the Jews' revised with so much acclaim by Pope Paul VI. Also the new text cannot but pray 'that even they [*i.e.*, Jews] may

recognise the redeemer of all, our Lord Jesus Christ' . . . and 'that those who
once were your chosen people will be able to attain to the fullness of grace in the
redemption' (quoted in full in *New York Times*, 1 April 1965, p. 9). See Toynbee's
statement on Israel's rejection and replacement by Christianity and Mohammedanism, on p. 25.

96. 'A Land of Refuge' (1907), in *Speeches, Articles, Letters* (ed. Maurice Simon)
(London, Soncino), 1937, p. 241. The *Stated* Clerk of the United Presbyterian
Church, Dr Eugene Carson Blake, expressed the idea of a clear division between
Judaism and Christianity as being in the interest of true religion. 'Judaism and
Christianity have a common mission to the modern world,' he said (*New York
Times*, 15 November 1965, p. 44), but such a mission cannot be undertaken
'unless we are willing to understand better than we have the central difference in
our faith. The dilution of either Christianity or Judaism into a kind of syncretistic
tolerance would result in the collapse of faith in God and the end of high religion
in favor of secularism.'

97. I am thinking of a case, trivial in isolation, but characteristic if it occurs often,
where, for instance, a non-Jewish neighbour in an English town felt offended by
the work done on Sunday by a pious Jew, who refrained from working on his
own Sabbath. A case 'for disturbing the peace' was finally brought before the
court. The judgment went in favour of the Jew. These Jewish and Christian
families and relatives ceased every social contact (*Jewish Chronicle*, 15 June 1962,
p. 43).

How often is the social contact between Jew and non-Jew cut off, or not even
established, if the Jew adheres (as many do) to the laws of *kashruth* and therefore
cannot partake in parties or private dinners at the house of his Gentile neighbour
or friend?

An example from a different area, but still within purely religious affairs, can
be quoted in the case of a Jewish labourer in Belgium whose right to unemploy-
ment benefit was contested because of his refusal to appear at the labour exchange
on the Sabbath. His claim was finally agreed to, not without the dismay and dis-
content of the labour challengers (*World Jewry*, London, September–October
1963, p. 6).

Revealing on the subject of the desire for separateness because of religious
practice is the decision of the Hassidic congregation, led by Rabbi Joseph Jacob
Twersky, to leave Williamsburg (Brooklyn) and to establish a town of their own
'so that they can make their laws to facilitate their religious practices'. The town
of Ramapo (New York) protested, but the New York Supreme Court ordered the
issue of the incorporation papers. Thus New Square (the Americanised form of
Skvir, the Russian town whence this group originated) came into being (*New York
Times*, 14 June 1961, p. 20). An interesting book giving an insight into the life of
Hassidim in Williamsburg was published a few years ago, Solomon Poll, *The
Hassidic Community of Williamsburg* (New York, Free Press), 1962.

A similar step, accompanied by a much louder controversy between Jews and
non-Jews, was taken by another Hassidic group of Brooklyn, who for purely
religious reasons wanted to separate themselves from the non-Jewish surroundings
and settle in a town of their own, which was, of course, also surrounded by non-
Jews. The group of Rabbi Joel Teitelbaum, a violent anti-Zionist (see his work
Vayoel Moshe, Brooklyn, 1961), acquired a 500-acre area in Mt Olive Township
(New Jersey), but the Township Council objected and tried every means to block
the project. A court case ensued, accompanied by charges on both sides of bias and
prejudice, and with the usual publicity. The New Jersey Superior Court decided
in favour of the Hassidim (*New York Times*, 7 June 1962, p. 28; and 25 September
1963, p. 36).

Or the incidents in New Hampden (Connecticut) come to mind, where, as a result of a communication from the New Haven Jewish Community Council, the school superintendent was asked to disallow both Chanukkah and Christmas celebrations (because they were constitutionally illegal religious practices at schools). When the superintendent acted according to this request, there resulted 'furious denunciations from Catholic and Protestant pulpits; a hectic public school board meeting which verged on the brink of mob-hysteria and open anti-Semitism, according to individuals present, a host of anti-Semitic chalk slogans, Nazi swastikas, and crank letters and, finally, a repudiation of the school super-intendent of his original directive. . . . To most observers it would appear that the pressure to heighten a "wall of separation" between Church and State not only failed to accomplish its ends, but measurably heightened the wall of separation between the various elements of the community' (Herbert Weiner, 'The Case for the Timorous Jew', in *Midstream*, December 1962, pp. 5–6).

98. Thus in England every few years, a law appertaining to the slaughter of animals is submitted to Parliament. In its proposed form it is apt to infringe on the method of slaughter (*Shechita*) Jews practice according to their religion. Press campaigns on both sides ensue; Members of Parliament are prodded by their respective constituents (pro or con, as the case may be). In short, a broad political campaign, embracing the whole country and every county where Jews live, develops on this matter, of the utmost importance to Jews observing their religious tenets. (See about such campaigns, the press reports and Parliamentary debates preceding the legislation on *Shechita* in 1928 [the Public General Acts, London, Chapter 29]; in 1933 [*ibid.* for the years 1932–3, Chapter 39]: and all sub-sequent attempts [Lords, 18 March 1948]; and 1954 [*ibid.*, House of Commons, 29 January 1954, and Standing Committee B, 17 February 1954]—and up to the debate in the House of Lords on 3 December 1962). It is noteworthy in this con-nection that the practice of *Shechita* is defended and supported by all Jewish religious denominations.

As another example, one could take the fight in New York, which has lasted for decades, to permit religious Jews who observe the Sabbath to open their shops on Sundays. Thanks to a wide political campaign, in the course of which mass delegations descended on Albany, senators and political leaders were asked to intervene, and lobbying was carried out on a broad front—in short, thanks to a full-fledged political campaign, to no small degree influenced by the vote of Jews in larger cities, the Fair Sabbath Law for New York City (only) was approved by the State Legislature in April 1963, while the political struggle for its application throughout the State continues.

99. Thus, when the question of a new code of ethics was under consideration by the New York Legislature, Rabbi Uri Miller, President of the Synagogue Council in America (representative body of the Orthodox, Conservative, and Reform branches of Judaism), suggested 'that such a code be not left to the legislators for a decision, but that it be prepared "by a special advisory committee of responsible citizens". I trust that since there are ethical and moral problems involved, members of the three-faith community will be represented on this committee—Catholic, Protestant, Jew' (*New York Times*, 26 October 1963, pp. 1, 12). This statement clearly indicates that every one of the religions has its own approach to these vital questions.

Or another example. Some 600 integrationists, about evenly divided between Roman Catholics and Episcopalians, assembled in November 1963, in Washington, D.C., 'to demonstrate the unanimity of religion in opposing racial segregation' (*New York Times*, 15 November 1963, p.21), and when the U.S. Supreme Court recently voided a ban on a film, Jewish, Protestant, and Catholic clergymen in a joint statement urged 'that religious leaders of all faiths in all communities stand together vociferously decrying the fact that the Court has presumed to recast the moral law' (*New York Times*, 1 September 1964, p. 37).

100. Even far-fetched aspects of religious institutions assume political importance when it is recalled that, for instance, the Church of England owns properties, stocks, and bonds, valued in 1963 at $840 million (*New York Times*, 3 November 1963, p. 3). It thus becomes unavoidably interested and involved in legislation affecting these investments, from which the Church derives a large part of its income.

101. *New York Times*, 26 October 1963, p. 3.

102. Lawrence H. Fuchs, *The Political Behavior of American Jews*, Glencoe (Free Press), 1956, pp. 191-9.

103. *Ibid.*, p. 178.

104. Fuchs, *op cit.*, p. 187.

105. *Ibid.*, p. 191.

106. Toynbee, 'Pioneer Destiny of Judaism', p. 8.

107. Where, for instance, Parliament, a purely political instrument, has to sanction all the ecclesiastical legislation of the Church of England, which needs must lead to political activities by those who are interested in ecclesiastical legislation (see C. Garbett, *Claims of the Church of England*, New York), 1947, and the literature referred to there.

108. See Max Lerner, *America as a Civilization* (New York, Simon and Schuster), 1957, particularly Chapter X. *Cf.* also Murray S. Stedman Jr, *Religion and Politics in America* (New York, Harcourt), 1964. As an example it may be useful to refer to the influence of religious affiliations in elections as seen in the 1965 Mayoral elections in New York (Samuel Lubell, 'Will Religion Decide Election?' in *New York World Telegram and Sun*, 25 October 1965, p. 4.) It must be stressed in this connection that all these issues have no relation to the question of division of Church and State.

109. As the United States B'Nai B'rith has done in South America.

110. Toynbee, 'Pioneer Destiny of Judaism', pp. 5-7; *idem.*, 'Future of Judaism', pp. 73-6.

111. Even where Jewish secular organisations attempt to intervene in religious matters through lobbying, they are rebuked by religious organisations as undignified, unauthorised, or harmful to Jewish religion. See, for instance, the statement by Moses Feuerstein, President of the Union of Orthodox Jewish Congregations in America, against intervention by secular agencies among the Catholic clergy at the Ecumenical Council, in *New York Times*, 10 May 1965, p. 10, *Jewish Chronicle*, 14 May 1960, p. 17; or the protest of religious circles against the American Jewish Congress for its intervention in matters of Federal support for religious schools (*The Day*, 17 April 1965, p. 1); or against lobbying by secular leaders regarding *Shechita* legislation (*The Day*, 28 May 1965, p. 2). This obviously shows that religious organisations fully subscribe to political activity for religious purposes and do not wish secular sections to interfere.

112. Toynbee, 'Future of Judaism', p. 77. A similar thought is expressed in *Reconsiderations*, p. 496.

113. Thus when two prominent Orthodox Rabbis called on Cardinal Spellman and, among other things, asked him to withdraw his opposition to long-standing legislative proposals to amend New York State Compulsory Sunday Law so as to exempt Jewish Sabbath-observers, the Cardinal replied that the U.S.A. was a Christian country and that accordingly Jews would have to comply with the customs and practices imposed by Christians (Leo Pfeffer, 'Counter-reflections on Church and State', in *Midstream*, December 1962, p. 20).

As another instance the speech may be quoted, on 3 December 1962, in the British House of Lords, by Lord Cohen of Birkenhead. He replied to a speech by Lord Huntington in the House on the occasion of the debate on Lord Somers' proposed 'Slaughter of Animals Bill', as follows: 'He made two statements which I hope your Lordships reject and resent. The first is that minorities in this country who have religious practices which are not accepted by the majority might look out because it might react upon them adversely. If he said that not directly, he implied it quite directly' (*Parliamentary Debates*, House of Lords, 4 December 1962, col. 39).

Very much along the same line of thought was a statement in the Jesuit magazine *America* of 28 August 1962. The decision by the Supreme Court of the United States, invalidating the recitation of the New York Regent's prayer in public schools (25 June 1962), was then widely acclaimed in Jewish religious circles. This induced the Jesuit weekly to turn in an editorial 'To our Jewish Friends' and to warn: 'We wonder whether it is not time for provident leaders of American Judaism to ask their more militant colleagues whether what is gained through the courts by such victories is worth the breakdown of community relations. . . . What will have been accomplished if our Jewish friends win all the legal immunities they seek, but thereby paint themselves into a corner of social and cultural alienations?' The principle of this statement is not altered by a subsequent friendly 'explanation' of this stand by the paper.

114. See, for instance, the many examples of good results in Leo Pfeffer, 'Counter-reflections on Church and State', in *Midstream*, December 1962, pp. 15–23. An interesting survey of the situation in the U.S.A. in the last half-century was published in *Look*, 4 June 1963, in '50-Year War on Prejudice. The Story of the Anti-Defamation League'. Or the conference of all three major faiths (Catholic, Protestant, Jew) in Washington in a drive for the Civil Rights Bill (*New York Times*, 10 April 1964, p. 1). A very interesting study showing the great progress made in the U.S.A. in the last half-century in the field of civil rights was prepared by Dr John P. Roche, *The Quest for a Dream*, for the Anti-Defamation League of B'nai B'rith (see *New York World Telegram*, 13 November 1963, p. 1).

115. *New York Times*, 19 January 1966, pp. 1, 18.

116. lv, 5.

117. Toynbee, *A Historian's Approach to Religion*, London, 1956, p. 252.

118. See in this connection the interesting study on toleration in history appertaining to Jews in Guido Kisch, 'Tolerans und Menschenwürder', in *Judentum ins Mittelalter* (Berlin, Gruyters & Co), 1965.

119. Toynbee, 'The Future of Judaism in Western Countries', p. 77.

120. Talmud *Berakhoth*, 47b. At this point an illuminating example is given of this thought: Once Rabbi Eliezer entered the house of worship but was unable to pray because instead of the required quorum of ten men only nine were assembled. He therefore set free a slave in order to count him among the ten. Thus the fulfilment of the Godly command was only possible through the humanitarian act preceding it.

121. *Psychology of the Transference* (New York, Bollinger XX), 1954, VII.

122. Toynbee, 'Pioneer Destiny of Judaism', p. 4.

123. Toynbee, *Study*, Vol. VIII, pp. 287–8.

124. Speech at the First Zionist Congress, in *Protocol* I, p. 25.

125. About the term 'emancipation' see Jacob Katz, 'The Term Jewish Emancipation', etc. in *Studies in Nineteenth-Century Jewish Intellectual History* (ed. A. Altmann) (Cambridge, Mass., Harvard), 1964, pp. 1–25.

126. *Study of History*, Vol. II, p. 240.

127. *Ibid.*, Vol. VIII, p. 287.

128. *Ibid.*, Vol. II, p. 252n.

129. Toynbee, 'Future of Judaism', p. 71.
130. See *Author's Note* in above.
131. *Ibid.*
132. Toynbee, *Reconsiderations*, p. 627.
133. This is the title of his article in *Issues*, New York, Summer 1960, Vol. XIV, No. *6*, p. 1.
134. Toynbee, 'Future of Judaism in the Western World', p. 69.
135. Toynbee, *Reconsiderations*, p. 628n. He repeated this same idea in an article 'Why I dislike Western Civilization', in the *New York Times Magazine* (10 May 1964, p. 15), when he wrote: 'Now that my German fellow-Westerners have murdered six million Jews, how can I be certain that my English fellow-countrymen might not do something similar equally criminal?'
136. Toynbee, *Reconsiderations*, p. 488.
137. *Ibid.*, pp. 494–5. See also *ibid.*, p. 622n. A similar thought is expressed in Rosenberg, *Der Mythos*, p. 462.
138. *Amos*, ix, 7.
139. *Leviticus*, xix–xx.
140. For instance, *Reconsiderations*, pp. 621–5.
141. *Ibid.*, p. 623.
142. *Ibid.*, pp. 621, 622.
143. *Ibid.*, p. 623.
144. Debate between Pieter Geyl and Toynbee on the BBC Third Programme on 4 January 1948, published by F. G. Krooner, Bussum, Holland.
145. Toynbee, *Study of History*, Vol. VIII, p. 290.
146. Toynbee, *Reconsiderations*, p. 609.
147. Toynbee, 'Pioneer Destiny of Judaism'.
148. Toynbee, 'Future of Judaism', p. 2.
149. *Ibid.*, p. 4.
150. Shakespeare, *King Richard III*, Act III, Sc. i.
151. See on this subject the section in this book 'A Natural Corollary' on p. 128.
152. See p. 25.
153. *Deuteronomy*, vii, 7.
154. Masaryk, *Otázka sociální* (The Social Question), Prague, 1898, p. 354.
155. Toynbee, *Study*, I, 46.
156. Lord Acton, 'The History of Freedom in Antiquity', in *Essays on Freedom and Power* (Boston, Beacon), 1948, p. 33.
157. *Ibid.*
158. Toynbee, *Reconsiderations*, p. 305.
159. *Ibid.*, p. 517.
160. Some Bible critics confine Deutero–Isaiah to Chapters xl–lv.
161. *Zohar Vayikra* 36a (author's translation).
162. By October 1963 some 5,000 Israeli experts were reported to be assisting twenty African new nations in the various problems of their development in every field of human endeavour. Also, students from various African countries enrolled at the various schools of higher learning in Israel. At the end of the summer term 1963, for instance, African student graduates at the Haifa 'International School for Social Workers and Educators' expressed their sentiments in a special song which began with the words: 'Africa will not forget what Israel did for her' (*The Day-Jewish Journal*, 22 October 1963, p. 4). See as a further instance a report on these Israeli activities in Africa in the *New York Times*, 29 October 1963, p. 6; and Ben Oyserman, 'What Israelis are doing in Africa' in *Jewish Chronicle*, 15 November 1963, p. 22; S. Izban, 'What African Countries learn from Israel', in *The Day-Jewish Journal*, 13 February 1965, p. 4; Mordechai M. Kreimin, *Israel and Africa:*

A Study in Technical Cooperation, New York, (Praeger), 1964; Sabbatai Tebeth, 'Israel's Special Position: Israel–Africa', in *Haaretz*, 30 April 1965, p. 2.

163. Letter dated 12 October 1963, addressed to the fortieth annual conference of the National Committee for Labor Israel in New York (*New York Times*, 28 November 1963, p. 47).

164. Message to Histadruth (*New York Times*, 29 November 1964, p. 68).

In this connection it seems right to mention the following facts:

During the years 1957 to 1963 more than 3,500 students from countries in Africa and Asia attended courses in Israel. When they returned to their countries of origin they had successful careers at home. This is brought out not only by the continuous demand for such courses from many of these countries, but also by the establishment of 'Israel Graduate Clubs', of which there were eight at the time of writing and by the large volume of correspondence between Afro-Asians who graduated in Israel and Israeli friends and tutors. In addition they continued their studies of Hebrew.

In the summer of 1961 hundreds of African students met in Jerusalem (at the Hebrew University) and established the 'African Students' Association in Israel'.

Foreign students publish since 1962 their own paper *Shalom* ('Peace') in Israel.

About these activities, their meaning and influence, see Yohanan Ramati, 'Popular Friendship for Israel', in *Jewish Observer and Middle East Review*, 22 November 1963, pp. 7–8; see also Godwin O. Nwafor, 'African Students in Israel', in *Jerusalem Post*, 12 June 1964, p. 3; and an interesting report about the training by Hadassah of doctors and nurses from African countries in Israel, in *New York Times*, 17 August 1964. Finally, see Mordechai E. Kreinin, *Israel and Africa* (London, Pall Mall Press), 1964.

It may be useful to compare the number of students from newly created nations in various countries in the world and the State of Israel. Thus at the time when little Israel had 3,500 such students, in Britain there were 16,000, in France 15,000, in West Germany 4,300, and Soviet Russia about 1,000 students from these territories (*New York Times*, 19 December 1963, p. 10; 21 December, p. 2; 22 December, p. 2. See also *The Observer* [London], 22 December 1963, p. 3, and *Sunday Times* [London], 22 December 1963, p. 5).

165. *Isaiah* ii, 3.

166. *Psalm* cxxvii, 1. Toynbee placed this verse on the title-page of Vol. VI of his *Study of History!*

167. *Psalm* cxlv, 6 and 7.

168. Toynbee, *Reconsiderations*, pp. 534, 617, 624. However, by 1962 he regarded Hinduism as the candidate *par excellence* for serving as the 'religion of coexistence' (Toynbee, *America and the World Revolution*, p. 49), and a year later he repeated that he felt that Indian religion alone was the 'kind of religion that is needed for our times' (Philip and Arnold Toynbee, *Comparing Notes*, pp. 13, 18).

169. Toynbee, *Reconsiderations*, p. 516.

170. Toynbee, *Study of History*, Vol. VI, p. 113.

171. Toynbee, *Reconsiderations*, p. 263.

172. *Ibid.*, pp. 486, 513.

173. *Ibid.*, p. 263.

174. Toynbee, *Study of History*, Vol. I, p. 212n.

175. Toynbee, *Reconsiderations*, p. 517.

176. *Ibid.*, p. 494.

177. Toynbee, *Study of History*, Vol. IX, p. 87.

178. Alfred Rosenberg, *Mythos*, p. 603 (author's translation). In another connection Rosenberg blames the Old Testament for 'Supplying poison to many a protestant movement to this day', (p. 109).

179. Philip and Arnold Toynbee, *Comparing Notes*, p. 22.
180. Toynbee, *Study of History*, Vol. V, p. 658.
181. *Ibid.*, Vol. IX, p. 95. A similar idea about Paul as a defender of Judaism, notwithstanding his criticism of Jewish law, is made by the Nazi leader Alfred Rosenberg, in *Mythos*, pp. 74–75f.
182. Chapter II, pp. 17–29; III, pp. 19–26; VII, pp. 7–25, and so on.
183. Toynbee, *Study in History*, Vol. V, p. 126.
184. Toynbee, *Reconsiderations*, p. 414.
185. *Ibid.*, p. 420n.
186. See, for instance, Professor Eduard König, *Das Antisemitische Dogma* (Bonn, Marcus & Webers), 1914, Chapter III, 'Juden und Galilaeer', pp. 41–60; and for a survey of the issue see Dr Samuel Klein, in *Encyclopaedia Judaica* (Berlin), 'Galilea', Vol. VII, col. 57. It is interesting that where Toynbee dislikes a theory about Jews or Judaism, he takes refuge in 'scholarship'. But general subjects are treated more considerately. For instance, with regard to racial characteristics of a psychic order, he writes: 'This dogma was a bare postulate which had never been borne out by any scientific demonstration down to the time of writing; and the burden of proof had still to be discharged by the credulous before the task of disproof need be shouldered by the sceptics.' But of course, in Jewish matters, he does not apply this cautious approach, and does not call for a 'burden of proof'. (Toynbee, *Study*, Vol. VIII, p. 579).
187. See, for example, Houston Chamberlain, *Grundlagen des neunzehnten Jahrhunderts* (Muenchen), 1919, Vol. I, pp. 246–358. (Toynbee refers to him in his *Study of History*, Vol. VI, p. 217, as one of the inspirers of racialism in Germany); Theodor Fritsch, *Der falsche Gott. Mein Beweismaterial gegen Jahwe* (Leipzig), 1913, pp. 118f; Alfred Rosenberg, *Der Mythos des 20. Jahrhunderts* (Muenchen), 1935, p. 76n.
188. Toynbee, 'The Future of Judaism', pp. 76–7. A similar thought is expressed in *Reconsiderations*, p. 496.
189. See *supra* p. 25, quoting *Reconsiderations*, p. 478.
190. The statistics are quoted from *Britannica Book of the Year*, p. 270.
191. Toynbee's characterisation.
192. Toynbee's characterisation.
193. Toynbee, *Reconsiderations*, p. 575. Blanche E. C. Dugdale, *Arthur James Balfour*, Vol. I (London), 1936, p. 22.
194. Toynbee, *Reconsiderations*, pp. 75–6. Dugdale, *Balfour*, Vol. I, pp. 50f.
195. Dugdale, *Balfour*, Vol. I, p. 52.
196. *Parliamentary Debates* (Commons), 19 July 1905, Vol. XX, 149, col. 154–5. It is recorded in the text in *oratio obliqua*.
197. Quotation from the 'Balfour Declaration'.
198. Toynbee dealt with these critics in *Reconsiderations*, pp. 76–7.
199. Toynbee, *Reconsiderations*, p. 478.
200. William Wordsworth, *Yes, it was the Mountain Echo*.
201. Thus, for instance, a 'Conference on Intermarriage and Jewish Life' was held in New York on February 13–14, 1960, to deal with this vexing problem (see the papers presented there in *Intermarriage and Jewish Life: A Symposium*, ed. by Werner J. Cahnman, New York, 1963). The seriousness of the problem was stressed particularly by Erich Rosenthal, 'Studies of Jewish Intermarriage in the United States', in *American Jewish Year Book 1963*, Vol. 64, pp. 3–53. See also Salo Baron, 'The Growing Number of Intermarriages Causes Pessimism among Jews', in *The Day*, 20 September 1964, p. 6. See also Albert I. Gordon, *Intermarriage: Interfaith—Interracial—Interethnic* (Boston, Beacon), 1962. See also *Ten Vital Jewish Issues*, ed. by Rabbi William Berkovitz (New York, Yoseloff), 1965.

Another conference on intermarriage was organised by the Federation of Jewish Philanthropies of New York (December 12–13 1964) in Long Beach, New York, in which 50 rabbis, social scientists, and communal leaders participated. Steps were discussed to stem the tide of intermarriage, which had lately shown that 70 per cent of children born to mixed marriages in the U.S.A. are lost to Judaism (*The Day*, 20 December 1964, p. 1).

202. 'That intermarriage usually spells the end of belonging to the Jewish group is demonstrated by the fact that in at least 70 per cent of the mixed families in Greater Washington the children were not identified with the Jewish group. This finding, which repeats earlier European experiences, takes on a special significance if viewed against the fact that fertility of the Jewish population in the United States is barely sufficient to maintain its present size' (Erich Rosenthal, *op. cit.*, p. 53).

203. Toynbee, 'The Future of Judaism', pp. 76–7.

204. Apart from the fact of the world-wide efforts by Christian denominations to make converts to Christianity through their well-financed missionary activities (see, for instance, G. Dalman, who wrote on the subject in Germany in 1893, and K. S. Latourette, *History of the Expansion of Christianity*, 7 volumes, 1938–46, with bibliography).

205. See, for instance, David Flinker, 'Missionaries in Israel', in *The Day-Jewish Journal*, 27 February 1963. *Cf.* also the correspondence in the London *Times*, 16 September 1963, p. 11 (J. Litvin); 20 September p. 13 (H. Sebag-Montefiore); 4 October 1963, p. 13 (J. Litvin).

206. 'Intermarriage: A Survey of Unresearched Problems', in *Intermarriage and Jewish Life* (ed. Cahnmann), p. 100.

207. *Ibid.*, p. 101 (Simon Marcson, 'A Theory of Intermarriage and Assimilation', in *Phylon* 4 [1951], pp. 457–63).

208. Rudyard Kipling, *The Female of the Species*.

209. Fred Werbell, in *Jewish Life* (New York, Vol. 31, March–April, 1964, p. 39).

210. Toynbee, 'The Future of Judaism', p. 77.

211. Toynbee, 'Pioneer Destiny of Judaism', p. 14.

212. Josephus, *Antiquities*, 13.9, 1 (257). Toynbee refers to this event in *Reconsiderations*, p. 502.

213. See about his Judaean nationality Solomon Zeitlin, 'Herod', in *Jewish Quarterly Review*, July 1963, pp. 4–8.

214. *Ibid.*, p. 6.

215. Toynbee describes this forced conversion in *Study of History*, Vol. II, p. 244; and Vol. VIII, p. 281. The quotation is from Vol. II, p. 248n.

216. Toynbee himself has expressed his astonishment over the reappearance after centuries of Marranos in important Jewish places and activities.

217. Alex Bein, *Theodor Herzl* (Vienna), 1934, p. 11.

218. Toynbee, 'The Future of Judaism', p. 77.

219. *Isaiah*, lvi, 8.

220. One of the eighteen blessings in the most important prayer (*Amidah*).

221. Toynbee, *Reconsiderations*, p. 515.

222. *Ibid.*, p. 514.

223. Toynbee, 'The Future of Judaism', p. 76.

224. Toynbee, *Reconsiderations*, p. 596.

225. *Ibid.*, p. 631.

226. This challenge came in 1961 in an invitation by an American Jewish journalist, David Horowitz, also active in Jewish proselytisation, to Toynbee to join the Jewish faith, if he believed, in his own words, that it is Judaism that mankind needed. Toynbee replied that he would not do so as long as Jewish religion

was centred on Palestine; and he might do so if Judaism became a denationalised Diaspora based on religion only (*The Day-Jewish Journal*, 19 September 1961, p. 3). This was a characteristic answer, for, while not at all satisfied with much of his Christian creed (*Reconsiderations*, p. 596), he nevertheless retains it, 'overlooking' the disagreements. Yet with regard to Judaism, Toynbee laid down his 'condition', although many Jews regard themselves as members of a denationalised religion only. Would it not be appropriate to join them in their struggle within Jewry for the concept? After all, if a man believes in high ideals, he should stand up and fight for them not from the outside but from within the fold; and he will not wait for 'victory' to be fought for by others and presented to him on a silver platter.

227. Toynbee, *Reconsiderations*, p. 475.

228. *Ibid.*, pp. 96, 97.

229. *Ibid.*, p. 643.

230. *Ibid.*, p. 307.

231. *Ibid.*

232. *Ibid.*, p. 643.

233. *Ibid.*, p. 466.

234. *Ibid.*, p. 475.

235. Toynbee, *Study of History*, Vol. II, p. 244.

236. *Ibid.*, Vol. V, p. 76.

237. Toynbee, *Reconsiderations*, p. 467.

238. Toynbee, *Study of History*, Vol. II, p. 253.

239. *Ibid.*, pp. 280-2.

240. Toynbee, 'Pioneer Destiny of Judaism', p. 9.

241. Toynbee, *Reconsiderations*, p. 211 (author's italics).

242. *Ibid.*, p. 483 (author's italics).

243. *Ibid.*, p. 486 (author's italics).

244. Toynbee, 'Future of Judaism', p. 68 (author's italics).

245. Toynbee in *Maariv* (Tel-Aviv), 27 July 1964, p. 11.

246. Toynbee, 'The Future of Judaism', p. 76. The speech was delivered in 1962.

247. Toynbee, *Reconsiderations*, p. 496.

248. Toynbee, *Reconsiderations*, p. 613.

249. About him see David Philipson, *Samuel Holdheim, Jewish Reformer* (Cincinnati), 1906.

250. Heinrich Graetz, *Geschichte der Juden*, Vol. XI (Leipzig), 1900, p. 515.

251. See *Reconsiderations*, pp. 481, 482, 494n, 502n, 503n, 504n, 505n, 507, 516.

252. Toynbee, *Reconsiderations*, p. 619.

253. *Ibid.*, p. 239.

254. *Jeremiah*, i, 5. Toynbee denies regarding himself as a prophet (*Reconsiderations*, pp. 3-4, 238-9), and I feel inclined to agree with him wholeheartedly in the light of so many 'prophecies' that he has projected in his career and which have come to naught.

255. Toynbee, 'Pioneer Destiny of Judaism', pp. 13-14.

256. Toynbee, *Reconsiderations*, p. 619.

257. 'In order to turn [the national States] into welfare agencies we have to deprive them of their traditional sovereignty and subordinate them, both legally and emotionally, to a higher authority', (*ibid.*, p. 620n).

258. Toynbee, 'Pioneer Destiny of Judaism', p. 8.

259. *Parliamentary Debates*, House of Lords, 1 August 1833.

260. Toynbee, *Study of History*, Vol. II, p. 240.

261. In August, 1912, Goldstein's article was headed: 'Deutschjuedischer Parnass' and was followed by a debate in the magazine over three issues. Avenarius, its editor, was a spiritual leader in Germany, free from bias and antisemitism.

A similar attitude was taken by Russian progressive writers against Jewish 'understanding' of Russian culture. Thus in 1909, when Shalom Asch read his story 'Orphan' before Russian literati, a leading progressive writer, N. Czirikov, spoke in the debate and said that 'Jewish literary critics who attained important positions in the Russian press and literary magazines cannot organically understand a true national and popular Russian literary work. This can only be understood by a Russian, to whom all this is his own inner national possession'. And another speaker that evening, K. Arabazhin, also a progressive writer, added that Czirikov's opinion 'is not that of an individual, but applies to the wider circles of Russian literati'. J. Weinberg, 'The New Course', in *Tribune* (Berlin, 1922), No. 30–1; p. 71.

Even an enlightened man, the world-famous Prof. Ernest (later Lord) Rutherford, had to accept this same 'distinction', as Dr Weizmann reveals in his memoirs: 'One morning, when I came into the common room, he thrust the London *Times* under my nose: "Look at that!" he roared. Israel Gollancz had been appointed professor of Old English literature at Queen's College [Weitzmann's mistake here; it should be King's College] London. "I understand that Gollancz's grandfather came here from Galicia! Not chemistry, or physics, mind you, but literature, something of national significance," and he finished up with a great burst of laughter. "You know, professor," I said, "if I had to appoint a professor of Hebrew literature at the Hebrew University in Jerusalem, I would not take an Englishman!" "There you are!" shot back Rutherford. "I always said you were narrow-minded, bigoted and jingoistic." "For England," I explained, "it doesn't matter much. Your culture is too well established. Gollancz may even bring a new note into the teaching of English literature, and England will profit by it. But if you had ten chairs of English literature, and ten Jews got them, what would you think of it?" "Oh, that!," roared Rutherford, "that would be a national calamity"' (*Trial and Error*, p. 154, London, Hamish Hamilton, 1949).

262. 'My inescapable Westernness makes it impossible for me to become culturally acclimatised in any of these other contemporary civilisations' (Toynbee, 'Why I Dislike Western Civilization', in *New York Times Magazine*, 10 May 1964, p. 15).

263. Arnold and Philip Toynbee, *Comparing Notes*, p. 100.

264. Toynbee, *Reconsiderations*, p. 596.

265. *Ibid.*, pp. 628–9.

266. Toynbee, *Study of History*, Vol. IX, pp. 536ff. (The volume was first published in 1954, but Toynbee mentions in it, p. 536, that this section was written in 1952.)

‡267. David Cushman Coyte, 'The United Nations and How it Works' (New York), 1960.

268. In a speech to the Labor Union Convention, in *New York Times*, 25 March 1964, p. 4.

269. Toynbee, *Reconsiderations*, p. 633.

270. Toynbee, *Study of History*, Vol. VIII, p. 580.

271. *Ibid.*, pp. 599, 600, 601. Toynbee chose as evidence of the Zealot–Agudath Israel parallelism only their strict adherence to the Law. He omitted entirely the conspiratorial military practices of this sect of 'Passionate Avengers' in ancient Palestine (see Graetz, *Geschichte*, Vol. III, pp. 452ff. and particularly pp. 457, 504ff.; Dubnow, *Weltgeschichte*, Vol. II, p. 412. See Toynbee himself on the Zealots' militant outbursts in *Study of History*, Vol. VI, p. 107).

And for the parallel with Liberalism, Toynbee selected that part of Herodianism which appertains to Herod's assimilationism to Hellenism and Rome, but omitted entirely his bloodthirsty murder of wife, children, friends, and foes, which are no less characteristic of Herodianism and not unlikely to have stemmed from its assimilationism (see Abraham Shalit, *Hordos Hamelech* (King Herod), Jerusalem 1960, particularly ch. VI, pp. 274–321; Solomon Zeitlin, 'Herod', in *J.Q.R.*, July 1963, pp. 1–27).

272. Toynbee, *Study of History*, Vol. V, p. 617n, for the first quoted paragraph; and *ibid.*, p. 76, for the second.

273. See, for instance, Toynbee, *Study of History*, Vol. V, pp. 76, 588–9; Vol. VI, pp. 128, 216; Vol. VIII, pp. 298–301, 600.

274. *Die Welt*, 31 May 1912, p. 658. *The Purpose and the Programme of the World Agudist Organization*, London, 1937, p. 4.

275. *Ibid.*, 2 August 1912, p. 931.

276. Royal Commission on Palestine, Report, Cmd. 5479 of 1937: *Minutes of Evidence Heard or Public Sessions*, Colonial Of. 1937, No. 134.

277. *Ibid.*

278. Full text of these memoranda in *Die Vertretung der Agudas Israel vor der Commission*, Frankfurt am Main, 1937. (The quotations are author's translation.)

279. *Ibid.*, p. 67.

280. *Ibid.*, p. 118.

281. Vol. I, pp. 376–7. The section 'The Development of the Jewish National Home' was written by Leonard Stein.

282. The Council (Va'ad Le'umi) was then the recognised organisation of Palestine Jewry. But there was no compulsion for individuals or congregations to come under its control. However, the organising of a second Jewish community was rejected (Toynbee, *Survey for 1925*, Vol. I, p. 377).

283. Petition from the Council of the Ashkenazic Jewish Community of Jerusalem, printed as Annex No. 8 to the *Minutes of the Seventh Session of the Permanent Mandates Commission*, pp. 181–3 (quoted in the *Survey*).

284. 'Conservative' here denotes strict Orthodoxy (as it was understood in Europe); not what in America is known as 'Conservative Judaism'.

285. Petition from the Ashkenazic Community, 22 November 1924, printed in *loc. cit.*; petition in support from *Agudath Israel*, 11 October 1925, printed as Annex No. 5 to the *Minutes of the Seventh Session of the Permanent Mandates Commission*, pp. 195–6 (quoted in the *Survey*).

286. Toynbee, *Study of History*, Vol. VIII, p. 300.

287. Toynbee, *Reconsiderations*, p. 516. I believe, however, judging from the context, that Toynbee portrays them as two different movements because of his ignorance of Jewish affairs rather than from an understanding of the differences between the various sectors of Liberal-Reform belief and theory.

288. About that school and the history of Biblical science see Max Soloweiczik and Zalman Rubashov (later Shazar, who became president), *Toledot Bikkoret Hamikra* (History of Biblical Research), Berlin, 1925.

289. Solomon Schechter, *Seminary Addresses* (Cincinnati), 1915 (26 March 1903).

290. Toynbee, *Survey for 1933*, p. 145.

291. Toynbee, *Reconsiderations*, p. 517.

292. *i.e.*, the Bible as we know it today.

293. Toynbee, *Reconsiderations*, p. 482.

294. Montefiore, *The Hibbert Lecture*, pp. 5 and 416.

295. Toynbee, *Reconsiderations*, p. 416.

296. Montefiore, *op. cit.*, p. 416. (Additional references *ibid.*, p. 6; *Rabbinic Literature and Gospel Teachings*, pp. 352–3; *The Synoptic Gospel*, p. civ.)

297. Toynbee, *Reconsiderations*, p. 425. (Additional references *ibid.*, p. 623.)

298. London, 1923.

299. Montefiore, *Hibbert Lecture*, p. 552.

300. Toynbee, 'Pioneer Destiny of Judaism', p. 14.

301. Montefiore, *Liberalism and Nationalism*, p. 10.

302. Toynbee, 'The Future of Judaism', p. 76.

303. See Theodor Herzl, 'Mr Claude Montefiore's Ansichten' (opinions), in *Die Welt*, No. 18, 1898, p. 1.

304. About this period and Montefiore's efforts at preventing the issuance of the Declaration, see Leonard Stein, *The Balfour Declaration*, pp. 525–6.

305. Apart from Stein, *op. cit.*, see also *Zionism* (Foreign Office Handbook No. 162), pp. 38–43; *cf.* also Montefiore's interview with Lord Milner, then a member of the War Cabinet of May 1917, in Oskar K. Rabinowicz, *Herzl, Architect of the Balfour Declaration*, p. 94.

306. In writing his book Toynbee 'was left an entirely free hand to carry it out' (Toynbee's letter to me of 21 June 1961).

307. 'Judaism and the Gospels', translated from the Hebrew by Leon Simon, in *Nationalism and the Jewish Ethos* (New York, Schocken), 1962, pp. 289–319. The quotation is *ibid.*, p. 319.

308. In his essay 'A Revaluation of Reform Judaism', in *Central Conference of American Rabbis' Year Book*, Vol. 34, 1925, p. 223.

309. *Jewish Year Book* for 1911.

310. *The Essentials of Liberal Judaism* (London, Routledge), 1947, p. 128.

311. *Ibid.*, p. 163.

312. *Esther*, Chapter ix.

313. 'I will bring you out from . . . Egypt . . . and I will take you to Me for a people; and I will be to you a God' (*Exodus*, vi, 6).

314. See the prayer 'Al Hanissim' for Hanukkah in every Prayer-Book.

315. For a full report, the resolutions, and the speeches, see *Jewish Chronicle*, 26 April 1963, pp. 12–13.

316. There are today Hebrew-speaking classes at the London Liberal Synagogue. [90, 26 April 1963, p. 7.]

317. 'Mr Claude Montefiore's Ansichten', *op. cit.*, p. 206–7.

318. Toynbee, 'Future of Judaism', p. 68.

319. Toynbee, *Reconsiderations*, p. 487.

320. Toynbee, *Study*, Vol. II, p. 253.

321. Toynbee, *Study*, Vol. II, pp. 253–4.

322. The first was accepted on 28 January 1790, but appertained only to the Spanish, Portuguese, and Avignon Jews in France. The second extended to all Jews (see about this, *Moniteur*, 1790, p. 243; 1791, 28 and 29 September).

323. The 'Decree' referred to was Duport's proposal of 23 December 1790, that 'no Frenchman can be deprived of active citizenship', which was rejected by the National Assembly (*Moniteur*, 1790, 23 December).

324. See p. 113.

325. We are not entering the debate on the actual emergence of 'emancipation' and the subsequent division of the 'emancipation periods' (see for these Dubnow, *Weltgeschichte*, Vol. VIII, pp. 69ff.; Baron, *A Social and Religious History of the Jews* (New York, Columbia), 1937, Vol. II, pp. 164f.; Jacob Katz, 'The Term "Jewish Emancipation": Its Origin and Historical Impact,' in *Studies in Nineteenth-Century Jewish Intellectual History*, ed. A. Altmann (Cambridge, Mass., Harvard), 1964, pp. 1–25.

326. See pp. 156ff.

327. *Ibid.*

328. Harry Sacher, *Jewish Emancipation: The Contract Myth* (London, Engl. Zionist Federation), 1917, p. 6.

329. *Protocol* II, pp. 4–5 (author's translation).
In order to avoid misunderstanding, it should be pointed out that the currently

NOTES

used yet still confusing terminology of 'nationalism', 'nation', 'nationality' frequently had different meanings and was frequently applied differently at the end of the eighteenth and beginning of the nineteenth century. In France, for instance, 'nation' was identical with 'State' (see Dubnow, *Weltgeschichte*, Vol. VIII, p. 96) and even in later decades French terminology has not developed an 'ethnic nationality' in its usage (see Akzin, *State and Nation*, p. 20). This explains why, when the Count from Clermont-Tonnerre in his support of Jewish equality uttered the famous words 'To the Jews as a Nation nothing is to be granted, to the Jews as human beings everything is to be granted' (*Moniteur*, 1790, 23 December), he had Statehood, or what Napoleon later called *une nation dans la nation*, a State within the State, in mind. He never even thought of applying it to what we call nationalism in Judaism aiming at independence (not in France but) in Palestine. These terms were, therefore, used in a connotation which can only be understood from the new concepts then formulated. Jews for centuries enjoyed their internal corporate life, in full religious, national, cultural, economic, juridical autonomy, as was described above in the part dealing with the 'Ghetto'. It could exist and survive in this state-like separateness because the non-Jewish society then consisted of corporations and States which also enjoyed full internal autonomy. When then, as Baron, developing this idea, pointed out, 'the modern State came into being and set out to destroy the medieval corporations and estates and to build a new citizenship, it could no longer suffer the existence of an autonomous Jewish corporation' ('Ghetto and Emancipation', in *Menorah*, p. 60).

330. Buber, *Three Speeches About Judaism*, Frankfurt a/Main, 1919, p. 26–7 (author's translation).

331. Toynbee, *Study*, Vol. VIII, p. 295.

332. Rosenberg, *Mythos*, p. 464.

333. *Zionism*, Handbook prepared under the direction of the Historical Section of the Foreign Office, London, 1920, p. 2.

334. Franz Rosenzweig, *Diary*, quoted in Nahum M. Glatzer, *Franz Rosenzweig, His Life and Deeds* (Hebrew) (Tel Aviv, Dvir), 1959, p. 67 (my translation). Rosenzweig regarded himself as a 'non-Zionist' (see 'Briefe eines Nicht-Zionisten an einen Anti-Zionisten' in *Der Jude*, Sonderheft zu Martin Bubers 50 Geburtstag, Berlin, March 1928, Vol. X, No. 1, pp. 81–5).

335. The *Zohar* is the basic work of the *Kabbala* (Jewish mysticism). It was translated into English (London, Soncino), five volumes, 1931–3. The quotation is from *Leviticus*, 93b.

336. *Ten Essays on Zionism and Judaism* (translated by Leon Simon) (London, Routledge), 1922, p. 212.

337. Hassidism, from the Hebrew *Hassid*, plural *Hassidim* (pious), is the name of a popular religious movement which arose in Poland in the first half of the eighteenth century.

338. In his preface to the first translation of the Bible into English in 1384. Quoted in Joseph L. Baron, *A Treasury of Jewish Quotations* (New York, Crown), 1956, p. 27.

339. Hans Kohn, 'Nationalism', in *Encyclopaedia Britannica* (1963).

340. Hans Kohn, *The Idea of Nationalism* (New York, Macmillan), 1946, p. 37.

341. Thomas G. Masaryk, 'Die philosophischen und soziologischen Grundlagen des Marxismus', in Karl Jentsch, 'Das Ende des Marxismus', *Die Zukunft*, Jahrg. 8, Bd. 29, pp. 119–28.

342. Thomas, *Jan Hus* (Prague, Bursik a Kohout), 1923, p. 132 (author's translation).

343. The confusion about the translation of the terms 'nation' or 'nationality' from a foreign language into English to which reference has been made applies

also to the Czech language. Masaryk in this text uses two terms: 'národ' (which I translate as 'nation', although it does not mean a political nation or a State), and 'národnost' (which I translate as 'nationality').

344. Kohn, *Idea of Nationalism*, p. 18, quoting Israel Zangwill, *The Principle of Nationalities* (London, Watts), 1917, p. 39, defines it with the same term.

345. Johannes Hus, lived 1369–1415.

346. Lord Acton, 'The History of Freedom in Antiquity', in *Essays on Freedom and Power* (Boston, Beacon), 1948, p. 33.

347. In his book *Nationality and the War* (1915) Toynbee suggested special arrangements for national minorities after World War I.

348. Dr E. Bernstein, *Der Zionismus* (Berlin, Juedischer Verlag), 1919, p. 27.

349. 'Zionism as Nationalism', in *Jewish Chronicle*, 27 August 1965, p. 7.

350. *Zionism*, p. 2.

351. *Nationalism*. A Report by a Study Group of the Royal Institute of International Affairs, London (Oxford), 1939, pp. 163–4.

352. Herzl, *Judenstaat*, p. 26.

353. Toynbee, *Reconsiderations*, p. 487.

354. *Ibid.*, p. 72.

355. Toynbee, *Study*, Vol. VIII, p. 301.

356. See *supra*, p. 182.

357. Toynbee, *Reconsiderations*, pp. 292–300; 479.

358. See pp. 118–19. In this connection it is worthy of note that other people longing for freedom go back to the 'aims and ethos of the generation of Joshua', such as, for instance, American Negroes and their leader, Dr Martin Luther King, the winner of the Nobel Prize for peace. Repeatedly in his speeches Dr King returned to the story of the fall of Jericho by peaceful means, as told in the Book of Joshua, and held it out as the symbol of non-violence (George Carmack, 'King Promises the Walls will Come Tumbling Down', in *New York World Telegram and Sun*, 26 March 1965, p. 2).

359. Toynbee, *New Europe*, p. 20.

360. Shakespeare, *A Midsummer Night's Dream*, I, i, 141.

361. Toynbee, *Nationality and the War*, p. 13.

362. Toynbee, *New Europe*, p. 19.

363. *Ibid.*, p. 20.

364. This thought was elaborated with deep insight into *the essence of Judaism* in Daniel Pasmanik, *Die Seele Israels* (Geneva, 1910).

365. See pp. 118–19.

366. Toynbee, *Reconsiderations*, p. 483.

367. See p. 112.

368. *Isaiah*, lx, 21.

369. Toynbee, *Study*, Vol. V, p. 617n.

370. For instance, Rabbi Joel Teitelbaum, who may be regarded as the contemporary spokesman of this conception, which he laid down in his bitter and hateful anti-Zionist and anti-Israel work *Vayoel Moshe* (Brooklyn), 1961.

371. Information given to me by Professor Moshe Davis, of the Hebrew University, Jerusalem, as recorded by Mr Zalman S. Shragai, a prominent Mizrachi leader who had heard it directly from the Rabbi.

372. The *Amidah* or *Shemoneh Esreh* is the Jewish central prayer, consisting originally of eighteen (now nineteen) benedictions. The words above are in the text of the fifteenth verse beginning 'Speedily cause the offspring of David, Thy servant, to flourish'.

373. As the Talmud indicates: 'If Israel would repent for one day only, the world would be immediately redeemed, and the Son of David would come right

away, for it is said (*Psalm* xcv, 7): "*today* if you would hearken to My voice.'" (*Sanhedrin* 98a.) An interesting confirmation of this hope of redemption 'any day' can be found in an anecdote related of the famous Rabbi Levi Yitzchak, of Berditchev (Russia). It tells of the invitation which he sent to his friends on the occasion of his daughter's marriage. It read: 'You are invited to my daughter's wedding, which will take place next Tuesday in the Holy City of Jerusalem. Should, however, the Messiah not have arrived by then, the marriage will be solemnised on that day in the House of Worship in Berditchev at 5 p.m.'

374. *Palestine Mandate*, Preamble.

375. Toynbee, *Reconsiderations*, p. 483. He used the same phrase also in his *Historian's Approach to Religion*, p. 88.

376. Toynbee, *Study*, Vol. VI, p. 39.

377. *Ibid.*, Vol. VIII, p. 290.

378. Published in German, Leipzig (Hammer), 1920.

379. Toynbee, *Reconsiderations*, p. 59.

380. Toynbee, *Study*, Vol. VIII, p. 294.

381. *Exodus*, xxxiii, 16.

382. *Jeremiah*, xxxi, 35–6.

383. *Theologico-Political Treatise*, Chapter 3.

384. *Coningsby* (New York–London), 1904, Vol. I, p. 293.

385. Religion is dealt with, pp. 48ff.

386. About the 'ghetto' as a national centre for preserving Jewry, see Daniel Pasmanik, *Die Seele Israels* (Geneva), 1910, pp. 15ff; Vladimir Jabotinsky, 'Weshalb wir die Diaspora nicht wollen in *Der Judenstaat* (Vienna, Glanz), 1936, pp. 7–12; also Salo W. Baron, 'Ghetto and Emancipation', *op. cit.*

387. Bezalel Sherman, 'The Jew in American Society', in *Forum IV*, Spring, 1959 (Jerusalem), pp. 284–6.

388. Nathan Glazer and Daniel Patrick Moynihan, *Beyond the Melting Pot* (section 'The Jews'), (Cambridge, Mass.), 1963, p. 161.

389. Dr Azriel Eisenberg, Executive Vice-President of the Jewish Education Committee, New York, in an interview in *New York Times*, 24 February 1965, p. 70.

390. See Pasmanik, *loc. cit.* Toynbee also dealt with this economic aspect of Diaspora Jewry in *Study*, Vol. VIII, pp. 284ff.

391. Tailoring and clothing generally, shoemaking, furniture, and jewellery are prominent examples of Jewish concentration in trades in recent times, and the law and medicine in the professions.

392. Samuel Johnson, Boswell's *Life*, Vol. III, p. 38, 12 April 1776.

393. Ahad Ha'am's call for 'learning' aptly applies in this connection. (See note 386, above.)

394. Toynbee, *The New Europe*, p. 10.

395. See for an analysis of the confusion on 'nationalism' a book by Benjamin Akzin, *Nation and State* (London, Hutchinson), 1964.

396. See p. 139.

397. Toynbee, *Reconsiderations*, pp. 223–314 ('Usage of Terms').

398. To which it must be added that Herzl's writings and the other Zionist classics were written in German and thus used a German terminology, which, with regard to 'nation', 'people', 'country', 'state', and so on, differs considerably from the Anglo-Saxon terminology.

399. Leo Baeck, *Wege im Judentum* (Berlin), 1933, p. 138.

400. Clarence J. Coleman, Jr., 'By their Aspiration, You Shall Know Them', in Bulletin of American Council of Judaism, 3 May 1963, p. 14.

401. About this group see Baruch Kurzweil, 'Essence and Sources of the "Young

Hebrews" ("Canaanites") Movement' in *Luach Haaretz* 5713 (1952–3), pp. 107–29. (The essay is in Hebrew.) See also S. Ephraim, 'The Canaanites', in *The Jewish Frontier* (New York), August 1952, No. 8 (208), pp. 25–6.

402. A case *sui generis* is that of Arthur Koestler, a former Zionist. He has stated his case and does not concern himself any more with the question of Zionism or Jewish peoplehood (see his *Promise and Fulfilment* [London, Macmillan], 1949, pp. 332–5).

403. Herzl, 'Protestrabbiner', in *Gesammelte Schriften*, p. 135.

404. Herzl, *Judenstaat*, p. 27.

405. *Protocol* I, p. 31 (author's italics).

406. Letter from Sir Clement Hill to Leopold J. Greenberg of 14 August 1903, reprinted in Oskar K. Rabinowicz, 'New Light on the East Africa Scheme', in *Rebirth of Israel*, ed. by Israel Cohen (London, Goldston), 1952, pp. 95–6.

407. Royal Institute of International Affairs, *Nationalism* (London; Oxford), 1939, p. xvii ('Note on the Use of Words').

408. Original in the British Museum, Additional MSS. 41178, Folios 1 and 3. (Author's italics.)

409. About the internal Jewish controversy preceding the Balfour Declaration see Stein, *Balfour Declaration*, pp. 442–61; 525f.

410. This term is used in Temperley's *History of the Peace Conference* when referring to the Balfour Declaration as 'in purpose a definite contract between the British Government and Jewry represented by the Zionists' (London, 1924, Vol. V, p. 173). Winston Churchill called it an 'agreement' (House of Commons *Debates*, 23 May 1939, Vol. 347, col. 2173).

411. Chief among them, Chaim Weizmann, the President of the English Zionist Federation. During World War I many a new country emerged as a result of similar 'contracts' entered into by individuals or groups who had been recognised by the one or other Allied nation (and, finally, by all of them) as representatives of their respective peoples; such as, for instance, Thomas G. Masaryk and Eduard Beneš for Czechoslovakia, Ignacy Jan Paderewsky for Poland, King Hussein and Emir Feisal for the Arabs, etc. It may be pointed out in this connection that the Balfour Declaration was not addressed and sent to the Zionist Organisation or its English branch, or to any of its prominent leaders. It was sent to Lord Rothschild, who was not a member of the Zionist Organisation. His was, however, at the time, 'the most potent name in Jewry' (Stein, *Balfour Declaration*, p. 548), he symbolised world Jewry.

412. 'It was in consequence of and on the basis of this pledge that we received important help in the War, and that after the War we received from the Allied and associated Powers the Mandate for Palestine' (Churchill in House of Commons *Debates*, 23 May 1939, Vol. 347, col. 2172). Toynbee also confirms this when he writes that in World War I 'a competition between the belligerents in courting the sympathy of Jewry' had broken out. 'To win Jewish support . . . was an object of great moment to both sides . . . and a trump card had been placed in their [the Allied] hands by a British conquest of Palestine, which put it in their power to offer satisfaction to Zionist aspirations . . .' The Jews responded to this measure so well calculated to help win a war in which the Allies were fighting for their lives'. (*Study*, Vol. VIII, p. 303).

413. *Documents on British Foreign Policy* 1919–39, Series I, Vol. VIII, p. 160.

414. Great Britain, *Cmd.* 1785, of 1922.

415. *Essential Facts about the League of Nations*, Geneva, 1939, pp. 34–5. The United States, although not a member at the time of the confirmation of the Mandate by the League of Nations, accepted it in full in the Anglo-American Treaty of 3 December 1924 (*Convention between the United Kingdom and the United*

States of America Respecting the Rights of the Governments of the Two Countries and their Respective Nationals in Palestine. Great Britain, *Cmd.* 2559 of 1925; Treaty Series No. 54, 3 June 1925). In addition, the Joint Resolution passed in both Houses on 3 June and 11 September 1922, respectively emphasised 'that the United States of America favors the establishment in Palestine of a *national* home for the *Jewish people*' (facsimile in Reuben Fink, *America and Palestine* (New York, Herald Square Press), 1945, p. 36. References on p. 43). The Resolution was signed by President Harding on 21 September 1922, on the recommendation of the State Department (letter of William Phillips, of the Department of State, to George B. Christian, Jr., Secretary to the President, of 21 September 1922, quoted from the official archives in Frank E. Manuel, *The Realities of American–Palestine Relations*, Washington [Public Affairs Press], 1949, pp. 283–4).

416. *Cmd.* 1700 of 1922, p. 18 (author's italics) (The 'Churchill White Paper').

417. House of Commons, *Parliamentary Debates*, 23 May 1939, Vol. 347, col. 2172 (author's italics).

418. This Memorial, which endorsed the Balfour Declaration and called upon the British Government to accept the appointment as Mandatory Power in Palestine, was signed by a large number of Members of Parliament and representatives of the Church, press, and literature. It was submitted in 1920 to the Government in which Churchill was Secretary for War ('The Memorial', in *Zionist Bulletin*, London, 30 April 1920, p. 3).

419. Toynbee, 'The Present Situation in Palestine', address at the Institute of International Affairs, London, 9 December 1930, in *International Affairs*, Vol. X, 1931, London, p. 39 (first paragraph): p. 49 (second paragraph).

420. Quotations from Art. 6 of the Palestine Mandate.

421. *Ibid.*

422. This subject is dealt with fully in the essay by an eminent authority on international law, Professor Nathan Feinberg, 'The Recognition of the Jewish People in International Law', in *The Jewish Yearbook of International Law* (Jerusalem, Massada), 1949, pp. 1–26.

423. Ernst Frankenstein, *Justice for My People* (London, Nicholson and Watson), 1943, p. 64. Also a French authority, Paul Fauchille, stated that these declarations 'undoubtedly constitute the recognition of the Jewish people as a nation' (*Traité de Droit International Public*, Paris 1921, I, pp. 314–15).

424. Toynbee, 'The Main Features of the Landscape', in *The Treaty of Versailles and After*, by Lord Riddell, Professor C. K. Webster, Arnold J. Toynbee, and others, London 1935, p. 82.

425. League of Nations. Permanent Mandates Commission. *Minutes* of the Twentieth Session, Geneva (9–27 June 1931), No. C.422, M.176, 1931. VI, p. 78 (italics in the original).

426. The letter, dated 13 February 1931, addressed by Ramsay MacDonald (Prime Minister) to Dr Weizmann, interpreted officially a number of statements of the *White Paper*, *Cmd.* 3692 of 1930 (see House of Commons *Debates*, Vol. 248, No. 58, col. 750). This letter 'was communicated as an official document to the League of Nations' (Toynbee, *Survey for 1930*, p. 301).

427. League of Nations. Permanent Mandates Commission. *Minutes, op. cit.*, p. 80.

428. *Ibid.*, p. 93.

429. *Encyclopaedia Britannica* (1963), Vol. XII, p. 521.

430. Georg Schwartzenberger, 'International Law', in *Chambers's Encyclopaedia* (1950), Vol. VII, p. 644.

431. This is not rendered invalid if political repression of Jews in any particular country prevents those who wish to from leaving in order to go to Israel—in the

U.S.S.R., for example, where it is generally offensive to the régime for any citizen to express a desire to go and live in another country and where Jews seeking visas to go to live in Israel are, except for a small trickle of émigrés with family already there, particularly subject to unpleasant pressures; or in those Arab countries which have forced aggressive wars on Israel or are in a state of unilaterally declared enmity to her and which maintain a state of terror on those native Jews who have been unable to leave. In both cases, the Jews stay there not out of desire but by *force majeure*.

432. League of Nations. Permanent Mandates Commission. *Minutes of the Thirty-second (Extraordinary) Session*, held in Geneva from 30 July to 18 August 1937, p. 18.

433. Toynbee, 'Pioneer Destiny of Judaism', p. 10.

434. *Esther*, iii, 8.

435. Salo Baron, *A Social and Religious History of the Jews* (Philadelphia, J.P.S.), Vol. V, 1958, p. 398.

436. Johann Andreas Eisenmenger, *Entdecktes Judentum* (Dresden), 1893, p. 96 (author's translation).

437. xxix, 7: 'And seek the peace of the city whither I have caused you to be carried away captive, and pray unto the Lord for it; for in the peace thereof shall ye have peace.'

438. Eisenmenger, of course, omitted to add that the principal part of this sentence is a quotation from *Jeremiah*, xxiii, 6.

439. *Debate in the House of Commons . . . For Removing the Civil Disabilities of the Jews* (London), 1934, pp. 12f.

440. This is the quotation from *Jeremiah* xxiii, 6, referred to above (footnote 437).

441. Sir Robert here quoted examples from history to that effect.

442. The literature of this sort is so vast that it cannot be quoted here. Any Jewish author of the period dealing with contemporary problems can be selected for corroboration.

443. As a few of many examples, see Hitler, *Mein Kampf*, pp. 333f; Peter Aldag, *Das Judentum in England* (Berlin, Nordland), 1940, Vol. I, pp. 277ff.

444. Max Nordau article 'Patriotism and Zionism', published 1903 in *L'Echo Sioniste*, Paris 1903, No. 2.

445. *Die Welt*, No. 40, 3 October 1906, p. 13. Geiger was a prominent historian and the son of Abraham Geiger, foremost theoretician of German Reform Judaism.

446. Geheimer Regierungsrat Professor Dr Ludwig Geiger, *Die deutschen Juden und der Kreig* (Berlin, Swetschke), 1916, p. 65 (author's translation).

447. Louis D. Brandeis, 'The Jewish Problem', address delivered in June 1915. Reprinted in *Brandeis on Zionism* (Washington), 1942, p. 28.

448. R. W. Seton-Watson, 'The Issue of the War', in *The War and Democracy*, by R. W. Seton-Watson, J. Dover Wilson, and others (London, Macmillan), 1914, p. 290 (quoted by Brandeis).

449. *Felix Frankfurter Reminisces*, recorded in Talks with Dr Harlan B. Phillips (New York, Reynal), 1960, pp. 145–64.

450. In a speech in Washington on 3 May 1965 (*Jewish Telegraphic Agency*, 3 May 1965).

451. President Johnson in announcing Justice Goldberg's appointment *New York Times*, Paris ed., 21 July 1965, p. 1).

452. *Ibid.*, 22 July 1965, p. 4.

453. *Jewish Chronicle* (London, 26 November 1954, p. 19). Just one of the numerous similar statements: 'We have learned that unquestioned, unqualified loyalty to this country is wholly consistent with strong spiritual and emotional ties to

Israel (the then Vice President, Hubert H. Humphrey at the 20th anniversary dinner of Yeshiva University, New York, in *Jewish Chronicle* [London], 12 March 1965, p. 21).

454. Toynbee, 'Pioneer Destiny of Judaism', p. 6.

455. Toynbee, 'Future of Judaism', p. 74.

456. 'The Call of Spirit in Israel'. From the *Government Year Book*, October 1951, quoted in David Ben Gurion, *Rebirth and Destiny of Israel* (New York, Philosophical Library), 1954, p. 489.

457. In *The American Zionist*, 5 February 1953, p. 13 (a quotation from the year 1948). A good survey of Zionist leaders' opinions on this issue, as well as on the relationship between Israel and the Diaspora, can be found in *Fundamental Issues of Zionism*, Jerusalem, 1952, and in *Forum for the Problems of Zionism, Jewry and the State of Israel*, Vols I-V, Jerusalem, 1958–62.

458. Debate between Pieter Geyl and Toynbee on the B.B.C. Third Programme, 4 January 1948, published by F. G. Krooner, Bussum, Holland.

459. See p. 160.

460. See *New York Times*, 11 September 1960 (Section 4), p. 1 (this quotation is from a statement of the 150 Protestant ministers who assembled in Washington under the chairmanship of the Rev. Norman Vincent Peale).

461. See p. 158.

462. President Kennedy's speech in Houston, 12 September 1960, as reported in *New York Times*, 13 September 1960, p. 1.

463. See Oskar K. Rabinowicz *Vladimir Jabotinsky's Conception of a Nation*, (New York, Beechhurst, 1946).

464. Yet can one think of any other group of people showing such loyalty as that described by Sir Stuart Samuel, British Commissioner in Poland after World War I: 'The Jewish soldiers in Poland do their duty to their country in the certainty that their country will not do its duty by them' (quoted in Israel Zangwill's *Voice from Jerusalem*, p. 18).

465. *New York Times*, 28 January 1961, p. 21; 30 May 1961, p. 34.

466. *Ibid.*, 7 October 1961, p. 1.

467. To refer to just one case: The court of Tallahassee (Florida) in June 1963 sentenced Rabbi Israel Dresner (Springfield, New Jersey) and Rabbi Martin Freedman (Patterson, New Jersey) to sixty days' imprisonment. They were sentenced together with two white Protestant and eight Negro clergymen for sitting together in a segregated restaurant (*Jewish Chronicle*, 7 August 1964, p. 12).

468. *New York Times*, 1 April 1965, p. 34.

469. *Ibid.*, 15 November 1965, p. 1.

470. Eduard Beneš, 'Masaryk's Philosophy of State', in *The Spirit of Czechoslovakia* (London), 31 July 1941, Nos. 6–7, p. 3 (italics in the original).

471. *The Litany.*

472. Toynbee, 'Pioneer Destiny of Judaism', p, 6.

473. Toynbee, 'Future of Judaism', p. 74.

474. Robert Murphy, *Diplomat Among Warriors* (New York, Doubleday), 1964, pp. 388–9.

475. President Eisenhower's reply to Premier Bulganin's vote of 5 November 1956, in *Middle Eastern Affairs*, Vol. VIII, No. 1, January 1957, p. 35.

476. *New York Times* editorial on Nasser, 1 November 1956, p. 38.

477. *The Statesman's Year-Book* (London), 1957, p. 565.

478. Adlai Stevenson, 'Middle East', telecast delivered on 1 November 1956, in Buffalo, New York, reprinted in *The New America* (New York), 1957, p. 34.

479. Richard P. Stebbins and The Research Staff of the Council on Foreign Relations, *The United States in World Affairs 1957* (New York, Harper), 1957,

p. 168. See also Emanuel Neumann's statement in *Haaretz* (Tel-Aviv), 28 June 1964, p. 6.

480. *New York Times*, 21 February 1957, p. 9.

481. *Ibid.*, 20 March 1957, p. 9.

482. Dated 11 February 1957, in *New York Times*, 20 February 1957, p. 9.

483. *Ibid.*, p. 1.

484. *Ibid.*, p. 9.

485. *Ibid.*, 28 January 1957, pp. 1, 3; 30 January, p. 10; 2 February, p. 3; 4 February, p. 3; 6 February, p. 5; 7 February, p. 12; and 14 February, p. 1.

486. Toynbee, 'Gaza After Seven Years', in *Between Niger and Nile*, p. 86.

487. *New York Times*, 24 June 1963, p. 7.

488. Toynbee, 'Future of Judaism', p. 74.

489. Toynbee, *Reconsiderations*, pp. 573–7, an entire autobiographical chapter.

490. Toynbee, 'Why I dislike Western Civilisation', in *New York Times Magazine*, 10 May 1964, p. 15.

491. Toynbee, *Reconsiderations*, p. 589.

492. *Ibid.*, p. 630.

493. *Ibid.*

494. *Ibid.*

495. *Ibid.*; see also pp. 631–2.

496. Toynbee, 'Encounters Between Civilizations', in *Civilisation on Trial and the World and the West* (New York, Meridian), 1959, pp. 196–7.

497. Toynbee, *Reconsiderations*, p. 210.
A similar tendency exists in his advice that 'if the human race is to survive . . . we shall have to transfer our paramount loyalty from our respective national fragments of the human race to the human race itself' (Toynbee, 'Again Nationalism Threatens', in *New York Times Magazine*, 3 November 1963, p. 111).

498. Quotation from Toynbee, *Reconsiderations* starting 'Thus normally the establishment of a universal state . . .' and ending with '. . . that have been incorporated in it,' on p. 210.

499. Toynbee, 'The Future of Judaism in the Western World,' p. 71.

500. Toynbee, *Study*, Vol. VIII, p. 294.

501. See *infra*, p. 181.

502. Toynbee, *Survey for 1933*, p. 157. A similar comparison in *Study*, Vol. II, p. 252n.

503. *Ibid.*, Vol. VIII, p. 288.

504. About Luther's hatred of Jews, see his *Von den Jueden und ihren Luegen*, 1538, *Die Vermahnung gegen die Jueden*, 1546, etc. . . .

505. Toynbee, *Reconsiderations*, p. 486.

506. Rosenberg, *Mythos*, p. 463.

507. Toynbee, *Survey for 1933*, p. 122.

508. It may be noted without comment that Toynbee accepted Gobineau's conception of societies as of 'greater extension . . . than national states or city states, or any other'.

509. Joseph Arthur Gobineau, *Essai sur l'inégalité des races humaines*, 2nd ed. 1884, in 2 vols.; Houston Stewart Chamberlain, *Die Grundlagen des XIX*.

510. 'How can we arrest racial decay? Must what Count Gobineau says come true?' he once asked Hermann Rauschning (*Hitler Speaks*, London, 1939, p. 227).

511. *Mein Kampf*, p. 135.

512. Toynbee, *Survey* for 1933, p. 158.

513. See p. 176.

514. *Ibid.*

515. Toynbee, *Study*, Vol. VIII, p. 294.

516. Kellner, Leon, ed. *Theodor Herzl's Zionistische Schriften*. Berlin, 1920, Vol. I. 'Autobiographie' mention of being Paris correspondent on p. 17–18.

517. *Judenstaat*, pp. 26, 29, 30.

518. *Ibid.*, p. 29.

519. Protocol of the First Zionist Congress (Prague), 1911, pp. 219–21; also Tulo Nussenblatt, *Theodor Herzl Jahrbuch* (Vienna), 1937, pp. 214–16.

520. About Marr and the subsequent developments in Germany, see Lucien Wolf, 'Antisemitism', in *Encyclopaedia Britannica* (11th ed.), Vol. II, reprinted in *Essays in Jewish History* (ed. by Cecil Roth), London, 1934, pp. 419ff.

521. *Ibid.*, p. 430.

522. *Ibid.*, p. 431.

523. *Ibid.*, p. 441.

524. N. Katzburg, 'Antisemitism in Hungary and its Place in Politics 1883–1887', in *Zion*, Vol. XXX, No. 1–2, 1965, p. 83. This whole essay (pp. 79–114) confirms my contention above.

525. *Encycl. Brit.*, *loc. cit.*

526. Hans Kohn, *Prophets and Peoples* (New York, Macmillan), 1946, p. 195.

527. *Encycl. Brit.*, *loc. cit.*

528. Toynbee, *Survey for 1933*, p. 112.

529. Hitler, *Mein Kampf*, pp. 131–2. This argumentation also confirms that Hitler's 'racialism' appertained to all non-Germanic nationalities, with specific emphasis on the Jews.

530. Toynbee, *Reconsiderations*, p. 532.

531. Toynbee, *Reconsiderations*, p. 239.

532. This was written in 1961. In an interview, however, given in 1962, Toynbee was quoted as saying, 'I am a determinist, but paradoxically I believe in free will' (Ved Mehta, 'Onward and Upward with the Arts', in *The New Yorker*, 8 December 1962, p. 92). It may one day be possible to find out what he really was . . .

533. *Study*, p. 270.

534. Toynbee, *Reconsiderations*, pp. 314–27.

535. *Ibid.*, p. 316.

536. See p. 176.

537. 'But I remember a master reading us news about the Dreyfus case; and that did arouse my feelings. . . . We didn't feel responsible, but there was certainly a very lively interest' (Arnold and Philip Toynbee, *Comparing Notes*, pp. 117–18).

538. Toynbee quoted it from James Parkes, *The Jewish Problem in the Modern World* (New York), 1946, p. 89.

539. Theodor Herzl, 'Zionism', published in the *North American Review*, 1899, reproduced in Theodor Herzl, *Zionistische Schriften* (Berlin, Jued. Verlag), 1920, pp. 255–66.

540. Toynbee, *Reconsiderations*, p. 245.

541. For an analysis of this aspect see Alex Bein, 'Herzl and the Dreyfus Trial', in *With Herzl and in his Steps* (Hebrew), (Tel-Aviv), 1954, pp. 25–33; see also my 'After Sixty Years—a Still Misunderstood Herzl', paper read at the acceptance ceremony of the Landau Prize Award presented for Zionist historiography on 7 July 1964, in Tel-Aviv at the Herzl Lodge.

542. Alfred Dreyfus, *Five Years of My Life* (London), 1901, pp. 19f.

543. See p. 181.

544. See, for instance, his reports in *Neue Freie Presse* between 1 November 1894, and 5 January 1895. Extracts from these reports are in Ludwig Lewisohn, *Theodor Herzl* (Cleveland and New York), 1955, pp. 194–207. They are fully recorded in Alex Bein, *Herzl and Dreyfus* (Hebrew), (Tel-Aviv, Newman), 1945.

545. As a result of the findings by Colonel Picquart, head of the Information Service, in the secret files appertaining to the case, which showed Dreyfus's innocence.

546. Alex Bein, *Theodor Herzl* (Vienna), 1934, p. 234.

547. The *Judenstaat* appeared in February 1896 (see Herzl, *Diaries*, I, p. 299).

548. Simon Dubnow, *Weltgeschichte des juedisches Volkes* (Berlin), 1929, x, p. 23. See also Hannah Arendt, *Elemente und Urspruenge totaler Herrschaft* (Frankfurt am Main, Europain Verlages), 1955, p. 176 ('Die Dreyfus-Affaire').

549. Hannah Arendt, *op. cit.*, p. 175.

550. See the specific references to French antisemitism in *Judenstaat*, pp. 26, 29–30, 34, 68.

551. *Diaries*, I, pp. 14–30.

552. See *Protocol*, I, pp. 15–20.

553. See *Die Welt*, No. 26, 26 November, 1897 p. 3 ('Die Woche'); No. 30, 24 December 1897, pp. 1–2 ('Französische Verhaltnisse').

554. *Protokol*, II, p. 20. He devoted the larger part of his speech (pp. 15–20) to the Dreyfus case.

555. Bernard Lazare, *L'affaire Dreyfus* (1897), quoted and repeatedly commented on in *Die Welt*, ed. by Herzl (see, for instance, January 21 1898, p. 68; 28 January p. 6; 11 February, p. 3; 18 February, p. 5; 25 February, pp. 4, 10, 11, etc.). Nordau, too, mentioned the cry 'Death to all Jews' in the streets of Paris in his speech at the Zionist Congress (see *Protokol*, II, p. 18), one year before Herzl referred to it in his article.

556. Selections from this *Youth Diary* were published in Tulo Nussenblatt, *Herzl Jahrbuch* (Vienna), 1937, pp. 21–52.

557. 'Rede in der Oestereichischen Israelitischen Union', of 7 November 1896, in *Gesammelte Schriften*, pp. 97–109.

558. *Diaries*, I, p. 4.

559. Eugen Duehring, *Die Judenfrage als Rassen-, Sitten-, und Culturfrage* (Nova Ves–Neudorf,) 1880.

560. Opening speech at the Second Zionist Congress (*Protokol*, II, p. 4).

561. His remarks on Jewish issues can be found there in his comments on the books by Victor Cherbuliez, *Samuel Brohl & Co.* (entry January 22 1882, pp. 24–5), and Wilhelm Jensen, *Die Juden von Coelln* (entry 8 February 1882, pp. 30–2).

562. This phrase is quoted from *Diaries*, I, p. 4.

563. *The Diaries of Franz Kafka*, ed. by Max Brod, translated by Martin Greenberg and Hannah Arendt (New York, Schocken), 1948, Vol. I, p. 125.

564. *Youth Diary* (entry 9 February 1882), quoted in full in Leon Kellner, *Theodor Herzls Lehrjahre* (Vienna and Berlin, Loweit), 1920, p. 127.

565. 'Inactive race' is Duehring's phrase. It reminds one of Toynbee's description of his 'fossil' theory of the Jewish community as 'a survival of something that is otherwise extinct' (*Reconsiderations*, p. 296).

566. *Diaries*, I. p. 4.

567. *Ibid.*

568. In the form of a novel (*ibid.*, p. 5).

569. *Ibid.*, p. 9 "We Jews have maintained ourselves . . . as a foreign body among the various nations').

570. This play was presented in an English version in London in the early 1900s. There is no existing manuscript as such of the English translation of *Das Neue Ghetto*.

571. *Das neue Ghetto* (Vienna), 1903, p. 100.

572. Kellner, Herzl, *op. cit.*, p. 147.

573. Bein, *Herzl*, p. 176.

574. *Diaries*, I, ii.

575. He attended services in his childhood regularly with his father (Bein, *Herzl*, p. 10).

576. *Protokol*, I. p. 16.

577. Toynbee, *Study*, Vol, II, pp. 242–3.

578. Vol. II of his *Study*, containing these anecdotes, appeared in 1934.

579. Chaim Weizmann, *Trial and Error* (London), 1949, pp. 11–43.

580. *Ibid.*, p. 123.

581. *Ibid.*, p. 67.

582. See about him and the further particulars mentioned: Baron David von Guenzberg, 'Der groesste juedische Bildhauer,' in *Ost und West* (Berlin), 1902, pp. 729–40; and Elias Guenzburg, 'Antokolski', *ibid.*, pp. 740–50.

583. See Weizmann, *Trial and Error*, p. 93; and Dr Israel Klausner, *Oppositzia le Herzl* (Jerusalem), 1960, pp. 45f.

584. *Protokol*, V, pp. 164–5. Regret that Antokolski depicted Ivan instead of Herod and a Vilna Saint instead of the Wilna 'Gaon' (rabbinical authority) was expressed by Ahad Ha'am in an essay, 'Herut Haruach' ('The Spiritual Revival'), in *Al Parashat Derachim*, Vol. II, pp. 120f.

585. *Trial and Error* (New York, London), 1949.

586. *Ibid.*, pp. 41–2.

587. One need only compare this simple reference to Isaiah with Toynbee's efforts at deracinating and dezionising the great prophet to understand the deep gulf between real Jewish life and Toynbee's missionary hopes.

588. Weizmann, *Trial and Error*, p. 21.

589. *Ibid.*, p. 67.

590. Isaac Naiditch (1863–1949) hailed from Pinsk (where Weizmann attended high school), and was a lifelong friend of Weizmann's and a leading Russian Zionist.

591. Weizmann, *Trial and Error*, p. 67.

592. See Toynbee, *Reconsiderations*, p. 117, and the passage quoted below at note 597.

593. *Ibid.*, p. 118n.

594. Toynbee, *Reconsiderations*, p. 121.

595. *Ibid.*, p. 47.

596. 'The Problem of Quantity in the Study of Human Affairs', particularly subsection 3 : 'Attempts to Bridge the Gap Between our Knowledge of Psychic and Social Phenomena and our Knowledge of the Acts of Individual Human Being', in *Reconsiderations*, pp. 114–24.

597. *Ibid.*, p. 117.

598. Toynbee, *Study*, Vol. I, pp. 1–50. See also Toynbee, *Reconsiderations*, pp. 103–58.

599. Toynbee, *Study*, Vol. I, p. 15.

600. Toynbee, *Reconsiderations*, pp. 133–4.

601. Toynbee, *Study of History*, Vol. II, p. 112.

602. In his essay 'Geudemann's National-Judentum', in *Gesammelte Schriften*, p. 114.

603. See p. 199.

604. *Psalms*, ii, 11.

605. *Proverbs*, i, 7.

606. Although it must be added that many an individual finds his way to religion through fear of or in confrontation with danger. A case in point is Winston Churchill, who once confessed: 'As it was, I passed [in 1896–1897] through

a violent and aggressive anti-religious phase which, had it lasted, might easily have made me a nuisance. My poise was restored during the next few years by frequent contact with danger. I found that whatever I might think and argue, I did not hesitate to ask for special protection when about to come under fire of the enemy; nor to feel sincerely grateful when I got home safe to tea' (*My Early Life* (London, Macmillan), 1941, pp. 129–30).

607. Toynbee, *Study*, Vol. VIII, p. 292.

608. 'Zionism', in *North American Review*, January, 1899, in *Gesammelte Schriften*, p. 256.

609. 'Zionism', *loc. cit.* He defined nationality on another occasion as follows: 'A nationality is an historical group of men united by clearly discernible ties, and held together by a common foe' (*Gesammelte Werke*, I, 474).

610. Herzl, *Judenstaat*, p. 38 (author's italics).

611. Mordecai M. Kaplan, 'The Rose of Palestine. The Conception of Nation-hood Through Jewish History', *Theodor Herzl, A Memorial* (ed. M. Weisgal, New York, 1929, p. 261).

612. Herzl, *The New Ghetto*. (For note about an English translation, see note 570 above).

613. see p. 20.

614. Herzl, *Judenstaat*, p. 23 (author's translation).

615. See quotation starting 'I believe I understand antisemitism' and ending '. . . I also recognise the element of unconscious self-protection.' *Der Judenstaat*, 6th ed., Cologne, 1908, pp. 9–10.

616. Toynbee, *Study*, Vol. II, p. 112.

617. *Protokol*, IV, pp. 3–4 (author's translation).

618. We eliminate Nazi Germany, of course, from these considerations, be-cause, in the first place, it had no bearing on the emergence of political Zionism at the end of the nineteenth century; and, anyhow, it is a case *sui generis*, an anti-semitism as an official part of State policy.

619. *Judenstaat*, p. 87.

620. *Ibid.*, p. 24.

621. see p. 176.

622. Quoted in Bentwich, *Magnes*, p. 114.

‡623. Buber, 'Wege zum Zionismus', in *Die Welt*, 20 December 1901.

624. Theodor Herzl, 'Der Baseler Kongress', *op. cit.*, pp. 158–9.

625. Toynbee, *Reconsiderations*, p. 140.

626. Toynbee, *Turkey: A Past and a Future*, p. 69.

627. This refers to Davis Trietsch, who in 1915 in a brochure suggested a 'German protectorate over the whole of Jewry'.

628. A 'protectorate' is contrasted with a 'national home'.

Part II

1. Toynbee, 'Jewish Rights in Palestine', in *Jewish Quarterly Review* (Philadelphia), Vol. LII, No. 1, pp. 1–11.

2. *Ibid.*, pp. 1 and 2.

3. *Ibid.*, p. 1. If this were to be taken to a logical conclusion, the 'disinteredness' of the United States in the Toynbeean sense, for instance, might become doubtful. For they claim an interest in Palestine based on rights, as Franklin D. Roosevelt wrote to King Ibn Saud in 1938: 'The interest which the American people have in Palestine is based on a number of considerations. They include those of a spiritual character as well as those flowing from the rights derived by the United

States in Palestine through the American-British Mandate Convention of 3 December 1924' (*Foreign Relations of the United States*, 1939, Vol. IV, p. 696).

4. Toynbee, *Reconsiderations*, pp. 58–9 (author's italics).

5. *Palestine and the Arabs* (London, Harrap), 1935.

6. *The Arab Awakening* (London, Hamish Hamilton), 1938.

7. *Palestine: A Reality* (London, Longmans, Green), 1939.

8. *The Arabs and the West* (London, Methuen), 1952.

9. *Arab and Jew in the Land of Canaan* (Chicago, Regnery), 1957.

10. *England and the Middle East. The Destruction of the Ottoman Empire* (London, Bowers), 1956.

11. *The Middle East 1945–1950*, published under the editorship of Arnold Toynbee. *Survey of International Affairs* (London; Oxford), 1954. It should be added on this last, author Arnold Toynbee has provided the following note: 'I edited Mr Kirk's contribution and passed it for press, but after this, while I was absent abroad, Mr Kirk altered my edited version of his script without my knowledge, and, on my return to London, I found that this altered version had been published. The altered version was polemical and discourteous. Chatham House decided to withdraw all still undistributed copies of this volume, and asked me to edit a new version of Mr Kirk's work. I did this. I revised the previously published version extensively.'

12. See Toynbee, *Reconsiderations*. See examples on pp. 2, 26–7, 46–7, 229, 639n, 649, and 651.

13. Toynbee, 'It is One World or No World', in *New York Times Magazine*, 5 April 1964, p. 35.

14. *Who's Who 1960*.

15. London and Toronto (Dent & Son), 1915.

16. With a Speech and Letter by Viscount Bryce (London-New York-Toronto, Hodder & Stoughton), 1915.

17. Preface by Viscount Bryce (London-New York-Toronto, Hodder & Stoughton), 1917.

18. New York (Doran), 1917.

19. Original in the Weizmann Archives, Rehovoth, published with their permission.

20. June, 1917, No. 27, pp. 532–6. The article is unsigned, but the text is identical with that in Toynbee's book. Stein, *Balfour Declaration*, pp. 321–2, dealing with the article, is unaware of Toynbee's authorship.

21. In the Weizmann Archives. Published with their permission. Also quoted by Stein, *Balfour Declaration*, p. 321n.

22. Lloyd George, *War Memoirs*, Vol. I, pp. 633–4.

23. Blanche Dugdale, *Arthur James Balfour* (London, Hutchinson), 1936, Vol. II, p. 241.

24. Stein, *Balfour Declaration*, p. 318.

25. Lloyd George, *War Memoirs*, Vol. I, p. 643. See also Josef Davis, *The Prime Minister's Secretariat* (Newport, Mon.), 1951.

26. Lloyd George, *War Memoirs*, loc. cit.

27. *Ibid.* and Stein, *Balfour Declaration*, p. 319.

28. Stein, *Balfour Declaration*, p. 321, based on the records of *The Round Table*.

29. *Ibid.*, p. 322.

30. *The Times History of War* (London), Vol. XIV, pp. 289–324.

31. *Ibid.*, pp. 321–2.

32. *Ibid.*, p. 322.

33. The survey is dated 15 January 1918.

34. *Ibid.*, p. 324. Even Toynbee's suggestion of dividing the area of the Ottoman

Empire, apart from Turkey proper, among Arabs, Armenians, and Jews was adopted in the *Times* survey.

35. Stein, *Balfour Declaration*, particularly pp. 309–483.
36. On 2 April 1917. Lloyd George, *War Memoirs*, Vol. I, p. 990.
37. Toynbee, *Study*, Vol. VIII, p. 303.
38. Vol. VI ('Palestine and Zionism', by Childs), pp. 172–3.
39. *Syria and Palestine*, p. 128.
40. Toynbee, *Study*, Vol. VIII, p. 303.
41. While British official circles seem to have become alarmed about the German efforts in favour of an 'alliance' with Zionism only in 1917, German official circles had thought on these lines since almost the outbreak of World War I. In an official document, 'Survey of the Agitation Activity Commenced in the Islam–Israel World', dated 16 August 1914, a special section was devoted to the Jews and it began as follows: 'We have succeeded in winning over the entire organisation of Zionists to us. At the head of the society is Professor Dr [Otto] Warburg, of this [Berlin] University. The society numbers more than 100,000 members and a great number of secret adherents. In the strictness of their organisation, the Zionists can be compared to a Jesuit Order. Like the Jesuits, the Zionists are obliged to offer strict discipline to their head. In the Zionist Organisation we shall acquire an instrument of immeasurable importance for our information service and propaganda activity abroad. Further, in view of the fact that almost all the deliveries of grain and livestock for the Russian army are in the hands of Jewish middlemen, we shall acquire through the Zionists effective means of making the progress of Russian operations and the provision of food for the Russian army more difficult' (Document A 17 520 of the German State Archives, published in Egmot Zeichlin, 'Friedensbestrebungen und Revolutionierungsversuche', in *Aus Politik und Zeitgeschichte* [Beilage zum 'Das Parlament' B 25/61, 21 June 1961, p. 364]).

These efforts failed, but attempts at their renewal never ceased throughout the war.

42. See p. 222.
43. Toynbee, *Reconsiderations*, pp. pp. 573–657.
44. Leipzig (Veit), 1915. Pamphlet No. 8 of the *Deutsches Vorderasienscomitee's* series: 'Laender und Voelker der Tuerkei'.
45. Toynbee, *Turkey: A Past and a Future*, pp. 66–9.
46. As referred to in Toynbee's quotation (see note 40 above), the 'Pale' had been 'ravaged' by the retreating Russians and 'liberated' by the Germans.
47. Toynbee here quotes Trietsch's brochure referred to in footnote 44, above. He erroneously gives him the title of 'Dr'.
48. About his description of Zionism as a negative concept some thirty years later, see *Author's Note*.
49. See pp. 345–7 of Toynbee's essay.
50. Toynbee's footnote at this point reads as follows: 'The Spanish-speaking Jews in Turkey are descended from refugees to whom the Ottoman Government gave shelter in the sixteenth century; the Arab-speaking Jews have been introduced into Palestine from the Yemen, by the Zionists, since 1908.' (Yemenite Jews actually began to emigrate to Palestine well before this; there are a couple of dozen references to their presence as immigrants in Jerusalem in the London *Jewish Chronicle* between the years 1882 and 1890—see *Cumulative Index to the J.C.* [1881–90 section] by J. M. Shaftesley.)
51. Both references are in Toynbee's essay, p. 71.
52. This refers to the Armenian massacres, which Toynbee described in a few publications (see *supra*, p. 220).

53. Toynbee, *Study*, Vol. VIII, p. 303.

54. Toynbee, *Turkey: A Past and A Future*, pp. 71–2.

55. *Foreign Relations of the United States. Paris Peace Conference*, Vol. III (Washington), 1943, p. 9, where it is stated: 'III. Technical Experts. Great Britain. Diplomatic Questions Mr A. J. Toynbee, Secretary in the Ministry of Foreign Affairs (Orient).'

56. Toynbee refers to his conversation with Weizmann in *Study*, Vol. II, p. 242. See also *ibid.*, pp. 287f.

57. *Ibid.* We know that his article in the Round Table was revised by Dr Weizmann and that Toynbee then (May 1917), wanted to meet the Zionist eader (see *supra*, p. 221).

58. I am most grateful to Mr Florian Sokolow for making this letter, addressed to his late father, available and permitting me to publish it for the first time (letter to me by Mr Sokolow of 21 May 1961); and to Professor Toynbee for permission to reproduce it here (Toynbee's letter to me of 3 July 1961). Sokolow's *History* was published by Longmans, Green & Co., London, 1919.

59. The other participants were: Dr Weizmann, Dr Victor Jacobson, Messra James de Rothschild, Alfred Zimmern, Julius Simon, Israel Rosoff, Bernard Flexner, and Benjamin Cohen, Commander Hogarth, Major the Hon. W. Ormsby-Gore, Mr Toynbee, Lieut.-Gen. Gribbon and Major Money.

60. See p. 220.

61. *Nationality and the War*, p. 493.

62. Toynbee at that early date already suggested the establishment of an international body and an executive organ to be responsible for post-war settlements.

63. Toynbee, *Survey for 1925*, Vol. I, pp. 347–8.

64. *Handbooks* prepared Under the Direction of the Historical Section of the Foreign Office, London, 1920. The Introduction informs us that the material for the *Handbooks* was prepared by the Section in the spring of 1917. These *Handbooks* were a collection 'the amplest and were generally felt to be more systematically and concisely arranged than either the American or French. Even members of the American and French delegations frequently consulted the little white books for enlightenment on obscure subjects on which they were called upon to pronounce or prophesy'. (Norwak, *Versailles*, p. 34.)

65. Apart from the similarities noticed in the texts of the *Handbooks* and in Toynbee's contemporary writings, there is also a common denominator underlying both: to fight German attempts to persuade Jewish opinion towards a pro-German attitude in the war. Both, for instance, refer to the Zionist struggle over the attempts of the German Jewish *Hilfsverein* to introduce German for certain subjects in Palestine Jewish schools in 1913–14 (*Handbook* No. 60, p. 63, and Toynbee's *Turkey: A Past and A Future*, p. 69).

66. Toynbee's letter to the author of 21 June 1961. Also letter from the British Consulate General, New York, to the author of 5 July 1961 (on behalf of the London Foreign Office).

67. Toynbee, letter to the author of 21 June 1961. The most prominent 'liberal circle' centred in World War I on the *Round Table* (see pp. 326f.).

68. *Syria and Palestine, Handbook* No. 60. Toynbee also in later years used this as an authoritative source (Toynbee, *Survey for 1925*, Vol. I, pp. 347–51). The first paragraph is quoted from that *Handbook*, pp. 16–17; and the second paragraph from pp. 56–7.

69. Toynbee, *Turkey: A Past and A Future*, p. 6 (for the first paragraph) and p. 64 (for the second).

70. The English reader may be interested in a book dealing with the pre-1914 period, significantly called *The Land That Is Desolate: An Account of a Tour in*

Palestine, by Sir Frederick Treves (New York, Dutton & Co.), 1912. A comprehensive list of the relevant literature on Palestine, in all languages, is contained in Peter Thomsen, *Systematische Bibliographie der Palaestina-Literatur*, Vol. I (1895–1904), Leipzig 1908; Vol. II (1905–9), *ibid.*, 1911; Vol. III (1910–14), *ibid.*, 1916; Vol. IV (1915–24), *ibid.*, 1927.

71. Arthur Ruppin, *Syrien als Wirtschaftsgebiet* (Berlin-Wien, Harz), 1920, p. 18. See also Dr Weizmann's statement before the Peace Conference, in U.S.A. *Foreign Relations: Paris Peace Conference*, Vol. IV, pp. 164–5.

72. *Handbook, Syria and Palestine*, p. 15.

73. *Ibid.* and Toynbee, *Turkey: A Past and A Future*, p. 65.

74. This emanates clearly from the literature quoted on p. 14, footnote 2, of the *Handbook*.

75. Great Britain, *H. o. C. Debates*, Vol. 156, 4 July 1922, col. 335.

76. In *Reform Advocate*, 1897, XIII, 208.

77. Toynbee, 'Jewish Rights in Palestine', p. 1.

78. *New York Times*, 19 May 1961 (under the heading: 'U.S. Favors Curb of Unfit Parents').

79. Toynbee, *Survey for 1930*, p. 231.

80. Toynbee, *Nationality and the War*, p. 493.

81. *Syria and Palestine*, p. 57.

82. Toynbee, *Nationality and the War*, p. 411.

83. *Idem.*, p. 379.

84. Toynbee, *Survey for 1925*, I, 351. See what he said about the Palestine 'Arabs in name who having nothing Arabic about them but their language' (*Turkey: A Past and A Future*, p. 66).

85. See *supra*, p. 221.

86. Toynbee, *Turkey: A Past and A Future*, pp. 6, 64–72.

87. This refers to the Russian revolution of March 1917, which brought the democratic regime under Kerensky to power.

88. As mentioned above, see p. 225, Toynbee set out the Zionist programme in the form of an answer to Trietsch, who had proposed a German–Jewish alliance for the fulfilment of the Zionist programme.

89. See U.S. Department of State, Near Eastern Series No. 1, *Mandate for Palestine*, Washington, 1931, p. 13.

90. See Josef Schechtmann, *Transjordanien im Bereiche des Palaestina Mandates* (Paris), 1929.

91. Oskar K. Rabinowicz, 'Zangwill's Plan for Population Transfer', in *Jewish Observer and Middle East Review*, 24 April 1963, p. 23.

92. Toynbee, 'The East after Lausanne', in *Foreign Affairs*, Vol. II, No. 1, September 1923, pp. 85–6.

93. Toynbee, *Survey for 1926*, p. 211.

94. *Ibid.*, p. 209.

95. Toynbee, 'Jewish Rights in Palestine', p. 5.

96. Toynbee, *Survey for 1925*, Vol. I, p. 387.

97. 'There was a moment during the First World War . . . when in Arab eyes Britain was the Arabs' champion, while France remained the villain' (Toynbee, 'Britain and the Arabs', in *International Affairs*, October 1964). See also Toynbee, *Survey for 1925*, Vol. I.

98. Toynbee, *Survey for 1930*, p. 257.

99. See Zionist Executive, *Reports to the XII Zionist Congress*: Political Report. London, 1921, pp. 43–57.

100. Clayton's statement of 9 July 1919, in Great Britain, Foreign Office, *Documents on British Foreign Policy 1919–1939*. Vol. IV, London, 1952, p. 333.

General Clayton's anti-Zionist stand can be gathered from his advice given in 1917 to Sir Mark Sykes, of the British War Cabinet, to refrain 'at present' from publishing a statement in favour of the Jewish National Home (see Leonard Stein, *Balfour Declaration*, pp. 522–3). Therefore his statement quoted above is of undoubted importance with regard to the issue under discussion.

101. Quoted above (p. 236).

102. Jon Kimche, 'Palestine as the Catalyst in Arab Unity', in *Jewish Observer and Middle East Review*, 26 March 1965, p. 27.

103. The Hussein-MacMahon correspondence of 1915–16 indicates that this was so. Eventually, several documents in the correspondence became the bases for the Hussein-MacMahon agreement. See also below, notes 114, 115, 117 and 118.

104. Toynbee, *Survey for 1925*, Vol. I.

105. *Ibid.*, p. 388.

106. Son of the above-mentioned King Hussein.

107. *Cmd.* 5479 (1937), p. 27.

108. David Hunter Miller, *My Diary of the Peace Conference of Paris* (New York), 1924.

109. Foreign Relations of the U.S.A., *Paris Peace Conference, op. cit.*, Vol. III, p. 888.

110. Full text of the letter in *Reports of the Zionist Organisation to the XII Zionist Congress*. I. Political Report. London, 1921, pp. 23–4.

111. *Doc. on Brit. Foreign Policy op. cit.*, Vol. IV, 1919, pp. 267–8.

112. Foreign Relations of the U.S.A., *Paris Peace Conference, op. cit.*, Vol. III, p. 1037.

113. *Ibid.*, p. 1028.

114. The correspondence ended in 1916. It was reproduced in Great Britain, *Cmd.* 5957. Misc. No. 3 (1939), London 1939.

115. Great Britain, *Cmd.* 1700 (1920), p. 20; *Cmd.* 5479 (Pal. Royal Commission), London, 1937, pp. 19, 20; *cf.* also *Documents Relating to the MacMahon Letters* (London, Jewish Agency), 1939, pp. 14–17.

116. Toynbee, *Survey for 1930*, p. 25.

117. Great Britain, *Cmd.* 5957 of 1939. Misc. No. 3 (1939), London, 1939, pp. 5, 6, 9, 11.

118. *Ibid.*, p. 12 (MacMahon to Hussein, December, 1915).

119. *Three Deserts* (Dutton), 1937, p. 302. Major Jarvis spent eighteen years living and working with the Arabs.

120. *Palestine, the Land of Three Faiths* (London, Jonathan Cape), 1923, pp. 112–13.

121. Toynbee, *Survey for 1925*, Vol. I, p. 44.

122. See, for instance, Feisal's statements in *Doc. Brit. Foreign Policy, op. cit.*, Vol. IV, 1919, pp. 407, 415, 417, 518; and a cable of his brother Abdullah, *ibid.*, p. 442.

123. *Ibid.*, p. 407.

124. *Ibid.*, pp. 415, 417, 418.

125. *Ibid.*, p. 442.

126. Toynbee, *Survey for 1925*, Vol. I, p. 272 (author's italics).

127. Great Britain, *H. o. C. Debates*, 23 May 1939, Vol. 347, col. 2174.

128. Toynbee, *The World After the Peace Conference*, p. 41.

129. See, for instance, Liddell Hart, *Colonel Lawrence* (New York, Mead), 1937, p. 58.

130. See *infra*, p. 251n.

131. Toynbee, *Survey for 1925*, Vol. I, p. 12 (for the first quotation), and p. 273 (for the second).

132. Great Britain, *Cmd.* 6808 (1946), p. 36.

133. Speech to the Arab Delegation in Jerusalem, 29 March 1921 in *Jewish Chronicle*, London, 8 April 1921, pp. 23–5. (The Arab response appeared in the 27 May issue of *Jewish Chronicle*.)

134. Toynbee, *Murderous Tyranny of the Turks*, p. 21.

135. See above, p. 245.

136. See pp. 246-47.

137. See *supra*, p. 245.

138. Aouni Bey Abdul Hadi, former member of the Palestine Arab Executive, 'The Balfour Declaration', in *Annals of American Academy of Political Sciences* (Philadelphia), November 1932, Vol. 164, p. 12.

139. Mimeographed folder of the provisional minutes of the General Assembly, folder A/C.1/P.V.33, p. 102.

140. Toynbee, *Survey for 1939–46* (Kirk), p. 315. The reference to this text is given in this *Survey* as: Musa Alami, 'The Lesson of Palestine', *Middle East Journal*, October 1949, III, 385.

141. 'Our Political Problem is a Moral Problem', in *Al-Arabi* (Kuwait), quoted in the *Jewish Observer and Middle East Review*, 7 June 1963, pp. 6–7.

142. Toynbee, *Turkey: A Past and A Future*, pp. 70–1.

143. See *supra*, pp. 245ff.

144. Toynbee once referred to those 'gold interests' as follows: 'The Arabs' price had been high, and with the barbarian's instinctive suspicion of the devices of civilisation, which in this case was fully justified by the event, they had insisted on being paid in gold, cash down, by all parties. King Husayn of the Hedjaz received from the British Government a subsidy of £200,000 sterling, then one million dollars a month from the time of his intervention in the war to the 1 February 1919 . . . this single subsidy must have amounted to about £6,000,000 [30 million dollars] from first to last. The Amir Sa'ud was paid at the more modest rate of £5,000 [$25,000] a month . . . it was not till later (1924) that British subsidies to Arabian princes ceased altogether' (Toynbee, *Survey for 1925*, Vol. I, p. 273).

145. Vladimir Jabotinsky, *Story of the Jewish Legion*. Translated by Samuel Katz. With a Foreword by Col. John Henry Patterson (New York, Ackerman), 1945. Lieut.-Col. J. H. Patterson, *With the Judaeans in the Palestine Campaign* (London, Hutchinson), 1922. The Jewish Legion, also called The Judaeans, were officially recorded as the 38th, 39th, and 40th (Jewish) Battalions of the Royal Fusiliers.

146. See pp. 245, 249.

147. *Syria and Palestine*, pp. 62–3.

148. Nili is an acronym formed from the initial letters of the Hebrew verse 'Netzah Yisrael Lo Yeshakker' (The Strength of Israel Will Not Lie), Samuel I, xv, 29. Their story has been repeatedly told. The latest in English is by Anita Engle, *The Nili Spies* (London, Hogarth), 1959.

149. See *supra*, p. 249.

150. Toynbee's excuse formulated for Arab unconcern (see *ibid.*).

151. *Military Operations Egypt and Palestine*, Part I. H.M. Stationery Office (London), 1930, pp. 176–7.

152. *Syria and Palestine*, p. 63.

153. *Ibid.*

154. The speech in full in Patterson, *With the Judaeans*, pp. 186–7.

155. Toynbee, *Nationality and the War*, p. 2.

156. Toynbee, *The World After the Peace Conference*, p. 43 (author's italics).

157. 'Speech to the Arab Delegation in Jerusalem', in *Jewish Chronicle*, 27 May 1921.

158. Toynbee, *Jewish Rights in Palestine*, p. 9.

159. Albert Hourani, *Arabic Thought in the Liberal Age*, 1798–1939 (London), 1962, p. 296.

160. See p. 247.

161. Toynbee, *Reconsiderations*, p. 571.

162. *Ibid.*, 610.

163. See above, p. 253.

164. See above, p. 254.

165. In *The Tablet*, 12 August 1939, p. 304, quoted in Toynbee, *Reconsiderations*, p. 611.

166. *Ibid.*, pp. 610–12.

167. See p. 254.

168. See p. 253.

169. Toynbee, *The World After the Peace Conference*, p. 41; see also p. 359.

170. Toynbee, *Survey for 1925*, Vol. I, p. 9. See *supra*, p. 247.

171. *Palestine Royal Commission*, Cmd. 5479, p. 24.

172. *Ibid.*

173. See *supra*, p. 253.

174. See *supra*, p. 215.

175. Toynbee, 'Jewish Rights in Palestine', p. 8.

176. Sir Frederick Pollock and Frederick W. Maitland, 'Ownership and Possession', in *Theories of Society* (Glencoe, Free Press), Vol. 1, 1961, p. 428.

177. Quotation from Pollock & Maitland article, 'Ownership and Possession', in *Theories of Society*, Vol. I (Free Press, Glencoe, 1961) starting 'the ownership is valid until an older is proved', and ending '. . . older right than that of the person whom he attacks', p. 428.

178. Toynbee, 'Jewish Rights', p. 10.

179. *Ibid.*, p. 4 ('Jews do, in my opinion, have a right to a special position in Palestine which no other present-day non-Palestinians possess').

180. Toynbee, *Reconsiderations*, pp. 32, 36, 39.

181. Toynbee, 'Mr Montague's Pound of Flesh', p. 147.

182. The then Prime Minister of Greece.

183. The Peace Conference in Paris, 1919.

184. He blamed Montagu, then Secretary of State for India, for Lloyd George's change of mind. (See Toynbee, 'Mr Montague's Pound of Flesh'.)

185. About the Palestine Arabs, see pp. 232–33.

186. Vol. VIII, p. 566n.

187. 'Toynbee Voices Regret', in *New York Times*, 22 December 1961.

188. This *volte face* in the face of physical power might serve as a lesson for those who accept Toynbee's idea of a Jewish community in the Diaspora based on religion only.

189. *International Law*, p. 667.

190. Herzl, 'Der Baseler Kongress', in *Zionistische Schriften*, p. 155 (author's translation).

191. All the subsequent quotations are from the Preamble of the Palestine Mandate.

192. Toynbee refers to foreign rule over the whole of Syria, including Palestine, in *Survey for 1925*, II, 348. For a comprehensive description of these various occupations and sovereignty exercised over Palestine from abroad see the several Jewish histories of the period and, in particular, Samuel Krauss, *Vier Jahrtausende Jüdischen Palästinas* (Frankfurt/Main, Kaufmann), 1922.

193. (Author's italics.)

194. (Author's italics.)

195. Toynbee, *Survey for 1925*, Vol. I, p. 348.

196. Toynbee, *Survey for 1930*, p. 261.
197. Toynbee, *Survey for 1925*, Vol. I, p. 347.
198. *Ibid.*, p. 355.
199. *I.e.*, of the Ottoman Empire.
200. Permanent Mandates Commission, *Minutes*, Seventeenth (Extraordinary) Session. 3–21 June 1930, p. 37.
201. This sentence, frequently used in those old days by Arab propaganda, has been taken up by Toynbee, although it was repeatedly proved to be wrong and untenable in international law. Toynbee did not confine this argument to Britain alone. As we have seen he also challenges the Jews' God, Jehovah, for having dared to promise Palestine to the Jews although 'the Land was not His'.
202. See p. 215.
203. See p. 233.
204. See p. 237.
205. *Syria and Palestine*, p. 3.
206. David Cushman Coyle, *The United Nations*. A Mentor Book. New York, 1960, pp. 62–3. *Cf.* also United Nations, *Annual Report of the Secretary-General on the Work of the Organisation 16 June 1959–15 June 1960*. Suppl. No. I (A/4390), p. 47.
207. *Supra*, p. 215.
208. Great Britain, *Documents of British Foreign Policy 1919–39*, First Series, Vol. VIII. International Conferences on High Policy 1920, H.M. Stationery Office, London, 1958, p. 160.
209. Great Britain, *Cmd.* 1785 of 1922. Miscellaneous No. 4 (1922).
210. *Essential Facts about the League of Nations* (Geneva), 1939, pp. 34–7.
211. Toynbee, *The World after the Peace Conference*. Being an Epilogue to the 'Survey of International Affairs 1920–23'. Oxford University Press, London, 1925, p. 53.
212. *Op. cit.*, p. 172 (the essay was written by W. J. M. Childs).
213. Great Britain, *H. o. C. Debates*, Vol. 347, 23 May 1939, Col. 2168/9.
214. 'The Palestine Situation Restated', in *Foreign Affairs* (Washington), April 1931, p. 414.
215. 'The Council of the League . . . has been unexpectedly successful in making the mandates system work. The chief reason is that it has succeeded in thinking out and creating the right instrument for this purpose in the shape of a body called the Permanent Mandates Commission. This Commission is a set of distinguished experts in colonial administration . . . whose duty it is to receive the annual reports of trustees—the so-called mandatory Powers—and to give the Council an expert opinion upon how manadates are being carried out' (Toynbee, 'The Main Features of the Landscape', Chap. III in *The Treaty of Versailles and After*, by Lord Riddell, Professor C. K. Webster, Professor Arnold J. Toynbee, and others (London), 1935, p. 82.
216. For instance, the Palestine Royal Commission. See its *Report*, H.M. Stationery Office, London, 1937, *Cmd.* 5479 and *Cmd.* 5779 (Minutes and Evidence).
217. Anglo-American Committee of Inquiry, *Report to the U.S. Government and His Majesty's Government in the United Kingdom*, Dept. of State, Publication No. 2536, Washington, 1946.
218. Unscop, *Report to the General Assembly*, Vols. I–V. Lake Success, New York, 1947. (Official Records of the 2nd Session of the General Assembly [GAOR], Supplement II, No. A/364/Add 1–4.)
219. Resolution 181 (II) in UN Official Records, 2nd Session of the G.A Resolutions (16 September–29 November 1957), pp. 131–50.
220. Verbatim text of questions and answers in GAOR, 3rd Session, 2nd Part,

Ad Hoc Political Committee, 46th–51st Meeting, 6–9 May 1949, pp. 248–361.

221. Resolution 273 (III) in GAOR, *op. cit.*, 207th Plenary Meeting, p. 330.

222. *Essential Facts About the League of Nations, loc. cit.*

223. Coyle, *The United Nations*, p. 216; see also *The Statesman's Year-Book 1957*, ed. by S. H. Steinberg (London, Macmillan), 1957, pp. 12–13; *Information Please Almanac 1960* (New York, McGraw-Hill), pp. 536 and 632.

224. *Reconsiderations*, p. 636.

225. Toynbee, 'Jewish Rights', pp. 1–11.

226. *Ibid.*, p. 5.

227. The original in the British Museum, Additional Ms. 41178, folios 1 and 3.

228. Toynbee, 'Jewish Rights', pp. 5–6.

229. *Ibid.*, pp. 4 and 11.

230. British Government. *Palestine. Disturbances in May 1921. Reports of the Commission of Inquiry with Correspondence Relating Thereto. Cmd.* 1540 of 1921, p. 52. When this statement regarding Arab attitudes towards Jewish immigration was made, 1,806 persons had immigrated in 1919, and 8,223 in 1920 (D. Gurevich and A. Gertz, *Statistical Handbook of Jewish Palestine* (Jerusalem, Jewish Agency), 1947, p. 99).

231. 'The Passfield White Paper', in Stephen S. Wise and Jacob de Haas, *The Great Betrayal* (New York, Brentano's), 1930, pp. 288–9.

232. Full text of the Palestine Mandate in British Government, *Cmd.* 1785 of 1922.

233. Toynbee, *Survey for 1930*, p. 229.

234. *Ibid.*, pp. 230–1.

235. Article 6 quoted above.

236. *Nationality and the War*, p. 487.

237. Permanent Mandates Commission, *Minutes of the Twentieth Session* 9–29 June 1930, p. 79.

238. Toynbee, *Survey for 1930*, p. 231.

239. See pp. 267ff.

240. See pp. 220–1 and p. 237.

241. Toynbee, 'The Non-Arab Territories of the Ottoman Empire Since the Armistice of the 30th October, 1918', in Temperley, *A History of the Peace Conference*, Vol. VI, p. 56.

242. Toynbee, *The Treatment of the Armenians in the Turkish Empire: Documents Presented to Viscount Grey of Fallodon, Secretary of State for Foreign Affairs. With a Preface by Lord Pryce.* British Government Blue Book, *Cmd.* 8325 of 1916. Misc. No. 31 (1916), p. 607.

243. *Ibid.*, p. 619.

244. Toynbee, 'The Non-Arab Territories', in Temperley, *History of the Peace Conference*, Vol. VI, p. 56.

245. Lloyd George, Prime Minister at the time, wrote: 'It was contemplated that . . . if the Jews had meanwhile responded to the opportunity afforded them by the idea of a National Home and had become a definite majority of the inhabitants, then Palestine would thus become a Jewish Commonwealth' (David Lloyd George, *The Truth About the Peace Treaties*, Vol. II, London, 1938, p. 1139). Arthur J. Balfour, the Foreign Secretary, who signed it and after whom it is named, said: 'It did not necessarily involve the early establishment of an independent Jewish State, which was a matter of gradual development' (*ibid.*, p. 1137).

The Report of the Royal Commission for Palestine (*Cmd.* 5479 of 1937, Chapter II, pp. 24–5) confirmed that the intention of the authors of the Balfour Declaration was that 'it would depend mainly on the zeal and enterprise of the Jews whether the Home would grow big enough to become a State.'

246. About the *Handbooks* see p. 337n.

247. *Zionism, Handbook* No. 162, p. 47.

248. *Syria and Palestine, Handbook* No. 60, p. 63.

249. Toynbee, *Turkey: A Past and A Future* (George H. Doran Co., New York), 1917, pp. 69 and 71.

250. Toynbee, *Civilization on Trial* and *The World and the West*, (New York, Meridian Books, Inc.), 1959, p. 11. This comprises a collection of essays 'written at different dates—several as long as twenty years ago. . . .'

251. Palestine Mandate, Preamble.

252. Weizmann's statement before the Council of Ten on 27 February 1919, in Foreign Relations of the U.S., *Paris Peace Conference*, Vol. IV (Washington), 1943, p. 169.

253. British Government, *White Paper of 1922*, Cmd. 1700, p. 18.

254. *Ibid.*, pp. 28–9.

255. Report, *op. cit.*, p. 33.

256. 'The Trouble in Palestine', in New Republic (New York), September 6 1922, p. 39.

257. See *supra*, pp. 220ff.

258. See *supra*, p. 229.

259. Resolution 181 (II), GAOR, 2nd Session, Resolutions (16 September–29 November, 1947), pp. 131–50.

260. Toynbee, 'The Present Situation in Palestine'. Address given at the Royal Institute of International Affairs, London, 9 December 1930. Reprinted in *International Affairs*, Vol. X, London, 1931. The quotation there is on p. 53.

261. The term 'prophesy' does not appear here accidentally. In the same speech Toynbee used it, as well as the phrase 'I predict', a number of times (see, for instance, *ibid.*, pp. 43, 44, 53, 58). It is noteworthy that Toynbee, when challenged by his critics that he writes or speaks as if he felt the spirit of prophecy over his head, denies this emphatically (*Reconsiderations*, pp. 3–4, 238–9).

262. Toynbee and Kenneth O. Kirkwood, *Turkey* (London, Beim), 1926, p. 262 (author's italics).

263. Vol. VI, Chapter I, Part III ('Palestine Since 30th October 1918,' by W. S. M. Childs), p. 176.

264. Toynbee, *East to West. A Journey Round the World.* ('The Spell of Palestine'), p. 202. This book was published in 1958, the tenth year of Israel's existence.

265. Toynbee, *Between Niger and Nile* ('African Solidarity and Arab Unity'), p. 121.

Part III

1. Toynbee, *Study*, Vol. VIII, pp. 290f.

2. 'The Middle East 1945–1950', by Kirk, pp. 260–1.

3. The *Survey* here quoted 'Dana Adams Smith in *New York Times*, 10 April 1948, reporting an interview given by the I.Z.I. immediately after the attack'; *cf.* Begin, *The Revolt*, pp. 162–3.

4. I.Z.I. is the abbreviation for Irgun Zva'i Le'umi (National Military Organisation), which was responsible for the attack.

5. The *Survey* here quoted: 'Four killed and nearly forty wounded, according to Begin (*loc. cit.*); eight killed and fifteen wounded, according to the commander of the attacking force, addressing an audience of New York Jews (*New York Times*, 30 November 1948).'

6. Menahem Begin, *The Revolt* (London), 1951, pp. 162f.

7. *Report* of the Executive submitted to the 23rd Zionist Congress in Jerusalem, 1951, p. 203.

8. *Loc. cit.*, p. 261.

9. *Proclamation*, dated Nisan 5708 (April 1948), reproduced in *Lohamey Heruth Yisrael*, Vol. II, Jerusalem, 1960, p. 989; also reprinted in full in Menahem Begin, *In the Underground* (Hebrew), Vol. I, Tel-Aviv, 1961, pp. 276–7.

10. Begin, *The Revolt, op. cit.*, p. 164.

11. In *Al-Urdun*, Amman (Jordan), 9 April 1953.

12. Vol. VIII, p. 289.

13. *Ibid.*, p. 290.

14. *Ibid.*

15. Vol. VIII, pp. 289–92.

16. Harry S. Truman, *Memoirs.*

17. *Report*, in U.N. Document A/AC. 21/0. 16 February 1948.

18. *Survey for 1939–46* (Kirk), p. 254.

19. *Ibid.*, p. 260.

20. *Minutes* for 15 May 1948, No. 66, pp. 10–11.

21. This referred to a cable from the Egyptian Government which had stated that 'horrible crimes, revolting to the conscience of humanity, have been perpetrated by these Zionist gangs. Arab women have been assaulted, pregnant women's stomachs ripped open, children killed before the very eyes of their mothers, and prisoners tortured and then brutally murdered' (*ibid.*, p. 3). No details were given in that cable, no places or names mentioned. Neither then nor later have such acts by Jews ever been proved. Had there existed even the slightest possibility of any such Jewish cruelties, no doubt Toynbee would have referred to them when identifying Jews with Nazis.

22. See, for instance, Toynbee, *Study of History*, Vol. VIII, pp. 298–300.

23. Toynbee, *Survey for 1939–46* (Kirk), pp. 254, 271.

24. Jon and David Kimche, *Both Sides of the Hill* (London), 1960, p. 140. Kfar Etzion, established in 1943, had a population of 174 in 1948 (Dr Georg Herlitz, *Das Jahr der Zionisten* Jeru.–Luzern, 1949, p. 152).

25. As one of the many examples, we refer to Toynbee, *Survey for 1939–46* (Kirk), where the Kfar Etzion massacre is mentioned on p. 254.

26. Toynbee, 'Pioneer Destiny of Judaism', in *Issues* (New York, Summer), 1960, p. 10.

27. Toynbee, *Study of History*, Vol. VIII, p. 298.

28. *Ibid.*, Vol. V, p. 387.

29. Toynbee, *Study of History*, Vol. V, p. 657.

30. *Ibid.*, p. 387.

31. *Ibid.*, Vol. VI, p. 103.

32. Toynbee, *War and Civilization*, Preface, p. x.

33. Toynbee, *Study of History* (abridged edition), Vol. II, p. 140.

34. Talmud, *Berakhot*, 58a (based on *Exodus*, xxii, 1).

35. Talmud, *Yoma*, 85b.

36. Toynbee, *Study of History*, Vol. V, p. 387. See above, p. 416.

37. Talmud, *Baba Metzia*, 62a.

38. Toynbee, *Survey for 1920–1925*, pp. 208, 281; *for 1936*, p. 473.

39. Karel Capek, *Hovory S. Masarykem* (Conversations with Masaryk), (Prague), 1932, Vol. II, p. 39.

40. Toynbee, *Reconsiderations*, p. 612.

41. Toynbee, *Study of History*, Vol. II, p. 286.

42. Toynbee, *War and Civilization*, Preface, pp. x, xi.

43. British Broadcasting Corporation News broadcast, 15 May 1948.

44. Toynbee uses this phrase, for instance, in another part of the quotation on p. 287.

45. *Survey for 1925*, Vol. II, p. 290.

46. *Ibid.*, pp. 288–9 (where the whole incident is described).

47. *Ibid.*, p. 293.

48. *Ibid.*

49. *Ibid.*, p. 291n.

50. Without mentioning the names, he obviously referred to the attacks against the *Banu Kainuka* and *Banu al-Nadir* tribes, both in the vicinity of Medina (see about these events, the massacres, and confiscation of Jewish property by Mohammed, Simon Dubnow, *Weltgeschichte des Juedischen Volkes*, Vol. III, p. 400).

51. Toynbee, *Study of History*, Vol. VIII, p. 283.

52. See, for instance, *Study*, Vol. III, p. 467; *Reconsiderations*, pp. 220, 462, 467.

53. Sura 59, 'The Emigration. Revealed in Medina'.

54. These are the Jews of the tribe of *Banu al-Nadir*.

55. This refers to the Jews of the tribe of *Banu Kainuka*.

56. See Toynbee, *Study*, Vol. VIII, p. 283.

57. It was not 'one single Jewish community' but all three of them in the Medina area (Toynbee omitted *Banu Kainuka* and *Banu al-Nadir*); and even when Mohammed conquered Chaybar, he permitted the Jews to stay there only because he made them his bondmen, as he needed their financial support: half of the income of their produce (Dubnow, *op. cit.*, pp. 398–405).

58. Toynbee, *Reconsiderations*, p. 220. 'religion of the same order as Christianity and on a par with it' (*ibid.*, p. 467).

59. Both meanings are in Webster.

60. *Reports of the Executive submitted to the Twenty-Third Zionist Congress* (Jerusalem), 1951, p. 190.

61. (Kirk), p. 11.

62. *Ibid.*, p. 253.

63. *Ibid.*

64. *Ibid.*, pp. 253, 254.

65. *Ibid.*, p. 263.

66. Toynbee, *Study of History*, Vol. VIII, p. 290.

67. Toynbee, *Survey for 1939–1946* (Kirk), p. 263.

68. Habib Issa, 'The Arab League and the Refugees', in *Al-Hoda* (daily newspaper of the Lebanese emigrant community in the U.S.A.), 8 June 1951.

69. *Bulletin of Research Group for European Migration Problems*, (The Hague), January–March, 1957, pp. 10–11.

70. *Daily Mail*, (London), 12 August 1948.

71. Toynbee, *Survey for 1939–1946* (Kirk), p. 264.

72. Begin, *The Revolt*, pp. 164–5.

73. Al-Urdun, Amman (Jordan), 9 April 1953.

74. Dated 3 December 1948. Published in the *Document Book*, The National Council for Jews in Palestine (Va'ad Le'umi), p. 331.

75. Issued on that day in Tel-Aviv (*ibid*).

76. See the *Proclamation of Independence*, dated 15 May 1948, in contemporary press.

77. Quotation from Edward Attiyah, *The Arabs*, dealing with the flight of the Arabs from Palestine before and during the 1948 war, starting with 'This wholesale exodus was partly due . . .' and ending '. . . the Palestinian Arabs enabled to re-enter and retake possession of their country.' Baltimore, 1955, p. 183.

78. *Telegraph* (daily), Beyrouth, 6 September 1948.

79. Special Political Committee of the U.N. General Assembly, 17 November 1960 (U.N. Doc. A/SPC/SR, 202, p. 9).

80. *Minutes* of Security Council, 18 May 1948, No. 68, p. 42.

81. The statement by Mahmoud Bey Fawzi in *Minutes* of Security Council, 22 May 1948, No. 72, p. 7.

82. In a statement by Yashya Hawash in *Falastin* (daily), in the Old City of Jerusalem, 30 March 1955.

83. Lebanese daily, appearing in New York, dated 8 June 1951.

84. A collection of such statements primarily from Arab sources was published with references by the Israel Embassy in U.S.A. in *Arab Propaganda . . . and Facts* (Washington), 1957; and another by the Israel Government (Ministry for Foreign Affairs: Information Department), (Jerusalem), 1961, *The Arab Refugees. Arab Statements and the Facts*.

85. Toynbee, *Reconsiderations*, pp. 627–8.

86. E. Berkovitz, *Judaism: Fossil or Ferment* (New York), 1956, pp. 108–12; Toynbee refers to: 'The unbridled vehemence of Toynbee's condemnation of Zionism is out of all proportion to the guilt on the Zionist side. Accusing Zionism of "Nazism" reveals the measure of Toynbee's condemnation of "Nazism" in his own West.'

87. See, for instance, *Reconsiderations*, p. 2: 'If I now tried to maintain all my previous positions, I would find myself at war with myself as well as with my critics.'

88. Toynbee, *Study of History*, Vol. VIII, p. 289.

89. See, for instance, Ben Gurion's speech in the Elected Assembly which met in Jerusalem on 2 October 1947, to prepare for Statehood. In an outline of the future tasks he said, *inter alia*: 'Now, if ever, we must do more than make peace with them [Arabs]; we must achieve collaboration and alliance on equal terms.' See *Rebirth and Destiny of Israel* (New York, Philosophical Library), p. 218.

90. Ordinance No. 12 of 5708—1948, of 24 June 1948, in *Laws of the State of Israel* (Jerusalem, the Government Printer), Vol. I, pp. 25–6.

91. *Davar*, 17 June 1951 (Peretz, p. 149).

92. *Laws of Israel*, Vol. IV, Nr. 20, pp. 68–82.

93. Which during World War II also applied to Palestine, where German property, for instance, was seized by the Mandatory Power (*Survey for 1952*, p. 235).

94. GAOR 5th Session, Suppl. No. 18, p. 17.

95. GAOR 194 (III/1). (3rd Session *Resolutions*, pp. 21–5); GAOR 1st Committee 3rd Session, Par. I, pp. 906/907. (Summary Records.)

96. Article 11, *ibid.*, p. 24.

97. Article 6, *ibid.*, pp. 22–3.

98. Article 11, *ibid.*, p. 24.

99. *Survey for 1939–1946*, Middle East (Kirk), *op. cit.*, pp. 315–16.

100. *New York Times*, 18 January 1960. Hussein's interview of 17 January. The *Times* also devoted to this statement a letter headed 'An Arab Voice of Reason' (19 January 1960).

101. Toynbee, *Survey for 1939–1946* (Kirk's essay), p. 244.

102. *Ibid.*, p. 680.

103. *Ibid.*, p. 245.

104. Official *Protocol* (Jerusalem), 1947, p. 20.

105. Preliminary figures in *Bulletin of the Press Bureau*, No. 7 (Jerusalem), 28 December 1960. The exact figures appear in the official *Protocol*, but are not changed fundamentally.

106. Toynbee, 'New Homes for Old', in *Between Niger and Nile*, p. 84.

107. *Ibid.*, p. 85.

108. Toynbee, *Study of History*, Vol. VIII, p. 290.

109. *Ibid.*

110. That such compensation is regarded by Israel most seriously is additionally confirmed by the fact that that, for instance, she paid compensation for the possessions of the German Templars and paid forty-five million Israeli pounds for them in accordance with the decision of the arbitrator appointed by both sides and accepted by them (*Neue Zuericher Zeitung*, issue no. 3193 29 July 1964, n.p. [p. 2]).

111. Toynbee, 'Pioneer Destiny of Judaism', p. 3; 'Future of Judaism', p. 74.

112. Toynbee, *Study of History*, Vol. VIII, p. 290.

113. *Survey for 1939–1946*. 'The Middle East in the War' (Kirk), p. 229.

114. M. Begin (Commander of the Irgun), *The Revolt* (London), 1951, p. 61.

115. Protocol of the 22nd Zionist Congress, p. 20 (Statistical tables for 1948–9).

116. *Ibid.*

117. Toynbee, *Study of History*, Vol. VIII, p. 290n.

118. *Ibid.*

119. *Ibid.*

120. *Ibid.*, p. 291.

121. *Ibid.*, p. 290.

122. Toynbee, *Reconsiderations*, p. 627.

123. Toynbee, 'Pioneer Destiny of Judaism', in *Issues* (New York, Summer), 1960, Vol. 14, no. 6, p. 8.

124. Toynbee, *Survey for 1939–1946*, p. 145.

125. *Ibid.*, pp. 156n–157n.

126. Toynbee, *Reconsiderations*, pp. 222–314.

Index

303, 310, 311, 316, 317, 318, 319, 320, 321, 322
Nestorians, 30
Nili spy ring, 252, 253
Nixon, Richard, 173
Nordau, Max, 60, 158, 188

Ormsby-Gore, Major, 154, 222

Palestine, *passim*; historical Jewish connection, 128ff., 263, 264; Christianity & Mohammedanism born in, 70; combination with Jewish spiritual creativity, 70; Jewry's aim of preserving distinct national identity, 128ff., 135; British Government's view as 'national home', 144ff.; 'no-man's-land' category', 231, 233, 234, 235, 247; neglect by Arabs, 233, 234, 235, 240, 245, 266; officially surrendered by Turkey, 264; increase of immigrants, 271, 272-3, 274, 276, 277; explusion of Arabs, 300-9; land seizure explained, 312ff.; payment of compensation for land, 313, 316, 317
Paris Peace Conference (1919), 192, 268, 276, 280
Parsees, reasons for survival, 29, 74
Paul, St, 32, 72, 77, 89, 103, 107; 'only differs from Jews in recognition of Christ's divinity', 74; repudiation of Torah, 74
'penalisations' theory, 18, 19, 20-32, 203, 293, 294; 'cause psychological complex' in Jews, 33ff.; penalisations in Jewish traditions, 26-8; inadequacy of, 28-30
'Pittsburgh Program', 109
Platonic conception of the State, 166
Popper-Lynkens, Josef, 183
Port, Adrien Du, 114
proselytisation, intermarriage &, 79, 84; Jewish attitude to, 81, 83; forced, 82

Rees, M. Van, 149, 265
Reform Judaism, 103, 104, 110, 142
Reinhardt, Max, 183
Renner, Karl, 183
Renouvier, Charles, 33
Rosenberg, Alfred, 73, 99, 179; on Jewish nationalism, 117
Rosenzweig, Franz, on Jewish Bible, 118
Rothschild, Lord, 270-1
Round Table, 221, 222, 225
Rousseau, 10, 114

Ruthard, Archbishop, 23, 24

Sartre, Jean-Paul, 36
Schechter, Solomon, 105
Schoenerer, Gustav, 182
'School of Higher Criticism', 104
Schwarzenberger, Professor, 262
Seton-Watson, R. W., on Jewish loyalty, 160
Sherman, Bezalel, on ghettoes, 136
Shields, Dr Drummond, 149
Sidonia, 134
Silver, Dr Abba Hillel, 162
Singer, Charles, 52
Sokolow, Dr Nahum, 229, 281
Spate, O. H. K., 183
Spinoza, 134
'Statute of limitations', 258-66; Toynbee misunderstands legal aspect, 259, 260; applied in Constantinople, 261; in Goa Question, 261
Stein, Leonard, 222, 223
Stekel, Wilhelm, on 'Judaic complex', 36
Stern Group, 315
Stevenson, Adlai, 171, 173
Streicher, 132
Suez War (1956), 168-75; Jewish opposition to Eisenhower-Dulles stand, 173
Survey of International Affairs for 1936, 100
Sykes, Sir Mark, 222

Talmud, The, 26, 32, 51, 105, 131, 295
The False God. My Evidence Against Yahveh (Fritsch), 132
Times History of the War, The, 223
Tiso, Mgr. Jozef, 24
Torah, The, 32, 72, 74, 105
Toynbee, Arnold, *passim*; anti-semitism, 31, 35-6, 38, 63, 74, 121, 217; superficial assessment of Zionism, 17; 'penalisations', theory, 18, 19, 20-32, 203, 294; negation of theory, 29-30; contempt for Diaspora, 31, 62, 75; on age of toleration, 58-9; expects disappearance of Jews through emancipation, 60, 61, 62, 112, 320; denial of 'chosenness', 65ff.; wants religious reinterpretation by Jews, 73; on intermarriage, 76ff.; reduces Zionism to geographical term, 67ff.; on denationalisation, 91-7, 141; on Jewish suicide from within, 88-9, 92; parallelism with Montefiore, 104-11; on Agudath Israel, 99ff.; on Liberal